Global Sport Business

In the global sport business industry, growth, and development within and across various sport businesses are essential for competitive advantage. This fascinating collection of chapters examines how the development and management of resources and opportunities in sport business is vital to success.

Commissioned by the World Association for Sport Management (WASM) and featuring global perspectives from leading international scholars and original research data drawn from both qualitative and quantitative inquiry, the book presents cases as diverse as customer demand in the NBA, sport and physical activity human resources in Spain and stakeholder relationships in Chinese football. Presented in three parts (global perspectives, managing resources, and managing opportunities), *Global Sport Business* examines key research and practical issues in sport business management and marketing studies in both global and local contexts.

This is an important read for professors, scholars, and students in sport business management, a useful resource for sport business management professionals and practitioners, and illuminating reading for anyone with an interest in sport management.

Brenda G. Pitts is Professor of Sport Management and Director of the Sport Business Research Laboratory at Georgia State University, USA.

James J. Zhang is Professor of Sport Management and Director of the International Center for Sport Management (ICSM) at the University of Georgia, USA.

World Association for Sport Management series

Series Editors:
Brenda G. Pitts, Georgia State University, USA
James J. Zhang, University of Georgia, USA

The World Association for Sport Management (WASM) was founded to facilitate sport management research, teaching, and learning excellence, and professional practice, across every continent. The WASM book series is designed to support those aims by presenting current research and scholarship, from well-established and emerging scholars and practitioners, on sport management theory, policy, and practice. Books in the series will explore contemporary issues and key challenges in sport management, and identify important new directions for research and professional practice. Above all, the series aims to encourage and highlight the development of international perspectives, international partnerships, and international best practice in sport management, recognizing the globalised nature of the contemporary sport industry.

Available in this series:

1. **Global Sport Management: Contemporary Issues and Inquiries**
   Edited by Brenda G. Pitts and James J. Zhang

2. **Contemporary Sport Marketing: Global Perspectives**
   Edited by James J. Zhang and Brenda G. Pitts

3. **The Global Football Industry: Marketing Perspectives**
   Edited by James J. Zhang and Brenda G. Pitts

4. **Global Sport Business: Managing Resources and Opportunities**
   Edited by Brenda G. Pitts and James J. Zhang

Global Sport Business

Managing Resources and Opportunities

Edited by Brenda G. Pitts and
James J. Zhang

LONDON AND NEW YORK

First published 2019
by Routledge
2 Park Square, Milton Park, Abingdon, Oxon OX14 4RN

and by Routledge
52 Vanderbilt Avenue, New York, NY 10017

Routledge is an imprint of the Taylor & Francis Group, an informa business

British Library Cataloguing-in-Publication Data
A catalogue record for this book is available from the British Library

Library of Congress Cataloging-in-Publication Data
A catalog record has been requested for this book

ISBN: 978-0-367-13288-0 (hbk)
ISBN: 978-0-429-02566-2 (ebk)

Typeset in Baskerville
by Swales & Willis Ltd, Exeter, Devon, UK

Printed and bound in Great Britain by
TJ International Ltd, Padstow, Cornwall

Contents

Contributors

Thomas A. Baker is Associate Professor in the Department of Kinesiology at the University of Georgia, Athens, USA.

Cristiana Buscarini is Associate Professor at the University of Rome "Foro Italico", Italy, where she is also the Scientific Director of the Laboratory of Economics and Management.

Kevin K. Byon is Associate Professor in the Department of Kinesiology at Indiana University Bloomington, USA.

Antonio Campos-Izquierdo is Professor in the Faculty of Physical Activity and Sport Sciences at the Technical University of Madrid, Spain.

Kenneth K. Chen is Assistant Professor in the Department of Physical Education at Hong Kong Baptist University, Hong Kong.

Wen-hao Winston Chou is PhD Student in Kinesiology at the University of Georgia, Athens, USA.

Luxiang Cui is Professor of Physical Education and Training at Shenyang Sport University, China.

Chun-hua Dong is Associate Professor in the School of Physical Education and Sport Training at Shanghai University of Sport, China.

Sara Franzini Gabrielli is Researcher in the Laboratory of Economics and Management at the University of Rome "Foro Italico", Italy.

Pablo Gálvez-Ruíz is Club Manager in Vivagym Málaga Centro and Assistant Professor in the Internet Education Department at the International University of La Rioja, Spain.

Jerónimo García-Fernández is Associate Professor of Sport Management and Sport Marketing at University of Seville, Spain.

Andy Gerow is Aquatic and Rink Program Supervisor at Park District of Oak Parkan, USA.

Moisés Grimaldi-Puyana has been a Sports Manager for ten years and has been a Professor at different universities in Spain for almost nine years.

Jori N. Hall is Associate Professor at the University of Georgia, Athens, USA.

Billy J. Hawkins is Professor at the University of Houston, USA.

Lauren M. Johnson is a PhD student in the Sport Management and Policy department at the University of Georgia, Athens, USA.

Wai Huen Kwan is a final year Student of a Bachelor's Degree in Sports and Recreation Management at the Technological and Higher Education Institute of Hong Kong, Hong Kong. She is also a taekwondo player and coach in Hong Kong.

Bing Liu is Professor in the School of Economy and Management at Shanghai University of Sport, China.

Harmania H. M. Lo is Teaching Fellow in the Faculty of Management and Hospitality at the Technological and Higher Education Institute of Hong Kong, Hong Kong.

Mark Lyberger is Associate Professor of Sport Administration at Kent State University, USA.

Jana Nová is Assistant Professor of Sport Management and Chief of Administration in the Faculty of Sports Studies, Masaryk University, Czech Republic.

Evica Obadić is Main Internal Auditor at Croatian Olympic Committee and is currently attending doctoral studies at University of Zagreb, Croatia.

Gregg Rich is Assistant Professor of Sport Management at Georgia Southern University, USA.

Antonio Jesús Sánchez-Oliver is Professor in the Faculty of Sport at the University of Pablo de Olavide, Spain, and in Human Motricity and Sports Performance Area at University of Seville, Spain.

James Santomier Jr. is Professor of Sport Management in the Department of Marketing and Sport Management, Sacred Heart University, USA.

Sanela Škorić is Assistant Professor in Economics and Management of Sport at University of Zagreb, Croatia.

Sten Söderman is Professor Emeritus of International Business at Stockholm University and Affiliated Researcher at Center for Sports and Business, Stockholm School of Economics, Sweden.

Ting-ting Xiao is Lecturer at the Sports Institute at Shanghai Normal University, China.

Tao Yang is Professor of Sport Management and Director of Shaanxi Province Sports Industry R&D Center at Xi'an Institute of Physical Education, China.

Cuixia Yi is Associate Professor of Physical Education and Training at Shaanxi Normal University, China.

Brian H. Yim is Assistant Professor of Sport Administration at Kent State University, USA.

Tyreal Yizhou Qian is PhD Candidate in the Sport Management & Policy program at the University of Georgia, Athens, USA.

Kun Zhang is Associate Professor of Sport Management at Shaanxi Normal University, China.

Mandy Y. Zhang is Associate Professor at the College of Sport Science, Shanghai University, China.

Part I

Global perspectives

Chapter 1

Managing resources and opportunities in globalized sport business

Lauren M. Johnson, James J. Zhang, and Brenda G. Pitts

Introduction

Today, managers and marketers in any industry who wish to expand opportunities, products, and services to new consumers and industrial sectors often look for international markets that can be penetrated. Reduced labor cost, new customers, and a desire to share and exchange cultural activities can be attributed to the desire for businesses to globally expand their reach. North American sport leagues rely heavily on international players and fans to present their products that are aimed to be competitive, inclusive, and entertaining. The largest retailers of sport products, such as Nike, Adidas, and Under Armour, penetrate into foreign markets to reduce production cost, increase scales, and even enhance innovations that results in an economic linkage through international entities. Sport has historically been an activity that is enjoyed and celebrated throughout the world and the amount of individuals who engage in sporting activities is increasing globally. This growth has tremendous economic impact that forces organizations to be knowledgeable on trends and practices throughout the world (Zhang, Pitts, & Kim, 2017). Parker (1998) defines globalization as "a phenomenon that encompasses the ability for businesses to pursue profits and achieve organizational, social, or political goals while permeating borders and interacting with different parts of the world" (p. 7). The globalization of the marketplace is categorized by a growing interlocking dependency of economies of different countries and regions, frequency of financial and product transactions, and competition presented globally to retain market share (Cavusgil, 1993).

Markets are becoming increasingly globalized and the benefits can be seen in four travel activities, including business, education, tourism, and electronic travel. These activities are responsible for the growing globalization of new markets, opportunities, and management practices in business settings. The growing globalization of organizations and opportunities all over the world has greatly increased the amount of employees being sent abroad. Beyond corporations, opportunities to expand to other countries and/or cultures extend to individuals who are not traditionally identified as members of the professional class; for example, today entrepreneurs are able to expand into new markets and benefit from widely accessible information and transportation. Educational opportunities in foreign countries present advancement for individuals who wish to acquire new knowledge and skills, experience different cultures in an academic setting, or have a chance for social mobility through the university system. International students bring cultural diversity to many places that actively embrace new people, ideas, and opportunities to connect to members of local communities. Because of these transplants, retail businesses have been encouraged to make available international products and hire individuals who contribute to the growing interactions of individuals from different parts of the world. Foreign students also add to the globalization of markets by starting new businesses in countries other than their own. The desire to attract tourists and increase the economic incentives brought by these visiting individuals have motivated governments to welcome new cultures to their societies and stimulate business activities that promote a tourist-friendly country. Managers directly or indirectly associated with the tourism industry, such as sports, must design their business plans and strategies to foster cultural integration and tackle global challenging issues. Globalization in this sense forces local communities to be knowledgeable on issues that affect the world outside of their local concerns. Tourism has affected the global business market tremendously and the sport industry has been one of the biggest contributors and also benefactors. The benefits and accessibility of electronic communication and information exchange are a large factor in the globalization of the marketplace. Frequently traveling to multiple countries can be expensive and logistically unfeasible; however, with technological advances, today managers can feel more confident pursuing opportunities in other countries. Video conferences, data transfers, and automotive analytic database systems allow people to work from anywhere. All of these activities must be properly managed in the sport industry for globalization to continue to grow and sustain (Parker, 1998; Pitts & Zhang, 2016).

The desire for everything to be like everything else, or convergence, has added to the globalization of markets across different sectors. This can be noted as a main factor in the globalization of markets. Technology has allowed for individuals across the world, which was at one time thought of as being inaccessible, to identify and desire products and services that are advanced and efficient regardless of location. Levitt (1993) acknowledges that the world's needs and desires have been irrevocably homogenized in the globalization process. The homogeneity of everything usable, enjoyed, and desired has led to managers seeking new ways to penetrate borders and make their product known as the standard or most elite. This has aided in organizations' initiative to build and market products that can be used throughout the world. It has changed how products and events are produced and marketed, and the people and initiatives chosen to endorse these products. Businesses in all markets are identifying this shift of having their services as the one that is imitated and desired throughout the world. Traditional studies have focused on the homogenization of raw materials; today, this trend has widely extended to such areas as transportation, banking, and leisure, which creates tremendous managerial challenges for organizations that have been established to deal with local, domestic, or regional issues at the best. To have a product or brand that is recognizable and used throughout the world brings new opportunities and challenges. Globalization has increased the reach in engaging with people's needs and desires across the world, as marketers now have to be cognizant that in order to grow and maintain market share, they must connect globally and remain relevant economically. It appears certain that the ability to stay content in a particular region without the threat of outside competition is unrealistic in today's globalized market environment.

Other than economic implications, organizations often put in their missions, goals, and values that they engage in global business activities to grow and expand their initiatives to other parts of the world that are at times lacking in resources or standard services of a certain market. Technological advances have aided many organizations in expanding their operations overseas. The internet has had a major role in connecting people from all over the world, and now managers may consider adopting new technological resources such as social media, video conferencing, and language translation applications to help facilitate the growth of international relationships. Just knowing the likes and dislikes of consumers in a foreign market is not enough to thrive globally. People doing international business must be aware of common and unique customs, way of life, beliefs, and days of remembrance in order to be respectful and cautious of their business clients and communities. This is especially relevant for North American sporting good manufacturers who are known for having manufacturers abroad.

Sport is seen throughout the world as a form of entertainment that can be consumed by families, friends, and individual enthusiasts. There are many examples in history where sports have brought people together, creating an undeniable power and a universal appeal of popular culture. The broad appeal of pursuing sport opportunities globally is its ability to break down barriers set by different cultures, languages, religions, races, and genders. Bringing sports to new territories with good intentions of enriching cultures could contribute to breaking down barriers between countries (Pitts & Zhang, 2016; Thibault, 2009). Sports are often considered as an entity that can reach various demographic segments. As different sport forms are already played and enjoyed globally, many businesses want to align themselves with this particular market context, which would help bring additional marketing opportunities, such as online commerce businesses, by sponsoring teams and leagues with a global vision and outreach. Many professional sport organizations have increasingly realized the financial opportunities present in overseas markets that are untapped in such areas as television programming, licensed apparel, and sponsorship agreements (Zhang, Pitts, & Kim, 2017). The advancement and increasing popularity of mega-sport events has helped the cultural significance of athletic events and what they represent throughout the world. Mega-sport events are defined as large-scale sporting events, such as the Olympics and European Football World Championships, which have international significance. These recurring events have become engrained in a society's cultural, economic, and global initiatives that bring new people, opportunities, and innovations to local areas. The prominence and media attention given to national and global events stimulates the desire for business in all markets. Mega-events are known to bring economic and political opportunities to host countries and cities. In return, these countries and cities get to showcase their entrepreneurialism, structural competence, and modernization (Gruneau & Horne, 2016).

The increasing diversity of employees and athletes, expanded mega-events, and financial incentives of broadening consumers due to the globalizing process, have created an elevated demand for resources. Institutions such as the Federation Internationale de Football Association (FIFA), the International Olympic Committee (IOC), and the National Basketball Association (NBA) have spurred the growth of organizations that increasingly rely on the expansion of their leagues, merchandise, and personnel to penetrate into and remain in new market environments. Resources must be put in place to assist the migration of athletes, coaches, and sport business professionals, develop an effective workforce management for the production of equipment and sportswear, and adapt technological tools that help visually and socially connect consumers throughout the world (Cunningham, 2013). For instance, sponsorship of athletes, leagues, teams, and companies has resulted in worldwide spending and opportunities to grow brand awareness. The marketing of organizations and individuals in women's athletics throughout the world has increased as well, due to the increase of support for elite female athletes (Farneti, 2016).

The need to manage resources and opportunities globally in the sport industry can be attributed to business people's desire to increase the distribution of consumer goods and entertainment products into new markets that may not be exposed to the same level of experiences (Lizandra & Gladden, 2005). The management of sport resources and opportunities is directly related to an organization's strategic plan set in place to reach its goals and compete in its industrial segment or market environment. Strategic planning provides a business with the opportunity to maximize success by translating the vision of the organization into measurable activities that can be implemented. Executing a strategic plan in any organization is not possible without the effective management of resources to capitalize on opportunities existing within the organization and in the marketplace (Zhang, Pitts, & Kim, 2017).

Managing resources in a globalized marketplace

Managing resources and opportunities effectively is necessary in today's competitive sport industry. In order to capitalize on an opportunity, it is important to define and discuss how managing resources and opportunities well can give an organization a competitive edge. Sport industry resources can include arenas, players, coaches, merchandise, and financial resources such as capital and infrastructure (Jones, 2016). In any organization, resources are finite. Resources cannot be properly executed without planning surrounding how the business gets its return on investment; in this process, strategic planning is usually conducted to improve the management and use of the resources. Organizations understand that well-spent resources add value and poorly-used resources can diminish company growth. A competitive edge will be held by the organization that has the lowest production costs and the best distribution channels (Summers, 2009; Zhang, Chen, & Kim, 2014). Public engagement of a sports team or facility is crucial to the success of a business. Administrators must manage resources that are used to facilitate positive communication with their communities. Communication can come through such channels as event marketing, advertising, and social media engagement. Resources, such as social media and app software development tools, and the ability to conduct and analyze research concerning consumer demographics and cultural preferences, demonstrate the organization's commitment to social consciousness to their consumers. Multiple perspectives of needs must be properly met and managed for maintaining, growing, and expanding a sport business (Sparvero & Chalip, 2007).

Successful long-term strategic planning answers three basic questions: what business is the organization really in? What does it take for the organization to compete successfully? What does the organization wish to become in the future? In a sport business context, it is beneficial for organizations to exist in multiple segments to attract consumers. Organizations that run a sport facility can define themselves both as an entertainment and health-fitness entity if they utilize their resources in a strategic way. Resources that can help in facility management include programs and equipment implemented for both leisure and fitness. Apps that allow consumers to follow and engage with their favorite teams, players, and sport apparel companies in an effort to execute a social consciousness are ways that an organization can use a resource in multiple ways to enhance its business. Loyal consumers in a sport business can help drive revenue and create a positive cash flow; meanwhile, there are many factors that can contribute to an organization's success in capturing market share. It is important for an organization to define if its success relies on game ticket sales, merchandise, player fees, online viewers, or any of other entities that help add to the success of the business. People are one of the most influential resources a sport organization can have. Through managing and cultivating resourceful administrators, players, coaches, and facility staff, an organization can come closer to reaching its full potential. As an organization strives to become an industry leader in its respective market, it must determine the resources and opportunities it will invest in to reach the stated goals (Summers, 2009).

Managing resources effectively helps increase value and enable an organization to accomplish its objectives. These resources can be tangible or intangible. For instance, an intangible is the creation of a culture that helps drive consumer behavior. A resource-based view holds that internal resources and the ability to manage these resources strategically increase a company's competitive advantage. Value-creating capabilities and the ability to pursue business-growing opportunities in a sport organization make the management of resources the basis of success (Sparvero & Chalip, 2007). Specific resources that must be managed in sports are critical in the operation of a facility, human resources, community relations, and finances. Sport facility managers are in charge of the operation of a stadium, gym, arena, or other entities serving the sport community. They must manage resources to strategically plan events, make financial decisions, conduct building operations and ticket sales, and serve many people who use these facilities. Human resources who manage inventory an equipment are essential, and will determine how quickly items get made, shipped, and repaired (Fried, 2015). Other human resources, such as financial management professionals, face unique challenges in sustaining a competitive business. They must try to find funding streams such as external funding, scholarships, sponsorship, and television deals. Businesses must invest in a solid financial team that organizes how money is being spent and acquired to meet organizational goals. Sport organizations must truly maximize their resources to compete with those who have a larger budget to gain market share and consumers (Howard & DeSchriver, 2005). It is important that sport business management professionals have resources to help recruit, train, and retain diverse individuals that help facilitate a company's mission and growth. Having people from diverse backgrounds presents more ways of solving problems and tasks; as a result, this would likely improve the quality of decision-making (Cunningham & Melton, 2011).

As businesses seek to expand to meet the globalizing trend of the sport business industry, sport business management professionals must realize the importance of arguably their most important resource: their employees. Any consideration in expanding to different markets includes a look into the labor resources currently or potentially available and competent. Businesses that wish to pursue opportunities in foreign markets have the challenge of getting the human knowledge, skills, and capabilities that are most needed. Creating a workforce that represents the goals and values of an organization can have unique challenges in different countries.

Employees who are relocating must be provided with cultural assimilation programs, financial benefits for themselves and their families, and a clear and concise plan of execution. When new products or headquarters are being established in foreign markets, it is often beneficial to hire from the local workforce. This requires an additional set of resources that must be utilized from the organization. When training a workforce from a different county, laws and customs must be followed to prevent any legal misconduct (Dessler, 2001).

New issues in managing resources

New issues occur when managing sport resources in the globalized marketplace. For instance, the online shopping industry has changed the way many sport businesses rely on growing revenue. Sport apparel companies must now invest in e-market software and resources that help improve shipping and handling efficiency. The increased globalization of sport sponsorship has resulted in more complete packages for companies who want to know the effectiveness of their marketing efforts, which has led to the need for data-driven analytical systems that can measure a return on investments. For sport business management professionals to justify overseas investments into their clients, partners, and investors, a detailed forecast must be produced that shows potential market share and financial gain (Zwick & Dieterle, 2005). The popularity of e-gaming, also known as fantasy sports, is growing, and fans across the world can participate in online communities that bring them closer to their favorite teams. Based on actual statistics from a professional team, e-gaming is a platform where sport fans can pick their favorite players and teams and compete against their friends. Recently, a popular American online sport betting service, Draftkings, has expanded to some European countries, which opens the door for other online entertainment entities to create resources used globally (Gouker, 2017).

With growing technological advances, it is important to identify what new resources must be allocated to entities. New resources that must be managed in sports include ridesharing companies that require additional spaces in arenas and personnel to ensure more consumers can attend events. With the shift to livestreaming games and events, it is important for businesses to appoint staff members who are knowledgeable in producing quality content. With the globalization of sport apparel companies and leagues, it is important that organizations equip employees with resources to help acclimatize them to a different culture. This can include language tutorials and family immersion programs (Fried, 2015). Standardizing transportation throughout the world is easing some businesses' minds while attempting to travel overseas. Ridesharing opportunities throughout the world are changing the way international travel is completed. Safety concerns today are at an all-time high due to terrorist threats and the reshaping of major

European countries such as the United Kingdom and Spain. Border control is heightened and reasons for travel in a business space are often examined with more scrutiny. Not all of the threats are physical, as cyber hacking and technological outages are now pertinent threats that can alter an event (Gruneau & Horne, 2016).

Economic incentives have added to the globalization of markets across multiple sectors as new resources and profits can be obtained from these new markets. Local businesses must address in their strategic plans that the exchange of money, services, and ideas can be held by people of different cultures and nations. Finance, banking, business regulations, and tax implications are all important items that are assessed by organizations entering into a global consumer space. The amount of business being conducted does have to be monitored by financial advisors. While globalization has expanded, so has the need for financial knowledge of international business expansion. Finance departments can help ensure what resources are available with the help of accountants and advisors who are knowledgeable in international governance and policies. Economics are a huge driving factor in efficient globalization efforts. Foreign economies, forecast of sales, and supply and demand should be monitored in all areas of operations. Operations that are moved overseas are often done so for tax implications and write-offs. This opportunity presents many advantages for businesses and individuals alike, that can identify resources needed to conduct business while abiding to regulations set by the government. Banking abroad for organizations presents opportunities whether the business currently has operations overseas or not. Overseas investments can be a chance to discover new products and resources not readily available in a local area.

The popular amateur sport structure in Europe and non-American countries are in the form of clubs that host multiple sports for children and up to the professional level. These clubs must be equipped with resources such as long-term local sponsorship, facility maintenance, innovation personnel, and online record-keeping of former and current players, families, and employees. For example, basketball players in many European markets must also be registered under FIBA in order to track their amateurism and club transactions. In the United States, many college coaches are seeking opportunities to recruit young players from Europe who often have more experience than American players. Colleges often try to help former athletes receive professional contracts in European countries. In order to find and market talent, coaches and athletic departments must invest in video software, transportation opportunities, and personnel that can help with adjusting to a new culture and way of life. While the development of youth in sports can have great benefits, it is important that these opportunities are ethical. The success and visibility of youth sports nationally and abroad has resulted in sponsorship of leagues, teams, and sports facilities by organizations that pride themselves on strategic global partnerships.

In a professional sport organization, youth sport academy, or collegiate institution, there must be various resources in place to help coaches and players adjust and perform at their best. These include access to transportation, academic advisors, strength and conditioning personnel, access to the latest equipment, healthcare, and other family benefits. An intrinsic resource to develop young players can lie in an institution's scouting network and ability to preserve a club's history, tradition, and alumni contributions (Taylor & McGraw, 2015).

Managing opportunities

Sport-based entrepreneurship theory is defined as "when an entity in sport acts collectively to respond to an opportunity to create value" (Ratten, 2010). Sport entrepreneurs are driven by innovation, the ability to be proactive, and risk-taking. The advancement of technology greatly influences innovation in sports. Virtual reality headsets are currently being used in the sport world to improve athlete training and sport viewership experiences. Wearable technology has likewise improved the way athletes are measured in their performances (Levski, 2016). Online technologies have increased the way individuals view sports and support their favorite sport organizations. This includes through blogs, social media, and e-gaming. Being proactive in sports is essential to creating opportunities for your organization, which includes the building of facilities with the most up-to-date advancements of technology. For example, in 2017 Atlanta opened a brand new baseball stadium, the SunTrust Park, and a new football stadium, the Mercedes Benz Stadium; the city has also started renovating the Philips Arena and building new training facilities for the National Basketball Association and Major League Soccer teams located in the metropolitan area. As a result of these proactive upgrading of facilities, the city has been selected to host major upcoming events, such as the College Football Playoffs, Super Bowl, and NCAA Men's Final Four. Opportunities do not come without risks. When professional sport organizations offer rookies multi-million dollar deals, they are doing it with the assumption that they will have a return on their investments. Sport businesses of all kinds must be diligent in assessing what opportunities to pursue or forgo by determining how much risk they are willing to take (Ratten, 2010).

Managing opportunities in sport requires that individual sport facilitators, organizations, and communities taking part in sports actively organize, monitor, and seek ways for their businesses to grow and advance, which requires a strategy that actively identifies, pursues, and maintains innovative ideas that can create value for an organization. Systems must be established that focus on identifying market trends and opportunities to assess internal needs. Companies may use innovation as a key business strategy and subsequently take risks that must be managed properly. There are several forms of entrepreneurship that sport business management professionals have the ability to engage in. They can pursue opportunities in youth sports, infrastructure, corporate sponsorship, technology, and fan communication, among others. Pursuing opportunities in different cultures is becoming more common in sports. For example, Nike released a Habib for Muslim women to participate in sports in 2017, which is the first of its kind. With youth sports growing into a billion-dollar industry, new organizations are being formed with the idea of capitalizing on its booming market share by pursuing opportunities in online streaming services for youth games, more specialized apparel, and unique training facilities geared towards developing young athletes. While innovation in a company's policy and execution can be beneficial for all, it is important to identify what businesses are likely to pursue opportunities. To identify companies that are willing to take risks, it is important to factor in their organizational capacities, reputations, resources, experiences, and financial health. Businesses that are actively pursuing opportunities need to make decisions based on whether these new innovations will increase a market share, result in profit, and attract new customers (Bekefi, Epstein, & Yuthas, 2008).

Those businesses making a commitment to manage opportunities must accomplish specific tasks that foster the overall development. These managing tasks include planning, organizing, staffing, implementation, and evaluating. Strategic planning is essential for identifying what future opportunities are most in line with the vision and goals of the organization. A clear understanding of past company performances can be an indication of how to best pursue new ideas. Competitors and market trends should be routinely monitored to assess individual performance and compare this with the market developmental trends. Innovation often comes from the vision to project the best way to make current trends and operations more efficient. Research should be conducted to forecast performances of a new product line, service, or internal operation. The feasibility of implementing an idea must be realistic without impacting the financial future of a business. Setting aside a budget directly for pursuing opportunities is an investment that can pay dividends by allowing for swift actions and a built-in cushion if results are not profitable. This should all be done to identify what opportunities it would make sense for a business to pursue. The organization of how to implement the identified opportunities involves designing a plan of action, drafting a budget, putting a task force of capable individuals in positions to succeed, and establishing a realistic timeline. Project management principles can be applied to the organizational stage to identify how to pursue opportunities efficiently while utilizing the least resources. Trained individuals within an organization will be responsible for making a new opportunity to come to life. Assigning tasks according to their strengths or expertise can reduce the amount of resources that has to be spent on teaching a new skill. Marketing of new products or services must be done in a way to entice new and loyal customers to engage with the company. Similar to the planning stage, research should be done on the overall effectiveness of implementing an opportunity, both internally and externally, which can be accomplished by gauging consumer perceptions, conducting sales analysis of existing services in addition to any new ones, and measuring past and present operational efficiency (Hernandez, 2002).

Due to globalization, sport organizations have growing opportunities to engage in corporate sponsorships and partnerships in more ways than ever before. Managerial opportunities exist in the area of streamlining meetings and further connecting with leaders in the sport industry throughout the world. Social media has helped aid this growth by fueling the conversations between consumers of sport organizations and the business they are aligned with. For example, the New England Patriots engage with their fans by their Patriots 365 rewards program that rewards their fans for shopping at partnered organizations. Among the organizations aligning with the Patriots are Dunkin' Donuts and Uber. Programs are designed for fans to actively engage with Dunkin' Donuts and Uber during games, adding to the visibility of these partnered organizations with other sport fans (New England Patriots, 2015). With the addition of Apple Pay and other convenient shopping facilities through mobile devices becoming more widespread, organizations have an opportunity to simplify the ticketing process for fans. Opportunities also exist in engaging female fans and athletes. Recently, NBA Live 18 incorporated WNBA players into their video games, expanding the league's demographic reach of videogame users (Winfield, 2017). Sport sponsorship is increasingly becoming popular in the social media marketing space, where companies from across the world are able to have their brands spread to new markets when athletes post an image or message in support of their brand. Sports teams and managers encourage athletes to produce fun and enjoyable contents on their social media pages to grow fans' and community involvement (Lizandra & Gladden, 2005).

The management of sport facilities relies increasingly on pursuing new opportunities. With the emphasis on mega-sport events, it is important to seek opportunities in undeveloped areas, and areas where temporary facilities can be constructed. Non-traditional sport businesses see it as a great opportunity to align themselves with sporting events that have a wide array of audiences. Movie companies advertise during games. Television and entertainment companies engage in partnerships to attract viewers to their networks by using sports. Partnerships of this form are common and, meanwhile, more partnerships that bring sports together with organizations that are not traditionally used in sport are using sports as an opportunity to grow their products. Sport organizations can also use these newly aligned businesses to expand their resources and opportunities (Fried, 2015). Sport arenas and venues invest in facility improvements that allow fans to experience events in luxury, with greater concession options, and interactive communication through the use of a smartphone or tablet (Howard and DeSchriver, 2005). Organizations see these upgrades as opportunities to create a better experience for loyal consumers and engage new fans. One of the fastest growing opportunities is in e-business and internet fan engagement. Sport business management professionals must be aware of the current opportunities to engage sport fans and non-fans by linking their sponsorships with high-frequency internet assets. A strategy to manage online opportunities is just as important as any other strategy a business can plan. This is because new ideas, inventions, and opinions are constantly being shared and transformed through interactions occurring on the internet (Zwick & Dieterle, 2005).

About this book

Oftentimes, an increasingly globalized sport marketplace has brought not only resources and opportunities for sport organizations but also risks and challenges. As these issues are critical to every business or organization, sport business professionals must strategically seek and utilize resources and procedures for their businesses to grow, advance, and stay successful; in the meantime, managing resources and opportunities requires sport organizations to carefully plan, organize, implement, monitor, and control the quality of their production and delivery of goods or services in order to avoid or minimize the risks and overcome the challenges associated with international operations. In an effort to critically examine contemporary issues, formulate theories, and identify best practices for managing resources and opportunities in the context of global sports, the co-editors of this book have selected research papers relevant to the topical issues. Including this introduction chapter, the book contains a total of 12 chapters that are organized into two main sections: managing resources and managing opportunities. The chapters are contributed by a total of 36 scholars from eight countries or territories around the world. Drs. Pitts and Zhang would like to take this opportunity to thank these eminent scholars for their remarkable contributions to the completion of this book project.

References

Bekefi, T., Epstein, M. J., & Yuthas, K. (2008). *Managing Opportunities and Risks.* Toronto, Canada: Certified Management Accountants.

Cavusgil, S. T. (1993). Globalization of Markets and Its Impact on Domestic Institutions. *Indiana Journal of Global Legal Studies, 1(1),* 83–99.

Cunningham, G. B. (2013). *Sport Management.* Cheltenham, UK and Northampton, MA: Edward Elgar Publishing.

Cunningham, G. B., & Melton, E. N (2011). The Benefits of Sexual Orientation Diversity in Sport Organization. *Journal of Homosexuality, 5,* 647–63.

Dessler, G. (2001). *Human Resource Management* (9th ed.). Upper Saddle River, NJ: Prentice Hall.

Farneti, C. (2016). Merchandising and Marketing Women's Sports. In E. J. Staurowsky (Ed.), *Women and Sport: Continuing a Journey of Liberation and Celebration* (pp. 229–46). Champaign, IL: Human Kinetics.

Fried, G. (2015). *Managing Sport Facilities* (3rd ed.). Champaign, IL: Human Kinetics.

Gouker, D. (2017). *Daily Fantasy Sports in Germany: DraftKings Expands with New Skills Games License.* Retrieved November 6, 2017 from www.legalsportsreport.com/12815/draftkings-fantasy-sports-germany/.

Gruneau, R., & Horne, J. (2016). *Mega-events and Globalization: Capital and Spectacle in a Changing World Order.* New York, NY: Routledge.

Hernandez, R. A. (2002). *Managing Sport Organizations.* Champaign, IL: Human Kinetics.

Howard, D. R., & DeSchriver, T. D. (2005). Financial Principles Applied to Sport Management. In L. P. Masteralexis, C. Barr, & M. A. Hums (Eds.), *Principles and Practice of Sport Management* (2nd ed.) (pp. 3–24). Sudbury, MA: Jones and Bartlett.

Jones, A. W. (2016). *At the Gate and Beyond: Outlook for the Sports Market in North America Through 2020.* Los Angeles, LA: PwC U.S. Sports Practice.

Levitt, T. (1993). The Globalization of Markets. In R. Z. Aliber & R. W. Click (Eds.), *Readings in International Business: A Decision Approach* (pp. 249–66). Cambridge, MA: MIT Press.

Levski, Y. (2016). *Why Virtual Reality and Sports are a Match Made in Heaven.* Retrieved October 5, 2017 from: https://appreal-vr.com/blog/5-virtual-reality-uses-in-sports.

Lizandra, M., & Gladden, J. M. (2005). International Sport. In L. P. Masteralexis, C. Barr, & M. A. Hums (Eds.), *Principles and Practice of Sport Management* (2nd ed.) (pp. 166–94). Sudbury, MA: Jones and Bartlett.

Parker, B. (1998). *Globalization and Business Practice: Managing Across Boundaries.* Thousand Oaks, CA: Sage.

New England Patriots. (2015). Patriots launch Patriots365 rewards program for season ticket members. Retrieved October 1, 2017 from www.patriots.com/news/2015/02/19/patriots-launch-patriots365-rewards-program-season-ticket-members.

Pitts, B. G., & Zhang, J. J. (2016). Introduction: The WASM Foundation Stone. In B. G. Pitts, & J. J. Zhang (Eds.), *Global Sport Management: Contemporary Issues and Inquiries* (pp. 3–17). London, UK: Routledge.

Ratten, V. (2010). Sport-based Entrepreneurship: Towards a New Theory of Entrepreneurship and Sport Management. *International Entrepreneurship and Management Journal, 1*, 57–69.

Sparvero, E., & Chalip, L. (2007). Professional Teams as Leverageable Assets: Strategic Creation of Community Value. *Sport Management Review, 10*, 1–30.

Summers, D. C. S. (2009). *Quality Management: Creating and Sustaining Organizational Effectiveness* (2nd ed.). Upper Saddle River, NJ: Prentice Hall.

Taylor, T. D., & McGraw, P. (2015). *Managing People in Sport Organizations: A Strategic Human Resource Management Perspective* (2nd ed.). New York, NY: Routledge.

Thibault, L. (2009). Globalization of Sport: An Inconvenient Truth. *Journal of Sport Management, 23*, 1–20.

Winfield, K. (2017). NBA Live 18' is the first video game to feature full WNBA rosters. Retrieved November 30, 2017 from www.sbnation.com/2017/8/3/16089730/nba-live-18-wnba-rosters-all-star-ea-sports-nba-2k.

Zhang, J. J., Chen, K. K., & Kim, J. J. (2014). Leadership on a Global Scale. In J. F. Borland, G. M. Kane, & L. J. Burton (Eds.), *Sport Leadership in the 21st Century* (pp. 327–46). Burlington, MA: Jones & Bartlett.

Zhang, J. J., Pitts, B. G., & Kim, E. (2017). Introduction: Sport Marketing in a Globalized Marketplace. In J. J. Zhang & B. G. Pitts (Eds.), *Contemporary Sport Marketing: Global Perspectives* (pp. 3–20). London, UK: Routledge.

Zwick, D., & Dieterle, O. (2005). The E-business of Sport Sponsorship. In J. Amis, J., & T. B. Cornwell (Eds.), *Global Sport Sponsorship* (pp. 147–62). New York, NY: Berg.

Part II

Managing resources

Chapter 2

Role of state funding in participation of Croatian athletes at major sports events

Sanela Škorić and Evica Obadić

Introduction

Sport is a complex social activity that in Croatia, similarly as in other European countries, encompasses several different segments. Those are physical and health education, competitive sports, sports recreation, kinesiotherapy, and sport for disabled people (Bartoluci & Škorić, 2009, pp. 16–19). Due to its "capacity to reach out to everyone, regardless of age or social origin, sport can play various roles in European society" (European Commission, 2007). These roles include health promotion, educational, social, recreational, and cultural roles. Although attainment of socially beneficial goals is priority, non-profit (sport) organizations pursue economic activities as well (European Commission, 2007). Consequently, sport generates various macro and micro-economic effects (Bartoluci & Škorić, 2009). Nevertheless, due to their goals and social functions, sport, i.e. some segments of sport, are considered as public goods, and therefore require the involvement of the entire community. This means that sport is being financed both from private and public resources. The main stakeholders of the sport sector are public sector i.e. national governments and local authorities, companies and individuals, "each of which plays a different role and pursues specific objectives" (Eurostrategies, 2011, p. 21). Of interest for this chapter are national governments and their role in governing the sport system.

Nowadays, in the majority of European countries sport is under jurisdiction of ministries in charge of education, culture, and arts (Institut za javne financije, 2012). Nevertheless, the executive role in sport governance usually belongs to non-governmental, non-profit organizations such as national Olympic committees or national federations of sport associations (Institut za javne financije, 2012). This means that "lying below central government agencies, and in addition to local government, most countries have sports policy bodies which act as vehicles for delivering central and local government initiatives or allocating finances to sport" (Downward, Dawson, & Dejonghe, 2009, p. 42). Not going into more detail on other possible factors influencing international success, the aim of this chapter is twofold. The first aim is to examine the amount and structure of funds that the Republic of Croatia invested in their athletes through the COC during the period from 2003 to 2015, for WCs, and 2016 for SOGs Additionally, a hypothesis that international success of Croatian athletes at various WCs and SOGs was positively correlated with state funds aimed for financing these competitions was tested.

Review of literature

According to Coalter (2007), governments' systematic interest in sport "despite nineteenth century beliefs about the contribution of sport to improved health and the construction of civic cultures" (p. 9), dates largely from the 1960s. Various researchers have identified several roles and functions governments fulfil when sport is concerned, either directly or by delegation (Nys, 2006). These are the legal role (promulgation of rules and imperative standards such as laws, decrees, and orders) and expertise function through evaluations, accreditations, and diplomas that it awards. Governments value and encourage universal sports participation, oversees the health of sportsmen and women, ensures the development of the country's image through the organization of international competitions, the preservation of national teams at a high level of competitiveness and by the election of national leaders in international federations, and fosters international cooperation and grants subsidies to less-developed countries.

Different reasons can be mentioned as to why governments

> (including the EU here as a quasi-government) do seek to influence and steer the sports system, even if the resources which are brought to bear in sport are a mixture of public, voluntary and commercial sector resources rather than solely public resources. The role of national government and/or the European Union is in part related to seeing that 'sport's goals' are not 'subverted' by commercial abuse, while also ensuring that governmental goals are pursued in the sports field.
>
> (Henry & Lee, 2004, p. 34)

Governments

> pursue various objectives such as education and social inclusion through sport, the health and well-being of the population, ensuring a viable and diversified offer of services, in a large variety of sport disciplines, for all citizens, and the country's good standing in international competitions.
>
> (Eurostrategies, 2011, p. 21)

According to Downward et al. (2009), the traditional emphases of sports policy were "aimed at raising general physical fitness and enhancing social welfare, but such initiatives have gradually been eroded in favour of the pursuit of elite success" (p. 59). Greater governmental interest in pursuing goals of achieving international success was seen after the Second World War and it is "with the Soviet Union's change of heart about international sport at the end of the Second World War that we have a significant example of a government devoting resources to achieving prestige through victory in competition" (Allison & Monnington, 2002, p. 114). However, all credits cannot be awarded to the Soviet Union. According to Yesentayev (2016), the constant increase of elite sports' popularity as well as the significance of successes in the international sports arena at the end of the twentieth and beginning of the twenty-first centuries resulted in a change of attitudes towards sport and achievements of national teams. "As a result in many countries elite sports became one of strategic spheres of functioning, factor of national prestige, consolidation and self-affirmation of nation, development of national identity and unity" (Yesentayev, 2016, p. 21). Furthermore, Houlihan (2006, p. 256) explained that sport has a significant value as a diplomatic resource.

> However, if governments were to be able to exploit fully the diplomatic opportunities that international sport offered, it was important that they had successful athletes who would be missed if they took part in a boycott or who would confer status on, or at least generate publicity for, the countries that they visited and the events/competitions in which they participated.

This, according to Houlihan (2006), means investing heavily in elite sports institutes and paying athletes to train full-time. Nowadays, a country's unofficial ranking concerning medal count "despite the International Olympic Committee's protestation that the Olympic medal table is not an order of merit" (De Bosscher et al., 2009, p. 113), has become crucial in some societies mostly due to political reasons (Allison & Monnington, 2002; De Bosscher et al., 2009; Haut, Prohl, & Emrich, 2014; Houlihan, 2006; Petracovschi & Terret, 2013; Yesentayev, 2016). It is quite clear that "there is a range of factors that lead to international success" (De Bosscher, De Knop, Van Bottenburg, & Shibli, 2006, p.186). In general, according to De Bosscher et al. (2006), these can be classified into three levels: macro-level (economic welfare, population, geographic and climatic variation, degree of urbanisation, political and cultural system), meso-level (sport policies and politics), and micro-level (the individual athlete and their close environment).

A number of scholars researched the connection between the success of a country measured by won medals at international competitions (mostly Olympic Games) and numerous economic, but also sociological and political variables (Čustonja & Škorić, 2011; De Bosscher et al., 2006; Škorić & Hodak, 2011), namely at the macro-level. All the results are based on econometric testing, mostly regression analysis, and find that GDP or GDP per capita and population are significant determinants of Olympic performances (Andreff, 2008). Although available researches did not take into account variable expenditure for sport, some of them refer to it indirectly through the level of GDP. For example, Matros and Namoro (2004) state in their research that they use variable GDP to capture sport budgets in a certain country. Other researchers assume that the countries with a higher standard measured by GDP or GDP per capita can have greater expenses for top level sport (Rathke & Woitek, 2007; Roberts, 2006). On the other hand, the research on factors leading to international success at the so-called meso-level has been rather scarce.

> These factors are fully or partially determined by sports policies and politics. All things being equal, elite athletes will have a greater chance of success subject to the effectiveness of policy and investment decisions made in elite sport. Taking into account all the various factors that determine elite sports success, meso-level factors are the only ones that can be influenced and changed.
>
> (De Bosscher et al., 2006, p. 193)

It is therefore clear that, in order to fulfil its functions and achieve desired objectives of international success (i.e. win more medals at various international events), formation of appropriate strategy (Yesentayev, 2016), as well as significant funding, is needed. Research presented in the paper by De Bosscher et al. (2009) states that "all key success drivers, which can be influenced by policies, can be distilled down into nine key areas or 'pillars' that are important during the different stages of athletic development" (p. 115). One of the pillars is financial support, which is considered as an input with an assumption that "countries that invest more in (elite) sport can create more opportunities for athletes to train under ideal circumstances" (De Bosscher et al., 2009, p. 115). In the research, only public funds (governments and lotteries) were included, due to problems with collection of data from local authorities as well as private investors in sport. Four pillars were suggested as key success drivers, including financial resources, athletic career support, training facilities, and coach development. However, achieving these "ideal circumstances" could prove to be a problem. In their research on stress in elite sport performers, Hanton, Fletcher, and Coughlan (2005) found that participants mentioned the competitive stressors less than the organizational stressors. Among other organizational stressors, "the most frequently cited themes within *Finances* were 'lack of financial support' and 'differential financial support'. Financial issues emerged as a particularly sensitive subject for the elite performers" (pp. 1134–5). Similarly, results of the research from 2001 (Woodman & Hardy, 2001) show that the main sources of organizational stress were: selection, training environment, finances, nutrition, goals and expectations, coaches and coaching styles, team atmosphere, roles, support network, and communication. In addition, according to research conducted by Škorić and Hodak (2011), national sport federations in Croatia report that their biggest management problem is availability (or the lack of) of public funding (56.25 percent of federations). However, the research indicated that "at the 5% reliability level, a hypothesis that at least 50% of federations find that the biggest management problem in their federation is the availability of public funding, can be rejected" (p. 459).

On the other hand, a number of researches report the problem of governmental subsidies reduction (Wicker & Breuer, 2013, 2015), as well as the fact that public authorities may be more inclined to link public funding to minimum standards of good governance, particularly in relation to financial subsidies and the deployment of public money by sports bodies (XG GG, 2013). Therefore, it is no surprise that some countries report the use of "practices that have been criticized as unacceptable in democratic societies: funding of medal-promising sports only, early selection and specialization of young athletes, authoritarian tendencies in sport policy" (Haut, Prohl, & Emrich, 2014, p. 1). Nevertheless, the fact remains that governments increasingly intervene in sport regardless of the reasons.

In EU countries public support for sport can take many different forms, such as: direct subsidies from public budgets; subsidies from fully or partly State-owned gambling operators, or direct revenues resulting from a license to provide gambling services; special tax rates; loans with lower interest rates; guarantees with lower commissions; public financing of sport facilities; acquisition of a public municipal facilities by a private club or institution at a low price; renting of sports facilities by public entities at a low price; payment for the construction or renovation of sport facilities by the local council; public works in private sport facilities; public acquisition of advertising spaces in sport facilities; land sales or donations or an exchange of land for sport facilities (European Commission, 2007). A significant amount of government funds comes from lotteries, betting, and gambling operators. They contribute to the funding of sport in one of three possible ways: by making payments to designated sporting bodies under statutory schemes or in accordance with the terms of their licence, or under non-statutory schemes; by making commercial payments to third parties active in sport (through advertising and sponsorship); and by paying corporate and local taxes to national and/or local governments, contributing to the overall budget from which governments annually define the amount of funding that is allocated to sport (Eurostrategies, 2011).

A founding assembly of the COC was held on August 20, 1991 which, thanks to a new law on sports from 1992 (NN 60/1992, article 42), became the national sports body in Croatia. Two days after the international recognition of the Republic of Croatia, on January 17, 1992, the executive committee of the International Olympic Committee (IOC) temporarily recognized the COC, thus enabling Croatian athletes to participate in Winter Olympic Games in Albertville as well as in the Olympic Games in Barcelona (Lugović, Jajčević, & Drpić, 2006). The COC was officially recognized on September 24, 1993. It is the highest sports body in Croatia, i.e. it is at the top of a pyramid managing organized sport (Bartoluci & Škorić, 2009), similarly as in many other countries (Wicker & Breuer, 2014). It acts independently as a non-profit, non-governmental organization. According to data from 2016, its members are 84 national sport federations/associations (NFs/NAs), 21 county associations as well as ten other associations of special interest for Croatian sport (COC, 2016a, 2016b, 2016c). The aims of the COC are (COC, 2015, article 12) to:

> Promote the Olympic principles, ethical and moral norms in sports; encourage, promote the entire Croatian sport and its representation before the International Olympic Committee and corresponding international sports organizations and associations; harmonize, encourage the activities of national sports federations/associations; develop and promote sport nationally and encourage the organization and harmonization of sport in counties, cities and municipalities.

Promoting Croatian athletes' top sports achievements and their participation as national team members in the Olympic and Mediterranean Games, world and European championships and other major events, is one of the COC's many activities stated in the Statute. One of the crucial ways in which the COC achieves its tasks and aims is by financing various programmes for athletes' participation at international sport events.

A majority of the COC's income comes from the state budget (Figure 1). The task of central government is to help the functioning of the entire sports system through determining the public needs in sport (at state and local level) and providing necessary funds to finance those needs. According to EUROSTAT data (Europa, 2017) in 2015, the Croatian government has invested about 0.1 percent of its total expenditure for recreational and sporting services. This is below EU-28 average (0.7 percent) and is actually the lowest percentage level. A majority of those funds goes to the COC, which acts as an executive body to which funds for financing public needs in sport at state level are distributed via the Ministry of Education and Sport. Similarly to the Czech Republic, state support through COC is "primarily aimed on the support of professional sport and national representation" (Hobza, Pospíšil, & Hobza, 2015).

In the observed period from 2003 until 2015, the income structure of the COC was as follows: from state budget 87.7 percent; own income 8.9 percent; income from Olympic solidarity 2.3 percent; and other income

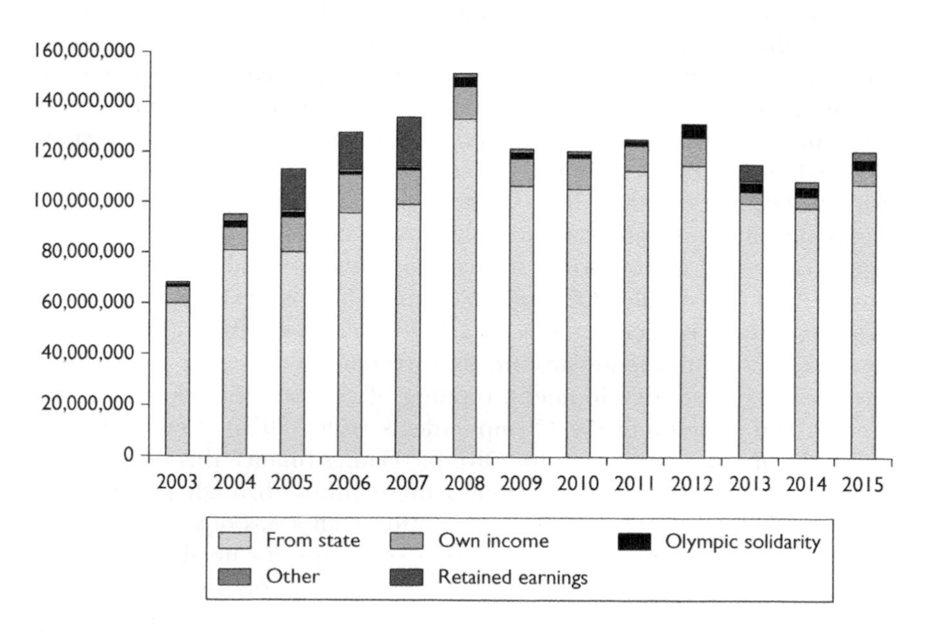

Figure 2.1 The structure of COC income from 2003 until 2015 (in kuna)

Source: based on data from COC's financial reports (formal permission to use data was obtained by Evica Obadić from Croatian Olympic Committee, registration number of the decision is 537/16 from June 6, 2016)

1.1 percent. As already previously mentioned, the most important source of income for the COC is state budget, which accounts to 87.7 percent of its total income. Depending on the year in question, its share ranges from 83 percent in 2005, to 91.9 percent in 2013. Funds coming from state budget encompass three different sources: games of chance (e.g., lottery, gambling, betting), general income, and budget reserves. The highest amount of the budget derives from games of chance. Act on Games of Chance (NN, 143/09) determines that 50 percent of funds from monthly fees or profits from various games of chance are allocated to various beneficiaries according to special regulations issued each year by the government. Among other organizations, those promoting the development of sports are regular users, and receive around 30 percent of these funds. Almost 69 percent of the total state budget for COC comes from games of chance (with the exception of 2013 and 2014 when COC received no revenue from this source). General state income and state budget reserves amount to 15.8 percent and 2.9 percent of total COC income respectively. However, budget reserves are not a usual source of income for COC. These funds were acquired in 2004, 2005, 2006, 2009, and 2010 based on COC's request due to insufficient funds for financing participation of Croatian athletes at Olympic Games. Although they are the most important source of income, funds coming from the state budget are usually insufficient for covering all the needs of Croatian sport and its athletes, so COC has to find ways to earn additional revenues. It does so through its own (marketing) revenue, based on membership fees, sponsor deals, donations, etc. Individual contract value of these projects ranges from 20.000 to 1.800.000 HRK (Croatian national currency).

Finally, although not amounting to much of COC's income (on average 2.3 percent) an important source of income for athletes and coaches comes from the so-called Olympic Solidarity. The aim of Olympic Solidarity is to organize assistance for all National Olympic Committees (NOCs), particularly those with the greatest needs, through multi-faceted programmes prioritizing athlete development, training of coaches and sports administrators, and promoting the Olympic ideals (IOC, 2016). Revenues from selling of broadcasting rights for Olympic Games finance this programme. Olympic Solidarity then redistributes these funds through programmes such as *World programmes* (cover and reinforce all areas of sports development), *Continental programmes* (meet some of the specific needs of each continent), *Olympic Games subsidies* (offer financial support to NOCs for the Games), and *Complementary programmes* (extended assistance offered in the framework of targeted projects). In the observed period, the COC used funds from all of the mentioned programmes. Nevertheless, the biggest amounts of money were received from the World programmes – Olympic scholarships for athletes (preparation of athletes for qualifying games for participation at Olympic Games).

The category entitled other income refers to revenue from refunding of various programmes, exchange rate differences, interest rates, etc. The COC's expenses consist of several categories that appear on a regular basis (every year), including NFs'/NAs' regular programmes, sport at local level, special programme projects, common programme tasks, Croatian Olympic Academy, programmes from the last year, Olympic solidarity (regularly from 2006), and reserves. In this chapter, only expenses whose aim is to finance the preparations and participation of Croatian athletes at international sport events will be analysed. Those are NFs'/NAs' regular programmes (Table 2.1) and special programme projects (Table 2.2).

The largest amount of expenses is reserved for the category entitled *NFs'/NAs' and other COC members' regular programmes*. The average share of total COC budget spent for regular programmes in the observed period of 13 years is 44.3 percent and varies from 27.8 percent in 2004 to 51.2 percent in 2014. Excluding expenses for sports recreation competitions, these funds are entirely directed towards financing athletes' participation at various events. They represent a base for financing athletes of all categories from cadets to seniors. Around 72 percent of all regular programmes' expenses finance preparations and competitions, followed by administration cost (around 24 percent). Again, there is no evident trend of growth or decline of these expenses. In the observed period of 13 years, a total amount of almost 470 million of HRK was invested solely in athletes' preparations for various events and their competing at those events, which amounts to almost 32 percent of all the COC's expenses in the same period.

The aims of these regular programmes are various. One of the major tasks is to support Croatian athletes' preparation and participation at international competitions, and other multisport events (mostly expenses for accommodation and nutrition of athletes and accompanying personnel, travel expenses, fees, etc.). In the period from 2003 until 2015 this project has undergone constant changes and improvements. Emergence of new sports resulted in the foundation of adequate associations, which became members and users of COC programmes. This resulted in a constant increase of the number of athletes and competitions financed from this item. In the first three observed years, on average 343 competitions were financed through these funds, and in 2015 almost double the number, i.e. 729. The most important competitions are world and European championships, which take up most of the finances. Payments for international membership fees (mostly for NFs/NAs), as well as support to expert group members and administration needs of all COC members, are also part of these funds (salaries for NFs'/NAs' main secretaries, directors, expert and administrative secretaries; rent and overhead expenses; other obligations emerging from piecework agreements).

Table 2.1 The structure of NFs'/NAs' regular programmes (in millions of HRK)

Year	*Competitions and preparation*	*NF's/NA's international obligations*	*Administration*
2003	15,721	1,281	5,952
2004	16,862	1,508	6,248
2005	40,160	1,746	7,916
2006	34,788	1,736	9,593
2007	43,109	1,934	11,582
2008	43,602	2,595	13,905
2009	39,687	1,602	13,863
2010	35,122	1,655	14,220
2011	41,821	2,194	14,905
2012	39,722	1,718	15,591
2013	38,667	2,046	14,385
2014	39,336	2,060	13,565
2015	41,021	2,334	14,789

Source: COC's financial reports (formal permission to use data was obtained by Evica Obadić from Croatian Olympic Committee, registration number of the decision is 537/16 from June 6, 2016)

Expenses connected with participation of athletes at sport events are also found in the category *special programme projects*, whose average share in total expenses in the observed period was 25.3 percent. These consist of health-care expenses (and doping); multisport programs (expenses for participation at various sport events – in the observed period a total of 22 sport events were financed); support for sports events (occurred from 2003 till 2009); development programmes (for athletes, coaches, research projects, testing of top level athletes, fees for foreign coaches, additional healthcare).

As can be seen from Table 2.2, the most important item in group special programme projects are expenses for multisport programmes, aimed mostly at financing preparation and participation of Croatian athletes at Olympic Games (summer and winter), Olympic Youth Games (summer and winter), European Youth Olympic Festival (summer and winter), Mediterranean Games, etc. In order to enable as many athletes as possible to qualify for Olympic Games, each of the games are accompanied by a *Project of preparation and participation of Croatian athletes at forthcoming Olympic Games*, which lasts four years. These projects ensure funds dedicated for additional preparations and competitions, Olympic scholarships, acquiring of special equipment needed for training process, health insurance, additional medical attention (medical examination, rehabilitation, etc.).

Health expenses, i.e., doping, refers to the conducting of doping tests for athletes. However, since 2013 when the Croatian anti-doping agency was founded, they are no longer a part of COC expenses. Expenses for support to sport events finance a part of organizational costs for staging various sport

Table 2.2 Structure of expenses for special programme projects

Year	*% Health (Doping)*	*% Multisport Programmes*	*% Support To Sport Events*	*% Development Programmes*
2003	0.51	58.58	5.25	35.66
2004	0.46	76.40	6.49	16.65
2005	2.33	67.24	4.69	25.74
2006	1.39	43.21	9.68	45.73
2007	0.48	49.49	6.82	43.21
2008	1.18	61.58	4.92	32.33
2009	1.22	41.09	5.51	52.18
2010	0.89	38.41	0.00	60.70
2011	1.28	38.00	0.00	60.72
2012	0.78	61.21	0.00	38.01
2013	0.00	44.01	0.00	55.99
2014	0.00	34.32	0.00	65.68
2015	0.00	52.32	0.00	47.68

Source: COC's financial reports (formal permission to use data was obtained by Evica Obadić from Croatian Olympic Committee, registration number of the decision is 537/16 from June 6, 2016)

events in Croatia. These funds can be used solely by NFs/NAs that gained the COC's and governmental support during candidature for staging the event in question. However, in 2010 this programme was abolished. In the observed period from 2003 until 2015 its share was on average 3.6 percent of total special programme project funds.

Development programmes refer to the expenses of athletes and coaches as an upgrade of the COC's and NFs'/NAs' programmes following development of each athlete, which starts when athletes show potential for achieving excellent results (i.e. candidature and participation at Olympic Games). These include rights to motor and functional testing, preparations, use of necessary sport facilities and equipment, healthcare and other insurances. Athletes gain the right to use scholarships with three levels of development programmes. All activities are built and conducted in cooperation with responsible NFs/NAs and are constantly enhanced. For example, in 2003 there was only one ("Individual programme of special care for young athletes"), and in 2016 six different development programs for athletes. These are the support programme for younger athletes (Programme I); individual programme of special care for young athletes (Programme II) which consists of individual programmes of special care for young athletes (Programme II/1) and young athletes participating in team sports (Programme II/2); support programme for qualitative athletes (Programme III); support programme for athletes in the pre-Olympic development programme (Programme IV); support programme for teams in pre-Olympic qualifying cycle (Programme V); and Olympic programme (Programme VI). This resulted in a 58 percent increase of funds in 2015 opposed to 2003 (from 1.5 million to just over 3.6 million HRK).

Additionally, development programmes for coaches finance their work with most successful athletes and teams, and aim to support expert knowledge and training skills and to develop and enhance sport results of top athletes. As was the case with the development programmes for athletes, in 2003 there was only one programme for coaches ("top" coaches), and in 2015 six: "top" level A and B coaches; coaches of Olympic team sports; "top" coaches; qualitative coaches; coaches of younger athletes; and coaches developing certain sport. Programmes for coaches experienced an even greater increase in funds, from 1.3 million to 7.1 million HRK. All development programmes strive to keep the achieved level of quality, promote the development of sport in Croatia, and especially ensure necessary expert, technical, material, and life conditions to most successful athletes and coaches.

Based on the previous analysis of income and expenses, it can be seen that the highest costs for regular and special programmes occurred in the year of COC's highest income, i.e., 2008. Constant fluctuation in expenses can be attributed to the government sporting and economic policy (Andreff, 2009), and as a consequence the level of COC's income, as well as sport calendars and destinations of sport competitions. For example, some sports host world and European championships every four, others every two, and some sports every year. Olympic Games are certainly the most important event for the COC. Therefore, it comes as no surprise that there is an increase in expenses for special programmes in the years before summer Olympic Games (2007, 2011, 2015) as well as in the years when the Games were held (Beijing in 2008 and London 2012). In addition, it is of importance whether competitions are held in Europe, the Americas, or Australia. Finally, as previously mentioned, there was a constant increase in the number of regular programme users (mainly NFs/NAs), from 68 in 2003, to 86 in 2015.

Method and results

In order to see if there is a connection between invested funds and achieved international success of Croatian athletes, a further correlation analysis was conducted using data presented in Appendix A. The main hypothesis was that international success of Croatian athletes at various WCs and SOGs was positively correlated with funds aimed for financing these competitions. International success was expressed by points awarded to medals won at WCs and SOGs (gold medal was awarded three points, silver medal two points, and bronze medal one point). Data on achieved success at WCs was summarized for 49 NFs/NAs. The underlying assumption was that each NF/NA had the same chance to participate and consequently win a medal, at each of the WCs. Data was missing from seven NFs/NAs, meaning that they either did not participate at any of the WCs, or they did participate but did not win any medals. According to the Kolmogorov-Smirnov test, all used variables were normally distributed. As can be seen from Tables 2.4 and 2.5 in Appendix A, Croatian athletes participated in total at almost 600 WCs (on average 45.69 each year), generated almost 3,000 trips (on average 213.92 per year) and won 810 medals (252 gold, 253 silver, and 305 bronze medals). It is necessary to note that the variable entitled "trips" was used and not the number of athletes due to possible overlapping of data; for instance, some athletes participated at more than one World Championship event within a calendar year.

Table 2.3 Correlation analysis for World Championships 2003–15

Variable	*N = 13*		
	Competitions and preparation	*NF's/NA's international obligations*	*Administration*
Trips	0.152	–0.028	–0.031
Medal points	0.061	0.328	0.440
World Championships	0.479	0.281	0.600*

* Significant at .05 level

Correlation analysis showed statistically significant correlation between variables number of World Championships and administration costs (Table 2.3). This can be explained by the previously mentioned increase in the number of federations/associations in the COC. Additionally, correlation analysis for SOGs reveals no statistically significant correlation between results achieved at SOGs and funds aimed at financing preparation and participation of athletes at Olympic Games. The correlation coefficient was -.372 between medal points and the multisport programmes and .233 between medal points and the development programmes, and neither was statistically significant ($p > .05$). Data used for correlational analysis for the World Championships and Olympic Games are presented in Tables 2.4 and 2.5.

Basic limitations that appeared in this study that should to be taken in consideration in future research are concerned with missing data and variables included in the analysis. First, as previously mentioned, international success was measured through won medals by awarding points to each medal (gold medal three points, silver medal two points, and bronze medal one point). However, it can be argued that international success at major sport competitions such as World Championships and Olympic Games cannot be measured only by won medals, meaning that as a measure of international success results encompassing at least first to eighth place should be taken into consideration. Furthermore, analysis included funds for preparations and participation at WCs for all NFs/NAs. However, not all of them participated and/or won medals. Future research should resolve this issue as well as the issue of the structure of these funds. Additionally, it is necessary to expand the scope of the research to include other variables, such as other sources of financing, including other championships.

Discussion

Achieving international success requires, besides athletes' talent and hard work, significant (financial) resources aimed at providing all necessary conditions for top athletes to prepare and compete at various sport events. The public, namely the government, usually secures (the majority of) these funds, as it has significant benefits arising from athletes' top results. The Croatian government has, in the observed period from 2003 until 2015, invested in its athletes, via various COC programmes, almost 1.3 billion HRK. An analysis showed that there has been a significant increase in the number of programmes and (consequently) the amount of money for development programmes for athletes and coaches. Therefore, one could say that the key role in the existing system of sport financing belongs to governing bodies as well as management of the COC and its members. Correlation analysis showed no statistically significant correlation between the total amount of expenses aimed for financing participation of Croatian athletes at various WCs and SOGs and medals won at these competitions. However, a more detailed analysis including other variables (such as other sources of financing, other championships, expanding the data on achieved international success to encompass results from first to eighth place, etc.) as well as deeper analysis of the structure of these funds is needed. The most important limitations of the study were missing data from some federations.

References

Allison, L., & Monnington, T. (2002). Sport, Prestige and International Relations. Retrieved September 1, 2016 from: http://s3.amazonaws.com/academia.edu.documents/43048421/Allison_Sport_and_prestige_in_International_Relations_Skaitytas.pdf?AWSAccessKeyId=AKIAJ56TQJRTWSMTNPEA&Expires=1473939770&Signature=AENBO3HR50JPWC0T9c1Z%2Bzrs7zI%3D&response-content-disposition=inline%3B%20filename%3DGOVERNMENT_AND_OPPOSITION_106_Sport_Pres.pdf.

Andreff, W. (2009). Sport Financing in Times of Global Recession. *Play the Game 2009 International Conference, Coventry, June 8–12, 2009.* Retrieved August 11, 2011 from www.playthegame.org/uploads/media/Wladimir_Andreff_-_Financing_of_sport_in_times_of_crisis_01.pdf.

Andreff, W. (2008). Sport in Developing Countries. Retrieved May 1, 2017 from: http://assets.sportanddev.org/downloads/79_sport_in_developing_countries.pdf.

Bartoluci, M. & Škorić, S. (2009). *Menadžment u sportu.* Zagreb: Odjel za izobrazbu trenera Društvenog veleučilišа u Zagrebu, Kineziološki fakultet Sveučilišta u Zagrebu.

Coalter, F. (2007). *A Wider Social Role for Sport: Who's Keeping the Score?* New York, NY: Routledge.

COC. (2015). Statut hrvatskog olimpijskog odbora. Retrieved August 1, 2016 from: www.hoo.hr/images/dokumenti/sport-olimpizam-hr/Statut__HOO-a-studeni_2015.pdf.

COC. (2016a). National Sports Federations. Retrieved August 1, 2016 from: www.hoo.hr/en/croatian-olympic-committee/national-sports-federations.

COC. (2016b). County Sports Associations. Retrieved August 1, 2016 from: www.hoo.hr/en/local-sport/county-sports-associations.

COC. (2016c). Other Associations. Retrieved August 1, 2016 from: www.hoo.hr/en/croatian-olympic-committee/other-associations-and-institutions/2045-other-associations.

Čustonja, Z., & Škorić, S. (2011). Winning Medals at the Olympic Games – Does Croatia have any Chance? *Kinesiology, 43(1),* 107–14.

De Bosscher, V., De Knop, P., Van Bottenburg, M. & Shibli, S. (2006). A Conceptual Framework for Analysing Sports Policy Factors Leading to International Sporting Success, *European Sport Management Quarterly, 6(2),* 185–215.

De Bosscher, V., De Knop, P., van Bottenburg, M., Shibli, S., & Bingham, J. (2009). Explaining International Sporting Success: An International Comparison of Elite Sport Systems and Policies in Six Countries, *Sport Management Review, 12,* 113–36.

Downward, P., Dawson, A., & Dejonghe, T. (2009). *Sports Economics: Theory, Evidence and Policy.* Oxford, UK: Elsevier.

Europa. (2017). File: Total general government expenditure on recreation, culture and religion, 2015. Retrieved May 1, 2017 from http://ec.europa.eu/eurostat/statistics-explained/index.php/File:Total_general_government_expenditure_on_recreation,_culture_and_religion,_2015_(%25_of_GDP_%25_of_total_expenditure).png.

European Commission. (2007). Commission Staff Working Document: The EU and Sport – Background and Context. Retrieved August 1, 2016 from: http://eur-lex.europa.eu/legal-content/EN/TXT/?uri=CELEX:52007SC0935.

Eurostrategies. (2011). Study on the Funding of Grassroots Sports in the EU. Deutsche Sportschule Köln. Retrieved August 1, 2016 from http://ec.europa.eu/internal_market/top_layer/docs/FinalReportVol1_en.pdf.

Hanton, S., Fletcher, D., & Coughlan, G. (2005). Stress in Elite Sport Performers: A Comparative Study of Competitive and Organizational Stressors. *Journal of Sport Sciences, 23(10),* 1129–41.

Haut, J., Prohl, R., & Emrich, E. (2014). Nothing but Medals? Attitudes Towards the Importance of Olympic Success, *International Review for the Sociology of Sport, 1,* 1–17.

Henry, I., & Lee, P.C. (2004). Governance and Ethics in Sport. In J. Beech & S. Chadwick (Eds.), *The Business of Ssport Management* (pp. 25–42). London, UK: Pearson Education.

Hobza, V., Pospíšil, R., & Hobza, V. (2015). Case Study: Proposal on Restructuring of Sport Support in the City of Litoměřice in the Favour of Grant-oriented Support, *Manager, 22,* 251–9.

Houlihan, B. (2006). Government Objectives and Sport. In W. Andreff & S. Szymanski (Eds.), *Handbook on the Economics of Sport* (pp. 254–9). Cheltenham, UK, and Northampton, MA: Edward Elgar.

Institut za javne financije (2012). Financiranje sporta u republici hrvatskoj s usporednim prikazom financiranja u Europskoj Uniji. Zagreb: Institut za javne financije. Retrieved August 1, 2016 from: http://public.mzos.hr/Default.aspx?sec=2379.

IOC. (2016). Olympic Solidarity. Retrieved September 1, 2016 from: www.olympic.org/olympic-solidarity.

Lugović, J. Jajčević, Z., & Drpić, A. (2006). *Na putu olimpizma: Hrvatski olimpijski odbor 1991–2006.* Zagreb, Croatia: Croatian Olympic Committee.

Matros, A., & Namoro, S. D. (2004). Economic Incentives of the Olympic Games. Retrieved September 1, 2004 from http://ssrn.com/abstract=588882.

Ministry of Science, Education and Sports (2007). Sports Act. Retrieved August 1, 2016 from: http://public.mzos.hr/Default.aspx?sec=2545.

NN. (2009). Act on Games of Chance. Retrieved September 1, 2016 from www.coe.int/t/dghl/monitoring/moneyval/Evaluations/Progress%20reports%202y/MONEYVAL(2011)4-ProgRep2HRVann_en.pdf.

Nys, J. F. (2006). Central Government and Sport. In W. Andreff and S. Szymanski (Eds), *Handbook on the Economics of Sport* (pp. 260–70). Cheltenham, UK, and Northampton, MA: Edward Elgar.

Petracovschi, S., & Terret, T. (2013). From Best to Worst? Romania and its Nostalgia for Olympic Successes. *The International Journal of the History of Sport, 30,* 774–88.

Rathke, A., & Woitek, U. (2007). Economics and Olympics: An Efficiency Analysis. Retrieved January 1, 2007 from: http://ssrn.com/abstract=967629.

Roberts, G. (2006). Accounting for Achievement in Athens: A Count Data Analysis of National Olympic Performance. Retrieved January 1, 2007 from: http://web.uvic.ca/econ/ewp0602.pdf.

Škorić, S., & Hodak, Z. (2011). The System of Sports Financing and Management in the Republic of Croatia (Preliminary Communication), *Zbornik radova Ekonomskog fakulteta u Rijeci – časopis za ekonomsku teoriju i praksu / Proceedings of Rijeka Faculty of Economics – Journal of economics and business, 29(2)*, 443–64.

Wicker, P. & Breuer, C. (2013). Exploring the Critical Determinants of Organizational Problems Using Data Mining Techniques: Evidence from Non-profit Sports Clubs in Germany, *Managing Leisure, 18(2)*, 118–34.

Wicker, P. & Breuer, C. (2014). Examining Financial Condition of Sport Governing Bodies: The Effects of Revenue Diversification and Organizational Success Factors, *Voluntas, 25*, 929–48.

Wicker, P., & Breuer, C. (2015). How the Economic and Financial Situation of the Community Affects Sport Club's Resources: Evidence from Multi-level Models. *International Journal of Financial Studies, 3*, 31–48.

Woodman, T., & Hardy, L. (2001). A Case Study of Organizational Stress in Elite Sport. *Journal of Applied Sport Psychology, 13*, 207–38.

XG GG. (2013). Deliverable 2: Principles of Good Governance in Sport. Retrieved February 10, 2014 from http://ec.europa.eu/sport/library/policy_documents/xg-gg-201307-dlvrbl2-sept2013.pdf.

Yesentayev, T. K. (2016). Political Influence on Sportsmen's Training System in Olympic Sports, *Pedagogics, Psychology, Medical-Biological Problems of Physical Training and Sports, 1*, 19–23.

Appendix A: data used for correlation analysis

Table 2.4 Data used for correlation analysis for World Championships

Year	Number of WCs	Trips	Medal points	Competitions and Preparations	NF's/NA's International Obligations	Administration
2003	36	247	87	15.721.030	1.281.008	5.952.871
2004	33	147	134	16.862.322	1.508.741	6.248.013
2005	37	215	76	40.160.447	1.746.741	7.916.487
2006	49	263	82	34.788.946	1.736.914	9.593.361
2007	43	254	69	43.109.631	1.934.198	11.582.502
2008	36	161	100	43.602.814	2.595.955	13.905.616
2009	59	231	121	39.687.455	1.602.929	13.863.062
2010	42	154	110	35.122.825	1.655.240	14.220.403
2011	52	236	112	41.821.991	2.194.578	14.905.171
2012	41	185	112	39.722.516	1.718.062	15.591.987
2013	58	272	183	38.667.046	2.046.937	14.385.910
2014	55	185	144	39.336.943	2.060.200	13.565.848
2015	53	231	181	41.021.350	2.334.398	14.789.911

Source: COC's reports (formal permission to use data was obtained by Evica Obadić from Croatian Olympic Committee, registration number of the decision is 537/16 from June 6, 2016)

Table 2.5 Data used for correlation analysis for Olympic Games

Year	Medal points	Multisport Programmes	Development Programmes
2004	9	36.956.316	11.201.170
2008	7	86.543.480	56.629.466
2012	13	56.118.139	61.452.575
2016	23	50.017.898	49.842.106

Source: COC's reports (formal permission to use data was obtained by Evica Obadić from Croatian Olympic Committee, registration number of the decision is 537/16 from June 6, 2016)

Chapter 3

Developing a demand model to estimate attendance at an individual NBA game from related-game attributes

Kenneth K. Chen, James J. Zhang, Brenda G. Pitts, Thomas A. Baker, and Kevin K. Byon

Introduction

Each game appears to be a unique product, and fan responses to different opponents are substantially different in various ways, including attendance. Such a phenomenon has puzzled sports team management and intrigued researchers for years, which leads to the following question: What are the real causes for such huge differentials in attendance for single games? In an effort to better understand the driving factors of attendance at professional sporting events, an extensive amount of research has been conducted to examine and/or estimate the demand trend using various game-related factors. Several factors have been reported to be positively related to attendance, such as income (Baade & Tiehen, 1990; Pan, Zhu, Gabert, & Brown, 1999; Wicker, Hallmann, & Zhang, 2012), population or community size (Baade & Tiehen, 1990; Robinson & DeSchriver, 2003), facility attributes (Byon, Zhang, & Baker, 2013; Roy, 2008; Wakefield & Sloan, 1995), team performance (Davis, 2009; McDonald & Rascher, 2000; Zhang, Pease, Hui, & Michaud, 1995; Zhang, Lam, Bennett, & Connaughton, 2003), schedule convenience (Cianfrone, Zhang, Pitts, & Byon, 2015; McDonald & Rascher, 2000; Zhang et al., 1995), star players (Byon et al., 2013; Baade & Tiehen, 1990; Rivers & DeSchriver, 2002), and game promotions (Boyd & Krehbiel, 2006; Gifis & Sommers, 2006; Henderson, Zhang, Byon, & Pitts, 2017; McDonald & Rascher, 2000). Conversely, other factors have been found to be negatively related to game attendance, such as ticket price (Donihue, Findlay, & Newberry, 2008; Zhang, Smith, Pease, & Jambor, 1997; Zhang et al., 2007), team roster turnover (Kahane & Shmanske, 1997), and alternative sports or entertainment options (Armstrong, 1999; Zhang et al., 1997).

Increasing attendance at games has been, and remains, one of the primary objectives of all professional sport marketers. Paid attendance is a major source of income for professional sport teams, and NBA teams rely heavily on gate receipts; attendance also leads to other sources of income on game days, such as revenues from concessions, printed program sales, parking, and apparel, souvenir sales, and broadcast programming (Howard & Crompton, 2004). Previous studies have either modeled variations in attendance figures among teams within a specific league (e.g., Davis, 2009) or identified general factors that affect ticket consumption, such as income, population, team payroll, facility attributes, and ticket price (e.g., Byon et al., 2013; Zhang et al., 1995). The findings in these studies suggest that team marketers should build new and improved stadiums, lower ticket prices, use promotions, and/or put together a strong (if not championship) team to increase overall attendance. However, some of these practices are often out of the marketing department's control, and others are simply unrealistic to execute without a long-term financial plan. It highlights the importance of understanding, in a practical sense, what makes certain games more appealing than others and how to estimate the demand for each game more precisely, which would then enable marketers to respond with specific promotional plans, event operational practices, and even differential game pricing. With the focus of research trained on different aspects of marketing, from general market demand to specific game demand studies, many of the frequently adopted variables in previous studies are neither adequate nor specific enough to explain the fluctuations in demand for a specific team.

Only a few studies have attempted to analyze attendance on a game-specific basis. Marcum and Greenstein (1985) examined the attendance of two Major League Baseball (MLB) teams and found that opponents' records, and the day of the week, were significant predictors of game attendance. Both of these variables were also found to be significant in explaining attendance, along with weather and sales promotion, in a study examining the effects of promotions on demand for a MLB game (McDonald & Rascher, 2000). However, using the win-loss record as the only measurement for the "opponent" variable in the study does not provide sufficient information to answer the question posed earlier, which has puzzled sport teams' managements. Additional information about the opponent might be useful and important for estimating game-specific demand, such as opponent star power, established rivalry, or a certain expected opponent interaction with the home team. Noticeably, most of the demand models in previous studies were built on MLB data because MLB has a wider range of attendance figures that are more readily available than those of the NBA (McDonald & Rascher, 2000), which likely results from the size of the stadiums and the large number of games. In a review of existing literature about the determinants of attendance from 1974 to 2003, Borland and MacDonald (2003) also found that an overwhelming majority of studies had been undertaken on baseball in the US and soccer in the UK. It might be constructive for the fairly narrow basis of the literature to expand into other sports, such as professional basketball.

Incorporating more detailed information about an opponent would enable marketers to be more precise in estimating the demand for each game and help prepare for event operations. As a result, more specific marketing strategies might then be implemented before each game, such as adopting different ticket pricing for different levels of market demand or packaging ticket sales by games, i.e., packaging low-demand games with high-demand games to increase overall ticket sales (Howard & Crompton, 2004). In addition, dynamic pricing has grown to be a new trend in the NBA and is expected to be the future trend of ticket pricing in sports (Rishe, 2012). Understandably, more accurate estimations of demand for each game are crucial to the success of these ticketing strategies, and it has become a major task for team management and sport marketers. Nonetheless, to date, we have found no study that has examined the fluctuation phenomenon of attendance at NBA games. Through a comprehensive review of the existing literature and using data from 1,188 NBA games, the purpose of this study was to develop a demand model from game-related attributes to estimate fluctuations in attendance, with the intention of providing sport marketers with guidelines for forming specific promotional strategies for each game.

Review of literature

In sport economic studies, the demand for sporting event attendance is often based on a consumer-based theory model, in which a consumer chooses to spend a limited budget on a sporting event or other goods or services. Determinants of the demand for attendance were categorized into five categories: (a) form of consumer preference; (b) economy; (c) quality of viewing; (d) characteristics of the contest; and (e) supply capacity (Borland & MacDonald, 2003). The aforementioned empirically tested variables fit perfectly into these theoretical categories. However, the proposed model in this study was designed to predict fluctuations in attendance on a game-specific basis by controlling for the home team and examining the attributes that are associated only with visiting teams. In so doing, most of the frequently adopted market-demand variables identified in previous studies would be fixed or controlled for in the model, such as income, population, team payroll, facility attributes, ticket price, and game promotion. Other variables would have to be measured in more specific and dynamic ways to capture fluctuations in a timely fashion. Through a comprehensive review of the literature, four major factors were found to fit the purpose of this study well. These four factors, i.e., game schedule, star power, team performance, and uncertainty of outcome, were selected as the main focus of the current model. Each of these factors is discussed in more detail below.

Game schedule

It is not difficult to understand why the scheduled game day is a major determinant of attendance. Consumers usually have more free time on weekends or holidays, which reduces opportunity costs and other constraints related to going to a sporting event. Schedule convenience has long been considered one of the most important factors influencing the market demand for sporting events (Braunstein, Zhang, Trail & Gibson, 2005; Zapalac, Zhang, & Pease, 2010; Zhang et al., 2003). Zhang et al. (1995) developed the Spectator Decision-Making Inventory (SDMI) to measure the variables that affect attendance at NBA games and found that four factors, i.e., game promotion, home team, opposing team, and schedule convenience, were related to attendance. Zhang et al. (2003) later confirmed these findings by administering the SDMI to a sample of NBA spectators and validated schedule convenience as a distinct factor in a scale that assessed market demand. Game Schedule was examined by testing the effect of the "day of week" in a study by Marcum and Greenstein (1985), which found that the day of the week on which a MLB game was held was significantly related to attendance. The same approach that used the day of the week dummy variable in the model can also be found in the studies conducted by Davis (2009), and Lemke, Leonard, and Tihokwane (2009). Instead of looking into the difference for each day of the week, Knowles, Sherony, and Haupert (1992) studied data from 861 MLB games and found that attendance was significantly higher when games were played on weekends and in the evenings. Apparently, the day of week would be an important predictor for the current study because it is directly related to the availability of free time for a consumer to attend a NBA game.

Another way to measure the impact of game schedule is to determine the supply of the game(s). If a consumer is deciding whether to attend a NBA game for the coming week, he/she can only decide to go if there is at least one scheduled game during the period of his/her available time. If there are multiple games that are tightly scheduled within a shorter period of time, he/she can choose to attend one preferable game during the period when he/she is available and a game that he/she desires to attend. As a result, attendance for certain games would likely decrease when games are scheduled close to each other, particularly if certain games are perceived as "better" than others. Research findings from Australian Rules football verify that attendance is higher when a series of games is spread across a longer time period (Borland & Lye, 1992). However, there are no similar variables that have been examined in MLB attendance studies, possibly because of the specific style of scheduling in the MLB. Baseball has 81 home games per season and often plays three to four games at home in a row; conversely, the interval between two home games could range from two to 17 days in the NBA. Game availability would therefore be an appropriate variable in the current model, in addition to day of week, and can be estimated by adding the number of days from the last home game to the next home game.

Star power

In sport market demand studies, star power has long been studied and considered a vital factor that positively influences the consumption of sports products (Braunstein & Zhang, 2005; Byon et al., 2013; Greenstein &

Marcum, 1981; Pifer, Mak, Bae, & Zhang, 2015; Zhang et al., 2003). A star player (or players) was utilized as one of the items measuring both home team and opposing team factors in the SDMI and was found to be related to attendance. Obviously, the existence of a star player on the opposing team is considered an important factor in attracting fans to attend games of professional sport leagues, such as the NBA (Braunstein et al., 2005; Zhang et al., 1995; Zhang, et al., 2003).

To test the hypothesis that certain spectators may be attracted to celebrity player(s) instead of a team's overall performance, Baade and Tiehen (1990) identified several star players and found their presence to be significantly related to attendance. Hausman and Leonard (1997) further demonstrated how certain players ("superstars") could positively impact the television ratings, attendance, and merchandise sales of NBA teams. However, authors subjectively selected the star players in these studies with no criterion provided. After a thorough search for an objective method of measuring star power, Rivers and DeSchriver (2002) adopted the MVP and Cy Young Award voting to capture the presence of star player(s) as a variable in their model that attempted to predict MLB attendance. Utilizing this metric, they did not find a significant effect in their study and concluded that a popular star might not necessarily be the player who had the best performance statistics. Although the researchers suggested that an elected All-Star game participant would be an excellent criterion to identify a star player, they decided not to use such data because the MLB did not allow fans to vote pitchers into the All-Star game. Conversely, the NBA All-Star balloting allows fans to vote for their favorite players as starters for each season's All-Star Game. The NBA typically reveals the results of the voting for the top ten players for each position (i.e., guards, forwards, and centers) and selects two guards, two forwards, and one center from each conference to start in the All-Star Game for such conference. The number of votes directly reflects the amount of support that each NBA player receives from his fans, which must be the best practical estimator of star power in the current model.

Team performance

The excellence and beauty of athletic performance are important characteristics that motivate consumers to attend sporting events (Madrigal, 2006). Team performance, as consistently shown in the literature, is one of the most significant demand factors related to attendance figures (e.g., Davis, 2008, 2009; McDonald & Rascher, 2000; Meehan, Nelson, & Richardson, 2007). A majority of these studies examined the effect of winning percentage on attendance using annual attendance data in a specific league (mostly MLB), including Alexander (2001), Davis (2008), and Schmidt and Berri (2006). These studies focus more on the performance of home teams and generally conclude that a team's winning percentage during the season is positively related to its seasonal attendance record. However, these models do not capture demand that changes from game to game. When trying to catch the demand fluctuation within the same season for a specific team, the team's winning percentage for the season is automatically fixed. Although a team's winning percentage usually has highs and lows during the season, its overall quality or performance level usually does not change significantly unless there is a major roster turnover (Kahane & Shmanske, 1997). Thus, home team performance within a season is more properly a constant and not a variable in the current model.

In the current model, a major star player change on a team's roster would be monitored by the star power variables (for both home and visiting teams), whereas the team performance variables would be mainly used to reflect the visiting team's performance level. A few studies have investigated the importance of winning on attendance, using data for individual games. Findings across these investigations generally confirm the conclusion that winning does increase attendance. For example, McDonald and Rascher (2000) examined 1,500 MLB games played during the 1996 season to test a demand model. Variables measuring player and team quality (e.g., team wins, starting pitcher wins) were included in the model and were found to be significantly related to attendance. Meehan et al. (2007) collected data from 7,189 games over the 2000 to 2002 seasons to test the relationship between competitive balance and game attendance in MLB. Several indices were used in the model to measure the quality of the teams. The findings of this study showed that the quality of both the home and visiting teams have significantly positive effects on attendance.

Nevertheless, as opposed to the current study, the goal of the models that were previously developed was to capture the relationship between certain variables and the variation of attendance within the league; these studies did not control for the home team. Davis (2009) analyzed the relationship between team success and MLB attendance using data from each home game played by 12 National League baseball teams from the 1979 to 2005 seasons; consequently, 12 separate regression models were tested for each team, and the results showed that winning significantly increased attendance for all teams. The author also devised ten dummy variables, with each variable representing one specific visiting team in the model, and found that different visiting teams had different effects on attendance. Boyd and Krehbiel (2006) used data from all 30 teams in the MLB and included 29 dummy variables to control for home teams in their model to test the effect of promotions on attendance. Both the home and visiting teams' winning percentages were found to have positive effects on attendance.

Conclusively, team performance is an important determinant of attendance, as shown in the literature. The current winning percentage is the most frequently used measure of team performance when analyzing game-to-game data. However, several shortcomings emerge when using this index. The first is that winning percentage is usually biased and fails to represent a team's real quality at the beginning of a season because of its small denominator. To adjust for this issue, Rascher (1999) multiplied the winning percentage by the percentage of games played and Meehan et al. (2007) dropped the first ten games from the sample for each season; nonetheless, neither of these studies truly corrected the problem. The second problem with this metric is that it does not always reflect fans' impressions of a team's quality. Few fans would spend the time to update each team's record on a daily basis; some might do that for their home or favorite team but would likely not do so for other teams. It usually takes time and consideration for consumers to form their impressions about a team.

In the demand literature, several indices are used to measure this impression, including wins over the last ten games (McDonald & Rascher, 2000), wins or playoff appearance in the previous season (Lemke et al., 2009; Meehan et al., 2007), and average or aggregate wins over the previous three seasons (Rishe & Mondello, 2004). A NBA team would have to win four rounds of playoff games to become the NBA champion. Because playoff games typically attract more attention from the media and the public, a team that plays in more playoff rounds would have a stronger image. Numbers of playoff rounds won by a team would be an appropriate measure of a team's performance level. The current model thus uses the accumulated number of playoff rounds won by a team over the previous three seasons as a measure of a team's performance level. In addition, a team's winning percentage over the previous half of a season would be used to capture the team's most recent performance in people's impressions. As illustrated earlier, current winning percentage has its bias and does not necessarily reflect people's impressions about a team's overall performance. McDonald and Rascher (2000) attempted to use wins over the last ten games to measure this feature but did not identify a significant effect in their model. A potential shortcoming of using wins over the last ten games is the lack of variation in this variable, and the number of games might be too small to make a difference in fan impressions. In this model, one-half of the NBA season (41 games) was considered a proper length for people to form their impression of a team's recent performance. A more detailed formulation of this variable is addressed in the methods section. Finally, although people's impression of a home team's performance would not alter much during the season, there may be certain exceptions, such as a long winning or losing streak. A long winning streak for the home team could stimulate fan attention and attract more people to the next or an upcoming game (Fort & Rosenman, 1998). Therefore, home team winning/losing streak is also included in the current model.

Uncertainty of outcome

In sports marketing studies, drama has long been recognized as an important factor in assessing the motivations of sport spectators (e.g., Madrigal, 2006; Mastromartino, Chou, & Zhang, 2017; Trail & James, 2001). It has been suggested that drama, which reflects the level of uncertainty of the game outcome, is one of the major motivations for spectators to watch or attend sporting events. Knowles et al. (1992) tried to estimate game attendance using the uncertainty of outcome and found that baseball attendance was maximized when the home team had a 60 percent chance of winning; additionally, the odds associated with a 60 percent probability of winning were actually more consistent with outcome certainty. Kochman (1995) concluded that the home team winning was more important than the presence of outcome uncertainty and attributed this difference in findings to the increased cost of attending a baseball game. Uncertainty of outcome does seem to affect the demand for a sporting event, but the research findings in the literature were not as consistent as expected. This result is not surprising when examining the spectator motivation literature because drama and vicarious achievement are typically what people seek when attending a sporting event (Madrigal, 2006; Mastromartino et al., 2017; Trail & James, 2001). Nonetheless, scholars on this topic are devoted to creating new indices to measure the uncertainty of outcome and to test these indices in different demand models (Borland & MacDonald, 2003).

This study attempts to capture the effect of the uncertainty of outcome using the betting odds posted for each game. Forrest and Simmons (2002) used betting odds to measure uncertainty and found that the attendance demand of English soccer reached its highest at maximum uncertainty. In the current study, a measure of uncertainty of outcome was included, using the point spread given by Las Vegas bookmakers for each home game. The point spread is used in sports betting to even the odds between two unevenly matched teams. In point spread betting, the favorite must win by more than the point spread for the favorite to win the wager (i.e., an underdog that loses by fewer points than the posted point spread wins the wager). The amount of the point spread usually reflects the expectation of a sporting event's outcome because bookmakers have to consider all possible information to create an equal number of wagers on either of the competition. People would expect a close game if the point spread were small, which would also mean that the uncertainty of the outcome is high. Accordingly, the absolute number of the point spread before each game would properly estimate the uncertainty of the outcome. Additionally, the sign of the odds would be a good indicator of whether the home team is favored to win the game. Moreover, as discussed above, the beauty of athletic performance is factors that motivate fans to attend sports events (Madrigal, 2006; Mastromartino et al., 2017; Trail & James, 2001). Style of play is another potential factor that influences demand.

In the NBA, certain teams are known for their strong defenses that usually keep game scores lower and the pace slower. Others might be acknowledged by efficient offenses that score more and play at a faster pace. This difference in style could attract consumers of different interests. The total points posted by Las Vegas bookmakers before each game represents the expected total scores of both teams in the game. A higher (lower) total score usually occurs in fast- (slow-) paced games, and vice versa. This makes the total points scored in each game another good index of the game style factor.

Model summary

A general structure for a game demand model can be summarized by classifying the explanatory variables into four groups of factors:

$$ATTENDANCE_{ijk} = \beta_0 + \beta_{1*}\ GAME\ SCHEDULE_{ijk} + \beta_{2*}\ STAR\ POWER_{ijk} + \beta_{3*}\ TEAM\ PERFORMANCE_{ijk} + \beta_{4*}\ UNCERTAINTY\ OF\ OUTCOME_{ijk} + \mu_{ij} + \varepsilon_{ijk} \quad (1)$$

where i is the team, j is the season of the game played, k is the game played, and μ_{ij} is the average home game attendance of the team during the season. Because μ_{ij} would be a constant in this study, the attendance variation from game to game may be expressed as the following equation:

$$ATTENDANCE\ VARIATION_{ijk} = ATTENDANCE_{ijk} - \mu_{ij} = \beta_0 + \beta_{1*}\ GAME\ SCHEDULE_{ijk} + \beta_{2*}\ STAR\ POWER_{ijk} + \beta_{3*}\ TEAM\ PERFORMANCE_{ijk} + \beta_{4*}\ UNCERTAINTY\ OF\ OUTCOMEijk + \varepsilon_{ijk} \quad (2)$$

Method

Data source

The current study aims to detect factors that affect demand for an NBA game. Because NBA teams play different number of games against division opponents and non-division opponents, we tried to select one team in each division to avoid possible bias. Table 3.1 shows the attendance record for 30 NBA teams from the 2006–07 to the 2010–11 seasons, in which the data were available for the study. The data were converted into a percentage of each stadium's capacity (to eliminate the effect of arena capacity). Another effort was made to avoid popular teams that have average attendance records over 90 percent in a single season to prevent a ceiling effect and to obtain a moderate amount of variation in demand. Under these criteria, the following six teams were selected as the sample for this study: the Philadelphia 76ers, Indiana Pacers, Washington Wizards, Sacramento Kings, Memphis Grizzlies, and Minnesota Timberwolves. Noticeably, all five teams in the Pacific Division had attendance records that exceeded the selection criterion.

The Sacramento Kings were eventually selected because the team generally had a wider relative range of attendance in the division, except for the 2006–07 season. Attendance data, stadium capacity, and other game information for home games played by the six teams during the 2006–07 to the 2010–11 seasons were

Table 3.1 Attendance record of 30 NBA teams in percentage

Division	*Year 1*	*Year 2*	*Year 3*	*Year 4*	*Year 5*
Atlantic					
Boston Celtics	100.0	100.0	97.6	100.0	100.0
Brooklyn Nets	78.3	75.8	69.1	80.6	75.5
New York Knicks	99.1	97.6	98.7	99.8	100.0
Philadelphia 76ers	72.7	79.7	70.0	72.6	86.1
Toronto Raptors	98.2	94.8	90.4	83.7	85.0
Central					
Chicago Bulls	101.3	97.6	97.1	104.2	105.9
Cleveland Cavaliers	99.5	97.3	100.0	97.8	77.5
Detroit Pistons	100.0	99.1	84.9	75.5	65.3
Indiana Pacers	66.6	78.1	78.2	74.5	78.0
Milwaukee Bucks	83.3	82.2	80.7	82.3	78.6
Southeast					
Atlanta Hawks	86.9	89.4	88.3	83.6	81.2
Charlotte Bobcats	77.4	76.3	82.9	83.1	77.4
Miami Heat	99.3	93.0	90.5	100.9	701.7
Orlando Magic	100.3	97.6	100.0	102.6	102.1
Washington Wizards	88.5	82.4	80.3	83.2	82.9
Pacific					
Golden State Warriors	100.2	96.7	92.0	95.4	96.2
Los Angeles Clippers	88.6	84.8	85.7	93.1	100.8
Los Angeles Lakers	98.5	99.7	99.7	99.7	99.7
Phoenix Suns	96.8	100.0	95.8	95.4	84.7
Sacramento Kings	81.7	72.6	76.5	80.2	83.8
Southwest					
Dallas Mavericks	105.6	104.4	104.1	104.7	105.9
Houston Rockets	94.7	96.9	91.6	89.7	85.1
Memphis Grizzlies	69.4	70.3	74.4	80.9	86.7
New Orleans Hornets	82.4	98.7	88.5	86.1	884
San Antonio Spurs	100.3	97.2	97.4	98.6	99.0
Northwest					
Denver Nuggets	90.6	89.9	93.9	88.2	88.9
Minnesota Timberwolves	76.2	74.9	78.0	78.8	90.4
Oklahoma City Thunder	78.2	97.7	98.9	99.7	100.0
Portland Trail Blazers	97.8	102.7	102.6	102.7	102.6
Utah Jazz	100.0	100.0	97.3	98.0	97.0

Note: Percentages of attendance were calculated by dividing the average attendance to the capacity of the stadium. It appears that teams in the NBA often oversold their tickets.

Table 3.2 Descriptive statistics of attendance record of each team

Teams	N	Min	Max	Mean	SD	*Stadium Capacity*	*# of sold-out games*
Philadelphia 76ers	205	9,317	20,809	14,899.5	3,007.04	21,315	0
Indiana Pacers	205	9,390	18,166	13,898.91	2,454.71	18,165	25
Washington Wizards	204	10,112	20,435	17,180.46	2,805.74	20,278	72
Sacramento Kings	164	10,021	17,641	13,505.62	1,858.03	17,317	12
Memphis Grizzlies	205	10,012	18,119	13,644.83	2,428.13	18,119	14
Minnesota Timberwolves	205	10,019	20,200	15,067.79	2,570.93	19,356	15

Note: Stadium capacity of each team was based on the official capacity announce by each stadium. # of sold-out games is based on the official capacity of the stadium.

collected from basketball-reference.com (2012). Descriptive statistics for the attendance figures of each team included in this study are presented in Table 3.2. The betting-line records for each game were collected from contests.covers.com (2012). The original sample contains 1,230 observations, each representing one specific game. The 2006–07 Sacramento Kings' data were excluded because the Kings had sold out all of its 41 games that season. The game played on November 10, 2006 between the Washington Wizards and the Milwaukee Bucks was also excluded from further analysis because of missing attendance records, which leaves the total sample size equal to 1,188 games.

Dependent variables

1 Attendance Variation (AV_{ijk}): To analyze how demand for each game deviated from the average demand for each team in a specific season, attendance variation was used as the dependent variable in the current model. It was calculated using the attendance for each game minus the seasonal average attendance for the home team.
2 Attendance Percentage (AP_{ijk}): The second dependent variable accounts for the diverse capacities of each arena. It was calculated by dividing the total attendance of each game by the capacity of each home arena to standardize the varying demand. A subsequent regression analysis was tested using AP_{ijk} as another dependent variable.

Independent variables

1 Home Team (PHI_{ijk}, IND_{ijk}, WAS_{ijk}, SAC_{ijk}, MEM_{ijk}): Six teams were selected in the current study. For models using all six teams, five dummy variables were used to control for differences among teams that might be caused by factors specific to each home team, e.g., income level,

population, and facility age, which is not the primary interest of this study and not the goal of our model.

2 Day of Week ($WEEKDAY_{ijk}$, $WEEKEND_{ijk}$): Based on the research findings of previous studies, the game-schedule effect often results in different demand between weekdays and weekends. To test how many levels of variables would be included in the demand model, a one-way ANOVA was first conducted to detect the differences in attendance on the seven days of the week, which revealed that Friday and Saturday games have significantly higher demand than Sunday games and Sunday games have higher attendance figures than Monday through Thursday games. Therefore, two dummy variables were included in the model to test the three levels of the day-of-week effect, i.e., Weekday and Weekend.

3 Game Availability ($GAMEAVA_{ijk}$): Game availability was calculated using the number of days from the last home game plus the number of days until the next home game.

4 Star Power on Visiting Team ($VTSTAR_{ijk}$): The NBA All-Star balloting allows each fan to select two guards, two forwards, and one center to start for each conference in the NBA All-Star Game. We utilize the voting results to identify the top ten guards, ten forwards, and five centers in each season's NBA All-Star balloting as the star players in this study. The total votes earned by a team's star players in the balloting represent a team's star power. The visiting star power is calculated for each game, and this number does not include players who were absent from the game. There are different causes of players' absence; some are announced in advance, but some are not. Although this could have had an effect on people's expectations for coming to the game, we decided to exclude data for all player absences in an effort to maintain consistency in the developed model.

5 Star Power on Home Team ($HTSTAR_{ijk}$): Although the home team is a controlled variable in this model, the star power on the home team is not. The data for this variable are calculated in the same process as that of the star power on the visiting team. Absent stars on the home team, who are most likely injured, were not counted under the Star Power on Home Team metric, which means that this measurement might fluctuate during a specific season.

6 Playoff Rounds Won for Last Three Years by Visiting Team ($VTPFWIN_{ijk}$): This variable is used to measure people's impression of a team's performance level. A team would score "1" if it advanced to the playoffs, "2" if it advanced to the second round of the playoffs, "3" if it advanced to the conference final, "4" for winning a conference championship, and "5" for winning a NBA title; these values are all measured over the previous three years.

7 Winning Percentage of Visiting Team ($VTWIN_{ijk}$): It takes time to change a consumer's impression about a team's quality or performance level, and the length of time might depend on how deeply he/she is

involved in the game (Davis, 2009). At the beginning of each season, fan impressions of a team's performance level would be largely based on how the team performed in the previous season, particularly if the second half of the season saw major changes on the roster (Kahane & Shmanske, 1997). As the season moves forward, the impression of a team could be gradually changed by their performance during the new season. Thus, it is reasonable to assume that one-half of a NBA season (41 games) would be long enough to change this impression in either direction. Therefore, we divided each NBA season into two halves. While the major roster change would be monitored by the star power variable in this model, a visiting team's winning percentage would be represented by its record from the previous half of the season (i.e., 41 games). For example, for the first 41 games in each season, each visiting team's winning percentage is calculated from their record in the second half of the previous season. When the game is played in the second half of the season, this variable is calculated using the visiting team's record for the 41 games in the first half of the same season. This variable thus accounts for a more up-to-date performance level of each team than the playoff rounds that the team has won over the last three years.

8 Home Team Winning/Losing Streak ($STREAK_{ijk}$): People's impressions of the performance level of the home team would not change much during the season, except for certain unusual circumstances, such as long winning or losing streaks (Fort & Rosenman, 1998). A long winning streak (e.g., five to ten games) might stimulate home team attendance, while a long losing streak could push people away from the game.
9 Betting Odds ($ODDS_{ijk}$): The point spread posted by Las Vegas bookmakers before each game is used to measure the uncertainty of outcome. A smaller (greater) absolute number of the point spread would mean a greater (smaller) uncertainty about the result of the match.
10 Betting total ($TOTAL_{ijk}$): The total points posted by Las Vegas bookmakers before each game represents the expected combined scores of both teams in the game. A higher total score usually happens in high-paced games, which might be more entertaining to certain consumers. It is expected that a higher total score would increase demand.
11 Home team favor to win ($FAVOR_{ijk}$): The positive or negative sign of a point spread would be used to measure whether the home team was favored to win the game. A negative sign would indicate the home team as the favorite in the game. This variable is coded as a dummy variable.

The demand model

To include the independent variables, the full demand model can be expressed as the following equation:

$$DV_{ijk}\ (AV_{ijk}/\ AP_{ijk}) = \beta_0 + \beta_{1*}PHI_{ijk} + \beta_{2*}IND_{ijk} + \beta_{3*}WAS_{ijk} + \beta_{4*}SAC_{ijk} + \beta_{5*}MEM_{ijk} + \beta_{6*}WEEKDAY_{ijk} + \beta_{7*}WEEKEND_{ijk} + \beta_{8*}GAMEAVA_{ijk} + \beta_{9*}VTSTAR_{ijk} + \beta_{10}{}^{*}HTSTAR_{ijk} + \beta_{11*}VTPFWIN_{ijk} + + \beta_{12*}VTWIN_{ijk} + \beta_{13*}STREAK_{ijk} + \beta_{14*}ODDS_{ijk} + \beta_{15*}\mathrm{TOTAL}_{ijk} + \beta_{16*}\mathrm{FAVOR}_{ijk} + \varepsilon_{ijk} \quad (3)$$

where i is the team and t is the game played.

Data analyses

A total of 1,188 observations were included in the analyses. Among these, the first and last games in each season for each team were excluded from further analyses to avoid potential bias. Various multiple linear regression assumptions (i.e., linearity, independence, normality, and equality of variances) were examined. Two multiple linear regression models were tested to examine the impact of game-related variables on the fluctuation of attendance from game to game, while controlling for potentially confounding variables in the model. Initially, a variety of different regression equations were tested to generate the best fitting model. Before executing the final regression equations, necessary transformations of independent variables were also computed as mentioned above.

Results

Table 3.3 presents the estimated coefficients from the two regression models, using attendance variation and attendance percentage as dependent variables. Each dependent variable is estimated using the ordinary least squares (OLS) method, containing 11 explaining variables and the fixed-team factors. Eight variables were found to significantly estimate attendance variance in the first model, including WEEKDAY (β = –1,044.48, $p < .01$), WEEKEND (β = 940.97, $p < .01$), GAMEAVA (β = 54.30, $p < .01$), VTSTAR (β = 583.46, $p < .01$), VTPFWIN (β = 92.32, $p < .01$), VTWIN (β = 1,065.10, $p < .05$), ODDS (β = 68.62, $p < .01$), TOTAL (β = 22.50, $p < .01$). These findings suggest that game schedule is a significant factor contributing to the attendance variation, as expected. The standardized β coefficients suggest that star power on the visiting team is the most influential variable (β = .349) that predicts attendance variations, followed by the game schedule variables WEEKDAY (β = –.216) and WEEKEND (β = .191). The negative coefficient of WEEKDAY indicates that games played on Mondays to Thursdays attract approximately 1,044 fewer fans than games played on Sundays in average; Friday and Saturday games attract approximately 940 more fans than Sunday games, when other variables are fixed. In terms of game availability, each day added to the number of days between games would bring 54 more people to the game.

Table 3.3 Summary of two regression models predicting attendance variation and attendance percentage

Independent Variables	*DV = AV_{ijk}*			*DV = AP_{ijk}*			VIF
	B	β	t	B	β	t	
Constant	−7,004.271**		−5.74	.472**		7.09	
PHI_{ijk}	99.828	.016	.49	−.077**	−.210**	−6.98	1.805
IND_{ijk}	−41.540	−.007	−.21	−.015	−.041	−1.36	1.795
WAS_{ijk}	92.740	.014	.47	.070**	.191**	6.55	1.686
SAC_{ijk}	179.561	.026	.83	.028*	.070*	2.39	1.705
MEM_{ijk}	−55.953	−.009	−.28	−.024*	−.064*	−2.17	1.748
$WEEKDAY_{ijk}$	−1,044.481**	−.216**	−5.12	−.055**	−.199**	−4.98	3.176
$WEEKEND_{ijk}$	940.974**	.191**	4.52	.046**	.161**	4.02	3.196
$GAMEAVA_{ijk}$	54.302**	.079**	3.32	.003**	.072**	3.18	1.015
$VTSTAR_{ijk}$	583.464**	.349**	10.85	.031**	.322**	10.58	1.845
$HTSTAR_{ijk}$	141.350	.029	1.11	.050**	.176**	7.15	1.202
$VTPFWIN_{ijk}$	92.318**	.121**	4.02	.004**	.098**	3.43	1.618
$VTWIN_{ijk}$	1,065.101*	.074*	2.25	.059*	.071*	2.30	1.910
$STREAK_{ijk}$	27.514	.034	1.38	.003*	.055*	2.36	1.093
$ODDS_{ijk}$	68.620**	.078**	3.22	.004**	.087**	3.81	1.035
$TOTAL_{ijk}$	22.495**	.098**	3.93	.001*	.059*	2.48	1.108
$FAVOR_{ijk}$	90.712	.019	.60	.011	.041	1.38	1.750
R2	.38				.44		
F	41.74*				54.89**		

* Significant at .05 level

** Significant at .01 level

Impact of the star power factor is well demonstrated by the findings in this study, which show that every increase of one million votes in the All-Star votes on the visiting team induces 583 more fans to come to the game. However, the absence of the home team star did not result in significant change in attendance. For the team performance factor, one more playoff round won in the past three years by the visiting team would attract approximately 90 more fans to the game. A one percent increase in the visiting team's winning percentage for the last 41 games would increase the attendance number by 1,065. The positive coefficient of ODDS suggests an opposite function with the uncertainty of outcome; every one-point increase in the betting odds actually brings approximately 70 more fans to the game. Attendance is also higher when the expected total score is higher.

When using the attendance percentage as the dependent variable, every independent variable was found to be significant except the FAVOR (β = .011, p = .17). Most of the results are consistent with the results derived in the

Table 3.4 Model summary predicting attendance variation and attendance percentage of individual teams

Teams	$DV = AV_{ijk}$			$DV = AP_{ijk}$		
	R^2	F	*Significant IVs*	R^2	F	*Significant IVs*
Philadelphia 76ers	.42	11.87**	VTSTAR (.456**) WEEKEND (.349**) TOTAL (.143**)	.42	12.15**	VTSTAR (.481**) WEEKEND (.328**) TOTAL (.124**)
Indiana Pacers	.41	11.62**	VTSTAR (.390**) WEEKEND (.239**) STREAK (.136*)	.48	15.40**	VTSTAR (.366**) HTSTAR (.332**) WEEKDAY (–.197**)
Washington Wizards	.48	15.05**	WEEKEND (.359**) VTSTAR (.285**) GAMEAVA (.132*)	.48	15.54**	WEEKEND (.304**) VTSTAR (.264**) HTSTAR (.234**) WEEKDAY (–.211*) ODDS (.114*)
Sacramento Kings	.44	11.41**	VTSTAR (.447**) TOTAL (.274**) WEEKEND (.243**) GAMEAVA(.165*)	.37	8.44**	VTSTAR (.376**) WEEKEND (.247**) TOTAL (.206**) GAMEAVA(.167*)
Memphis Grizzlies	.43	12.35**	VTSTAR (.422**) VTPFWIN (.222**) FAVOR (.172**) TOTAL (.117*)	.41	11.76**	VTSTAR (.399**) HTSTAR (.243**) VTPFWIN (.186*) TOTAL (.120*)
Minnesota Timberwolves	.42	11.78**	WEEKDAY (–.575**) ODDS (.153*) VTPFWIN (.150*)	.44	12.86**	WEEKDAY (–.544**) HTSTAR (.301**) ODDS (.153*) VTPFWIN (.149*) TOTAL (.130*)

* Significant at .05 level

** Significant at .01 level

first regression model, although star power change on home team ($\beta = .05$, $p < .01$) and winning or losing streak ($\beta = .003$, $p < .05$) were found to be significantly related to the increase of attendance in this model. The difference between the models suggests that star power on home team and winning or losing streak are more influential in predicting attendance fluctuations over seasons. Every increase of one million votes in the all-star votes on the home team would stimulate an attendance increase of five percent, and winning ten games in a row for the home team would bring three percent more fans to the game. Low variance inflation factors (VIFs) for all independent variables eliminate concerns about multicollinearity.

The same regression models were tested for individual teams by running the model separately using data from each team. The results are summarized in Table 3.4. Although star power on the visiting team and game schedule variables are generally the most influential variables, teams demonstrate different patterns in their prediction models. In Minnesota, it is difficult to attract fans to weekday games; weekday games have 2,853 fewer fans than games played on Sundays on average, and there is no significant difference between Friday or Saturday games and Sunday games. Fans did not show much interest for visiting star players ($\beta = 170.34$, $p > .05$). On the opposite side of the coin, the Memphis Grizzles' fans care about visiting star players more than any other variables (standardized $\beta = .422$, $p < .01$), followed by the visiting team's winning percentage (standardized $\beta = .222$, $p < .01$). Game schedule variables did not have significant impact on the game attendance of Memphis Grizzlies fans.

Discussion

A better estimation of the demand for each game ahead of time would be an essential piece of information for a more efficient and effective marketing and ticketing plan. This is especially true for the NBA in recent years because NBA teams are devoted to creating various ticket packages to bundle high-demand games with low-interest games. There is also the trend that an increasing number of teams in the NBA have adopted: dynamic ticket pricing strategies, which allow teams to price each game differently, based on demand. This study analyzed the most recent attendance records of six teams in the NBA to test demand models that were built on the most frequently discussed factors both in the literature and in practice. The proposed models were supported by the research findings of this study and showed excellent predictive power for game attendance, with R2 values that ranged from .38 to .48. Although the results vary from model to model, star power on the visiting team and game schedule variables are generally the two most influential variables of the proposed game-demand factors. Hausman and Leonard (1997) referred to the abilities of star players to generate extra revenue for other teams as so-called superstar externality, and they illustrated this effect with the economic impacts of six star players. They found that the superstar from the Chicago Bulls, Michael Jordan, generated US$53 million in revenue for teams other than his specific employer. In general, the findings of our estimation model are consistent with these findings.

Morse, Shapiro, McEvoy, and Rascher (2008) measured the effect of roster turnover on the demand of NBA games and found that losing a star player on a team did not have a significant effect on attendance. The researchers explained the insignificant effect by indicating that teams usually replaced a star player with a player or players of similar salary and abilities, and/or in most cases, teams change rosters to improve the over quality of the team. The results of this study suggest that changing star players has a different impact within a season and over different seasons. The star power on the home team was not significant in the first model because the dependent variable was controlled for the season. Nonetheless, the same variable was a significant predictor of attendance variation over seasons in the second model. The explanation offered by Morse et al. is partially supported by the results of this study when the quality of star players is measured using the all-star voting. Rivers and DeShriver (2002) also found that when a star player is able to enhance a team's performance, this player would have a significant positive impact on attendance. Their conclusion is confirmed by the findings of this study because both the team performance and star power variables were found to significantly contribute to attendance figures.

More consistent with previous research findings, the effects of game scheduling were found to be significant across models. Nonetheless, the current study still contributes to the demand literature by recognizing three levels of the "day of week" effect, in addition to the influence of game availability. As a frequently examined factor in demand models, the day of the week is either tested by incorporating a seven-level dummy variable, i.e., Monday to Sunday (e.g., Meehan et al., 2007) or a two-level dummy variable (weekday and weekend) (e.g., Knowles et al., 1992). Through a pretest, this study adopted a three-level dummy variable (Monday to Thursday, Friday and Saturday, and Sunday) in the tested model and found significant differences among the three levels. Although most people do not work on Sundays, some still go to church, spend time with family, or prepare for work the next day. The attendance demand of Sunday games is significantly lower than that of Friday and Saturday games, but it is still significantly higher than for games that are scheduled on Monday through Thursday.

A similar effect of game availability derived from a study on Australian Rules football was confirmed in the current study, where attendance is higher when a series of games is spread across a longer time period (Drever & McDonald, 1981; Borland & Lye, 1992). The game availability variable was never investigated in the North American demand literature to our knowledge, which may be because a majority of demand studies in North American focused on MLB attendance, which has an idiosyncratic style of schedule, as discussed above. Measured by the sum of the number of days from the last home game to the number of days to the next home game, the game availability effect was tested and confirmed in the current study. This particular variable was found to be significantly and positively related to attendance in both models.

Research findings associated with the effect of uncertainty of outcome on game demand in this study would likely lead to the most controversial debates. Knowles et al. (1992) found that uncertainty of outcome is a significant determinant of attendance and that attendance reaches its maximum when the home team is slightly favored to win. These authors suggest that competitive balance plus a home team advantage are desirable for professional sports leagues to maximize overall attendance. Forrest and Simmons (2002) also found a significant relationship between uncertainty of outcome and attendance in the English soccer league. However, they did not consider the idea that competing teams are rarely evenly balanced because the home court advantage reduces the uncertainty of outcome in a match between two evenly strong teams. Beckman, Cai, Esrock, and Lemke (2011) found insignificant effects of uncertainty of outcome on game demand and concluded that spectators want to see a home team victory more than they want to see a competitive match. Contrary to these research findings, the findings of this study showed a significant positive relationship between the absolute numbers of betting odds to the demand variation. Combined with the finding that whether the home team is favored to win was not significant related to attendance, the models tested in this study showed the polar opposite result from what Forrest and Simmons (2002) and Knowles et al. (1992) found.

One possible explanation of the conflicting finding might be the distinctive characteristic of the sample included in this study. To avoid the ceiling effect, ensure the range of variation in attendance, and increase its generalizability, this study systematically selected one team from each division of the NBA. However, the six NBA teams in this study were not strong teams, as defined by their records during the sampling period. During the five NBA seasons under examination, these six teams together appeared in playoff games a total of seven times; these teams together finished the season with a winning record only five times. In this case, higher betting odds could imply that the home team is playing against a stronger team that has a better chance to win. According to our research findings, we believe that there might be a moderating effect of the home team's quality (e.g., winning percentage) on the relationship between uncertainty of outcome of the game and game demand. More specifically, when the quality of performance level of a home team is high, uncertainty of outcome might be positively related to attendance. Conversely, when a home team has low quality or a lower level of performance, uncertainty of outcome might have a negative effect or no effect on attendance. This might also provide a good explanation of the mixed and controversial effect found in the demand literature; it is certainly worthy of further investigation. Because competitive balance in professional team sports has been an important academic and practical issue, future research is needed to reach a more consistent conclusion on the relationship between uncertainty of outcome of the game and game demand.

The results from single-team regression models may have significant implications for marketers who wish to estimate attendance for their teams. For the Minnesota Timberwolves, for instance, it is very difficult to attract fans to games on weekdays. Unlike other teams in this study, the data from the Timberwolves revealed that "Weekday" was the most influential variable predicting attendance and that star power on the visiting team was not significant. This may be the result of the severe weather conditions in the winter season, which might result in additional obstructions for fans coming to weekday night games. There may be other causes that would require extra effort to discover; nonetheless, what we try to demonstrate here is that the six teams in this study have shown different patterns in their regression models. Although it might be ideal if we can find a perfect model for each team in the NBA, the reality is that every team must be considered different. The 30 NBA teams are located in different cities that are not only across a wide range of geographic areas but also have a huge variation in their demographics. It would be unrealistic for marketers to ignore the different aspects of the geographical, demographical, historical, cultural, economic, and financial backgrounds of local communities. Some of these geographic factors, such as city or market area population, region of the country, accessibility, or the presence of teams from contiguous areas have occasionally been part of studies on sports attendance (Baade & Tiehen, 1990; Fisher, 1998; Byon et al., 2018; Leonard, 2005; Zhang et al., 2004). Fans from different backgrounds might have diverse consumer taste, which requires team marketers to put forth extra effort to identify what attributes of their products (games) are appealing to local consumers. These attributes determine the appeal of a specific sports team to its local community and help the team form a culture among its fans in the long term. It also helps teams build rivalries both among and between teams and among/between individuals, which give fans a team to cheer for and a team to cheer against, which, in turn, increases fan involvement, identification and attendance (Henderson, Leopkey, & Zhang, 2018; Luellen & Wann, 2010; Trail, Robinson, Dick, & Gillentine, 2003). All these factors need to be considered to adjust the general equation individually when estimating attendance for different teams.

Among the factors that drive fan support, demographics might have the most contribution to the difference from team to team. Individual age, gender, and/or ethnicity have been long acknowledged by researchers as affecting spectator consumption of sporting events (Baade & Tiehen, 1990; Greenstein & Marcum, 1981; Henderson et al., 2018; Zhang et al., 1995). Based on Mullin, Hardy, and Sutton (2014), Pitts and Stotlar (2013), Wicker et al. (2012), and Zhang et al. (2003, 2007), consumer income, education level, and occupation are also important demographic variables that may impinge on social class distinction and, in turn, affect sports consumption. Demographics influence what sport consumers choose to watch and play and make certain game-related attributes more attractive than others. These variables may serve as a point of identification between the team and the individual and increase team attractiveness to an individual as he/she develops identification with the team (Fisher, 1998; Zhang et al., 2004). The NBA featured 84 international players from 37 countries and territories on the opening-night rosters for the 2012–13 season. Twenty-nine of the 30 teams feature at least one international player (NBA.com, 2012). These international players represent different social constructions of race, ethnicity, and nationality that might connect their teams to certain populations (Larmer, 2005). Although we tried to select and measure game-related attributes as objectively as possible, some attributes must be treated more subjectively, to a certain degree. Star power, for instance, is certainly one of them. The attractiveness of certain star players might vary from city to city because of the background of the players, in addition to the different ethnic composition in a local population. When a NBA player is a local hero who played for college in the area or was actually from the area, he may have more support from local fans compared to fans in other cities. Marketers might pay more attention to the roster of each visiting team and utilize this information to adjust the regression model and arrive at a marketing plan targeting specific populations.

To summarize, the purpose of this study was to build and test a demand model that allows NBA teams to better estimate the demand of each home game. In this study, various demand factors were incorporated into the model through a comprehensive review of both the theoretical and empirical literature. The proposed model was tested using an empirical data set of a total of 1,189 NBA games played by six teams over five seasons. The resulted prediction models may be useful for estimating the demand of attendance because this study confirmed the strong effect of star power on demand, clarified the three-level day-of-week variable, added and verified the effect of the game availability variable, incorporated and validated new and more accurate variables to capture team performance, and discovered the potential moderating effect of the home team's quality on the relationship between uncertainty of outcome and game demand. The findings of this study might provide team management and marketing practitioners with accessible and expedient information when they are formulating marketing plans, ticketing strategies, trying to improve their team rosters, or even discussing new policies related to the league's competitive balance. Noticeably, it was not our intention to stimulate attendance by manipulating game-related factors, although some of these factors were identified as more influential than other factors.

There are several limitations of this study. The first and primary limitation is the systematic sampling method used in this study, which might cause a lack of generalizability beyond the population of NBA games played. The findings of this study might also cause difficulty in generalizing them to every team in the NBA unless a larger sample is included in future studies. When applying the proposed equation to a specific team, the aforementioned individual differences should be considered. Second, the star power on each team was calculated according to the box score of each game, which excluded those star players who were on the team's roster but did not play in the game. A player's absence from a game could be due to numerous reasons, of which some are expected ahead of time but others are not. A fan's knowledge of the absence of a star player (or players) could not be controlled in this study. Additionally, the NBA All-Star balloting usually starts in November and ends in January; thus, it could also be a bias estimation of people's impression of a star's popularity for games played during the beginning or ending period of a season. Finally, as in all other demand studies, the current study adopted past attendance to develop and test our model. However, average attendance figures would not be known until the end of the season. This factor might trouble managers who try to use this variable to predict demand for an incoming event. Of course, a team's average attendance would not dramatically change from season to season unless there were a major roster turnover (Kahane & Shmanske, 1997), a major renovation or the construction of a new stadium (Coffin, 1996), or special promotions (Boyd & Krehbiel, 2006). Team management usually would not have problems figuring out a baseline number, for instance, by adopting the previous season's average attendance figure or the average attendance figures for the last 41 games. In this case, our model would still be able to provide a good estimate of demand. Notably, researchers of future studies may consider working with NBA teams to conduct cross-validation studies for the developed prediction models.

References

Alexander, D. L. (2001). Major League Baseball: Monopoly Pricing and Profit-Maximizing Behavior. *Journal of Sports Economics, 2*, 341–55.

Armstrong, K. (1999). A Quest for a Market: A Profile of the Consumers of a Professional Women's Basketball Team and the Marketing Implications. *Women's Sport and Physical Activity Journal, 8*, 103–26.

Baade, R. A., & Tiehen, L. J. (1990). An Analysis of Major League Baseball Attendance, 1969–1987. *Journal of Sport and social Issues, 14*, 14–32.

Basketball-reference.com. (2012). *Basketball Statistics and History - 2007 to 2011.* Retrieved January 11, 2012 from www.basketball-reference.com/.

Beckman, E. M., Cai, W., Esrock, R. M., & Lemke, R. J. (2011). Explaining Game-to-Game Ticket Sales for Major League Baseball Games Over Time. *Journal of Sports Economics,* 1–18.

Borland, J., & Lye, J. (1992). Attendance at Australian Rules Football: A Panel Study. *Applied Economics, 24,* 1053–58.

Borland, J., & MacDonald, R. (2003). Demand for Sport. *Oxford Review of Economic Policy, 19,* 478–502.

Boyd, T. C., & Krehbiel, T. C. (2006). An Analysis of the Effects of Specific Promotion Types on Attendance at Major League Baseball Games. *Mid-American Journal of Business, 21*(2), 21–32.

Braunstein, J. R., & Zhang, J. J. (2005). Dimensions of Athletic Star Power Associated with Generation Y Sports Consumption. *International Journal of Sports Marketing & Sponsorship, 6,* 242–67.

Braunstein, J. R., Zhang, J. J., Trail, G. T., & Gibson, H. J. (2005). Dimensions of Market Demand Associated with Pre-season Training: Development of a Scale for Major League Baseball Spring Training. *Sport Management Review, 8,* 271–96.

Byon, K. K., Zhang, J. J., & Baker, T. A. (2013). Impact of Market Demand and Game Support Programs on Consumption Levels of Professional Team Sport Spectators as Mediated by Perceived Value. *European Sport Management Quarterly, 13,* 232–63.

Byon, K. K., Zhang, M. Y., Hsu, N. Y., Drane, D., Pitts, B. G., & Zhang, J. J. (2018). General Game Support Programs Associated with Professional Team Sports. In J. J. Zhang & B. G. Pitts (Eds.), *The Global Football Industry: Marketing Perspectives* (pp. 303–30). London, UK: Routledge.

Cianfrone, B. A., Zhang, J. J., Pitts, B., & Byon, K. K. (2015). Identifying Key Market Demand Factors Associated with State High School Basketball Tournament. *Sport Marketing Quarterly, 24,* 91–104.

Coffin, D. (1996). If you Build it Will they Come? Attendance and New Stadium Construction. In J. Fizel, E. Gustafson, & L. Hadley (Eds.), *Baseball Economics: Current Research* (pp. 33–46). Westport, CT: Praeger.

Contests.covers.com. (2012). *NBA Matchups - 2007 to 2011.* Retrieved January 11, 2012 from www.covers.com/sports/nba/basketball-matchups.aspx.

Davis, M. C. (2008). The Interaction Between Attendance and Winning Percentage: A VAR Analysis. *International Journal of Sport Finance, 3,* 58–73.

Davis, M. C. (2009). Analyzing the Relationship Between Team Success and MLB Attendance with GARCH effects. *Journal of Sports Economics, 10,* 44–58.

Donihue, M. R., Findlay, D. W., & Newberry, P. W. (2008). An Analysis of Attendance at Major League Spring Training Games. *Journal of Sports Economics, 8,* 39–128.

Drever, P., & McDonald, J. (1981). Attendances at South Australian Football Games. *International Review of Sport Sociology, 16,* 103–13.

Fisher, R. J. (1998). Group-derived Consumption: The Role of Similarity and Attractiveness in Identification with a Favorite Sports Team. *Advances in Consumer Research, 25,* 283–328.

Forrest, D., & Simmons, R. (2002). Outcome Uncertainty and Attendance Demand in Sport: The Case of English Soccer. *The Statistician, 51,* 229–41.

Fort, R., & Rosenman, R. (1998). Winning and Managing Streaks for Baseball. *American Statistical Association, 1998 Proceedings of the Section on Statistics in Sports*, 11–15.

Gifis, L. S., & Sommers, P. M. (2006). Promotions and Attendance in Minor League Baseball. *Atlantic Economic Journal, 34*, 513–14.

Greenstein, T. N., & Marcum, J. P. (1981). Factors Affecting Attendance of Major League Baseball: Team Performance. *Review of Sport & Leisure, 6*(2), 21–34.

Hausman, J., & Leonard, G. (1997). Superstars in the National Basketball Association: Economic Value and Policy. *Journal of Labor Economics, 15*, 586–624.

Henderson, C., Leopkey, R., & Zhang, J. J. (2018). The Equalizer: Feminist Themes in NWSL Club Marketing. In J. J. Zhang & B. G. Pitts (Eds.), *The Global Football Industry: Marketing Perspectives* (pp. 269–302). London, UK: Routledge.

Henderson, C., Zhang, J. J., Byon, K. K., & Pitts, B. G. (2017). Gender, Advertising Techniques, and Consumer Response in NASCAR. In J. J. Zhang, & B. G. Pitts (Eds.), *Contemporary Sport Marketing: Global Perspectives* (pp. 214–43). London, UK: Routledge.

Howard, D., & Crompton, J. (2004). Tactics Used by Sports Organizations in the United States to Increase Ticket Sales. *Managing Leisure, 9*, 87–95.

Kahane, L., & Shmanske, S. (1997). Team Roster Turnover and Attendance in Major League Baseball. *Applied Economics, 29*, 425–31.

Knowles, G., Sherony, K., & Haupert, M. (1992). The Demand for Major League Baseball: A Test of the Uncertainty of Outcome Hypothesis. *The American Economist, 36*, 72–80.

Kochman, L. M. (1995), Major League Baseball: What Really Puts Fans in the Stands? *Sport Marketing Quarterly, 4*, 9–11.

Larmer, B. (2005). *Operation Yao Ming: The Chinese Sports Empire, American Big Business, and the Making of an NBA Superstar.* New York, NY: Gotham.

Lemke, R., Leonard, M., & Tihokwane, K. (2009). Estimating Attendance at Major League Baseball Games for the 2007 season. *Journal of Sports Economics, 11*, 316–48.

Leonard, J. M. (2005). The Geography of Visitor Attendance at College Football Games. *Journal of Sport Behavior, 28*, 231–52.

Luellen, T. B., & Wann, D. L. (2010). Rival Salience and Sport Team Identification. *Sport Marketing Quarterly, 19*, 97–106.

Madrigal, R. (2006). Measuring the Multidimensional Nature of Sporting Event Consumption. *Journal of Leisure Research, 38*, 267–329.

Marcum, J. P., & Greenstein, T. N. (1985). Factors Affecting Attendance of Major League Baseball: 11. Within-season Analysis. *Sociology of Sport Journal, 2*, 314–22.

Mastromartino, B., Chou, W. W., & Zhang, J. J. (2017). The Passion that Unites Us All – The Culture and Consumption of Sport Fans. In C. L. Wang (Ed.), *Exploring the Rise of Fandom in Contemporary Consumer Culture* (pp. 52–70). Hershey, PA: IGI Global.

Morse, A. L., Shapiro, S. L., McEvoy, C. D., & Rascher, D. A. (2008). The Effects of Roster Turnover on Demand in the National Basketball Association. *International Journal of Sport Finance, 3*, 8–18.

McDonald, M., & Rascher, D. (2000). Does Bat Day Make Cents? The Effect of Promotions on the Demand for Major League Baseball. *Journal of Sport Management, 14*, 8–27.

Meehan, J. W. Jr., Nelson, R. A., & Richardson, T. V. (2007). Competitive Balance and Game Attendance in Major League Baseball. *Journal of Sports Economics, 8,* 563–80.

Mullin, B. J., Hardy, S., & Sutton, W. A. (2014). *Sport Marketing* (4th ed.). Champaign, IL: Human Kinetics.

NBA.com. (2012, October 30). Record-tying 84 International Players on Opening-night Rosters. Retrieved January 11, 2013 from www.nba.com/global/international_players_rosters_2012_10_30.html.

Pan, D. W., Zhu, Z., Gabert, T. E., & Brown, J. (1999). Team Performance, Market Characteristics, and Attendance of Major League Baseball: A Panel Data Analysis. *The Mid-Atlantic Journal of Business, 35(2/3)*, 77–91.

Pifer, N. D., Mak, J., Bae, W. Y., & Zhang, J. J. (2015). Star Struck: Examining the Relationship Between Star Player Characteristics and the Branding Process of Professional Sport Team. *Marketing Management Journal, 25,* 88–106.

Pitts, B., & Stotlar, D. (2013). *Fundamentals of Sport Marketing* (4th ed.). Morgantown, WV: Fitness Information Technology.

Rascher, D. A. (1999). The Optimal Distribution of Talent in Major League Baseball. In L. Hadley, E. Gustafson, & J. Fizel (Eds.), *Sports Economics: Current Research* (pp. 27–45). Westport, CT: Praeger.

Rivers, D., & DeSchriver, T. D. (2002). Star Players, Payroll Distribution and Major League Baseball Attendance. *Sport Marketing Quarterly, 11,* 164–73.

Rishe, P. (2012, January 6). Dynamic Pricing: The Future of Ticket Pricing in Sports. *Forbes.* Retrieved January 16, 2012, from www.forbes.com/sites/prishe/2012/01/06/dynamic pricing-the-future-of-ticket-pricing-in-sports/.

Rishe, P., & Mondello, M. (2004). Ticket Price Determination in Professional Sports: An Empirical Analysis of the NBA, NFL, NHL, and Major League Baseball. *Sport Marketing Quarterly, 13,* 104–12.

Robinson, M. J., & DeSchriver, T. D. (2003). Consumer Differences Across Large and Small Market Teams in the National Professional Soccer League. *Sport Marketing Quarterly, 12,* 80–87.

Roy, D. P. (2008). Impact of New Minor League Baseball Stadiums on Game Attendance. *Sport Marketing Quarterly, 17,* 146–53.

Schmidt, M. B., & Berri, D. J. (2006). What Takes Them Out to the Ball Game? *Journal of Sports Economics, 7,* 222–33.

Trail, G. T., & James, J. D. (2001). The Motivation Scale for Sport Consumption: Assessment of the Scale's Psychometric Properties. *Journal of Sport Behavior, 24,* 108–27.

Trail, G., Robinson, M., Dick, R., & Gillentine, A. (2003). Motives and Points of Attachment: Fans Versus Spectators in Intercollegiate Athletics. *Sport Marketing Quarterly, 12,* 217–27.

Wakefield, K. L., & Sloan, H. J. (1995). The Effects of Team Loyalty and Selected Stadium Factors on Spectator Attendance. *Journal of Sport Management, 9,* 153–72.

Wicker, P., Hallmann, K., & Zhang, J. J. (2012). What is Influencing Expenditure and Intention to Revisit? An Investigation of Marathon Events. *Journal of Sport & Tourism, 17,* 165–82.

Zapalac, R., Zhang, J. J., & Pease, D. G. (2010). Market Demand Factors Associated with Women's Intercollegiate Volleyball Games. *International Journal of Sports Marketing and Sponsorship, 12,* 320–43.

Zhang, J. J., Connaughton, D. P., Byrd, C. E., Cianfrone, B. A., Byon, K. K., & Kim, D. H. (2007). Formulating a Questionnaire for Marketing Studies of Professional Basketball Game Attendance: A Review of Literature. In J. James (Ed.), *Sport Marketing in the New Millennium* (pp. 193–212). Morgantown, WV: Fitness Information Technology.

Zhang, J. J., Lam, E. T. C., Bennett, G., & Connaughton, D. P. (2003). Confirmatory Factor Analysis of the Spectator Decision Making Inventory (SDMI). *Measurement in Physical Education and Exercise Science, 7*, 57–70.

Zhang, J. J., Lam, E. T. C. & Connaughton, D. P. (2003). General Market Demand Variables Associated with Professional Sport Consumption. *International Journal of Sports Marketing & Sponsorship, 5*, 33–55.

Zhang, J. J., Pease, D. G., Hui, S. C. & Michaud, T. J. (1995). Variables Affecting the Spectator Decision to Attend NBA Game. *Sport Marketing Quarterly, 4*, 29–39.

Zhang, J. J., Pease, D. G., Smith, D. W., Wall, K. A., & Saffici, C. L., Pennington-Gray, L., & Connaughton, D. P. (2004). Spectator Satisfaction with the Support Programs of Professional Basketball Games. In B. G. Pitts (Ed.), *Sharing Best Practices in Sport Marketing* (pp. 207–29). Morgantown, WV: Fitness Information Technology.

Zhang, J. J., Pennington-Gray, L., Connaughton, D. P., Braunstein, J. R., Ellis, M. H., Lam, E. T. C., Williamson, D. (2003). Understanding Women's Professional Basketball Game Spectators: Sociodemographics, Game Consumption, and Entertainment Options. *Sport Marketing Quarterly, 12*, 228–43.

Zhang, J. J. & Smith, D. W. (1997). Impact of Broadcasting on the Attendance of Professional Basketball Game. *Sport Marketing Quarterly, 6*, 23–29.

Zhang, J. J., Smith, D. W., Pease, D. G., & Jambor, E. A. (1997). Negative Influence of Market Competitors on the Attendance of Professional Sport Games: The Case of a Minor League Hockey Team. *Sport Marketing Quarterly, 6*, 31–40.

Chapter 4

Sport and physical activity human resources in Spain

A managerial perspective

Antonio Campos-Izquierdo[1]

Introduction

Our current society is composed of and structured by a diversity of organizations which create, offer, and develop services (Chelladurai, 2001; Gibson, Ivancevich, & Donnelly, 1994; Slack & Parent, 2006). All these organizations have a basic and central element: The human resources. Without them, the organizations and services could not even exist (Becker & Gerhart, 1996; Campos-Izquierdo, 2010; Koontz & Weihrich, 2007). Moreover, the human resources characterize and differentiate each organization and service (Becker, Huselid, & Ulrich, 2001; Chelladurai, 1999; Pfeffer, 1994; Wright & McMahan, 1992). Therefore, the human resources are a central and essential element of the services being offered and developed in today's society.

Sport and physical activity (SPA) has become one of the most important phenomenon of the last decades of the twentieth century and of the current century. This social phenomenon is continuously growing and expanding as SPA's demand and supply increases both in volume and diversification (García & Llopis, 2011; González-Rivera & Campos-Izquierdo, 2014). In addition, SPA has a great potential and impact on health (both preventive and therapeutic), social integration and cohesion, education, pleasure, and economic of citizens and society. SPA also exists as a service, since it generates these benefits to people, and improves the quality of life of citizens and social welfare, satisfying social and individual demands (Commission of the European Communities, 2007; European Observatoire of Sport and Employment [EOSE], 2014). Thus, different organizations emerge to offer a wide and diverse range of physical activities and sports services.

The benefits concerning health, education, economy, and social issues generated by the services of SPA depend on the human resources involved, mostly SPA human resources. Hence, the importance of proper management of human resources in SPA organizations, especially of SPA human resources, ensuring quality, efficiency, and professionalism of the service offered. Besides, if the practice of SPA is not done properly due to an inadequate performance of SPA human resources, instead of the potential benefits, one may incur health risks and hazards affecting an individual's safety and education and therefore the society, even translating into economic costs (Campos-Izquierdo, 2010; Tojal, 2004).

Sport and physical activity human resources

Human resources are "the people that staff and operate an organization" (Tracey, 2004, p. 322). Actually, human resources can be understood as the capabilities, knowledge, experience, abilities, and commitments of the workers of SPA organizations (Cabrera & Bonache, 2004; Fernández-Ríos, 1999). The classification of Campos-Izquierdo (2005, 2010) and Campos-Izquierdo, González-Rivera, and Taks (2016) can be used to identify, analyze, structure, and manage the human resources in the different SPA services in any organization or facility in Spain. This classification establishes two types of human resources, one of which is in turn divided into two other groups:

- Indirect (non-specific) sport and physical activity human resources: Employees who work in SPA services but who carry out functions which are not specific of SPA. Subdivided into two groups:
  - Workers who do not belong to any particular professional group but are salaried: cleaning, maintenance, etc.
  - Workers who belong to a profession but not of SPA working with athletes or users of sport facilities: physicians, physiotherapists, architects, psychologists, etc.
- Sport and physical activity human resources (sport and physical activity professionals): Workers who carry out functions specific of SPA.

In Spain, the SPA human resources are defined by Campos et al. (2016) as "SPA professionals" and in the legislation as "Sport Professionals". These SPA professionals are the center of services and SPA organizations (Campos-Izquierdo, 2005; González-Rivera, 2008; Martínez, 2007; Mestre, 1995). The SPA human resources are workers who use (design, plan, lead, guide, develop, and assess) SPA and exercise as a fundamental and central element of their professional practice or professional performance (Campos-Izquierdo et al., 2016; Spanish National Sports Council, 1991) in its different manifestations. The laws which regulate the sport professions in some regions of Spain (i.e., Catalonia, Madrid, and Extremadura) and draft bills to the sport professions of Spain establish that SPA professionals are the ones who apply the knowledge (practical, theoretical, and scientific), procedures, and specific techniques of SPA sciences in their professional practice. Their competences are acquired through SPA specific training in official qualifications of SPA (certificate, diploma or title, official document issued by an official awarding body) (Campos-Izquierdo & Martín-Acero, 2016; European Centre for the Development of Vocational Training [CEDEFOP], 2014).

The regulating laws of sport professions of regions of Cataluña, Madrid, and Extremadura and draft bill on sport professions in Spain requires official SPA qualifications in SPA occupations in order to guarantee the quality and efficiency of the service as well as the health, safety, and education of individuals. Furthermore, in Spain, Campos-Izquierdo et al. (2016) establish that SPA human resources (SPA professionals) carry out basic functions specific of SPA in the following occupations: Sports instructor; physical education teacher; extracurricular physical education teacher; sport coach; personal trainer or physical trainer; physical-sport readaptator or physical trainer in health; fitness instructor; sport animator; sport manager; SPA inspector; and SPA technical advisor.

Management and physical activity human resources

The laws regulating the sport professions of regions of Catalonia, Madrid, and Extremadura and draft law of sport professions in Spain define the "Sport Manager" as the "SPA professional" who manages, organizes, plans, coordinates, and assesses SPA and SPA human resources (SPA professionals) in any service, facility, and organization applying the knowledge (practical, theoretical, and scientific), specific procedures, and techniques of SPA sciences as well as the corresponding competencies. These laws establish a Sport Manager having the following duties and tasks:

- Managing, planning, programming, coordinating, promoting, controlling, evaluating, and assessing SPA.
- Managing, planning, coordinating, supervising, and assessing professional practice or professional performance (performance appraisal) and services of SPA human resources (SPA professionals).

The human resources management is a key aspect for the success of any organization and service (Becker & Gerhart, 1996; Fernández-Ríos, 1999; Huselid, 1995; Wright & McMahan, 1992). One of the core elements for the excellence in services is the efficient management of human resources (European Foundation for Quality Management, 2003). On management process, all the strategies depend on people, and money, materials, and facilities only become resources when the people use them efficiently (Chelladurai, 2001; Gómez & Mestre, 2005). For this importance, a great amount of research and literature about the subject of human resources' management in a wide range of contexts and situations is being produced (Pérez & Garrido, 2006; Trenberth, 2010). In the case of SPA organizations and services, the appropriate and efficient management of SPA human resources is essential in order to ensure the quality and the benefits of these services (Campos-Izquierdo, 2010).

The management of human resources consists mainly in orientating the employee's performance through a certain philosophy and the strategies, systems, and techniques for the organization to achieve its objectives efficiently (Cabrera & Bonache, 2004; Fernández-Ríos, 1999). In this process it is necessary to emphasize the role of the human resources on the success of the organization in connection with organizational efficiency. For this reason they should be considered in all analysis, objectives, strategies, actions, processes, and elements of the organization having a central role (Becker et al., 2001; Campos-Izquierdo, 2010; Claver, Gascó, & Llopis, 1996; Leal, Román, Alfaro, & Rodríguez, 1999). The human resource's management should be the responsibility of all managers and be the backbone of the organization (Cabrera & Bonache, 2004; Campos-Izquierdo, 2010; Claver et al., 1996).

The management of SPA human resources must be understood and take place from a broad, comprehensive, macro-organizational, and cross-cutting perspective. In this regard, the professional ethics, legislative, social responsibility, professionalism, and quality of SPA services should be taken into account. One of the main purposes of the SPA human resources management is to promote, develop, ensure, and enhance the various benefits generated by SPA as well as avoid creating security, educational, social, and health problems for the individuals and to the whole society (Campos-Izquierdo, 2010).

Organization in SPA human resources management

For an appropriate and efficient management of human resources, the organization and the services it provides, among other aspects, the following elements are essential: the selection (Dolan, Valle, Jackson, & Schuler, 2003; Peiró, 1992; Soucie, 2002); the organizational philosophy (Heinemann, 1998; Norton & Kaplan, 2004; Pires, 2007; Teruelo, 1996); the organizational chart of the human resources (Mestre, 2008; Mintzberg, 2003); job analysis and description (Fernández-Ríos, 1995; Gael, 1983; McCormick, 1976); and of its competencies (Boyatzis, 1982; Levy-Leboyer, 1997, Pereda & Berrocal, 1999); performance appraisal (Campos-Izquierdo, 2010; Chelladurai, 1999; Soucie, 2002). In Spain, in the particular case of public organizations, Regulation 7/2007 settles that the previously mentioned elements are mandatory, and are understood and assimilated by all employees.

The selection of personnel is constituted by the recruitment processes, selection, and incorporation of workers. These processes are preceded and influenced by the job description (Fernandez-Ríos, 1995; Mestre, 1995; Soucie, 2002). The recruitment is "the first step in the process of matching job descriptions and applicant specifications with people. The process of surveying all sources of personnel, inside and outside the organization, is to locate and attract the best possible candidates for new or vacated positions" (Tracey, 2004, p. 566). Afterwards, a selection is performed, a systematic process by which the most adequate candidate for the job position is chosen among the candidates recruited (Peiró, 1992, Pereda & Berrocal, 1999). Then, the incorporation phase takes place. During this phase the candidate gets to know the organization, his work, and the professional performance. During this phase, the candidate must be informed in detail, among other aspects, about the organization philosophy, organizational chart, job description, and the performance appraisal (Barranco, 2000; Bayón, 2002; Campos-Izquierdo, 2010; Claver et al., 1996) in order to prevent initial confusion and to facilitate the employee's integration within the organization (Leal et al., 1999; Pereda & Berrocal, 1999) and to know the professional performance expected (Campos-Izquierdo, 2010). Within this phase there is a trial period as established by the labor legislation, this period is a phase of orientation, training, adaptation, and performance appraisal (Bayon, 2002; Pereda & Berrocal, 1999). This period is a very important part of the selection process. Once the worker becomes part of the organization, and for this period of time, the job adaption and the professional performance of the individual selected can be assessed (Barranco, 2000; Bayón, 2002; Campos-Izquierdo, 2010; Claver et al., 1996; Pereda & Berrocal, 1999). Therefore, in this period the performance appraisal and job description are critical.

The job analysis and description and the performance appraisal are essential and central elements for the management of human resources and therefore in SPA management. The process of job analysis (which focuses on the duties, tasks, and elements that make up a job position) and description results in a document that describes the duties, functions, task, work activities, job demands, equipment, work performance, job context, personal data, and requirements of the job (Fernández-Ríos, 1995; Gael, 1983; McCormick, 1970; Tracey, 2005), as well as the competencies, qualifications, and training needs (Campos-Izquierdo, 2010; Pereda & Berrocal, 1999). The performance appraisal is a systematic process of

> periodic review and analysis of employees' performance with the objective of improving that performance so that employees can realize their full potentials. Ideally, it measures how well people do the job compared with a set of performance standards, communicates that information to them, gets agreement on strengths and weaknesses, and results in a plan of action to enhance strengths and shore up weaknesses.
>
> (Tracey, 2004, p. 508).

In Regulation 7/2007 performance appraisal is defined as the process by which the professional conduct and professional performance or achievement of results of the worker belonging to an organization is measured and valued.

The organization's philosophy and organizational chart are very important elements and processes in management of human resources, and in

SPA management. The philosophy of organization is "a statement of the fundamental beliefs and values that underlie and govern the actions of an organization and its people and provides guidelines for management planning and decision making. Philosophy deals with principles, truths, and ultimate ends. It typically states the purposes and obligations of an organization" (Tracey, 2004, p. 517).

In Spain, and in the most of the organizations, the management of SPA human resources does not do or does incompletely or inadequately the job analysis and description and performance appraisal (Campos-Izquierdo, 2010; Gómez & Mestre, 2005; González-Rivera, 2008; Martínez, 2007). Also, in human resources management it is very important that the workers know and understand the different elements and processes affecting them (Barranco, 2000; Campos-Izquierdo, 2010; Gómez & Mestre, 2005; Martínez, 2008). So, it is necessary to the employees to have the necessary information to carry out efficiently and successfully their professional performance (Bayón, 2002; Campos-Izquierdo, 2010). The lack of information generates negative consequences for their professional performance and the integration of workers (Claver et al., 1996). A lot of sport managers fail to provide the detailed information of these processes to SPA human resources in Spain (Campos-Izquierdo, 2005; González-Rivera, 2008; Martínez, 2007).

In this context, the purpose of the study is to analyze the selection process and the knowledge that SPA human resources (SPA professionals) have about different and fundamental processes that affect them. The specific objectives of this research are:

1 To describe the recruitment process and the instruments used during the selection process of the SPA human resources in Spain.
2 To analyze the recruitment process and the instruments used in the selection process of the SPA human resources in Spain according to the organization type.
3 To describe the perception of the importance of a variety of factors for the SPA human resources for getting their current job.
4 To describe the SPA human resources' knowledge in Spain about: organizational philosophy, organization charts, job description, and performance appraisal.
5 To analyze the SPA human resources' knowledge in Spain about: organizational philosophy, organization chartz, job description, and performance evaluation according to the organization type.

Method

The methodology followed in this investigation has been descriptive. In developing this methodology, the procedures followed were those of a sectional survey (Alvira, 2004; García, 2002). This research project was approved by the Ethics Committee of the Technical University of Madrid, Spain.

Participants

The participants in this study were 2500 workers who carry out SPA functions (SPA human resources) in 1797 sports facilities (1512 organizations) in 696 different municipalities in all of the Spanish provinces and regions, of whom 71 percent were men and 29 percent were women. The participants' ages ranged from 16–70 years with a mean age of 33.4 and the standard deviation 10.29 (Campos-Izquierdo et al., 2016). The study is working with a confidence interval of 95.5 percent and if it is assuming the population variance in the worst case of p equal to 50 percent, then q = 50 percent, the margin of error sampling allowed would be + 2 percent (Cea, 1998; Sierra, 2001).

Instrument

To collect the information for the purposes of the study, we used a standardized interview questionnaire PROAFIDE: Sport and physical activity human resources (Campos-Izquierdo, 2011). The structured interview was composed of 57 closed questions which covered five dimensions: socio-demographic characteristics, SPA functions, specific professional performance, work characteristics, and training characteristics of these SPA human resources (SPA professionals). The dimensions and questions related to the objectives of the present study were selected from the questionnaire: work characteristics (selection process and knowledge and understanding of organizational philosophy, organizational chart, job description, and performance appraisal) and their interrelation with the type of organization. In two questions a Likert scale of 1–5 was used.

On the question regarding the factors on the selection processes, the reliability index obtained through the calculation of the Cronbach's alpha coefficient (alpha = 0.720) indicated an acceptable internal consistency. On the question regarding knowledge of the selection processes, the reliability index obtained through the calculation of the Cronbach's alpha coefficient (alpha = 0.760) indicated an acceptable internal consistency.

Procedure

The research was cross-sectional given that the data collection was carried out in one single period (the year 2011) although it was divided into four seasons (winter, spring, summer, and autumn), in order to have deeper and more rigorous knowledge of the studied population, as many of the SPA services are seasonal. The interviews were carried out personally and individually face to face with each of the employees selected for the sample in the sports facilities and took an average of 15 minutes. Controls and supervisory tasks were carried out during the fieldwork and at its completion. There were 19 interviewers in the study and they were trained by the research team to make sure that the interviews were carried out correctly.

Data analyses

Data was recorded, entered into a computer, and analyzed using a univariate and bivariate descriptive analysis as well as an inferential analysis that included the Pearson's Chi-square value and Cronbach's alpha coefficient. All the statistical analyses were done using the statistical software package SPSS Version 19.0.

Results and discussion

In the results and discussion are described the recruitment process and instruments used in the selection process of SPA human resources in Spain, and equally, the perception of the importance of a variety of factors for the SPA human resources for getting their current job. Also, in this section is described the SPA human resources knowledge and understanding about: the organizational philosophy, the organization chart, the job description and the performance appraisal.

Selection of human resources

The selection process, in the great majority of SPA human resources and organizations (in all types of organizations: public, non-profit, and for-profit), is carried out by the organizations (98 percent employees), and only two percent of employees were hired with selection companies. This percentage is similar to studies by Campos-Izquierdo (2005), González-Rivera (2008), and Martínez (2007). The typology of recruitment of SPA human resources is fundamentally external (94 percent workers). Only six percent of workers come from the organization. These data are similar to other research in Spain (e.g., Campos-Izquierdo, 2005; González-Rivera, 2008; Martínez, 2007). The recruitment type (external or internal to the organization) depends on the circumstances and needs of the organization and new or vacated positions; both types have advantages and disadvantages (Chiavenato, 2007; Dolan et al., 1999). Therefore, sport managers should consider these characteristics in the management of SPA human resources.

According to Dolan et al. (2003), one of the most important phases of recruitment is the identification, selection, and maintenance of sources that might provide candidates. In this regard, the external recruitment SPA human resources indicates that recruitment and knowledge of the job

Table 4.1 Description of external recruitment of the SPA human resources

Recruitment and knowledge of the job offers	%
Informal recruitment through employees or acquaintances	58
Jobs offers and announcements on the website	25
Jobs advertisement in sports facilities and training centers	10
Labor Exchange	4
Public organizations specialized in job search	2
Companies specialized in job search	1

offers has been: informal recruitment through employees or acquaintances (58 percent), job offers and announcements on the website (25 percent) and job advertisements in sports facilities and training centers (ten percent). Public organizations or companies that specialize in the job search are not usually used in recruitment (Table 4.1). This external recruitment is similar to other employees in Spain (Salgado, Moscoso, & Lado, 2004). In addition, a specific characteristic of recruitment of SPA human resources are job advertisements in sports facilities and training centers (Campos-Izquierdo & González-Rivera, 2010; Martínez-Serrano, 2007). In external recruitment it is very important to promote the use of the internet. In the last decade there has been an important change with an increasing use of the Internet, both from the corporate site itself and in the diffusion or candidate search portals or employment websites. In addition, this decision reduces the time and economic costs and provides more information about the organization and opportunities for individuals (Paz, 2004).

The most used instrument in the selection of SPA human resources is "references or contacts" (36 percent of answers and 60 percent of workers), then it is the "curriculum vitae" (30 percent of answers and 51 percent of workers), subsequently the "interviews" (24 percent of answers and 41 percent of workers) and after professional tests (theoretical and practical) (11 percent of answers and 21 percent of workers) (Table 4.2). These data confirm that SPA organizations generally carry out a traditional selection process similar to other organizations in Spain (Salgado et al., 2004) and they also indicate that there is a wide range of instruments that are not used in the selection process (Levy-Leboyer, 1997, Pereda & Berrocal, 1999) and could be used in the future. In addition, it is necessary to carry out a constant monitoring and assessment of each of the procedures, techniques, and instruments used in the selection process. The objective is to examine their validity and reliability and their usefulness in predicting the future performance of the candidates (Pereda & Berrocal, 1999). In the case of public organizations, in the selection process, the Regulation 7/2007 requires to comply with the principles of equality, publicity, transparency, merit, and capacity. Also, professional testing (practical or theoretical) and personality tests are fundamentally used in the selection processes of public organizations of SPA (more 85 percent of workers in this instrument).

The element called "references or contacts" is more used and highly diversified: To be or to have been a client of the organization or sports facility, to be or to have been a student of the educational center, have been a member of the sport club, to know the manager or his relatives, to be friend of a manager or employee. This instrument is common and is characteristic in the SPA management. This situation is worrying and might negatively affect quality, efficiency, and professionalism of the SPA service (Campos-Izquierdo, 2005, 2010; González-Rivera, 2008; Mestre, 2008). In these cases, the adequacy and logic of the selection process and the criteria used are not appropriate. Furthermore, this situation is more serious if the employee is selected without appropriate training (official SPA qualifications appropriate to SPA occupation). The great majority of employees selected through "reference or contacts" (more than 75 percent of workers selected through this instrument) do not have official SPA qualifications appropriate to the job.

The second most used instrument is the "curriculum vitae". This instrument and the interviews are key elements in the selection process. A lot of people selected by "curriculum vitae" do not have official SPA appropriate qualifications and they do not have professional experience in SPA. This situation determines the uncertainty about the criteria of the selection process. In the training of future SPA professionals it will be necessary to stress the importance of a curriculum vitae and the interview in order to access a good job position. In the case of sport manager, the training should also include contents about "curriculum vitae" and interview for an efficient and adequate SPA management.

The selection mainly used a set of two instruments (52 percent of workers) and used jointly "references or contacts" and "curriculum vitae". Later, only one instrument was used (48 percent of workers). In this case, the two most used instruments are the "references or contacts" or "curriculum vitae". Then, with a lower percentage, it is the use of three instruments (20 percent of employees), in which the majority used jointly "references or contacts", "curriculum vitae" and interview (Table 4.3).

Table 4.2 Instruments used in the selection of SPA human resources

Instrument	*% Answers*	*% Workers*
References or contacts	34	60
Curriculum vitae	30	51
Unstructured interview	24	41
Professional testing (practical or theoretical)	11	21
Personality tests	1	1

Table 4.3 Number of instruments used in the selection of SPA human resources

Instrument	%
Two instruments	52
One instrument	48
Three instruments	20
Four instruments	2

According to the typology of the organization, the most used instrument in public organizations is the professional test (47 percent). The element "references or contacts" is present in all types of organizations. In the case of public organizations, these organizations should obey in their selection process Regulation 7/2007 that settles the terms of equality, publicity, transparency, merit, and capacity. In companies, the use of "curriculum vitae", interviews and "references or contacts" are balanced. In the case of associative organizations, the most used instrument is "references or contacts". It is determined that the selection process in these organizations is more inappropriate and inefficient than in other type of organizations ($X^2 = 1{,}468.753$; $p = .000$) (Table 4.4).

In the perception of importance of a variety of factors for the SPA human resources for getting their current job, the workers believe that contacts and personal skills have been very important for getting the job (more than 60 percent). Also the factors of qualifications, professional experience in SPA occupations, and ongoing training are perceived as important in the selection process (Table 4.5).

Overall, the selection process is a dualism: some employees are appropriately selected but in many cases the process is inadequate, inconsistent, or non-existent. This situation determines the need to improve the management of SPA human resources as it affects the quality and efficiency of SPA services and organizations (Campos-Izquierdo, 2010; Mestre, 1995). In addition, a lot of SPA organizations do not comply with the legislations of different regions of Spain which require official SPA qualifications in SPA occupations for guaranteeing health, safety, and education of citizens in SPA services.

Table 4.4 Instruments used in the selection according to type of organization

Organization Type	*% References or contacts*	*% Curriculum vitae*	*% Interview*	*% Professional test*
Public organizations	19	24	10	47
Companies	32	32	32	4
Associative organizations	60	16	21	3

Table 4.5 Perception of importance of variety of factors for the SPA human resources for getting their current job

Factors in Selection Process	*% Little or No Importance*	*% Some Importance*	*% Fairly or Very Important*	*M (1–5)*	*SD*
References or contacts	33	4	63	3.5	1.76
Personal skills	23	16	61	3.5	1.48
Qualifications	38	8	54	3.3	1.8
Professional experience	36	13	51	3.2	1.67
Ongoing training	38	13	49	3	1.67
Athlete	49	12	39	2.7	1.71
Physical appearance	54	16	30	2.5	1.51
New technology	78	11	11	1.7	1.14
Foreign language	84	16	10	1.5	1.06

Knowledge of SPA human resources

The majority of employees (69 percent) have a fair amount or much knowledge of the organizational philosophy and the general behaviour expected, although the percentage obtained is slightly lower than in other sectors in Spain, such as in the tourism sector (Ortega, Molina, & Garrido, 2006) (Table 4.6). This situation might hinder the efficiency and adequate professional performance desired by the organization (Bayon, 2002; Pires, 2007).

A majority of SPA human resources (66 percent) have a fair amount or much knowledge of the organizational chart (Table 4.6). In addition, the organization chart must be functional (Campos-Izquierdo, 2010; Celma, 2004; Fernández-Ríos, 2005). Although it has been observed that many of the organizational charts are neither adequate nor efficient, the great majority of SPA human resources have low or no knowledge of the job description (80 percent) (Table 4.6). This situation affirms that, in Spain, the majority of SPA organizations do not carry out the analysis and description of the job (Campos-Izquierdo, 2010; Gomez & Mestre, 2005; González-Rivera, 2008). Campos-Izquierdo (2010) states that the job description is not explained at the selection process. This determines that many workers do not know or understand professional performance (what to do, how, when, and why in detail), and this results in inadequate and inefficient professional performance. Likewise, the majority of SPA human resources have low or no knowledge of the performance appraisal (60 percent). The employees should know and understand with detail the performance appraisal process (Chiavenato, 2007, Pereda & Berrocal, 1999; Soucie, 2002). Both situations needs to be improved for adequate and efficient SPA management in all types of organizations and SPA services.

Table 4.6 Knowledge and understanding of organizational philosophy, organizational chart, job description, and performance appraisal by human resources of physical activity and sport

Concept	*% Little or no knowledge*	*% Some knowledge*	*% A fair amount or much knowledge*	*M (1–5)*	*SD*
Organizational philosophy	17	17	66	3.8	1.321
Organizational chart	17	14	69	3.92	1.406
Job description	80	7	13	1.7	1.299
Performance appraisal	60	12	28	2.42	1.566

About the organizational philosophy and general behaviour, most of the workers have fair or deep knowledge in all types of organizations. In public organizations and associative organizations, the percentage is higher (X^2 = 62,486; p = .000) (Table 4.7). Similarly, the majority of SPA professionals have fair or deep knowledge of the organizational chart in all types of organizations. In public organizations and associative organizations the percentage is higher (X^2=171,842; p = .000). However, the majority of the workers have little or no knowledge of the job description in all types of organizations (X^2 = 59,496; p = .000). In associative organizations and companies, most of the SPA human resources (81 percent and 51 percent) have little knowledge or do not have knowledge at all about the performance appraisal. In the public organizations the employees have little or no knowledge about the performance appraisal (45%) (X^2 = 403,390; p = .000) (Table 4.7).

Table 4.7 Knowledge of organizational philosophy, organization chart, job description and performance appraisal of SPA human resources according to organization type

Concept	*% Type*	*% Little or no knowledge*	*% Some knowledge*	*% A fair amount or much knowledge*
Organizational philosophy	Public	13	14	73
	Non-profit	12	11	77
	For-profit	15	17	68
Organizational chart	Public	11	11	78
	Non-profit	14	9	76
	For-profit	23	20	57
Job description	Public	83	4	13
	Non-profit	86	5	9
	For-profit	75	8	17
Performance appraisal	Public	45	11	44
	Non-profit	81	7	12
	For-profit	51	17	32

Many of the public organizations breach the regulations on performance appraisal and job description. The differences between public and private organizations could be that public organizations should comply with the Regulations related to performance appraisal and to report to all the workers about the process but in public organizations the percentage of lack of awareness is very high. The SPA human resources management must improve in all the organizations in relation to the performance appraisal and job analysis and description of job. It is necessary to emphasize that the trial period is fundamental during the selection process and that the lack of knowledge about the job description and performance appraisal can generate problems in the process or make it inefficient (Campos Izquierdo, 2010; Chiavenato, 2007; Pereda & Berrocal, 1999).

Conclusion

In most of the cases the selection process is carried out by the SPA human resources and organizations. Furthermore, the SPA human resources recruitment is mainly of external staff (external recruitment). The external recruitment of the SPA human resources is made mainly by the traditional tools. This recruitment is in most of the cases informal recruitment made through employees or acquaintances, job offers and announcements on the web, and job announcements in sports facilities and training centers.

The most used instrument in the selection of SPA human resources are the "references or contacts", followed by "curriculum vitae" and "interviews". References or contacts are used in all types of organizations, with higher percentages in associations and lower percentages in public organizations. The "curriculum vitae" and interview are used in all types of organizations. In addition, generally, in the selection process only one or two instruments are used. Personal and interpersonal skills are important in the selecting of SPA human resources, and this question must be considered in their training. Training (qualification and continuous training) and experience are important factors in selection process. Regarding the selection process, a lot of SPA organizations and managers do not comply with legislation from different regions of Spain that requires official SPA qualifications in SPA occupations for guaranteeing the health, safety, and education of the individuals in SPA services.

The knowledge of organizational philosophy and organizational charts of SPA human resources is high in all the organization types. Although a majority of SPA human resources have little or no understanding of job description and performance appraisal in all types of organizations. This question determines the inadequate and inefficient SPA management in many SPA organizations. In several public organizations in the SPA human resources management do not comply with Regulation 7/2007.

It is very important to carry out a scientific, continuous, and systematic process of monitoring and assessment of the procedures, techniques, and instruments used in the selection process, in the job description and performance appraisal. The objective of this process is to analyze their validity and reliability and their usefulness and suitability. According to the results, in different typologies of SPA organizations in Spain, there is a need to improve several processes of management of SPA human resources to ensure the quality, security, efficiency, and professionalism of the SPA services offered as well as to guarantee health, education, and social benefits to individuals and to society.

Note

1 The research is a part of the Fundamental Research Project I+D+i DEP2009–12828 which has been funded by the Ministry of Science and Innovation of Spain.

References

Alvira, F. (2004). *La encuesta: una perspectiva general metodológica.* Madrid: Centro de Investigaciones Sociológicas.

Barranco, F. J. (2000). *Marketing interno y recursos humanos.* Madrid, Spain: Pirámide.

Bayón, F. (2002). *Organizaciones y recursos humanos.* Madrid, Spain: Síntesis.

Becker, B., & Gerhart, B. (1996). The Impact of Human Resource Management on Organizational Performance: Progress and Prospects. *Academy of Management Journal, 39(4),* 779–801.

Becker, B., Huselid, M., & Ulrich, D. (2001). *El cuadro de mando de recursos humanos.* Barcelona, Spain: Editorial Gestión 2000.

Boyatzis, R. E. (1982). *The Competent Manager: A Model for Effective Performance.* New York, NY: John Wiley & Sons.

Cabrera, A., & Bonache, J. (2004). Recursos humanos y ventaja competitiva. In J. Bonache, & A. Cabrera (Eds.), *Dirección estratégica de personas* (pp. 4–26). Madrid, Spain: Pearsons Educación.

Campos Izquierdo, A. (2011). Diseño y validación de la entrevista estandarizada por medio de cuestionario "PROAFIDE. Recursos humanos de la actividad física y del deporte, *Actividad Física y Deporte: Ciencia y Profesión, 15,* 53–62.

Campos-Izquierdo, A., & González-Rivera, M. D. (2010). Selección de los recursos humanos de la actividad física y del deporte en las empresas. *Dirección y Organización, 41,* 44–57.

Campos-Izquierdo, A., & Martín-Acero, R. (2016). Percepción de las competencias profesionales de los Graduados en Ciencias de la Actividad Física y del Deporte. *Revista de Psicología del Deporte, 25(2),* 339–46.

Campos-Izquierdo, A. (2005). *Situación profesional de las personas que trabajan en funciones de actividad física y deporte en la Comunidad Autónoma Valenciana (2005).* Doctoral Thesis. Facultad de Ciencias de la Actividad Física y el Deporte, Universidad de Valencia, España. http://dialnet.unirioja.es/servlet/tesis?codigo=7194.

Campos-Izquierdo, A. (2010). *Dirección de recursos humanos en las organizaciones de la actividad física y del deporte.* Madrid, Spain: Síntesis.

Campos-Izquierdo, A., González-Rivera, M. D., & Taks, M. (2016). Multi-functionality and Occupations of Sport and Physical Activity Professionals in Spain. *European Sport Management Quarterly, 16(1)*, 106–26.

Cea, M. A. (1998). *Metodología cuantitativa. Estrategias y técnicas de investigación social.* Madrid, Spain: Síntesis.

Celma, J. (2004). *ABC del gestor deportivo.* Barcelona, Spain: Inde.

Chelladurai, P. (1999). *Human Resource Management in Sport and Recreation.* Champaign, IL: Human Kinetics.

Chelladurai, P. (2001). *Managing Organizations for Sport and Physical Activity: A System's Perspective.* Scottsdale, AZ: Holcomb & Hathaway.

Chiavenato, I. (2007). *Administración de recursos humanos.* México City, México: McGraw-Hill.

Claver, E., Gascó, J. L., & Llopis, J. (1996). *Los recursos humanos en la empresa: un enfoque directivo.* Madrid: Civitas.

Commission of the European Communities (2007). *White Paper on Sport.* Brussels, Belgium: Commission of the European Communities.

Dolan, S.L., Valle, R., Jackson, S. E., & Schuler, R. E. (2003). *La gestión de los recursos humanos. Preparando profesionales para el siglo XXI.* Madrid, Spain: McGraw-Hill.

European Centre for the Development of Vocational Training [CEDEFOP] (2014). *Terminology of European Education and Training Policy – A Selection of 130 Key Terms.* Luxembourg: Publications Office.

European Foundation for Quality Management. (2003). *EFQM. Introducción a la Excelencia.* Bruselas: EFQM. www.efqm.org.uploads/introducing spanish.pdf.

European Observatoire of Sport and Employment [EOSE]. (2014). *VSport: Strategy for a Competent Workforce.* Lyon, France: EOSE.

Fernández-Ríos, M. (1995). *Análisis y descripción de puestos de trabajo: teoría, métodos y ejercicios.* Madrid, Spain: Díaz de Santos.

Fernández-Ríos, M. (1999). *Diccionario de recursos humanos.* Madrid, Spain: Díaz de Santos

Gael, S. (1983). *Job Analysis.* San Francisco, CA: Jossey Bass.

García, M. (2002). La encuesta. In F. Alvira, M. García, & J. Ibáñez (Eds.) *El análisis de la realidad social. Métodos y técnicas de investigación* (pp. 167–202). Madrid, Spain: Alianza Editorial.

García, M., & Llopis, R. (2011). *Ideal democrático y bienestar personal. Encuesta sobre hábitos deportivos en España 2010.* Madrid, Spain: Consejo Superior de Deportes.

Gibson, J. L., Ivanicevich, J. M. & Donnelly, J. H. (1994). *Las organizaciones.* Buenos Aires, Argentina: Addison-Wesley.

Gómez, A., & Mestre, J. A. (2005). *La importancia del gestor deportivo en el municipio.* Barcelona, Spain: Inde.

González-Rivera, M. (2008). *El deporte escolar en la Comunidad Autónoma de Madrid: intervención didáctica y recursos humanos en las actividades físico-deportivas extraescolares en los centros educativos.* Doctoral Thesis. Facultad de Ciencias de la Actividad Física y el Deporte. Universidad de Valencia, España.

González-Rivera, M.D. & Campos-Izquierdo, A. (2014). *Intervención docente en Educación Física en secundaria y en el deporte escolar.* Madrid, Spain: Síntesis.

Heinemann, K. (1998). *Introducción a la economía del deporte.* Barcelona, Spain: Paidotribo.

Huselid, M. A. (1995). The Impact of Human Resource Management Practices on Turnover, Productivity, and Corporate Financial Performance. *Academy of Management Journal, 38*, 635–72.

Koontz, H., & Weihrich, H. (2007). *Administración: una perspectiva global.* México City, Mexico: McGraw-Hill.

Le Roux, N., Chantelat, P., & Camy, J. (1999). *Sport and Employment in Europe.* Brusseles, Belgium: European Commission, DGX.

Leal, A., Román, M., Alfaro, A., & Rodríguez, L. (1999). *El factor humano en las relaciones laborales. Manual de dirección y gestión.* Madrid, Spain: Pirámide.

Levy-Leboyer, C. (1997). *Gestión por competencias.* Barcelona, Spain: Gestión 2000.

Martínez, G. (2007). *Los recursos humanos de la actividad física y del deporte en la Comunidad Valenciana.* Doctoral Thesis. Facultad de Ciencias de la Actividad Física y el Deporte, Universidad de Valencia, España.

McCormick, E. J. (1976). Job and Task Analysis. In M. Dunnette (Ed.) *Handbook of Industrial and Organizational Psychology* (pp. 651–95). New York, NY: Amazon.

Mestre, J. A. (2008). *Planificación estratégica del deporte: Hacia la sostenibilidad.* Madrid, Spain: Síntesis.

Mestre, J. A. (1995). *Planificación deportiva. Teoría y práctica.* Barcelona, Spain: Inde.

Mintzberg, H. (2003). *Diseño de organizaciones eficientes.* Buenos Aires, Argentina: El Ateneo.

Norton D. P. & Kaplan, R. S. (2004). La disponibilidad estratégica de los activos intangibles. *Harvard Deusto Business Review, 122*, 38–51.

Ortega, R., Molina, J. A., & Garrido, A. (2006). *Recursos humanos y turismo en Aragón: Análisis del impacto socioeconómico de la Expo-2008.* Zaragoza, Spain: Fundear.

Paz, M. (2004). Nuevos procedimientos en el proceso empresarial de provisión de candidatos: el reclutamiento "on line". *Cuadernos de Ciencias económicas y empresariales, 47*, 89–110.

Peiró, J. M. (1992). *Psicología de las organizaciones.* Madrid, Spain: UNED.

Pereda, S., & Berrocal, F. (1999). *Gestión de recursos humanos por competencias.* Madrid, Spain: Ramón Areces.

Pérez, M. P., & Garrido, M. J. (2006). La investigación en recursos humanos en España. *Investigaciones Europeas de Dirección y Economía de la Empresa, 12(2)*, 119–36.

Pfeffer, J. (1994). *Competitive Advantage Through People.* Boston, MA: Harvard Business School.

Pires, G. (2007). *Agôn. Gestao do desporto. O Jogo de Zeus.* Porto, Spain: Porto editora.

Regulation 7/2007, of 12 April, Basic Statute of Public Employees. Boletín Oficial del Estado, April 13, 2007.

Salgado, J. F., Moscoso, S., & Lado, M. (2004). Reclutamiento y selección. In Bonache, J. & Cabrera, A. (Eds.), *Dirección estratégica de personas* (pp. 97–134). Madrid, Spain: Pearsons Educación.

Sierra, R. (2001). *Técnicas de investigación social. Teoría y ejercicios.* Madrid, Spain: Paraninfo.

Slack, T., & Parent, M. M. (2006). *Understanding Sport Organizations: The Application of Organization Theory.* Champaign, IL: Human Kinetics.

Soucie, D. (2002). *Administración, organización y gestión deportiva.* Barcelona, Spain: Inde.

Spanish National Sports Council. (1991). *Reforma de las enseñanzas y titulaciones deportivas. Propuesta para el debate.* Madrid: National Sports Council.

Teruelo, B. (1996). Dos herramientas para mejorar la gestión de las entidades deportivas municipales: la planificación estratégica y la gestión de la calidad de los servicios (1). *Apunts: Educación Física y Deportes, 46,* 103–12.

Tojal, J. B. (2004). *Da educaçao física à motricidades humana. a preparaçao do profissional.* Lisboa, Portugal: Instituto Piaget.

Tracey, W. R. (2004). *The Human Resources Glossary: The Complete Desk Reference for HR Executives, Managers and Practitioners.* Boca Raton, FL: CRC.

Trenberth, L. (2010). Organizing and Human Resource Management. In S. Hamil & S. Chadwick (Eds.), *Managing Football: An International Perspective* (pp. 169–84). Oxford, UK: Elsevier.

Wright, P. M., & McMahan, G. C. (1992). Theoretical Perspectives for Strategic Human Resource Management. *Journal of Management, 18,* 295–320.

Chapter 5

Relationships between standard sports facilities and elite sport development in taekwondo

Wai Huen Kwan and Harmania H. M. Lo

Introduction

Sport is a great channel for the public to improve their relationships. In addition, sports can greatly promote a healthy lifestyle, and the famous sports can bring economic benefit to the Hong Kong Government. Therefore, the Hong Kong Sport Institute Limited (HKSI) started supporting selected sports with facilities and subsidies. For example, athletes of tier A* and tier A sports can enjoy the facilities in HKSI, like training venues, gym rooms, sports performance laboratories, and medical support. Tier A* and tier A sports are the sports which show good performance in international competitions, such as the Asian Games and even the Olympics. Those selected sports developed faster under facility and subsidy supports.

On the other hand, under the effort of Hong Kong Taekwondo Association (HKTKDA), taekwondo had become a tier B sport, which can receive money support from Hong Kong Sport Institute Limited. However, according to the interview with Wan Leuk Hon, the coach of the Hong Kong National Taekwondo Team, "taekwondo facilities in Hong Kong could not satisfy elite taekwondo players' needs" (Chan, 2016). Apart from this, there is no facility specifically for taekwondo. According to the information of Hong Kong Taekwondo Association (HKTKDA, 2016), there are 44 taekwondo unions under HKTKDA, and each of the unions had their own training venue (Dojang). All dojangs are of different size and safety standard. If the Hong Kong Government could not give a comprehensive facility for the elite taekwondo athletes, it would be difficult for the athletes to enhance their performance and obtain good results in the international competitions. Quality of facilities is one of the factors to enhance elite taekwondo development.

Compared to the tier A* and tier A sport, like table tennis, badminton, and wind surfing, taekwondo is not a popular sport in Hong Kong. In order to promote taekwondo, taekwondo players need to get good results in the international competitions, for instance, Asian Games and East Asian Games, to gain the public's awareness. Hong Kong Taekwondo Association should find some methods to enhance elite taekwondo development, thus to gain better results. There are many factors that need to be considered in order to improve the above situation. For example, mass media, government policies, facilities, etc. Different factors may enhance elite taekwondo development in different ways. The purpose of the study is to find out the relationship between the standard of sports facilities and elite sport development in taekwondo, and to give some useful ideas to the government and the sports association to improve the taekwondo facilities, hence to develop taekwondo. To date, there is no study investigating elite taekwondo development in Hong Kong; the findings of this study can redound taekwondo development, and also to let people know about the importance of the standard of sport facilities, such as training venues, fitness rooms, recovery zone, etc. This study will also lead to the improvement of sport facilities. People can make use of the findings in this study to understand the current situation and improve elite taekwondo facilities in Hong Kong in the future. According to the previous research, the standard of the sports facility is one of the important factors to motivate athletes, and to improve elite athletes' performance (Jeroh, 2012), therefore this study will find out whether the existing sports facilities in Hong Kong could motivate athletes and improve athletes' performance in taekwondo.

Review of literature

Taekwondo is a Korean martial art and a combat sport which focuses on kicking techniques and punches. Taekwondo players need to have power, speed, flexibility, and balance during kicking and free style sparring. Taekwondo started to develop during the 1940s and 1950s. A number of martial artists incorporate the elements of karate and Chinese Martial Arts, like Subak and Taekkyeon. In order to develop taekwondo, the World Taekwondo Federation (WTF) and International Taekwon-Do Federation (ITF) were founded in 1973 and 1972, respectively. Under the efforts of the Taekwondo Association, "Gyeorugi", which means free style sparring, has become an Olympic event, since the 2000 Sydney Olympics. The rules of taekwondo in Olympic Games are set by the World Taekwondo Federation (WTF). Generally, people refer to WTF taekwondo as 'Olympic-taekwondo' or 'sport taekwondo' (Moenig, 2015).

Gyeorugi takes place between two competitors in the contest area. By referring to the standard of International Olympic Committee (IOC), the safety area should be an 11.2m × 11.2m area, players need to play the game in an 8m × 8m octagonal-shape flat area inside the safety area, which is called the competition area. The safety area and competition area should be in different colors, which can show the safety area and contest area clearly. The whole contest area is covered by a safety mat, which is shown in Figure 5.1. Each match consists of three rounds, and the length of each round is two

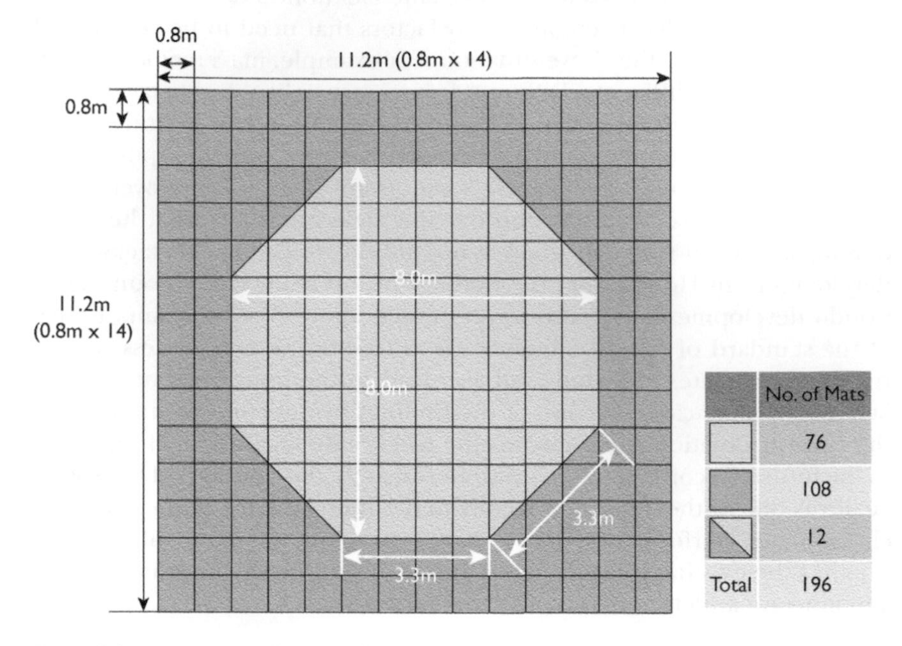

Figure 5.1 International Olympic Committee (IOC) standard taekwondo competition area

Figure 5.2 Sample of taekwondo competition area

minutes. Competitors need to attack the opponent with permitted techniques to gain points. The player wins when (a) a player gain more points after three rounds of Gyeorugi, (b) a player gains 12 points more than their

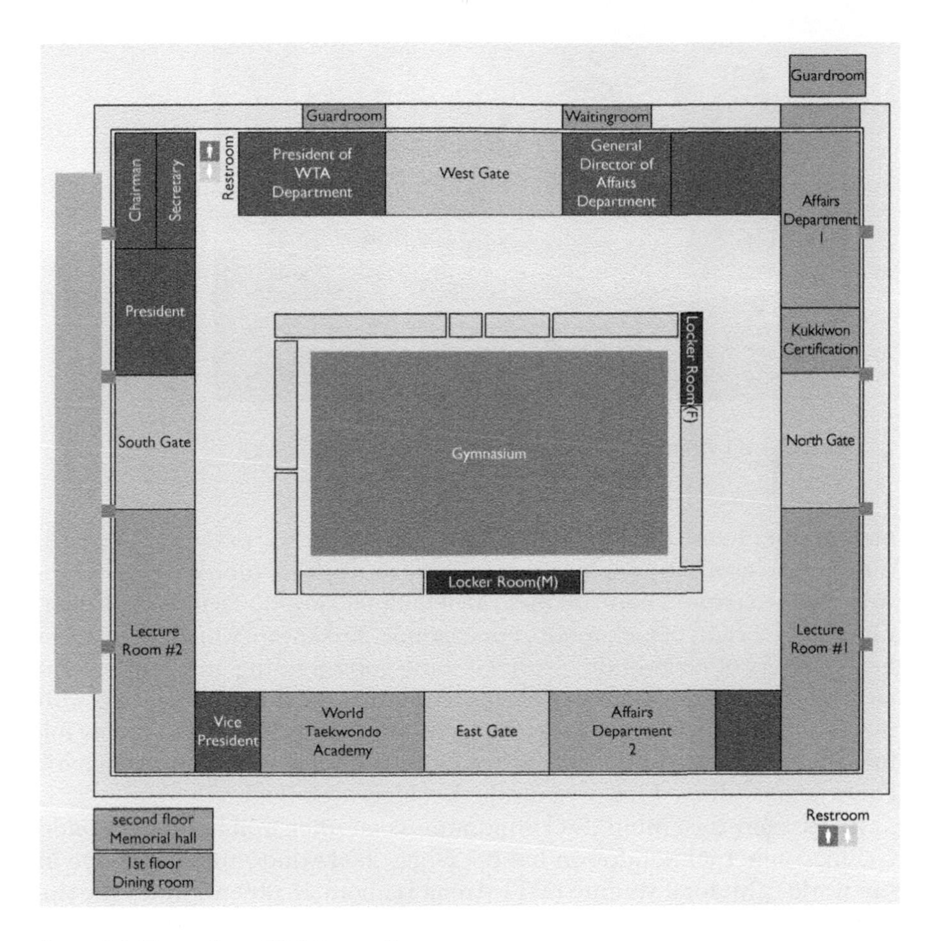

Figure 5.3 Floor plan of Kukkiwon, Korea

opponents, or (c) a player knocks out their opponent. The valid points are divided as follow: one point will be scored with a permitted attack on the trunk protector; two points will be scored by a valid turning kick attack on the trunk protector; three points will be scored with a valid kick attack to the head, and four points will be scored by a valid turning kick to the head. Taekwondo athletes need to wear proper gear to protect the full body during sparring. The full gear includes padded helmets, and feet, shin, groin, hand, and forearms protectors. Athletes will be disqualified if wearing improper gear, or when any one of the protectors is missing.

According to the Taekwondo Explanatory Guide of Rio Olympics (2015), the training venue will include changing rooms and showers, taekwondo equipment storage, a weigh-in room, medical facilities, four safety mats which are at competition standard, a lounge area, and catering services.

Figure 5.4 T1 Arena, Muju Taekwondowon

On the other hand, the competition area of taekwondo is in Carioca Arena 3, with a capacity of 850 people. A medical post and information center are provided in the venue. There are many well-built taekwondo facilities in Korea, which is the origin of taekwondo. For example, Kukkiwon, which is the world headquarters of taekwondo, provided some good training and competition facilities for athletes. There is a big gymnasium in the training building, with men's and women's locker room and restrooms. The gymnasium strictly follows the WTF standard, which is with a 11.2m × 11.2m safety area, and a 8m × 8m octagonal-shaped flat area inside the safety area (Figure 5.3).

Apart from this, Muju Taekwondowon is another well-built taekwondo facility. Muju Taekwondowon has the largest taekwondo training venue in the world. The total volume of T1 Arena is about 18,000m^3, with four storeys and two basement levels, and has capacity for 4,571. T1 Arena has six competition area (Figure 5.4). In contrast, according to the information of Hong Kong Taekwondo Association (HKTKDA), there are 44 taekwondo unions under HKTKDA, and each of the unions have their own training venue (dojang). All dojang are of different sizes and safety standards.

Elite taekwondo development in Hong Kong

The Hong Kong Government uses an 'Elite Vote Support System (EVSS)' to evaluate and choose sports with higher performance for support. The three key elements of EVSS include (1) a four-year support cycle, (2) a generic scoring table and (3) a three-tier structure. According to the guideline of Home Affairs Bureau – Hong Kong Sport Institute limited (2016), tier A* and tier A sports can enjoy enhanced support and full support respectively from the Hong Kong Government. All tier A* and tier A sports can attend the Elite Training Program that is organized by Hong Kong Sport Institute

(HKSI). Those athletes can use all the facilities in HKSI, including training venues, gym rooms, and also science and medicine support services. However, tier B sports can only enjoy the basic support, like funding support, but cannot enjoy the facilities in the Hong Kong Sport Institute. Tier B athletes can receive a Sports Aid Grant, which is for non-Olympic and Asian Games sports, or an Elite Training Grant, which is for Olympic and Asian Games sports.

Hong Kong Taekwondo Association was found in 1967. In order to develop Taekwondo in Hong Kong, Hong Kong Taekwondo Association organized the Hong Kong National Taekwondo Team, and appointed some elite athletes to attend the international competitions, including Olympics and Asian Games. Under the efforts of HKTKDA and the Hong Kong National Taekwondo Team, taekwondo was chosen to be a tier B sport in 2015, which can receive more subsidies from the government. Since taekwondo is an Olympic and Asian Games sport, since 2000 and 1986 respectively, elite athletes of taekwondo can receive the Elite Training Grant from 2015 after taekwondo became a tier B sport. Referring to the interview of Wan Leuk Hon, the coach of the Hong Kong National Taekwondo Team, he stated that

> The Hong Kong National Taekwondo has its training in Judo room of Pei Ho Street Sports Centre in Pei Ho Street Municipal Services Building on Monday and Thursday. They are training in activity room on Shek Kep Mei Park Sports Centre on Wednesday and Sunday, and those venues will not provide the safety mats for HK team. Since both hardware (facilities) and software (subsidies) are important for training an elite athlete, therefore no regular training venue is the most serious obstruction of elite taekwondo development.
>
> (Chan, 2016)

The commissioner for sports, Mr. Yeung Tak-Keung, stated that the registered sports association in Hong Kong can have the priority when renting the facilities under the Leisure and Cultural Services Department (LCSD). However LCSD also need to consider the balanced usage of the facilities between the sports associations and the public. If the facilities which the sport association would like to use are fully booked, LCSD cannot guarantee the sport association can use the desirable facilities. Eventually, the Hong Kong National Taekwondo Team could not have a suitable venue with a large area and safety mats to train in most of the time.

Training injuries in elite taekwondo

Usually, injuries would occur when people are participating in sports (Lystad, Graham, & Poulos, 2015). Taekwondo is a contact sport involving fighting with the opponent, and involves a lot of motor skills, such as speed, balance, muscle strength and coordination, etc. Therefore, training injuries are common. Lystad et al. (2015) conducted a survey about the injuries of taekwondo athletes in Australia during training and competitions. 239 Australian taekwondo athletes took part in the survey. It found 173 reported injuries, and 141 out of the 173 reported injuries happened during training. According to the proportions and frequencies of training injuries by types of injury, 19.9 percent of taekwondo players got muscle strain, 16.3 percent of athletes got joint sprain, 14.2 percent of athletes received contusion during training. On the other hand, there were 31.3 percent of athletes who had attended taekwondo competition and received contusion during matches. Apart from this, 43.3 percent of the athletes who were injured during training sessions needed to rest for less than one week, and 56.7 percent of injured athletes needed to rest for more than one week. 27.7 percent of athletes needed to rest for more than 28 days. The injuries may lead to retirement of athletes, since the injuries may affect the total performance of the athletes.

Du and Tsai (2007) conducted a research regarding the reasons for retirement of elite athletes in Hong Kong, which showed that physiological factors, including health status and injuries, were the major reasons that caused the retirement of athletes. Injury is one of the reasons that leads to athletes being unsatisfied with their current sport life. Safety is one of the considerations of sport facilities, especially taekwondo facilities. The results of the survey show that the probability of injury of taekwondo athletes during training and competition is high. Increasing the safety level of facilities can lower the probability of injuries; therefore, a safe facility can retain talented athletes.

Standard of sport facilities

Jeroh (2012) conducted a survey in a Nigerian University, which focused on the relationship between school facilities and students' sports performance. All of the respondents were made up of sports officials, such as coaches and directors of sports, and the team leaders of the sports in the Nigerian University Game Association competition. According the results of the survey, about 70 percent of respondents showed their agreement that the standard of sport facilities could be the predictor of elite athletes to have a better performance (Jeroh, 2012). Hence, the standard of the sports facility is one of the important factors to motivate athletes, and to improve elite athletes' performance. The results also stated that the standard and safety of facilities can prevent injuries and enhance elite athletes' performance.

Physical fitness is important to elite taekwondo athletes. The athletes need to decrease the percentage of body fat and increase the body mass to ensure they can compete in the most suitable weight category to gain an advantage. Also, the physical techniques, for example, power and muscular endurance, are important for the elite taekwondo athletes for enhancing their performance (Zar, Gilani, Ebrahim, & Gorbani, 2008). On the other hand, the core training can also enhance the performance of taekwondo athletes. According to the experiment done by Seong-Deok Yoon, Dong-Hun Sung, and Gi Duck Park, the performance of experimented taekwondo athletes improved after fitness exercise for eight weeks (Yoon, Sung, & Park, 2015). Therefore, taekwondo needs to use gym facilities for training, which can enhance the performance of athletes, thus to the development of elite taekwondo.

Physical therapy helps athletes to recover from their injuries. The time of recovery without therapy is much slower than that with the treatments of therapy. Also, the physical therapy can relax the pain of muscles after intensive training and exercise, which can prevent injuries like muscles strain, etc. (Geier, 2012). Therefore, therapy facilities can also help the elite taekwondo athletes to decrease the time of recovery, which also can prevent injuries. Because the injuries may affect the sport careers of taekwondo athletes (Du & Tsai, 2007), appropriate therapy facilities can enhance elite taekwondo development.

In the twenty-first century, tennis is one of the sports growing rapidly in the USA. USA Government, the United States Tennis Association (USTA), and United Stated Professional Tennis Association (USPTA) paid great efforts to promoting tennis and building new standard of facilities for tennis. Providing high quality facilities and equipment is one of the elements of Mass Sport Development in USA. The increase of high quality tennis facilities can increase the number of participants in tennis-playing, and also enhance elite tennis performance in USA. According to the research in the USA (Smolianov, Gallo, & Naylor, 2014), tennis coaches believe that high quality of training centers is an important element to enhance the athletes' performance. Therefore, increasing the standard and quality of tennis training centers would be an indicator to advance the performance of elite athletes. This theory might be also applicable to other sports. This research would focus on the relationships between sports facilities and elite sport development in taekwondo. Therefore, the above topics would be covered. The definitions can let the readers know more about taekwondo and sports facilities, and the others literature reviews can let the readers know why the sports facilities are important to enhance sport development.

Method

This study is focused on the elite taekwondo players' development in Hong Kong. Since there are not many elite taekwondo players in Hong Kong, the researcher chose to use the qualitative research design to figure out the study. This could help getting more details and in-depth opinions and comments from the respondents. The interview sample will be narrowed to two types of taekwondo stakeholders: (a) certified taekwondo coach and (b) taekwondo athlete with international competition experience. Face-to-face, one-on-one interview was adopted in this study, as it would be more spontaneous and would not be influenced by the other participants (Opdenakker, 2006). Interviewees could express their opinions on their own without hesitation and without an extended reflection. All interviews would be tape recorded with the permission of the interviewee. Interview questions were set to cover three main areas: (a) the current situation of Hong Kong taekwondo facilities, (b) the training and competition venuess overseas, and (c) the possible future development of taekwondo in Hong Kong.

Participants and procedures

Purposive sampling has been used in the study since the researcher could find the individuals who have the information related to the research, and obtain rich data (Blankenship, 2010). All the respondents are familiar with taekwondo, half of them were certified taekwondo coaches with teaching experience and leading elite athletes' experience in attending local or international competitions; and the other half were the elite taekwondo players and had represented Hong Kongwith local or international competition experience. Besides this, the interviewees should have obtained experience in overseas training before. All subjects were actively participating in taekwondo at the moment. The reason for inviting both taekwondo coaches and players to participate in the study is to make the data collected comprehensive. For instance, taekwondo athletes know what facilities need to be upgraded or improved to enhance their performance, while the taekwondo coaches can observe the taekwondo athletes' needs, and know what facilities need to be added.

Excluding the pre-interview briefing section, the interview section lasted about 30–45 minutes. All interviews had been recorded by audio recorder. The data had been collected once only. If the interviewees felt any discomfort during the interview, they could have the right to stop the interview at any time without any consequences, and the recording of the withdrawal respondent would not be used in the study. No interview data will be used for other purposes. The researcher will keep the data strictly confidential and used for the research only, the supervisor of the study will store the data, and the research data will be kept for a year.

Results

The researcher invited six respondents for data collection, three of them were athletes and the other three were coach in taekwondo. Basic information of the respondents is shown in Table 5.1. The age range of all the interviewed athletes is 18– to 25 years, while the age of the interviewed

Table 5.1 Demographic information of the respondents

Interviewee	*Age*	*Gender*	*Practicing TKD (Year)*	*National TKD Representation*	*Certified TKD coach*	*Attended International Competition*	*Teaching elite TKD (Year)*
Athlete A	18–25	Male	10–15	Yes	Yes	Yes	-
Athlete B	18–25	Male	15+	Yes	Yes	Yes	-
Athlete C	18–25	Male	15+	Yes	Yes	Yes	-
Coach A	45–50	Male	15+	-	Yes	-	15+
Coach B	30–35	Male	15+	-	Yes	-	15+
Coach C	45–50	Male	15+	-	Yes	-	1–5

coaches ranged from 30 to 50 years. The education level of the respondents range from secondary school to bachelor degree level. All the respondents were male. All the interviewed athletes are practicing in taekwondo at the moment. Two of them have initial contact with taekwondo for more than 15 years, while the other has initial contact with taekwondo of between ten and 15 years. All of them are Hong Kong National Taekwondo Team representatives, while they have attended international competitions within the past two years. All of the coaching respondents are certificated taekwondo coaches. All the interviewed coaches have initial contact with taekwondo for more than 15 years and they are all certified taekwondo coaches in Hong Kong. Two of them have already taught elite taekwondo athletes for more than 15 years, while the other one has taught elite taekwondo athletes for between one and five years.

Training venue

In terms of facility, the respondents stated that there are not enough taekwondo facilities in Hong Kong, since the elite athletes cannot have regular training in the same training venues. Also, the places in which they are having training are not specific for taekwondo. In fact, according to the guideline of Home Affairs Bureau – Hong Kong Sport Institute Limited (2016), taekwondo is a tier B sport in Hong Kong under the three-tier structure set by the Hong Kong Government. The athletes can only enjoy the funding support, but cannot enjoy the facilities in the Hong Kong Sport Institute. Therefore, the elite athletes cannot use the comprehensive facilities in HKSI, and can only use the facilities under Leisure and Cultural Service Department, which need to be shared with users from the public. The interviewees mentioned about the spaces of training venues eight times. "The training venues of elite taekwondo athletes are small, we need to stay in a small activity room for training even there are many athletes", one athlete said. Besides, one of the interviewed coaches mentioned that, "The size of activity rooms in LCSD's sport centers are not big, which are not good places for teaching and training taekwondo."

In addition, research about tennis development in USA stated that the increasing of tennis facilities can increase the participants in tennis, and also enhance the elite tennis performance in USA (Smolianov et al., 2014). It is believed that more taekwondo facilities help the elite sport development of taekwondo in Hong Kong. Therefore, the researcher claims that lack of government support is one of the reasons why the athletes and coaches expressed that there are not enough taekwondo facilities in Hong Kong. On the other hand, the respondents expressed they are not satisfied with the small training venues in Hong Kong. The majority of the respondents stated that the large training venues overseas are much better than that in Hong Kong, and it can accommodate more elite athletes together for training. According to the interview, the respondents expressed that, "Many activity rooms in the sport center of LCSD are not suitable for teaching and training taekwondo if the size is too small."

The respondents stated that the facilities overseas such as in Korea and Taiwan are much better than in Hong Kong. In the previous findings, the training venue in Muju Taekwondowon in Korea contains six competition areas, where the elite athletes can have different training in the same area. This can explain why the athletes are not satisfied with the taekwondo facilities in Hong Kong, after they experience the good quality facilities in other countries. In addition, the respondent expressed that a specific taekwondo training venue with well-equipped facilities can enhance elite sport development in taekwondo. The respondents define that a specific taekwondo training venue should include both training rooms and comprehensive supporting facilities. The previous findings claim that the standard of sport facilities is a predictor for elite athletes to have a better performance (Jeroh, 2012). In addition, research in USA claim that a high quality of training center is important to enhance the athletes' performance (Smolianov et al., 2014). The researcher used the findings in this research as an example, claiming that the specific training venue with comprehensive facilities can enhance athletes' performance, thus enhance elite taekwondo development. It can explain why the interviewees were concerned about specific taekwondo training venues.

In terms of location, the respondents expressed that the location is one of the considerations of attending the training. During the interviews for this research, the respondents expressed that the training venues in the other countries had halls for the elite athletes to live in the training center directly, which is convenient for the elite athletes. The interviewees were concerned about the convenience of taekwondo facilities and training venue, respondents had mentioned "convenience" eight times. "The elite athletes need to use many times on transportation which even more than time of practices", a coach mentioned during the interview. This finding can fit the previous findings of a study in China, the long travel distance between living place and sports facilities, poor quality of facilities and services, and also short opening hours are the factors which affect the motivation to participate in sport for rural residents of China (Zheng & An, 2015). If the location of the training venue always changed or was not convenient to the elite taekwondo athletes, it cannot motivate the elite athletes to attend the training frequently, so that it will be difficult to enhance the elite taekwondo athletes' performance. Since there is no specific taekwondo training center in Hong Kong, it is believed that it is difficult to develop elite taekwondo in Hong Kong.

Professional taekwondo facilities and equipment

In terms of the professional taekwondo facility, all the athletes and coaches expressed that the bad quality of taekwondo safety mats affected their training, which may increase the chances of injuries during training. Most of the athletes were concerned about the problems of taekwondo safety mats used in training, problems included the condition of mats, the size of the mats or the elasticity of mats, etc. An athlete stated the following:

> Hong Kong National Taekwondo Team has regular trainings in judo room in Pei Ho Street Sports Centre, which is under LCSD's administration. We are using judo safety mats during training, unfortunately, the judo mat is different from taekwondo mat, which cannot buckle each mat together, therefore when we are practicing footwork and sparring, the judo mat will shift, therefore it cannot give us a good protection, even some athletes got ankle sprain because of the inappropriate mats.

The interviewed athletes mentioned problems of safety mats 11 times, which shows they are concerned about the quality of safety mats, while the interviewed coaches only mentioned about problems of safety mats four times. The safety mats, which the elite taekwondo athletes are using, may not be the specific taekwondo safety mats, with all the mats not gripping with each other. The athletes may get ankle sprain because of the inappropriate safety mats. This showed the elite athletes' serious concern about the safety of the facilities. If they get serious injuries, they need to rest for several days, or even several months, it will be hard to recover, and keep in good condition after recovery. If they are seriously injured, they may need to retire from their sports careers. This finding supports the previous findings of Du and Tsai (2007). Injuries led to the dissatisfaction of the athletes with their current sport life. Both athletes and coaches mentioned about injuries during interviews nine times in total. One of the respondents mentioned that, "Some elite athletes need to retire because of the injuries during training."

In terms of taekwondo equipment, the coaches expressed that they are concerned about the quality of training equipment in taekwondo facilities. The training equipment included body protectors, hand targets, etc. The body protector is useful for protecting the body of the athletes, and can prevent injuries during training and competitions. A possible description of the finding is that the proper equipment can lower the chance of injuries, which injuries may affect the performance of elite taekwondo athletes, which also fits with the findings of Du and Tsai (2007). Moreover, the researcher found that the interviewed coaches were concerned about the training equipment in taekwondo facilities, they mentioned about "training equipment" seven times, while the athletes only mentioned once about the training facilities while talking about the current situation of taekwondo facilities in Hong Kong. One of the respondents indicated that

> The training equipment for Hong Kong National Taekwondo Team is not in a good quality. For example, if the hand targets, speed targets or sandbag damaged or became old, the athletes need to continue using the damaged equipment until the government provide subsidies to Hong Kong Taekwondo Association for buying new equipment after a long time.

Apart from the above elements, the respondents also stated that there are few facilities that are specific for taekwondo. "There are no standard facilities of taekwondo. Nowadays, Hong Kong Government or Hong Kong Taekwondo Association cannot provide a facility which fit the standard of taekwondo to the elite athletes", a respondent said. Therefore, the bad quality of professional taekwondo facilities and equipment in Hong Kong will affect the elite sport development in taekwondo.

Supporting facilities

There is a lack of supporting facilities for taekwondo in Hong Kong. The coaches had mentioned about the lack of supporting facilities in Hong Kong five times, while the athletes did not mention it. A coach commented that

> Use the taekwondo facilities overseas as an example, their facilities are comprehensive and well-equipped, for example there are gym facilities, swimming pools, and massage table, etc. But in Hong Kong, elite

> athletes cannot enjoy these supporting facilities even they are Hong Kong National Taekwondo Team's representatives.

The interviewees mentioned that the quality of gym facilities used by elite taekwondo athletes are not good enough to enhance their performance. Respondents mentioned "gym" or facilities in gym rooms 12 times. Two interviewees said the following, respectively:

> The gym room in LCSD cannot satisfy the needs of elite taekwondo athletes, since there is not enough gym equipment for all teammates, and we need to share the gym room with the public. Therefore, it is inconvenient for the coaches to train the athletes, and at the same time we may disrupt the public to use gym rooms.
>
> Majority of the gym rooms in Hong Kong are not well-equipped, even some of the gym rooms have no dumbbells. There should be a high quality of gym room which the equipment there can be used for training the whole body's muscles.

One of the previous findings mentioned that appropriate physical fitness is important to athletes, since power, muscular endurance, and core training are all important for enhancing performance (Zar et al., 2008). This kind of training should be done in the gym rooms. By comparing the experience training overseas and training in Hong Kong, the gym facilities in the other countries are well-equipped with a large number of machines and free weight equipment. Also, the machines and free weight equipment can train the whole body of the athletes. The athletes can use the same model of machine at the same time, and it is convenient for the coaches to guide the athletes during training. However, the gym rooms in Hong Kong are not well-equipped for the elite taekwondo athletes. Also, they need to share the gym room with the public, which is inconvenient for coaches to train the athletes.

Except gym facilities, the respondents also expressed that the physical therapy facilities can enhance athletes' performance, thus developing elite taekwondo in Hong Kong. According to the previous findings of Lystad et al. (2015), training injuries are commonly occurring in elite taekwondo athletes. On the other hand, therapy facilities help the athletes to recover from their injuries and release their pain (Geier, 2012), so physical therapy facilities are needed to enhance elite taekwondo development. Therefore, the researcher claims that lack of supporting facilities, like gym and physical therapy facilities, will badly affect the elite sport development in taekwondo. Other than this, the respondents also mentioned about hygiene of facilities, shower compartments, physical therapy facilities and that the facilities can be rented by the public, etc. Details are listed in Table 5.2.

Table 5.2 Perceptions of taekwondo facilities in Hong Kong between elite athletes and coaches

Situation of Hong Kong	*Athletes*	*Coaches*	*Total*
Not enough taekwondo facilities	12	6	18
Problems of taekwondo safety mats	11	4	15
Convenience	3	5	8
Dedicated	5	1	6
Gym	5	7	12
Injuries	4	5	9
Hygiene	2	3	5
Safety	4	3	7
Physical therapy facilities	2	2	4
Training spaces	3	5	8
Shower compartment	3	3	6
Few facilities specific for taekwondo	3	2	5
Training equipment	1	7	8
Lack of supporting facilities	0	5	5
Rent by the public	3	1	4

Competition venue

In terms of competition venue, the respondents stated that the competition venues of the other countries are much bigger than the competition venues in Hong Kong. Also, overseas' competition venues are well-equipped with first-aid facilities, spectator's stand, warm-up area, changing rooms, etc. From the previous findings, the quality of sports facilities will greatly affect the participation in sports (Zheng & An, 2015), and the higher sport participation can enhance sport development since the more participants, the more talented players can be found (Smolianov et al., 2014), which can enhance elite sport development. Hence, the responses of the interviewees in data collection fit the above findings. A respondent stated the following:

> The competition venue in Taiwan is much bigger than the competition venue in Hong Kong. There are eight competition areas, while there are mostly three competition areas in Hong Kong. Besides, Taiwan was already using the octagonal-shape competition area, while the competitions in Hong Kong still using the old one, which is in square shape.

In terms of warm-up areas in the competition venues in the other countries, the respondents stated that the overseas' warm-up areas are much bigger than the warm-up area in the taekwondo competitions in Hong Kong.

The warm-up area in competition venues is also one of the considerations of the interviewees. They had mentioned the warm up area overseas six times. An interviewee indicated that "Actually, the competitions in Hong Kong are the most difficult competitions for taekwondo athletes since there is not enough space for warm-up. The competitions in the other countries got a large area (nearly the same size of the whole competition area) for warm up, stretching and practicing."

The quality and the size of the facilities will affect the elite sports development in taekwondo. One of the findings stated that aerobic components, for example, kicking and running, are the main part of the conventional warm-up in taekwondo, which can increase the body and muscle temperature (Behm & Haddad, 2013). Dynamic stretching will be used for warm-up, which needs to be done in a large space. Therefore, the response of the interviewees can fit the previous findings. On the other hand, the respondents had mentioned that the competition venues overseas are convenient for the public and spectators six times. The respondent stated that "The competition venues overseas can accommodate nearly ten thousand spectators to watch the competitions. Although some of them cannot see the match clearly, they can sit down and watch the whole competition comfortably."

Discussion

With the experience in training or attending competitions overseas, the respondents experienced the good quality of facilities, including the training venues, supporting facilities such as gym facilities, physical therapy facilities, changing rooms with shower compartment, etc., and the competition venues. There is a big difference between the taekwondo facilities in Hong Kong and overseas. Therefore, facility is one of the considerations in order to develop elite taekwondo in Hong Kong, since a good facility can improve elite athletes' performance and motivate the elite to attend training and competitions. On the other hand, the researcher found that there are some differences in views between elite taekwondo athletes and coaches, in which the athletes are concerned about safety of the facilities, while the coaches considered more the quality of professional taekwondo facilities and supporting facilities. This topic can be discussed in the next research.

Based on the results and discussion, the researcher claims that there are four main factors that will affect the taekwondo facilities and elite sport development of taekwondo in Hong Kong. They are: (a) lack of government support, (b) lack of specific taekwondo training venues, (c) bad quality of professional taekwondo facilities and equipment, and (d) lack of supporting facilities for elite taekwondo athletes in Hong Kong. The practical application will eliminate the above limitations that affect the elite taekwondo development in Hong Kong.

The government support for elite taekwondo development is limited in that the government gave limited support in providing facilities for elite taekwondo athletes. Although the government gives funding subsidies to taekwondo athletes, lack of professional taekwondo facilities and supporting facilities still appear in elite taekwondo industry in Hong Kong now. Therefore, the researcher suggests that elite taekwondo athletes use the facilities in Hong Kong Sport Institute (HKSI). According to the facilities presentation in Hong Kong Sports Institute Facilities Brochure (2016), they are a big fitness-training center with comprehensive fitness equipment. In addition, the wushu hall in the sports complex annex is suitable for taekwondo training, where they have some large safety mats that are similar to the taekwondo safety mats. The researcher suggests that elite taekwondo can use the wushu hall for regular training when the wushu athletes are not using that facility. Apart from this, since muscle endurance is useful in elite taekwondo training (Zar et al., 2008), the researcher suggests that the government can provide some special time slots for elite athletes to use the gym rooms in the Leisure and Cultural Service Department. Hence, the elite taekwondo athletes do need to share the gym facilities with the public, and specific time slots would be convenient for taekwondo athletes for regular fitness training.

On the other hand, if the elite athletes gain some good results in high-level international competitions in the future, the government can provide a specific taekwondo training venue for elite taekwondo athletes. The Kai Tak Park Project (2016) is one of the important investments of the Hong Kong Government in the sports industry, in which the Hong Kong Government is planning to build a sports park for citizens in Kai Tak. One of the objectives of the Kai Tak Sports Park is to support elite athletes. In order to enhance elite taekwondo development, the government may build a specific taekwondo training venue with a good quality of professional taekwondo facilities and equipment within the Kai Tak Sports Park. Therefore, the elite taekwondo athletes can use the supporting facilities, such as fitness training facilities and physical therapy facilities, in Kai Tak Sports Park.

The researcher believes that promotion of taekwondo is one important element to increase the number of taekwondo facilities in Hong Kong. Higher sport participation can enhance sport development (Smolianov et al., 2014). If taekwondo becomes a famous sport in Hong Kong, more talented taekwondo athletes can be found. According to the guideline of Home Affairs Bureau – Hong Kong Sport Institute limited (2016), tier A* and tier A sports can enjoy the enhanced support and full support respectively from the Hong Kong Government. The tier A* and tier A sports are some famous sports in Hong Kong, which can also gain good results in the international competitions. This means that if taekwondo becomes more famous, the Hong Kong Government will give more support for elite taekwondo development. In order to promote taekwondo in Hong Kong, the

Hong Kong Taekwondo Association can organize more taekwondo competitions to attract spectators to watch the competitions. Sport media is one of the key elements to enhance sport participation (Nicholson, 2015). Besides, referring to research about the relationship of fantasy football participation with NFL television rating (2011), broadcasting of the sport events can attract people to participate in sport. Hence, HKTKDA can organize broadcasting on the internet for the spectators and public to watch the live matches. To sum up, the above practical application can improve the taekwondo facilities and standard of supporting facilities in Hong Kong. Therefore, this can help to enhance elite taekwondo development.

References

Blankenship, D. (2010). *Applied Research and Evaluation Methods in Recreation.* Champaign, IL: Human Kinetics.

Behm, D., & Haddad, M. (2013). Stretching During the Warmup and to Increase Flexibility for Taekwondo. *Performance Optimization in Taekwondo: From Laboratory to Field,* 1–6, available at www.researchgate.net/publication/254258354_Stretching_during_the_Warm-up_and_to_increase_Flexibility_for_taekwondo.

Chan, S. Y. (Reporter). (2016, October 8). Prehistoric Force [Television series episode]. In *News Magazine.* Hong Kong: TVB Jade.

Du, M. M. & Tsai, E. (2007). Reasons for Retirement and the Influence of Retirement on the Life Adjustment amongst Hong Kong Elite Athlete. *Journal of Physical Education & Recreation (Hong Kong), 13 (1),* 29–35.

Fortunato, J. A. (2011). The Relationship of Fantasy Football Participation with NFL Television Ratings. *Journal of Sport Administration & Supervision, 3(1),* 74–90.

Fried, G. (2010). *Managing Sport Facilities* (2nd ed.). Champaign, IL: Human Kinetics.

Geier, C. D. (2012). Injury Recovery and the Youth Athlete. *Rehab Management: The Interdisciplinary Journal of Rehabilitation, 25(8),* 26–30.

Home Affairs Bureau (2016). *Hong Kong Sport Institute Limited,* Hong Kong, 7–15.

Hong Kong Sports Institute (2016). *Welcome to Hong Kong Sports Institute Facilities Brochure,* Retrieved May 10, 2017, from www.hksi.org.hk/f/page/28/1469/HKSI_Facilities_presentation.pdf.

Hong Kong Taekwondo Association (2014). Retrieved October 27, 2016, from www.hktkda.com/index.html.

Jeroh, E. J. (2012). Standard Sports Facilities as Predictor for Elite Sports Performance. *Journal of Physical Education and Sport, 12(1),* 44–47.

Kai Tak Sports Park Project. (2016). Retrieved May 16, 2017, from www.kaitaksportspark.hk/en/index.html.

Lacey, A., & Luff, D. (2007). Qualitative Research Analysis. *Nottingham: The NIHR RDS for the East Midlands/Yorkshire & the Humber.*

Lystad, R., Graham, P., & Poulos, R. (2015). Epidemiology of Training Injuries in Amateur Taekwondo Athletes: A Retrospective Cohort Study. *Biol Sport Biology of Sport, 32(3),* 213–18.

Meriwether, N. (2001). *12 Easy Steps to Successful Research Papers* (2nd ed.). Lincolnwood, IL: National Textbook.

Moenig, U. (2015). *Routledge Research in Sports History: Taekwondo: From a Martial Art to a Martial Sport.* Abingdon: Routledge.

Nicholson, M. (2015). *Sport and the Media: Managing the Nexus.* Abingdon: Routledge.

Ochieng, P. A (2009). An Analysis of Strengths and Limitations of Qualitative and Quantitative Research Paradigms. *Problems of Education in the 21st Century, 13,* 13–18.

Opdenakker, R. (2006). Advantages and Disadvantages of Four Interview Techniques in Qualitative Research. *Forum Qualitative Sozialforschung / Forum: Qualitative Social Research, 7(4),* Art. 11.

Singh, P. (2006). *Facilities, Equipment and Supplies.* Retrieved October 28, 2016 from South African National Archery Association, at www.sabs.co.za.

Smolianov, P., Gallo, J., & Naylor, A. H. (2014). Comparing the Practices of USA Tennis Against a Global Model for Integrated Development of Mass Participation and High Performance Sport. *Managing Leisure, 19*(4), 283–304.

Taekwondo Explanatory Guide (2015). *Rio Olympic 2016.* Retrieved October 10, 2016 from International Olympic Committee. Web site: www.tpenoc.net/download/Rio2016/SportExplanatoryGuides/Taekwondo.pdf.

Taekwondowon. (2010). Retrieved October 27, 2016, from Taekwondo Promotion Foundation. Web site: www.tkdwon.kr/en/.

World Taekwondo Federation Competition Rules & Interpretation (2015), World Taekwondo Federation. Retrieved October, 16, 2016. Web site: www.worldtaekwondofederation.net/rules/.

World Taekwondo Headquarters. (2016). Retrieved October 27, 2016, from Kukkiwon. Web site: www.kukkiwon.or.kr/eng/index.action.

Zheng, J. & An, R. (2015). Satisfaction with Local Exercise Facility: A Rural-Urban Comparison in China. *The International Electronic Journal of Rural and Remote Health Research, Education, Practice and Policy,* 2–9.

Yoon, S., Sung, D., & Park, G. D. (2015). The Effect of Active Core Exercise on Fitness and Foot Pressure in Taekwondo Club Students. *Journal of Physical Therapy Science, 27(2),* 509–11.

Zar, A., Gilani, A., Ebrahim, K., & Gorbani, M. (2008). A Survey of the Physical Fitness of the Male Taekwondo Athletes of the Iranian National Team. *Physical Education and Sport, 6(1),* 21–29.

Chapter 6

Public relations network, absorptive capacity, and achievement level of traditional soccer schools

Bing Liu, Chun-hua Dong, Ting-ting Xiao, and Wen-hao Winston Chou

Introduction

Promoting soccer activity on school campuses is fundamental to the development of soccer in China in paving its way to become a powerful sports nation. As emphasized in the latest promulgated "China Soccer Reform and Development Program", the development of school soccer will expand the size of the soccer population and promote the cultivation of soccer talent. Throughout the country, there are approximately 5,000 primary and secondary schools specialized in soccer and this number is expected to reach 50,000 by 2025. Youth soccer population is predicted to increase substantially, which makes soccer one of the most popular participation sports in China (Wilson, 2015). With the government's support, the development of school soccer seems to heading in a favorable direction. However, the progressively fierce competition and conflict in education and soccer industry capitals triggers more complexity and uncertainty in soccer development on campus. Previous research indicated that school soccer development requires more than mere accumulation of favorable factors (Liu & Ji, 2012), and these schools specialized in soccer cannot thrive solely relying on their own resources (He, 2015). Under such a circumstance, it would be more fruitful for these schools to associate with possible resources to promote the sustainable development of school soccer (Liang, 2014).

In today's society, no organization can survive alone or develop well by itself without networking or building cooperative relationships with its partners. In an empirical analysis of German high-tech industries, Gemünden, Ritter, and Heydebreck (1996) identified seven different types of cooperation network configurations and explained how the intensity and structure of a firm's network contribute to its success. The same rule should apply to most of the countries where youth soccer organizations and programs thrive by means of well-established public relations networks and relationships with other relevant organizations in their society. In fact, there is a rapidly expanding body of theoretical and empirical literature showing that a public relations network constitutes a valuable means for integrating complementary resources into the development processes of school soccer in China (Liang, 2014; Li, He, Dong, & Xu, 2012; Wu, 2015; Wang, Wang, & Kang, 2014). Chinese scholars revealed that some local education departments and schools made unnecessary interventions by keeping social capital away from soccer activity on campus which cost the significant progress of overall soccer development in this country (Gong, 2011). Moreover, the results of their longitudinal studies indicated that a well-developed public relations network should be able to facilitate the absorption and utilization of resources such as information and knowledge in schools, which imply a correlation between a strong public relations network and absorptive ability in the context of school soccer program's achievement level (Wu, 2011). While considerable research suggests that a public relations network has a positive impact on a better development of school soccer in China, little is known about what constitutes an effective public relations network, and how a school's public relations network strength and its absorptive capacity may influence its soccer program's achievement level. This current research aims to address these issues.

In accordance with the aforementioned "China Soccer Reform and Development Program", a school's public relations network is composed of the school soccer-related interest groups including: Governing bodies (e.g., education and sports department), schools, soccer products suppliers, soccer facilities, counsellors, intermediaries, research and social training institutions, sponsors, professional soccer clubs, media, and volunteer organizations. The strength of public relations network is determined by how well the schools build and maintain cooperative relationships with these entities. In the process of school soccer development, a stronger public relations network should promote the popularity of soccer in schools and lead to a better cultivation of soccer talent. Previous research has shown that a rich and strong public relations network is one of the main reasons why youth soccer programs have been prospering for decades in Germany, Britain, and other developed countries (Mao & Liu, 2015; Yu, 2015). In China, although not many, a few public relations networks have been developed. As examples we can look to the following: Each professional soccer club assisted the training of soccer teachers for primary schools in Hangzhou city; in Huanggu district of Shenyang city, innovative soccer activities on a primary school campus were designed by a professional counseling soccer club; in Qingxiu district of Nanning city, soccer activities on campus were well planned by a local sport event company and received tremendous feedback from participating students; also in Zhengzhou city of Henan province, Brazilian soccer star Ronaldo opened one of his prospective 30 soccer schools in China.

Although it looks like school soccer in some provinces and cities in China has built a certain network with other cooperative partners, these public relations networks are susceptible to a variety of variables that impact their effectiveness. Research has found that one crucial factor is the strength of public relations network; that is, the extent of coordination and cooperation among the members of the network. Derived from Granovetter's (1973) definition of the strength of an interpersonal tie, the strength of public relations network is defined as a combination of the amount of time, emotional intensity, intimacy, and reciprocal services which characterized the tie between people or organizations. A given tie of the network could be strong, weak, or absent. When the strength of network is strong, it characterizes more collaborative time, stronger emotions and dependencies, as well as a higher degree of mutual benefit between organizations. If a public relations network does not demonstrate these characteristics, the strength of network is weak. The intensity of relationship will affect the acquisition, transmission, and creation of knowledge between organizations. The bulk of research on the strength of network in organization concerns its impact on performance of organization. That research finds that a strong network facilitates collaboration among organizations and expedites development and innovation processes within the organization. Despite some counter-arguments that an organization featuring a weak network with others might be more innovative by keeping its independence, a series of studies have shown that this contribution of a weak network is accidental and cannot be reduplicated or applied to the majority of organizations. In general, only a strong network can bring in full information and capital to organizations in order to achieve their objectives of healthy development. Similarly, it should be beneficial for a school aiming in developing soccer activity on campus when its strength of public relations network is strong. This makes intuitive sense since information and capital are crucial to schools for accomplishing their goals as well.

Many scholars in China have recognized the benefits of public relations networks; however, they also suggest that a public relations network may not be the only variable influencing the achievement level of a school's soccer program. In recent years, researchers have used absorptive capacity in their analyses of organizational performance and importance of absorptive capacity has been noted across the management field. Zahra and George (2002) recognize absorptive capacity as a dynamic capability that influences the nature and sustainability of an organization's competitive advantage. Building upon previous research, absorptive capacity is defined as a set of organizational routines and processes, by which organizations acquire, assimilate, transform, and exploit knowledge to produce a dynamic organizational capability. These four capabilities represent four dimensions of absorptive capacity and play different, but complementary roles, in explaining how absorptive capacity can influence organizational outcomes. Recognizing the roles and importance of a school's absorptive capacity and its influence on school soccer performance is central to the analysis of a school's evolution, knowledge management, and development of dynamic capabilities. Many scholars in China attribute the low achievement level of school soccer to the lack of facilities, coaches, and support; however, we believe the lack of absorptive capacity may be another critical factor.

Regarding the role of organizational social network, most of the current studies are based on how organizational performance is influenced by the network's composition and structure. In spite of this, theories from various areas remain insufficient to discuss and analyze organizational performance and innovation from the perspective of network intensity. Although greater differences exist between schools and firms, all organizations share the pursuit of building a good public relations network, forming a mutually supportive network, and promoting organizational performance effectively. Especially considering school soccer growth in a very competitive environment, it is undoubtedly helpful and obviously significant to borrow enterprise management philosophy to improve the overall performance of school soccer.

Based on the aforementioned argument and the existing theoretical framework, this study implemented an empirical investigation whose participants were from 90 Shanghai primary and secondary schools traditionally specialized in soccer, which are listed by the Ministry of Education of the People's Republic of China in July 2015 (Xinhuanet, 2015). This study was conducted to explore the relationship between strength of public relations network, absorptive capacity, and school soccer program's achievement level. The researchers aimed to see if during the process of current school soccer development the problem exists in the strength of the public relations network, in schools' absorptive capacity, or in both. At the same time, this study set the types and the locations of these schools as control variables to further analyze their impact on this relationship. The result of this current study should be practically and theoretically significant for improving contemporary school soccer performance and fostering the cooperative development of school soccer in China.

Theoretical framework

Relationship between public relations network and achievement level

Liang (2014) defined the public relations network from the perspective of the participants in his analysis of network pathway integration and multiple resources supply of English school soccer, which is the relationship between the network of government agencies, enterprises, communities and associations, such as Sport England, soccer foundations, sponsors, professional sports clubs, community clubs, and volunteer associations. Together these entities participate in the design, development, promotion, and completion of soccer activities on campus. Their interaction leads to a direct or indirect, mutually beneficial and flexible cooperative relationship. Similarly, from the integrated research of Chinese soccer folk tournament, *Who is the King*, Tian (2015) also found the interaction between communities, schools, and media improved their relationship and promoted a more positive atmosphere. Furthermore, Harris, Coles, and Dickson (2000) proposed a synergistic effect that a cooperative network among organizations results in better organizational performance and creativity than that of a single organization. Deriving from the research results of these scholars, the benefits of the construction of public relations networks can be summarized as the following points: (1) schools can access high-quality, external resources of soccer (e.g., experts, coaches, know-how of professional soccer clubs, coaches); (2) sponsors and enterprises can improve the efficiency of their investment in soccer activity on campus; (3) more soccer talent can be introduced and involved in better school soccer leagues and international youth soccer events; (4) media can be coordinated to share and disperse more information; (5) public departments can realize multi-participation, technology sharing, and common improvement by purchasing better soccer services from schools.

Although the construction of a public relations network can bring many advantages for the development of school soccer, the substantial improvement in achievement level of a school soccer program lies in the strength of the public relations network. At present, scholars argue that the advantages of public relations networks are determined by the acquisition of external resources and knowledge, that is, the improvement of a school soccer program's achievement is related to how strong the strength of public relations network is between schools and entities that provide resources and knowledge. Some scholars, while studying the effects of social network, found that a strong network can help organizations absorbing knowledge from outside because it generates trust and dependence. As Hao Ping, the former vice minister of education of the People's Republic of China, investigated the school soccer in Shanghai, he claimed that the development of school soccer in China can only be carried out by the cooperation of social forces together instead of by schools solely.

Also in the summit forum for 2016 China (Shanghai) International Youth Soccer Invitational, Eckhard Krautzun, the former head coach of the Chinese National Under-20 Soccer Team, stated, "Chinese soccer coaches are full of enthusiasm, but their knowledge is very limited. Many of them are master in sports other than soccer, while some of them never kick the ball in their life" (Song, 2016). This famous veteran coach emphasized that cognitive and athletic ability should be of equal importance for soccer players. We might pay more attention to the improvement of youngsters' athletic ability rather than to their cognitive ability; however, cognitive ability is the key to the formation of soccer-related knowledge and the essence of soccer culture. These statements indicate that a school soccer program's achievement level can only be effectively promoted by a strong public relations network existing within these school soccer participating entities when they are more willing to share the knowledge and ideas of soccer and expand the scope of cooperation. From the perspective of transaction cost economics, a strong public relations network is also beneficial for promoting school soccer program's achievement level because the strong organizational relationship network can reduce the cost of organizational learning and then internalize the external knowledge.

Some scholars believe that a weak relationship network can maintain the independence of the organization, which is more favorable to organizational innovation; however, Koberg, Detienne, and Heppard (2003) argued that some of the contingencies, such as the environment, mechanisms, and other elements, should not be ignored when discussing the strength of network. In China, the strength of school soccer network has been weak for a long time, which is the reason why the achievement level of school soccer programs is difficult to improve. As Krautzun mentioned, people's enthusiasm for soccer cannot guarantee the acquisition of soccer-related knowledge. Meanwhile, the general capability of Chinese primary and secondary schools to improve soccer development is so week that the overall performance of school soccer has to be improved through the cooperation of other related entities. Thus, it is reasonable to conclude that the significant and long-term development of school soccer can only be accomplished through building a strong public relations network. If true, one would predict:

> **H_1**: The strength of public relations network has a significantly positive correlation with the achievement level of school soccer program.

Relationship between public relations network and absorptive capacity

Absorptive capacity is a variable originating from the management literature, which explains how capable a firm is in acquiring, assimilating, transforming, and exploiting resources such as external information and knowledge. With growing use of this construct, a firm's absorptive capacity has been an important criterion for evaluating organizational learning. Its related theories are well developed and widely applied to diverse research of organizational development. For example, Ge, Fan, and Xiao (2016) explored the role of social capital in rural cooperative organizations by using absorptive capacity as a mediator, while Liu (2012) also evaluated how absorptive capacity mediated the performance of scientific research team in high schools. Analysis of past research reveals that definitions and operationalization of this construct vary widely, and Cohen and Levinthal (1990) offered the first definition of absorptive capacity. In the 1990s, as corporate competition intensified, Cohen and Levinthal realized the fact that firms of higher competitiveness in the market are more sensitive to external information and knowledge; these firms also pay more attention to their capacity to process, assimilate, and exploit valuable information. Thus, Cohen and Levinthal termed this phenomenon as the absorptive capacity of a firm and broke it down into three dimensions: Knowledge acquisition, knowledge assimilation, and knowledge exploitation. First, knowledge acquisition refers to a firm's ability to recognize the value of external information and knowledge that is critical to its development. Second, knowledge assimilation refers to a firm's ability to complement its lack of knowledge or create new knowledge by assimilating acquired information and existing knowledge. Third, knowledge exploitation refers to a firm's ability to apply the complementary and new knowledge to enhance its organizational efficiency and performance according to its development goals.

After Cohen and Levinthal defined absorptive capacity (ACAP) as a three-dimensional concept (i.e., a firm's ability to value, assimilate, and apply new knowledge), many scholars have proposed different definitions, such as two-dimensional, four-dimensional, or even five-dimensional components, for the application of absorptive capacity in their specific research fields. For example, entrepreneurship researchers Zahra and George (2002) suggested that absorptive capacity exists as two subsets of potential and realized absorptive capacities. The importance of absorptive capacity has been noted at different levels of analysis while adopting multiple measures of this construct, but it remains unclear if these measurements are capturing the same attributes of absorptive capacity. As Cohen and Levinthal have offered the most widely cited definition (Zahra & George, 2002), we would use their three-dimensional model of absorptive capacity in this study.

Although the effect of the public relations network has been explored in the previous research (Liang, 2014), few researchers have considered the relationship between strength of public relations network and schools' absorptive capability. Tian (2015) found that establishment of a strong network can effectively promote a favorable atmosphere for soccer; however, it is unclear whether this outcome was contributed by factors from outside or within schools. It is possible that the absorptive capacity of schools plays a crucial role when they build a cooperative network and then value, assimilate, and apply new soccer-related knowledge received from these outside partners. These relationships have not been empirically verified yet, but at least scholars have agreed that a well-established public relations network is beneficial to school soccer development.

Taking a further look into the practical process, it is helpful to improve the participants' sensitivity of soccer-related knowledge and deepen their understanding of soccer culture when schools receive external resources from professional soccer clubs, which is confirmed in related news reports. Research shows that a close long-term cooperative relationship between an organization and its network partners can facilitate its utilization of resources, dissemination of information, integration of knowledge, and improvement of absorptive capacity. According to Murovec and Prodan (2009), the importance of organizational absorptive capacity and difficulty of knowledge are positively related, and a firm's absorptive capacity becomes even more important when a firm deals with complicated and difficult knowledge. As Krautzun pointed out, the lack of soccer-related knowledge and culture is a main problem for the school soccer development in China, so it is necessary to identify conditions under which schools can be more capable to absorb complicated knowledge they receive from external soccer network. The argument above led to the following hypothesis:

> **H_2**: The strength of public relations network has a significantly positive correlation with the school's absorptive capacity.

Relationship between absorptive capacity and achievement level

The ultimate goal of the school is not only to enhance its capacity to absorb soccer-related knowledge, but to improve its soccer program's achievement level through its enhanced absorptive capacity. In their previous research, Chinese scholars concluded that the poor performance of school soccer in China is generally due to insufficient facilities, malfunction of school soccer system, shortage of coaches, overlook of school and family, and lack of soccer culture (Dong, Gong, & Yan, 2011; He & Liu, 2013; Li & He, 2011). Building on the results, Mao, Liu, and Zang (2015) proposed a top-down model of school soccer development emphasizing the key role of two 'P's, which are principals and parents. Indeed, these scholars have spotted problems related to the development of school soccer in China, and suggested different countermeasures to improve the school soccer program's achievement level based on their own experience. However, one important factor is neglected, which is absorptive capacity. The key function of absorptive capacity is to value, assimilate, and apply soccer-related knowledge that is new to organizations. Even if principals and parents recognize the importance of developing school soccer programs in China, there is no way they can be productive in fostering soccer culture on campus if they are unable to understand soccer-related knowledge. Furthermore, Cohen and other scholars suggested one more component of absorptive capacity, predictability, in their follow-up study. Therefore, as a principal of a primary or secondary school in China, he/she needs to be able to locate the problems and predict accurately the future directions of school soccer development by knowing how to use external resources to improve his/her knowledge of school soccer in addition to learning characteristics and international trends of youth soccer development.

Kostopoulos, Papalexandris, Papachroni, and Ioannou (2011) believe that absorptive capacity can guarantee the improvement of organizational performance, especially in promoting innovation. Hamel (1991) also suggests that the improvement of a firm's absorptive capacity can promote organizational outcomes by breaking the ceiling of competence. In the context of school soccer, it is reasonable that schools can improve the outcomes by enhancing their absorptive capacity. For example, school soccer managers will clearly understand characteristics and the latest trends of youth soccer development by recognizing the value of external information, and then they can change the routine path and update the ideas of school soccer development by assimilating and applying new knowledge in actual process. Application of knowledge often requires a good mechanism in order to transfer beneficial information into sustainable outcomes of school soccer development. The existing research indicates that the poor mechanism costs significant progress of school soccer development by increasing the difficulty of assimilating and applying soccer-related knowledge. Studies also show that continuous knowledge assimilation and application is critical to an organization's innovative capabilities, and, in turn, higher performance can be reached. Comparing the school soccer development gap between China, Japan, and South Korea (Wang, Wang, & Kang, 2014; Wu, 2015), researchers found a relatively lower cognitive level of soccer-related knowledge in the Chinese younger generation, and schools failed to build a multiple understanding of competition rules, soccer facilities, and coaching for their students, therefore, the overall achievement level of the school soccer program in China is low. Based on arguments above, this is the third hypothesis proposed:

> **H_3**: The schools' absorptive capacity has a significantly positive correlation with the achievement level of school soccer program.

Method

Data collection

The data was collected from 90 Shanghai primary and secondary schools specialized in soccer, which were listed by the Ministry of Education of the People's Republic of China in 2015. These schools were selected because Shanghai is one of the pioneering cities early initiating soccer activity on campus, where relatively sufficient soccer-related resources and information – such as a large amount of professional soccer clubs, a high level of economic development, a good base of soccer participants, and strong awareness of soccer – leads to a higher level of school soccer development across the country. Moreover, these 90 schools with better conditions for school soccer development are in an urgent need of understanding how to improve the achievement level of their soccer program. If the path to better performance could be revealed, the pattern of Shanghai schools could be an example for carrying out the nationwide development of school soccer. Therefore, the principles of sampling are: (1) including all Shanghai primary and secondary schools traditionally specialized in soccer; (2) including different types of schools (e.g., complete primary school, junior high school, complete middle school, and nine-year compulsory education school, etc.); (3) including different natures of schools (e.g., public, private, and other, etc.).

With the support of the Shanghai School Soccer League, the contact information of all potential subjects was provided. Subjects who participated in this study were contacted and confirmed by telephone that they were willing to fill out the questionnaire (one participant per school). They must be full-time teachers engaging in soccer coaching (in fact, some of them were outsourcing soccer coaches through a long-term contract) who comprehensively understand the status quo of their school soccer programs. They should also know about their public relations network, especially the cooperative relationship with professional soccer clubs, sponsors, soccer research institutions, education and sports departments, etc. In this way, their responses can be ensured to accurately reflect the relationship between public relations network, absorption capacity, and achievement level of school soccer programs.

Due to the variables in questionnaire derived from social and business organizations, the preliminary questionnaire was submitted to a panel of experts for face and content validity. The panel of experts included three senior practitioners in the field of youth sports: Mr. Song-hui Yu (the secretary-general of Shanghai School Soccer League), Mr. Shao Bin (the secretary-general of Shanghai Collegiate Soccer League), and Mr. Sun-wei Huang from Shanghai Youth Sports Center. Each panel member examined the relevance, representativeness, clarity of each item in the questionnaire. Before finalizing the questionnaire, we interviewed full-time school soccer coaches from the Wujiaochang Primary School in the Yangpu District, the Anshan Junior High School, and the First Affiliated Middle School of Tongji University for testing the questionnaire. Based on feedback from the above, the preliminary questionnaire was modified, revised, and improved to ensure that each item was concise and easy to comprehend. Ninety questionnaires were issued, and a total of 79 valid responses were recorded through the data collection procedure (87.8 percent). Descriptive statistics of the type, area, and nature of school are presented in Table 6.1.

Table 6.1 Descriptive statistics of Shanghai school specialized in soccer (N=79)

Variable	n	%
Type of school		
Primary school	32	19.0
Junior high school	18	27.8
Nine-year compulsory education school	7	15.2
Senior high school	15	29.1
Complete middle school	4	5.1
Twelve-year compulsory school	1	1.3
Vocational school	2	2.5
Location of school		
Pudong	17	15.2
Huangpu	3	2.5
Xuhui	4	3.8
Jing'an	4	3.8
Yangpu	4	3.8
Baoshan	6	7.6
Hongkou	2	5.1
Putuo	7	14.0
Changning	2	6.3
Minhang	7	7.6
Jiading	6	6.3
Chongming	3	3.8
Songjiang	3	7.6
Jinshan	6	6.3
Qingpu	3	3.8
Fengxian	2	2.5
Nature of school		
Public	75	94.9
Private	1	1.3
Other	3	3.8

Variables and measures

Strength of public relations network. Despite the difference between schools and firms, the research indicates that the relationship strength scale of enterprise network can be used in measuring the strength of a school's public relations network after appropriate modification. There are many scales measuring the strength of relationship among organizations, however, given the unique background of social environment and culture in China, the study adopted the questionnaire originally developed by Chinese scholars (Pan & Zheng, 2011). It was then modified to fit the context of school soccer.

The modified version of the questionnaire consisted of 13 items from four dimensions including cooperation time, cooperation scope, school investment, and cooperation reciprocity, which evaluates how strong the relationship is between these schools and their partners in the network, such as professional or social soccer clubs, sponsors, sports colleges and research institutes, soccer training institutions, associations of soccer events, venues and facilities suppliers, education and sports departments, and community sports organizations. The seven-point Likert scale was used in these question items, with 1 meaning strongly disagree, and 7 meaning strongly agree, and participants rated how much they agreed/disagreed with the statements that are consistent with the actual situation of their current public relations network. A higher score indicates a stronger public relations network.

School's absorptive capacity. The absorptive capacity of organization is a common variable in management literature, which is widely applied in various types of organizations other than firms. In this research, Cohen and Levinthal's (1990) three-dimension model was adopted to construct relevant indicators of how capable schools can absorb soccer-related knowledge. Nine questionnaire items were finalized by weighing the reality of school soccer in China, which consist of four items for knowledge acquisition, three items for knowledge assimilation, and two items for knowledge exploitation. In order to optimize participants' understanding of these items whereby they provided reasonable evaluation, each item was explained by additional description and examples. An example of a knowledge acquisition item is, "The school has established an informal way to obtain external resources of soccer", which was followed by an additional explanation, "The school encourages teachers and students to contact different kinds of cooperative partners individually to introduce more external resource into campus for developing soccer activity." The seven-point Likert scale was used in these question items, with 1 meaning strongly disagree, and 7 meaning strongly agree, and participants rated how much they agreed/disagreed with the statements that are consistent with the actual situation of school's absorptive capacity. A higher score indicates a higher absorptive capacity.

Achievement level of school soccer program. There is no existing scale for evaluating the performance of a school soccer program; however, the review of relevant literature indicated that popularity, recognition, and improvement are a common index of a school soccer program's achievement level in China. The achievement level of a school soccer program was evaluated by six items using a seven-point Likert scale (strongly disagree/strongly agree), which are, "Comparing with other schools specialized in soccer, our school's soccer program has received better social repercussion", "Comparing with other schools specialized in soccer, our school soccer structure is more reasonable", "Comparing with other schools specialized in soccer, our students have a higher participation and enthusiasm in soccer activities on campus", "Comparing with other schools specialized in soccer, our school receives higher returns from the investment in soccer program", "Our school has established a more mature model of school soccer program", and "Comparing with other schools specialized in soccer, the teaching skill and technique level of our coaches is improved more quickly." The participants rated how much they agree/disagree with these statements. A higher score indicates a higher achievement level of school soccer program.

Control variables. The control variables in this study are type, location, and nature of school. The difference between schools might impact their soccer program's achievement level when taking into account their economic and cultural conditions which will lead to different strength of public relations network. This study was conducted in Shanghai only, so if these control variables will affect the school soccer program's achievement level, then these variables will be of more importance when conducting nationwide research.

Measurement properties

The reliability of strength of public relations network, absorptive capacity, and achievement level of school soccer program is more than .90, indicating that the research scale is reliable (see Table 6.2). For the content validity, the measurement was referring to the verified scales, and experts in the field of

Table 6.2 Results of confirmatory factor analysis: reliability coefficient, factor loadings, construct reliability, and average variance extracted (AVE)

Factor	*Reliability Coefficient*	*Factor Loadings*	*Construct Reliability*	*AVE*
Strength of public relations network	.976		.9545	.8401
FN1. Cooperation time	.904	.869		
FN2. School investment	.952	.950		
FN3. Cooperation scope	.953	.958*		
FN4. Cooperation reciprocity	.946	.886		
Absorptive capacity of school	.979		.9853	.9572
FA1. Knowledge acquisition	.941	.970*		
FA2. Knowledge assimilation	.953	.986*		
FA3. Knowledge exploitation	.967	.979*		
Achievement level of soccer program	.977		.972	.9204
FP1. Social repercussion	.915	.950		
FP2. Program operation	.967	.968*		
FP3. Return on investment	.947	.960*		
Threshold	>.5	.50 –.95	>.6	>.5

*Significant at .05 level

campus soccer were invited to ensure that the questionnaire can reflect the purpose of study in the process of scale modification. As for the construct validity, the confirmatory factor analysis was conducted and factor loading of some index is more than .95, which is due to small sample size (N=79). In the future, the scope of study should be expended from Shanghai to Yangtze River Delta, or even further. Other fit indicators were within reasonable limits.

Results

Correlational analyses

Table 6.3 shows the means, standard deviations, and correlation coefficients of all variables involved in this study, which indicates that there was a positive correlation between strength of public relations network, absorptive capacity, and achievement level of school soccer program. The initial results of the correlation analysis showed that three hypotheses proposed in this paper are reasonable; however, further analysis is still required for more accurate verification.

In this study, structural equation modeling (SEM) analyses were performed with Analysis of Moment Structure (AMOS) 21.0 to verify the direct influence of public relations network strength on school soccer program's achievement level (see Model 1 in Figure 6.1) and to find out the interaction of absorptive capacity as a mediator (see Model 2 in Figure 6.2). As shown in Figure 6.1, strength of public relations network has a statistically significant and positive impact on campus soccer performance ($\beta = .81$, $p < .001$) when there is no mediating effect of absorptive capacity. Hypothesis 1 is supported.

Table 6.3 Means, standard deviations (SD) and correlations among variables

Variable	*Mean*	*SD*	*1*	*2*	*3*	*4*	*5*	*6*
1 Type of school	2.87	1.436	1					
2 Location of school	8.33	4.006	−.229*	1				
3 Nature of school	1.11	.531	.137	−.144	1			
4 Strength of public relations network	4.309	1.809	.080	−.117	.014	1		
5 Absorptive capacity of school	4.358	1.863	−.022	−.073	−.069	.859**	1	
6 Achievement level of soccer program	4.665	1.820	.032	−.154	−.079	799**	.830**	1

* Significant at .05 level
** Significant at .01 level

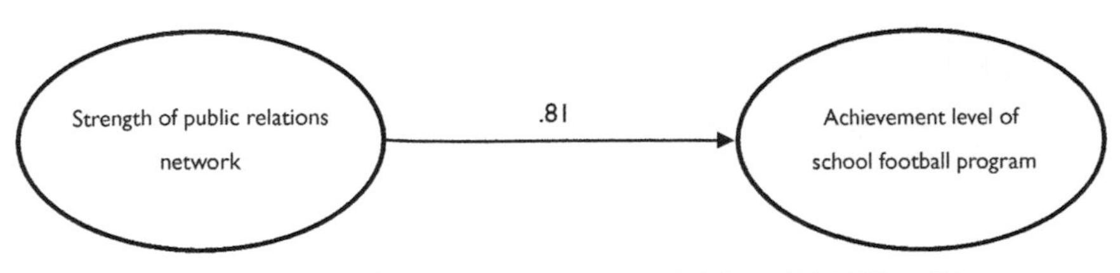

χ^2 = 22.178 (p = .053), χ^2/df = 1.706, NFI = .971, RFI = .953, CFI = .988, RMSEA = .095

Figure 6.1 Model 1

As for Model 2, the initial result showed that the model should be respecified according to the factor loadings and goodness-of-fit indices (see Table 6.4). After respecifying for six times, goodness-of-fit indices revealed that respecified Model 2 fit the data well. More specifically, the chi-square statistics were not significant ($\chi^2 = 35.844$, $p > .05$), indicating there was no statistically significant difference between the hypothesized model and the observed model. The model fit was evaluated by examining the ratio of the chi-square to its degrees of freedom, and the normed chi-square value (χ^2/df=1.38) ranged less than 3.0 (Kline, 2010), which indicated a better fit. Other goodness-of-fit indices were also examined, including the root-mean-square-error (RMSEA), NFI, RFI, and CFI, whereas only the value of RMSEA (.07) showed a reasonable fit but other indices indicated a good fitting model (Rong, 2007). Therefore, this respecified model is the finalized model for verifying all three hypotheses.

As showed in Figure 6.2 and Table 6.4, it can be determined that: (1) Strength of public relations network has a significantly positive correlation with achievement level of school soccer program (β = .37, p < .01), and H1 is supported; (2) strength of public relations network has a significantly positive correlation with absorptive capacity of school (β = .85, p < .001), and H2 is supported; (3) absorptive capacity of school has a significantly positive influence on achievement level of school soccer program (β = .51, p < .001), and H3 is supported.

In Model 1 and Model 2, we found that strength of public relations network had a positive impact on achievement level of school soccer programs, which means the enhancement of relationship strength is also important when building the public relations network for a better performance of school soccer programs. In Model 2, we found that the direct effect of public relations network strength on a school soccer program's achievement level is .37, but the indirect influence of public relations network strength through absorptive capacity of school on a school soccer program's achievement level is .43 (.846 × .511 = .432). Therefore, the school's absorptive capacity plays a very important mediating role between the strength of public relations network and school soccer program achievement level.

Table 6.4 Path coefficients and reports of significance of the respecified Model 2

Path			*Unstandardized coefficient*	*Standard error*	*C.R.*	p	*Std. coefficient*
Absorptive capacity of school	←	Strength of public relations network	.956	.097	9.856	***	.846
Achievement level of soccer program	←	Strength of public relations network	.381	.134	2.846	.004	.374
Achievement level of soccer program	←	Absorptive capacity of school	.460	.116	3.953	***	.511
Cooperation time	←	Strength of public relations network	1.000				.869
School investment	←	Strength of public relations network	1.069	.082	13.105	***	.950
Cooperation scope	←	Strength of public relations network	1.085	.081	13.372	***	.958
Cooperation reciprocity	←	Strength of public relations network	.999	.089	11.256	***	.886
Social repercussion	←	Achievement level of soccer program	1.000				.950
Program operation	←	Achievement level of soccer program	1.058	.051	20.636	***	.968
Knowledge exploitation	←	Absorptive capacity of school	1.000				.979
Knowledge assimilation	←	Absorptive capacity of school	1.005	.032	31.064	***	.986
Knowledge acquisition	←	Absorptive capacity of school	.899	.052	17.240	***	.970
Return on investment	←	Achievement level of soccer program	1.050	.053	19.738	***	.960

*** Significant at .001 level

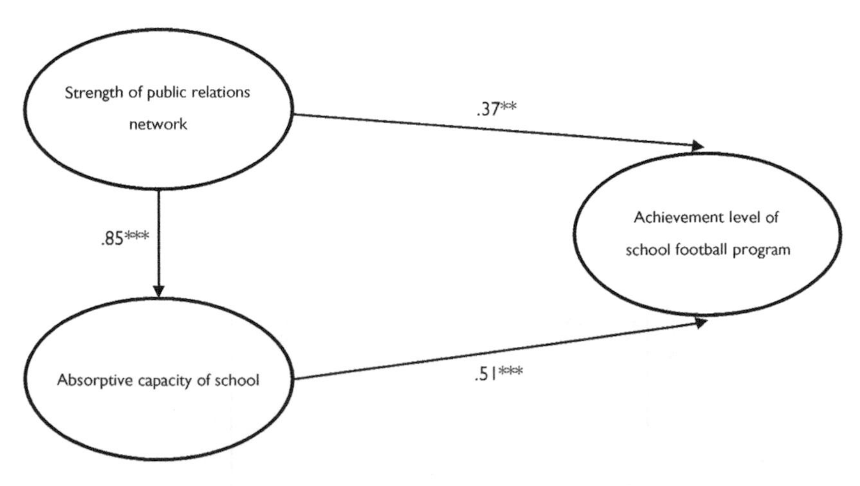

Figure 6.2 Model 2

Effect of control variables

The nature of school (i.e., public, private, or other) was planned to be one of three control variables in this study; however, 75 of 79 valid responses were from public schools and more than 90 percent of Shanghai primary and secondary schools specialized in soccer are public. Therefore, the nature of school was excluded as a control variable in the analysis of impact on school soccer program achievement level. As for the other two control variables, the location and type of school, all categories were combined into two major parts due to small sample size. The location of school was re-categorized as urban and suburban, while the type of school was re-categorized into primary and secondary school. After re-categorization, 39 subjects were from the urban area (nine distinctions including Huangpu, Xuhui, Jing'an, Yangpu, Baoshan, Changning, Minhang, Hongkou, and Putuo) and 40 subjects were from suburban area (seven distinctions including Pudong, Jinshan, Jiading, Chongming, Fengxian, Qingpu, and Songjiang). As for the type of school, one category was combining primary school and nine-year compulsory education school (39 subjects), and the other category was combining complete middle school, vocational school, junior and senior high school (39 subjects). The only one subject from twelve-year compulsory education school was excluded from data analysis.

As showed in Table 6.5, the results of model analysis changed after adding two control variables (i.e., location and type of school). For secondary and urban schools, all three hypotheses remained to be supported; however, it was

Table 6.5 Fit indices for the measurement models

Path			*Model 1*	*Model 2*	*Model 3*		*Model 4*	
					Primary	*Secondary*	*Suburban*	*Urban*
Achievement level of soccer program	←	Strength of public relations network (H1)	.815***	.374**	.142	.424*	.567	.551***
Absorptive capacity of school	←	Strength of public relations network (H2)		.846***	.868***	.787***	.924***	.816***
Achievement level of soccer program	←	Absorptive capacity of school (H3)		.511***	.830***	.412*	.311	.338*
Fit Indices								
Chi–square ($\chi 2/df$)			22.178 (1.706)	35.884 (.094)	31.346 (1.081)	43.563 (1.405)	34.763 (1.288)	25.855 (1.034)
P			.053	1.380	.349	.165	.145	.415
NFI			.971	.972	.956	.941	.947	.962
RFI			.953	.951	.932	.912	.912	.932
CFI			.988	.991	.996	.987	.987	.999
RMSEA			.095	.070	.046	.081	.086	.030

* Significant at .05 level

** Significant at .01 level

*** Significant at .001 level

not the case in primary and suburban schools. Specifically in primary school, H1 was not supported but the indirect effect of school's absorptive capacity was significantly higher than that of secondary school (.868 × .830 = .72), which means primary school required higher absorption capacity of soccer-related knowledge. In the suburban school, H2 was supported, while H1 or H3 were not supported. This result indicated that the mediating effect of school's absorptive capacity was not significant because the importance of public relations network strength has not yet been recognized in suburban schools or the establishment of a public relations network is still difficult for those teachers participating in the survey.

Mediating effect of absorptive capacity

The regression model was used for robustness testing for mediating effect of absorptive capacity instead of the structural equation model, which is widely adopted by contemporary scholars. The first step was to analyze the regression of strength of public relations network on achievement level of school soccer program, and then to analyze the regression of absorptive capacity of school on achievement level of school soccer program, and finally to analyze the interaction of strength of public relations network and absorptive capacity of school on achievement level of school soccer program by using SPSS21.0. As shown in Table 6.6, the three regression models were all significant, and all three hypotheses were supported. In addition, the regression coefficient of strength of public relations network on achievement level of school soccer program decreased by .422 after adding

Table 6.6 Robustness testing for mediating effect

Independent variables	*Dependent Variable*		*Dependent Variable*
	Achievement level of soccer program		*Absorptive capacity of school*
	Model 1	*Model 2*	*Model 3*
Type of school	.145	.083	.128
Location of school	.039	.035	.008
Nature of school	.221	.118	.212
Strength of public relations network	.772***	.350***	.869***
Absorptive capacity of school		.486***	
R square	.671	.731	.755
Adjusted R^2	.653	.713	.742
F-value	37.677	39.749	56.977

*** Significant at .001 level

absorptive capacity of school as mediator, which indicated a stronger mediating effect. The results of regression models were highly consistent with the structural equation models, indicating that mediator effect of absorptive capacity is robust.

Discussion

The purpose of this study is to explore phenomena and problems existing in the development of school soccer in China by applying relevant theories of social and business organization, which is the first empirical research analyzing the conundrum of campus soccer from this specific perspective in order to provide different solutions and insights. More specifically, this empirical investigation was conducted to explore the relationship among strength of public relations network, absorptive capacity of school, and achievement level of school soccer program, whose participants were soccer coaches from 90 Shanghai primary and secondary schools traditionally specialized in soccer, which were listed by the Ministry of Education of the People's Republic of China in July 2015. The results indicated three major conclusions as followings.

First, as was expected (H1), when the strength of public relations network is stronger, it is more likely the achievement level of the school soccer program will improve. This finding is consistent with previous research conducted in social and business organizations, which indicated the positive impact high network strength on organizational outcomes could have in the context of school soccer. In comparison with previous research (Chen & Liang, 2013; Mao et al., 2015), this finding extends the idea that the success of a school soccer program could rely on strengthening the relationship between schools and their cooperative partners in the network.

Second, as was expected (H2 and H3), the strength of public relations network is the major factor determining how good the school's absorptive capability and its soccer program achievement will be. A school's absorptive capacity is determined by how well the staff members of the school understand and recognize the objectives of school soccer development. This also influences its school soccer program achievement. Previous research rarely focused on school's absorptive capacity when studying the development of school soccer, therefore, there is little research elaborating on how to build a strong public relations network from where schools can acquire, assimilate, and exploit soccer-related knowledge. For example, one study comparing the difference of school soccer development between China and two other countries (Japan and South Korea) failed to point out the key factor to their success is actually how practitioners and participants of their school soccer program identify, understand, learn, and apply the knowledge of soccer (Jiao, 2013). Thus, the findings of this study illuminated not only the importance of public relations network strength, but also the irreplaceability of the school's absorptive capacity as a mediator.

Third, the aforementioned relationships among strength of public relations network, absorptive capacity, and achievement level of school soccer program were further analyzed by controlling two different types (primary/secondary) and locations (urban/suburban) of schools. The results showed that all proposed hypotheses were supported only in the secondary and urban schools. For primary schools, the relationship between strength of public relations network and achievement level of school soccer program was not significant, and the impact of public relations network strength on a school soccer program's achievement level was indirect through school's absorptive capacity. This finding indicated the lack of emphasis on building strong public relations networks in the Shanghai primary schools. These primary schools might improve their soccer program achievement level on their own resources instead of collaborating with other organizations. This kind of closed environment might cause the gap between China and other neighbors where school soccer is highly developed. For suburban schools, on the other hand, only H2 was supported that the strength of public relations network influenced the school's absorptive capacity. The difference between urban and suburban schools might be caused by the knowledge gap due to geographical disadvantages. The effect of suburban schools' absorptive capacity on their soccer program achievement level is so limited that they can only carry out restricted soccer activities on campus based on their own conditions.

Implications

The prosperity of soccer is crucial to a powerful sports nation, whereas school soccer is fundamental to the development of soccer in China. Thus, the findings of this study can be beneficial by providing implications of management for all participants of school soccer, especially officials of departments governing school soccer and the staff of schools who are specialized in soccer.

A school soccer program's achievement level can be improved by enhancing the strength of public relations network. The first implication of the study is that school soccer practitioners need to make more efforts to enhance the strength of public relations network when they devote themselves to the development of the school soccer program. It is necessary to build a stable network with other cooperative partners, such as education and sports departments, professional and social soccer clubs, soccer training institutions, sports colleges and research institutes, and youth soccer sponsors, etc. But establishment of a public relations network is only the first step, which should be followed by keeping a strong relationship with their partners in the network and sharing soccer-related knowledge and information with each other through a series of formal or informal routines. For the cities with professional soccer clubs, the government should actively build different platforms between schools and professional soccer clubs to facilitate cooperation. A few suggestions would include: constructing history museums of professional soccer clubs, increasing the way and time of professional players service on school soccer activity, providing an interaction zone and youth soccer factory in the home court, developing mobile app and software of the soccer game and education, establishing soccer forums, and leveraging all stakeholders, especially parents. For the cities without professional soccer clubs, the government should focus on building networks for schools that need more resources for coaching soccer, organizing soccer events, constructing soccer facilities, and conducting research. Communities, schools, social soccer organizations, and sport scientific research institutions should establish cooperative relationship. Meanwhile, these efforts of collaboration should be evaluated objectively and the result of evaluations should be released periodically. Furthermore, practitioners should pay more attention to primary and suburban schools by emphasizing the cultivation of strong public relations network if they want their school soccer programs to reach a higher achievement level.

The strategic importance of absorptive capacity on improving achievement level of school soccer progam. The study also draws the implication that absorptive capacity of school should be a prior factor to be considered if practitioners want to effectively improve the outcomes of a school soccer program. One of the reasons why school soccer in China has lagged for years is the lack of soccer-related knowledge management system on campus. This system should provide values, missions, objectives, and know-how of the school soccer program to all staff in schools, including but not limited to soccer coaches and physical education (PE) teachers, administrators at all levels, teachers of other disciplines and mentors of all grades. Only when all practitioners get involved in the process of learning and sharing soccer-related knowledge could they possibly form the correct values of soccer development, and then consciously maintain the universality of this value. In this way, the school's absorptive capacity can be truly enhanced and schools can more effectively acquire, assimilate, and apply soccer-related knowledge. With more information dispersed within campus, the strategic priority of the school soccer program can be promoted and then a centripetal force will form. Given that the goals of the schools are diverse and school soccer program development is only one of them, the importance of school soccer program needs to be widely recognized before any significant and sustainable outcomes can be realized. Building on that, the improvement of school soccer program achievement cannot only rely on school soccer program coaches and PE teachers, but also on all other staff members of school.

Limitations and future research

There are several limitations that need to be addressed in future research along this line of inquiry. First, the small sample size cost the independence of items and generalization of the results despite the high reliability. Larger sample size is suggested for future studies in order to further explore the importance of public relations network strength and urgency of improving school's absorptive capability. For instance, more data can be collected from additional Shanghai schools specialized in soccer that were lastly listed by the Ministry of Education of the People's Republic of China in July 2016, or extending to schools in the Yangtze River Delta region. Second, the findings of this study are limited to the relationship among only three variables without including other possible variables in the public relations network, such as the form and composition of the network. Future researchers could also investigate the effect of these variables on a school soccer program's achievement. Lastly, entities in the public relations network might have different levels of influence on a school soccer program's achievement, but the differences were not unveiled in this study. For example, what is the difference between education departments and professional soccer clubs when considering their attribution to one school's soccer program achievement? Which entity is more impactful in this process? Researchers examining this topic in the future should expand their investigation beyond schools and into other entities that may have a different impact on the school soccer program's achievement level.

References

Chen, H., & Liang, B. (2013). The Evolution and Enlightenment of British Youth Campus Football Development *Sports Culture Guide, 9,* 111–14.

Cohen, W. M., & Levinthal, D. A. (1990). Absorptive Capacity: A New Perspective on Learning and Innovation. *Administrative Science Quarterly,* 128–52.

Dong, Z., Gong, B., & Yan, Z. (2011). Discussion of Issues on Carrying Out Campus Football Activities. *Journal of Shanghai University of Sport, 35(2),* 91–94.

Ge, J., Fan, M., & Xiao, L. (2016). Research on the Mechanism of Social Capital's Effect on Innovation Performance of Farmer Cooperatives: Use Absorptive Capacity as a Mediator. *Journal of Agrotechnical, (1),* 118–27.

Gemünden, H. G., Ritter, T., & Heydebreck, P. (1996). Network Configuration and Innovation Success: An Empirical Analysis in German High-Tech Industries. *International Journal of Research in Marketing, 13(5),* 449–62.

Gong, B. (2011). Inspiration to Innovation of Chinese Football by View of Modern Transformation of Japanese Civilization and its Success in Football. *Journal of Tianjin University of Sport, 26(4),* 310–15.

Granovetter, M. S. (1973). The Strength of Weak Ties. *American Journal of Sociology,* 1360–80.

Hamel, G. (1991). Competition for Competence and Interpartner Learning Within International Strategic Alliances. *Strategic Management Journal, 12(S1),* 83–103.

Harris, L., Coles, A. M., & Dickson, K. (2000). Building Innovation Networks: Issues of Strategy and Expertise. *Technology Analysis & Strategic Management, 12(2),* 229–41.

He, Q. (2015). Cool Contemplation of Campus Football Heat. *Journal of Physical Education, 22(2),* 5–10.

He, X., & Liu, Y. (2013). Discussion on Several Problems of Campus Football Activities in China. *Journal of Beijing University of Physical Education, 11*, 108–13.

Jiao, Y. (2013). *The Analysis of Modern Football Development in China, Japan and South Korea.* Dalian, Liaoning Normal University.

Kline, R.B. (2010). *Principles and Practice of Structural Equation Modeling* (3rd ed.). New York: Guilford.

Koberg, C. S., Detienne, D. R., & Heppard, K. A. (2003). An Empirical Test of Environmental, Organizational, and Process Factors Affecting Incremental and Radical Innovation. *The Journal of High Technology Management Research, 14(1)*, 21–45.

Kostopoulos, K., Papalexandris, A., Papachroni, M., & Ioannou, G. (2011). Absorptive Capacity, Innovation, and Financial Performance. *Journal of Business Research, 64(12)*, 1335–43.

Li, J., He, Z., Dong, Z., & Xu, Y. (2012). On the Development Bottleneck and its Breakthrough in National Youth School Football Activity. *Journal of Shanghai University of Sport, 36(3)*, 83–86.

Li, W., & He, Z. (2011). Thoughts of National Youth Campus Football Sustainable Development. *Sports Culture Guide, 3(3)*, 106–08.

Liang, B. (2014). Inspiration from English School Football of Charter Standard Scheme: Network Pathway Integration and Multiple Resources Supply. *Shandong Sports Science & Technology, 36(1)*, 105–08.

Liu, H., & Ji, L. (2012). Effects of Campus Football Training System from Primary Schools to Universities in Shanghai. *Journal of Wuhan Institute of Physical Education, 46(7)*, 84–90.

Liu, Y. (2012). *Impact of Social Capital and Absorptive Capacity on Team Performance: An Empirical Study Based on the University Research Team.* Shijiazhuang, Hebei University of Technology, China.

Mao, Z., & Liu, T. (2015). Top-level Design of "New School Football": Chinese School Football as Seen from Development of German Juvenile Footballers. *Journal of Wuhan Institute of Physical Education, 49(6)*, 5–11.

Mao, Z., Liu, T., & Zang, L. (2015). Top-level Design of Future Campus Football. *Journal of Wuhan Institute of Physical Education, 49(3)*, 58–62.

Murovec, N., & Prodan, I. (2009). Absorptive Capacity, its Determinants, and Influence on Innovation Output: Cross-cultural Validation of the Structural Model. *Technovation, 29(12)*, 859–72.

Pan, S., & Zheng, Y. (2011). The Strength of Network Tie and Enterprise's Technological Innovation – The Empirical Study Based on Exploration Learning and Exploitation Learning. *Studies in Science of Science, 29(11)*, 1736–43.

Rong, T. (2007). *Amos and Methodology.* Taipei: Wu-Nan Book Inc.

Song, J. (2016, July 19). 2016 China (Shanghai) International Youth Campus Football Invitational Tournament Summit was held. *Ceweekly.cn.* Retrieved from www.ceweekly.cn/2016/0719/157942.shtml.

Tian, L. (2015). Enlightenment on China Folk Football Champions "Who is the King": Network Path Integration and Multiple Resources Configuration. *Zhejiang Sport Science, 37(4)*, 6–9.

Wang, W., Wang, L., & Kang, H. (2014). Comparison of Chinese and Japanese Youth Football Development. *Journal of Xi'an Institute of Physical Education, 31(6)*, 690–93.

Wilson, C. (2015, Mar 14). The General Office of the State Council publishes the 'Chinese Football Reform and Development Program'. Retrieved from https://wildeastfootball.net/2016/02/read-chinese-footballs-50-point-reform-plan-in-full-exclusive-translation/.

Wu, J. (2015). *A Comparative Study of Campus Football Management System between China and Korea.* (Master's thesis). Changchun: Jilin University, China.

Wu, M. (2011). *Interpersonal Interaction on Internet: The Basic Vision of Ideological and Political Education.* (Doctoral dissertation). Chengdu: University of Electronic Science and Technology of China, China.

Xinhuanet. (2015, July 28). Ministry of Education Announced 8651 Schools Specialized in Football: 90 Primary and Secondary Schools in Shanghai made the List. Retrieved from http://sh.xinhuanet.com/2015-07/28/c_134454833.htm.

Yu, K. (2015). Campus Football: How German Won Championships. *Shanghai Education, 2*, 48–49.

Zahra, S. A., & George, G. (2002). Absorptive Capacity: A Review, Reconceptualization, and Extension. *Academy of Management Review, 27(2)*, 185–203.

Chapter 7

Soccer feasibility study

Assessment, value, and demand – a traditional approach

Brian H. Yim, Mark Lyberger, and Andy Gerow

Introduction

Whether or not a sport facility developer can pay off the mortgage and generate additional revenue is the most important consideration before the mortgage lender and investors make their investment decisions (Apanavičienė, Daugėlienė, Baltramonaitis, & Maliene, 2015; Sangree, 2012). Therefore, lenders and investors often require a feasibility study to be conducted by an independent third-party, at the expense of the potential facility developers. Typically, this analysis is performed by an independent third-party consultant who specializes in analyzing the feasibility and performance of similar facilities. The consultant assesses whether or not the value of proposed project equals or exceeds the development and operational costs when completed. The third-party consultant will conduct the feasibility analysis to determine the value of proposed project by including revenue, operational costs and expenses, principals and interests, and the net income. Specifically, the consultant seeks to ascertain whether commercial concession services and facilities are of investment scale to which a capable private operator under lease agreement could achieve economic success, as well as offer such services and facilities at reasonable prices to the general public and fulfill financial obligations. Simply said, the feasibility study will help the investor and lenders to make the go/not to go decision.

Although the inclusion of a feasibility study is considered good practice it is not always required, or included, within the preliminary plans for proposal funding. However, feasibility studies serve a critical function in independently evaluating a plan or planned course of action, assessing assumptions behind it, the risks it faces, and its chances of success. Feasibility studies were invented to avoid bad investment decisions, prevent businesses from targeting non-existent markets and to flag risks and pitfalls in even the most well thought-out investment or strategic plans (Clarke & Kelleher, 2016). Hence, why outside investors, bankers, and others should insist on getting an independent assessment. When the owner/designer and the investor are one and the same person, the tendency is to try to cut costs by doing their own feasibility study and bias can often accompany the results.

Designers, engineers, inventors, and CEOs get attached to their own ideas. They discount problems, wish away concerns, and believe in themselves. The drive for profits can taint an analysis. According to Novak (1996), consultants are often under an enormous amount of pressure to provide a positive assessment of a project and while an analyst cannot ethically be biased, pressure may produce subtle compromises in objectivity. Biased studies are not just produced by neophyte analysts; they are more often done by incompetent staff. In reviewing a report, the reader should attempt to decipher whether it was performed by a principal in the analysis firm or a subordinate. If the person who wrote the study is inexperienced, there is a greater potential for bias, misrepresentation of data, or presenting only best-case outcomes and scenarios.

Market and feasibility studies are quite complex. However, since capital is becoming more difficult to acquire and regulatory considerations are becoming more complex, the importance of these studies is not going to decrease (Novak, 1996). According to Novak (1996), people often lump market and feasibility studies together, but they are two different entities and typically occur at different times in the development process. In general, a market analysis searches for the intersection of demand and supply that will create a market for a product at a given price, and a feasibility analysis tests whether a certain product will meet certain financial or social goals in the market. Hence, a market analysis is performed early in the process, while a feasibility analysis is performed after initial design and during design refinements. This study highlights components, outcomes, and methods employed in the feasibility process. It accentuates in the competitive world of real estate development that the investor with the best information is going to be the most successful (Novak, 1996).

One of the soccer management organizations in Midwestern Town in the United States submitted an indoor soccer facility construction project proposal to an investment bank headquartered in the Midwest for four million US dollars mortgage. The bank was not able to make the go or not to go decision based on the materials the soccer management organization provided and therefore asked for an economic feasibility study from a third-party consultant to make their decision. Specifically, the bank's concern was that the indoor sport facility market may be saturated since there may be too many indoor sport facilities around the area that would compete with this facility. Another concern was that there is a risk that the indoor facility has peak season (i.e., winter months) and off-peak season (i.e., spring, summer, and fall months) meaning it is a seasonal business that can create the revenue only five months a year. To address those concerns of the lender, not only a traditional economic feasibility study but also a market analysis was needed to analyze the market and the future market demands. A hired consultants group (herein, Consultants) identified a Center from a Midwestern state institution (herein, Center) as a qualified candidate to conduct a market demand analysis and feasibility study that would provide objective, research-based guidance to the prospective development of a new sports facility to be constructed in the Midwest.

The purpose of this study was to ascertain the feasibility of constructing an indoor sports complex to be located off of Road X in the Midwest United States. The Center conducted an examination of proposed facility function and identified future growth opportunities that may exist specific to needs and market feasibility specific to the said facility.

Major components in the feasibility study

There are several major components included in a market feasibility and financial analysis study. The following lists the major components: (a) market overview and analysis, (b) market demand survey, and (c) analysis of ProFormas.

Market overview and analysis

It is important to understand the market in which the proposed new sports complex would operate. As such, this section of the report profiles select market characteristics including demographic/economic data, area employment, accessibility, and climate.

Segmentation and demographic analysis. Assessing the demographic environment entails observing and monitoring population trends. Demographic and economic indicators are pertinent to estimating demand for youth and amateur sports. The Village was located in Northeastern quadrant of state, approximately ten miles southeast of Metropolitan City. The Village was located in a County adjacent to a National Park. The Village had a population of 2,034 (according to the 2010 US Census) and consists of approximately 3,615 acres of land. Approximately 97 percent of the Village population were white, with roughly an even split in males and females. Crime rates were far lower than the statewide and national averages. Median household income was around $85,833, with renters median at $54,107 and owner's at $90,208. The median household income was complementary to the median home value of $250K. The unemployment rate was 3.9 percent. The Village itself was located ten miles southeast of the Midwestern Metropolis, while median family income in the metropolis area was $49,715.

According to the US Census Bureau, the County had a population in 2014 of 1,259,858, making it the most populous county in state. The population had a one percent decrease from the 1,280,122 estimated in 2010. The County was bordered by a County to the northeast, with an estimated population of 229,230; a County to the east, population 94,295; a County to the southeast, population 161,882; a County to the south, population 541,943; a County to the southwest, population of 176,029; and a County to the west, with an estimated population of 304,216. Table 7.1 illustrates the breakdown

Table 7.1 Age segmentation county/city

Age Group	*% County NE*		*% Village*	
Under 18	21.5	271,079	19.1	378
18–64	62	781,399	62.3	1230
64+	16.5	207,350	18.6	367

of age groups of the total population that represent the Village, the County, State, and the entire United States. This analysis shows the percentage of people and the number of people in each particular age group throughout these regions.

Table 7.1 breaks down the age groups throughout the County and the Village. As shown below, the largest grouping of residents in both areas encompasses those aging from 18–64 and the second largest are those under the age of 18. This norm is advantageous to the Sport Facility for it further illustrates target market potential, above the norms, for sports participants in the area. Upon further analysis, data suggests that there are 2,756 people per square mile and 457.1 total square miles in the County. The Village had a total population of 2,034 in a total of 5.4 miles. The median household income, as stated earlier, was $85,833 which is 1.5 times higher than State's median income at $48,849. Table 7.3 illustrates a breakdown of income in the Village, County, State, and the US. The Village contains a population where the majority of average annual household incomes were between $50,000 and $200,000. This differs dramatically from the County, State, and the US as the majority of those residing in these locations are under $50,000.

Demographic/economic data. Event activity at the proposed new sports complex could potentially include a diverse set of outdoor and indoor sports. In addition, tournament producers typically place more emphasis on accessibility, the type and quality of facilities provided and surrounding infrastructure (e.g., restaurants, attractions, etc.) rather than local population, age, and income characteristics.

Market dynamics will also impact the amount, type, and success of any future ancillary development near the proposed new sports complex in the Village. In order to assess the relative size of the target market, key demographic statistics were analyzed for the following proximal radials, 25-mile, 100-mile, and 200-mile radii from the Village. A secondary marketing profile was created to accentuate demographic information specific to population density, average household size, and percentage of youth. Total population within a 25-mile radius was 2.2 million with 25.5 percent representing youth. Additionally, 67 percent of the population within the 25-mile radius had a household with two-plus people. The 100 mile radius revealed a population of 6.8 million of which 25.8 were youth. Approximately 70 percent of the 100-mile radius population had two-plus people households. Within the 200-mile radius, the total population was 23.6 million of which roughly 5.8 million were youth. Approximately 70.8 percent of the residents within the 200-mile radius had households with two-plus people.

Sports participation trends. The purpose of this section is to provide an overview of sports participation trends in the United States and the region. An analysis of these trends helps to articulate an understanding at a national, regional, and local level. In addition, it provides a framework from which to assess potential demand for the proposed Sports Complex.

The statistical data presented in this section was derived from a variety of sources. The Center was a member of the many identified organizations below and, therefore, had access to many of noted publications. The Sports & Fitness Industry Association (SFIA), formally known as The Sporting Goods Manufacturers Association (SGMA), is the trade association of leading industry sports and fitness brands, suppliers, retailers, and partners whose mission is, to "Promote Sports and Fitness Participation and Industry Vitality" by focusing on core product areas for the industry. Research information from the SFIA was derived from a study based on approximately 40,000 interviews encompassing youth and adult sports participation. Sports Business Research Network (SBRNet) serves those with an interest in the business of sports with "one-stop" access to multiple resources, including Industry-Developed Market Research, Government Statistics, Facility Reports and News, International Market Publications, Customized Research, and Directories. The National Sporting Goods Association (NSGA) publishes a comprehensive annual report of sports participation in the United States. The reports contain participation data which is gathered to analyze trends and patterns within 51 sports and activities. Each year, the Physical Activity Council (PAC) produces a Sports, Fitness and Leisure Activities Topline Participation Report. The report is the result of the partnership of six major trade associations within the US sports, fitness, and leisure industries. Each association partner produces detailed data on its specific areas of expertise, and submits its overall participation data to this "topline" report. These six associations are the Sports and Fitness Industry Association (SFIA) formerly SMGA, the International Health, Racquet and Sportsclub Association (IHRSA), the Outdoor Foundation (OF), the Snow Sports Industries America (SIA), the National Golf Foundation (NGF) and the Tennis Industry Association (TIA) in collaboration with the United States Tennis Association (USTA).

In order to gain a better understanding of sport participation amongst active US individuals, a secondary source of data was utilized. The Sports & Fitness Industry Association (SFIA) is the trade association of top sporting goods in the United States. Their mission is to "Promote Sports and Fitness Participation and Industry Vitality". One primary focus of this association was to meet the needs of active individuals and providing a healthier lifestyle amongst everyone in the United States. In 2016, SFIA implemented a nationwide online survey to 32,658 residents. Of those recipients, a total sample of 15,167 individual and 17,491 household surveys were completed. The overall objective of this survey was to gain a better understanding of participation trends in sport and also levels of activity amongst those aged six and older. A weighting technique was used to balance the data to reflect the total US population aged six and above. The following variables were used: gender, age, income, household income, size, region, population density, and panel join date. The total population figure used was 294,141,894 people aged six and older. These surveys have been conducted for a number of years.

According to SFIA (2016) in 2015, basketball (23.4 million) and volleyball (6.4 million) have the highest national participation levels among sports requiring a court. Soccer (12.6 million), baseball (13.7 million) and softball (7.1 million) have the highest national participation levels among sports requiring fields. Basketball has the highest number of CORE participants (15.6 million), followed by baseball (8.9 million), soccer (5.9 million), softball (4.1 million), volleyball (3.6 million), and tackle soccer (3.4 million). Cheerleading has experienced an approximate 9.1 percent growth in casual users from 2012 to 2015, the largest among targeted court sports. Other court sports experiencing growth in total participation from 2012 to 2015 include basketball (1.8 percent), volleyball (3.7 percent) and wrestling (4.6 percent). Specific to field sports in the past three years, rugby has experienced the largest growth in the past three years with a 21.4 percent increase. Other increases in field sports from 2012–15 include lacrosse (13.4 percent), field hockey (13.2 percent), baseball (7.0 percent), softball (2.2 percent) and flag soccer (1.7 percent). Participation levels in soccer have remained consistent over the past five years according to SFIA, but still has the highest level of frequent participation among outdoor sports and second only to basketball in terms of all targeted indoor and outdoor sports. CORE participation rates for softball (3.7 percent) and touch soccer (–5.6 percent) have experienced the largest decline for targeted field sports since 2010.

Targeted individual sports have remained consistent over the past five years. Cross training is a newly identified individual sport that has only been researched for the previous two years by SFIA but has experienced a 3.9 percent growth in total participation from 2014 to 2015. Casual participation levels increased 6.2 percent and frequent participation has increased 1.7 percent. Weight training has experienced an increase of casual users from 2010 to 2015 by 1.7 percent. From 2014 to 2015, running/jogging participation rate in all categories has dropped off. In addition to analyzing the most recent year's sports participation levels, it is also important to assess historical participation trends in order to understand which sports are experiencing a rise in popularity and which ones are remaining constant or declining in popularity. According to the most recently released 2016 *Sports, Fitness and Leisure Activities Topline Participation Report*, 27.7 percent of the population of Americans, aged six and older, are inactive, meaning that 72.3 percent of Americans are active. The report breaks down the number of active Americans based on low- to high-calorie activities and beyond. The results of the study indicate a figure of 72.3 percent of Americans or 212.6 million individuals age six and older that are active to a healthy level and beyond. This also may create targeted opportunities for the Sports Complex staff to develop and accentuate protocol targeted to this inactive population. Figure 7.1 shows that soccer has remained consistent in both levels of participation for the past five years and has only shown a minor drop off of casual users from 2011–12.

Sports participation is often very much tied to age. The proposed Sports Complex in the Village was utilized by a variety of age groups, and it was important to understand which sports appeal to each age group in order to develop appropriate programming. The following percentages, presented in Table 7.2, were compiled from the 2016 SFIA Topline Report. The seven to 11 and 12 to 17 year-old age groups represent the largest percentage of national sports participants, with an average of approximately 51 percent participating in targeted court sports, and approximately 47 percent participating in targeted field sports. Gymnastics had the highest levels of participation (41.3 percent) among seven to 11 year-olds, followed by soccer (33.7 percent), cheerleading (27.7 percent), baseball (24.6 percent), tackle soccer (24 percent), flag soccer (23.3 percent) and lacrosse (22.9 percent). Tackle soccer comprised the largest percentage of 12 to 17 year-olds (40.8 percent), followed by cheerleading (39.3 percent), wrestling (31 percent), volleyball (26.4 percent), flag soccer (25.4 percent) and lacrosse (25 percent).

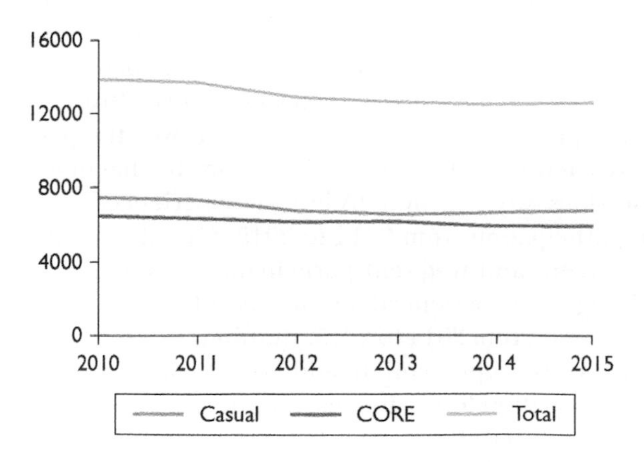

Figure 7.1 Soccer participation for the past five years. *2016 Sports, Fitness and Leisure Activities Topline Participation Report.*

Table 7.2 National sports participation by age groups for field sports

Ages	*Baseball*	*Flag Football*	*Lacrosse*	*Football*	*Softball*	*Tackle Football*	*Touch Football*	*Average*
7–11	24.6%	23.3%	22.9%	33.7%	14.6%	24.0%	18.6%	23.1%
12–17	20.6%	25.4%	25.0%	20.2%	17.2%	40.8%	20.6%	24.3%
18–24	12.5%	14.6%	14.8%	13.9%	14.3%	13.3%	13.2%	13.8%
25–34	15.9%	18.5%	17.8%	16.6%	19.7%	12.1%	24.1%	17.8%
35–44	13.1%	10.2%	11.2%	9.4%	17.6%	6.0%	12.8%	11.5%
45–54	8.1%	4.6%	6.6%	4.7%	9.2%	2.8%	7.4%	6.2%
55–64	4.1%	2.5%	1.3%	1.1%	5.0%	1.0%	2.3%	2.5%
65–74	1.1%	0.7%	0.4%%	0.2%	1.8%		0.7%	0.8%
75+		0.2%		0.2%	0.6%		0.4%	0.4%

*Source 2016 Sports, Fitness and Leisure Activities Topline Participation Report.

Table 7.2 illustrates select field sport participation for those aging seven to 11, 12 to 17, and 18 to 24 years of age, as well as for a variety of adult age ranges. Among the sports with the highest national participation levels, soccer reported the highest combined participation levels among seven to 17 year-olds (54 percent). Baseball (45 percent), basketball (40 percent), volleyball (36 percent) and softball (32 percent) had relatively high participation rates among seven to 17 year-olds. Sports that reported high participation levels among seven to 17 year-olds, but do not report high overall participation levels, included tackle soccer (65 percent), gymnastics (61 percent), wrestling (51 percent), flag soccer (49 percent), and lacrosse (48 percent).

Trends in sport spending. Youth team sports business survived the height of the recession due to the inherent resiliency of the youth athletics industry (Mitchell, 2012). Youth sports participation has been continuously increased (Kim, Zhang, & Connaughton, 2010) and youth team sports marketers have witnessed that, in good times and bad, parents will continue to support their children's desires to play sports and – in turn – provide the required sports equipment, apparel, shoes and accessories (Mitchell, 2012). Parents are spending thousands of dollars a year on kids' sports. The travel expenses alone for youth sports nationwide reach $7 billion a year, according to a recent report from CNBC. And there is still a bevy of other expenses, including club memberships, clinics, camps, individual coaching, and equipment, all of which run up the bill even more (Hageman, 2015). According to SFIA Grassroots Sports Participation in American Study, youth category spending is highest around the cost of registering for events/leagues – with an average annual spend of $125 for active youth participants and $115 for general population participants (Figure 7.2).

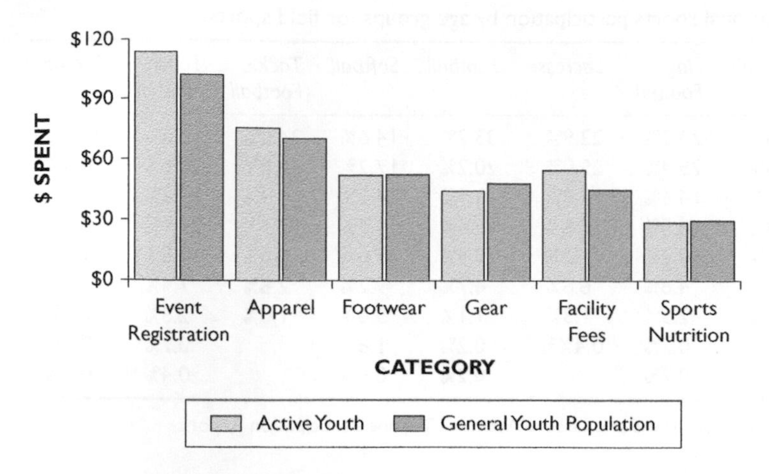

Figure 7.2 Youth average spending by category. *2016 Sports, Fitness and Leisure Activities Topline Participation Report.*

For youth sports, gymnastics and martial arts lead total annual spending with both active and general population participants spending nearly $1,000 annually to participate in these sports (Figure 7.3).

Seasonality. Seasons in State are often unpredictable and vary considerably. The seasonal changes in the Village can be dramatic and add to complexity of how residents may utilize the Sports Complex. Prevailing winds in late fall, winter, and early spring can limit outdoor recreational opportunities

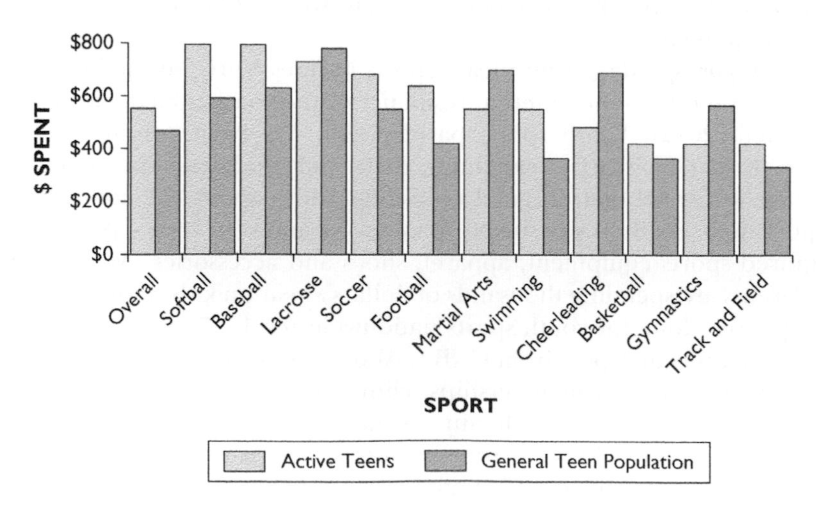

Figure 7.3 Youth average spending by sport. *2016 Sports, Fitness and Leisure Activities Topline Participation Report.*

Table 7.3 Overall average climate trends 2011–15

	City C	*City A*	*City M*	*City T*	*City Y*	*City E*
Average Temp	50.1	49.1	49.4	51.0	49.4	49.8
Average High	59.8	59.0	58.7	60.2	58.8	57.3
Average Low	42.6	41.7	41.9	41.2	41.7	42.3

*Data received from the National Climactic Data Center (NCDC)

for potential users and can impact demand characteristics specific to facility use, although specific to this analysis, that may result in a positive impact. The Village borders both the primary and secondary snowbelt corridor. The primary snowbelt gets anywhere from 60 to 110-plus inches of snow per year. It consists of the eastern half of said County, and all of the northeast surrounding counties. In addition, there were a number of municipalities in this area. The secondary snowbelt usually gets 40 to 80 inches of snow per winter and consists of the western half of the County, two adjacent counties, plus the portions of three other surrounding counties north of a local Interstate make up the remaining secondary snowbelt corridor. Table 7.3 indicates overall average yearly climate trends in 2011 to 2015.

Table 7.3 demonstrates the monthly average temperatures of the Village area over a 35-year period. These temperatures provide for a limited summer season and may adversely impact the usability of outdoor space in the region but further substantiate the need for indoor multipurpose facilities in the community. Table 7.4 illustrates precipitation trends for a 45-year period specific to the region. Planning to offset and accommodate climate conditions may help to ensure success of the Sports Complex. In addition, climate and seasonal changes may afford opportunities to expand the array of leisure offerings.

During the warm season, which lasted from May 28 to September 18, there was a 46 percent average chance that precipitation was observed at some point during a given day. When precipitation did occur, it was most often in the form of thunderstorms (36 percent of days with precipitation have, at worst, thunderstorms), light rain (32 percent), and moderate rain (27 percent) observed during 21 percent of all days. Moderate rain was the most severe precipitation observed during 20 percent of those days with precipitation. It was most likely around May 22, when it is observed during 15 percent of all days. Thunderstorms were the most severe precipitation observed during 14 percent of those days with precipitation. They were most likely around July 12, when it was observed during 20 percent of all days. The warm season lasted from May 28 to September 18 with an average daily high temperature above 72°F. The hottest day of the year was noted as July 24, with an average high of 82°F and low of 65°F. The cold season

Table 7.4 Historical climate data, 1981–2015 NCDC Normal

Element	*JAN*	*FEB*	*MAR*	*APR*	*MAY*	*JUN*	*JUL*	*AUG*	*SEP*	*OCT*	*NOV*	*DEC*	*ANN*
Max °F	33.1	36.7	46.6	59.6	69.3	78.0	82.0	80.3	73.0	61.0	49.2	37.0	58.8
Min °F	19.1	21.3	28.5	38.8	48.5	57.7	61.9	60.6	53.3	42.5	33.9	23.9	40.8
Mean °F	26.1	29.0	37.6	49.2	58.9	67.9	72.0	70.5	63.1	51.7	41.5	30.4	49.8
HDD base 65	1206	1008	851	481	225	49	6	14	119	416	704	1071	6150
CDD base 65	0	−7777	−7777	6	36	135	222	183	64	6	−7777	−7777	652

*Data received from the National Climactic Data Center (NCDC)

lasted from December 2 to March 7 with an average daily high temperature below 43°F. The coldest day of the year was identified as January 29, with an average low of 19°F and high of 33°F.

During the cold season, which lasted from December 2 to March 7, there was a 74 percent average chance that precipitation would be observed at some point during the given day. When precipitation did occur, it was most often in the form of light snow (55 percent of days with precipitation have at worst light snow), moderate snow (15 percent), light rain (13 percent), and moderate rain (nine percent). The probability that precipitation would have been observed at this location varied throughout the year. Precipitation was most likely around December 30, occurring in 77 percent of days. Precipitation was least likely around August 5, occurring in 44 percent of days. One would assume April to typically be the wettest month and although April was noted as the wettest month on record, on average the wettest months were, in rank order, May, July, June, August, April, then September.

Over the entire year, the most common forms of precipitation were light snow, light rain, moderate rain, and thunderstorms. Light snow was the most severe precipitation observed during 26 percent of those days with precipitation. It was most likely around January 17, when it is observed during 47 percent of all days. Light rain was the most severe precipitation observed during 26 percent of those days with precipitation. It was most likely around April 26, when it was observed during 21 percent of all days. Moderate rain was the most severe precipitation observed during 20 percent of those days with precipitation. It was most likely around May 22, when it was observed during 15 percent of all days. Thunderstorms were the most severe precipitation observed during 14 percent of those days with precipitation. They were most likely around July 12, when it was observed during 20 percent of all days. The warm season lasted from May 28 to September 18 with an average daily high temperature above 72°F. The hottest day of the year was July 24, with an average high of 82°F and low of 65°F. The cold season lasts from December 2 to March 7 with an average daily high temperature below 43°F. The coldest day of the year was January 29, with an average low of 19°F and high of 33°F.

Market demand survey

Data collection. In addition to the secondary market analysis data, the primary data were collected through an online survey questionnaire. Data were collected from soccer club directors in the Midwest. This study followed Hinkin's (1995) suggestion and maintained an item-to-response ratio range between 1:4 and 1:10 for factor analysis. Because the total number of items used in this study was nine, our target number of subjects was at approximately 36. Fifty-five individuals were invited to participate in this study through an online survey and the final number in the data set was 33.

Survey questionnaire. In the current study, an online questionnaire was developed and validated by a research team, consisting of two faculty members and four graduate students in the Sport Administration Program at the University, to measure the current demand of indoor fields among the soccer clubs. The current market demands and needs, and potential revenue generation opportunities through indoor facility utilization during summer, were examined via the online survey using nine items measured on a 7-point Likert scale (1 = strongly agree, 7 = strongly disagree).

Analysis and results. Data were analyzed via descriptive statistics and ANOVA using IBM SPSS Statistics 21. Out of 33 participants, one responded "strongly agree", four responded "agree", and four answered "somewhat agree". These nine respondents were grouped as *Enough Access* group. Three participants answered they neither agreed nor disagreed, four answered "somewhat disagree", eight responded "disagree", and another eight answered "strongly disagree", and these 20 were categorized as *Not Enough Access* group. Figure 7.4 shows that 64 percent of the sample did not have enough access to the indoor facilities indicating that there is high demand and not enough supply of indoor soccer facilities in the northeastern quadrant of the state.

Next, researchers asked the respondents' perception of the need for another indoor facility in the Village area. Almost all respondents (97 percent) answered that there is a need for an additional indoor facility in the Village area (i.e., 23 "strongly agree", six "agree", and three "somewhat agree"). The results were further examined within each of the two groups that were divided based on whether there was sufficient access to the indoor facilities. IBM SPSS Statistics 21 was used to conduct ANOVA test in order to investigate the group difference. The test result was significant, $F(2,32) = 6.150$, $p = .005$. Post hoc analysis using the Scheffe post hoc criterion for significance indicated that the "*not enough access*" group's perception of need for another indoor facility in the Village was significantly higher ($M = 1.17$, $SD = 0.49$) than the group that has enough access to the indoor facilities

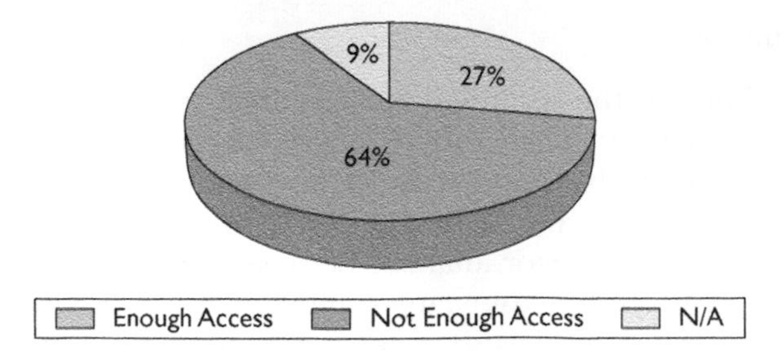

Figure 7.4 Access to indoor facilities

(M=2.11, SD= 1.05). The results indicated that the soccer clubs who do not have enough access to the indoor facilities more likely answered that there was a need of additional indoor facilities in the Village area.

The travel convenience to the Sports Complex was examined with the following item. Most of the respondents answered that the Village location was convenient for them to travel. Again, the results were further examined within each of the two groups to find the group difference. The ANOVA test result for the travel convenience to the Sports Complex was also significant, $F(2,32) = 6.864$, $p = .003$. Post hoc analysis using the Scheffe post hoc criterion for significance indicated that the "*not enough access*" group's perception of travel convenience to the Village was significantly higher (M=1.22, SD= 0.85) than the group that has enough access to the indoor facilities (M=2.78, SD= 1.71). The results suggest that the soccer clubs who do not have enough access to the indoor facilities perceived the Village location more convenient than the other group, indicating the Village location meets the market demand.

In order to measure the soccer club managers' perception of the competitiveness of the Village indoor facility, researchers asked the question, "if the Sports Complex would be a direct competitor of the facility you currently use". Over 60 percent of the participants responded that the Sports Complex would be the direct competitor of the indoor facility they are currently using (i.e., two "strongly agree", seven "agree", and 11 "somewhat agree"). The respondents answered this question solely based on the information of the facility location. They were unaware of the quality, size, or number of fields in the facility, therefore, the perception of the competitiveness of the Village indoor facility to the competitors will be increased after marketing activation and promotions.

Next, the soccer clubs expenditure on indoor facility usage was examined. The soccer club paid $157.67 per hour on average. Specifically, 27 percent paid less than $100, 50 percent paid between $101 and $200, 17 percent paid between $201 and $300, and six percent paid more than $301 an hour (Figure 7.5). Per season indoor facility usage expenditure was also surveyed. On average each club spent $20,226.43 per season (38 percent paid less than $10,000, 19 percent paid between $10,001 and $20,000, 19 percent paid between $20,001 and $30,000, and 24 percent paid more than $30,001). Per season expenditure/per hour expenditure implies that a soccer club used 128 hours of indoor facilities on average.

One of the main concerns of operating an indoor facility in Northeastern Ohio area would be the revenue decrease during the summer months. The current indoor facility industry trends of summer operation have been investigated and participants' suggestions were collected. The results show that only 59 percent (n=19) of the facilities operate during the summer months. Overall, the most popular sports played in indoor facilities are lacrosse (n=22), baseball (n=18), soccer/flag soccer (n=17), futsal (n=15),

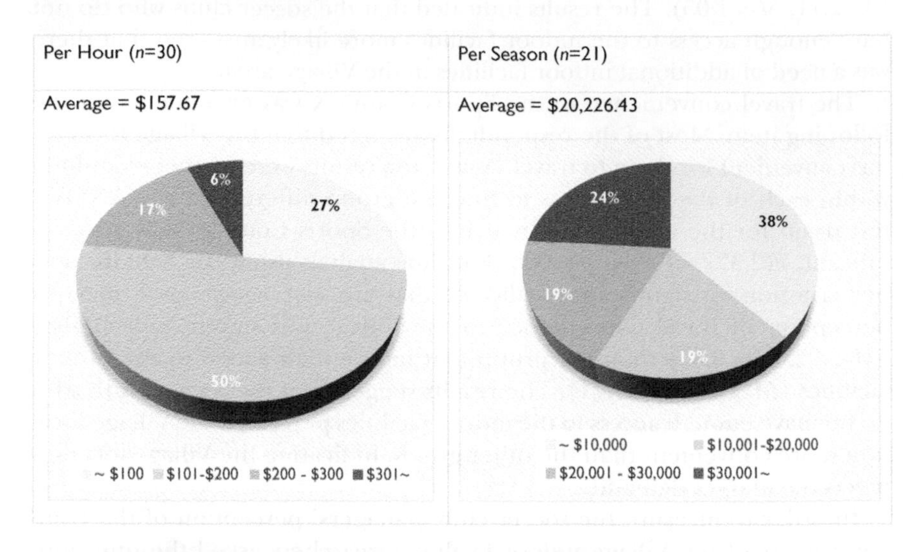

Figure 7.5 Expenditure on indoor facilities usage

and softball (n=12). When we identified the sports during the summer months, the number of these sports decreased almost to half. Basketball and volleyball did not show much difference during the summer months. One plausible explanation would be they are inherently considered as an indoor sport and hence do not show any difference. One interesting response was that the number for cheerleading participants indeed increased during the summer months. Eleven respondents answered "other sports" were utilized during the summer and they were personal training, group training, golf, tennis, and soccer. Indoor facility managers should consider these sports during the summer months. Respondents were asked if they would utilize the Sports Complex during the summer months (May-August) and 61 percent (*n*=20) answered "yes" and 39 percent (*n*=13) answered "no". This result was almost identical to the number of indoor facilities operated during the summer months. Lastly, respondents were asked to recommend suggestions to the Sports Complex.

Analysis of ProFormas

General assumptions. Based on input from the client group, several assumptions were used to develop estimates of event activity and financial operations for the proposed new multi-sport facility. It should be noted that these assumptions were preliminary and will continue to be refined as decisions related to the building program and other operating characteristics evolve.

These assumptions include the following:

1 The building program outline consists of three indoor fields.
2 The proposed multi-sport facility would be owned and operated by Sports Complex and staffed by personnel that specializes in marketing/management of sporting events and has established contacts and strong relationships with local and regional sports teams.
3 The proposed multi-sport facility would primarily focus on hosting youth sporting events.
4 A high level of quality customer service would be provided.
5 The selected site would be adequate in terms of visibility, parking, safety, and other similar issues.
6 Sufficient supporting infrastructure was located nearby (i.e. hotel rooms, restaurants, retail, entertainment, vehicular access, etc.).
7 No other similar, competitive/comparable facilities were built in the region.
8 Different amounts were presented that reflect a stabilized years of operations as well as break-even points.

Usage/event activity assumptions. The financial analyses were based on several factors including an estimate of usage/event activity that was developed from research on the youth sport market. Center summarized the market analysis including input from the client groups, market characteristics, industry trends, event activity at area facilities, input from potential demand generators, information on comparable facilities, as well as other research. Overall, utilization at any facility was identified as typically dependent on a number of factors (e.g., market size; accessibility; nearby amenities; size, configuration and quality of the facilities offered; effectiveness of the management team in booking the facility; date availability; cost, etc.). As such, the estimated range of utilization shown in the table below represents a stabilized year of operations.

1 It was anticipated that the league activity would accommodate high-level participants such as boys' and girls' premier youth travel teams that regularly play other regional teams and are supportive of the complex's efforts to draw regional and national tournaments.
2 In addition, there were residential-based parks and recreation type leagues that could be complimentary to the travel leagues at the proposed complex.
3 Since tournaments can be a revenue generator and are important to indoor facilities, the usage estimate included three tournaments with an average of 100 teams per tournament utilizing the proposed multi-sport facility on Saturday and Sunday.

4 For tournament activity, an event day was defined as three games being played at each hour starting at 8 am and running till 11 pm on Saturday and starting at 8 am and running till 10 pm on Sunday.
5 For example, three two-day tournaments with 100 teams paying $500 per team equates to $103,000 in revenue, which reflects the loss the facility would take from forfeiting the weekend hours to league activity.

The Center conducted an analysis of financial statements provided. The Center assumed the information contained within was valid and, therefore, conducted an analysis to determine feasibility and verify accuracy as it related to construction and operation of the Sports Complex facility. Both horizontal and vertical strategies were employed. The analysis took into consideration the critical areas that potentially created material impact in the results of the business operations, therefore, the Center assessment revealed relationships between components, their increments, and denouements, as they relate to plausibility, feasibility, and efficiency.

The Center's focus would be the critical points that make it possible for the Sports Complex to survive a general condition of economic downturn. The accuracy of this assessment was limited by the validity of the assumptions used in creating the financial sheet and economic demands. The Center utilized analytical tools and techniques to general-purpose financial statements and related data to derive estimates and inferences useful in business analysis. The analysis reduced reliance on hunches, guesses, and intuition for business decisions and decreased the uncertainty of business analysis. However, it did not lessen the need for expert judgement but, instead, provided a systematic and effective basis for defining feasibility as it related to the proposed development.

The Center understands that when you develop a business plan, financial projections and cash flow analysis are among the most critical elements, and that businesses that need financing will have to demonstrate the profit potential of their enterprise in order to convince a lender to provide needed funding. Therefore, the preliminary analysis contained within illustrated and referenced these important concepts. This analysis would help the consultant to assist its client in making informed decisions by helping structure the decision task through an evaluation of a company's business environment, its strategies, and its financial position and performance.

Field rental. The revenues generated from sports complexes are typically derived from field rental that can be charged per hour, per game, or per tournament based on the user, number of fields utilized, and the services provided. Facility management would likely negotiate rental terms for leagues and tournaments based on factors such as potential economic impact and/or the ability to execute multi-year contracts. Based on comparable facility data, complex rentals typically represent a significant revenue source. Rental revenue was largely dependent on the mix of business (tournaments versus leagues), mission of the facility (local league use versus economic impact) and ownership/management operating strategy (turn-key or full-service). From our research and the usage grid estimates it shows revenues associated with field rental operating at 100 percent occupancy during the 22-week Peak Time were $621,720 in revenue. From our usage grid, the revenues from the 30-week Off Peak Time rentals at 100 percent occupancy were $847,800. For our projections we calculated a conservative 75 percent occupancy rate during the 22-week Peak Time and 30 percent occupancy rate during the 30-week Off Peak Time that produced $466,290 and 254,340 in revenue respectively. These conservative calculations totaled $720,630 in revenue from the field usage.

Concessions. The operation and management of concession sales are generally handled by one of two methods. The first method allows an independent concessionaire exclusive rights to facility events with the facility taking either a percentage of gross sales or a flat fee per month. The second method allows for the facility owner to own and operate the concession service. Under this method, the facility owner captures all food and beverage sales but also incurs expense items related to purchase and maintenance of equipment, labor costs, and costs of goods sold. It has not yet been decided whether the proposed multi-sport facility will contract with a third party for concession operations or perform this function in-house. For purposes of this analysis, a net concession amount was estimated. Based on experience at comparable sports complexes concession revenue potential was relatively limited given the nature of event activity, relatively low margin food/beverage sales, and the common practice/desire of attendees to bring their own food and beverages.

Advertising/sponsorship. Advertising and sponsorship opportunities are diverse and can range from temporary signage at a single event to permanent signage on scoreboards or billboards located throughout one or more fields to advertising in a program to sponsoring team uniforms to sponsoring an entire event/tournament. Sponsorship could be specific to facility, team, tournaments, and even individual players and depend upon the strategic approach undertaken.

Salaries and wages. Although the staffing requirements and subsequent salaries and wages can represent a significant expense, permanent full-time staffing plans can vary. This variance in staffing levels was generally attributed to multiple factors. One factor relates to the management philosophy of maintaining event-related personnel as full-time or part-time staff. Another factor related to the management and physical relationship the facility might have to other public facilities. For example, the staffing plan for a complex only offering outdoor fields is different than that for an indoor/outdoor multi-sport facility. Ownership/management structure also plays a role in the staffing plan where a facility operated by the local parks and recreation department can often share administrative and maintenance costs with the broader municipal department. The number and type of fields, the overall mission of the complex, the level of competition, and primary uses can also impact staffing levels. In addition, the extent that contracted services and/or organized labor are used also impacts staffing at a facility. As a point of reference, the number of full-time equivalent staff ranged from four to ten at comparable complexes.

Repairs and maintenance. This line item includes labor, equipment, and materials associated with maintaining the fields and the general grounds. Depending on their management/ownership philosophy, some comparable facilities provided repairs and maintenance internally while others contract this service to a third party.

Marketing. Providing a new sports complex alone will not bring events to the facility. An aggressive marketing strategy will need to be undertaken to better allow the proposed sports complex to diversify and enhance its event base, particularly for large tournaments. This was consistent with industry practices and was considered critical in order to help establish the new venue as a major sports complex and enhance its on-going marketability.

Reserve for replacement. It was recommended that the Sports Complex owner and operator plan for an annual payment specifically designated as a reserve for replacement fund in order to safeguard its investment. This fund was intended to cover any extraordinary annual/future capital repairs or improvements to the sports complex. For purposes of this analysis, the reserve for replacement fund was estimated to be six percent of operating revenues.

Field Rental Matrix assessment. The Center conducted an assessment of the Field Rental Matrix with a variety of peak and non-peak season and usage rates. These calculations only utilized field usage revenue streams. These assessments can be found in Tables 7.5 and 7.6. At a 75 percent occupancy rate "peak season" and 30 percent occupancy "non-peak season", results revealed $513,177 in net revenue, prior to mortgage distribution. The revenue calculation at 75 percent occupancy included three tournaments, as proposed in the business plan ($50,000 per tournament). A deduction was made for the loss of weekend usage due to the tournaments. The deduction amount was $46,980. The net income after mortgage payment equates to $127,808. This revenue is only in relation to field use and does not account for other areas of revenue such as concessions, daytime use during the week, and auxiliary areas. Additionally, with concessions revenue included, net revenue exceeds $600,000 before mortgage payment with 75 percent occupancy during the 22-week "peak time" and 30 percent occupancy during the 30-week "non-peak time". With the addition of concessions revenue, the break-even point for the 22-week "peak time" as well as the 30-week "off-peak time" were 51 percent and 22 percent respectively. Table 7.5 provides the break-even occupancy for multiple 22-week peak times and 30-week off-peak times usage rates. The left side references the occupancy percentage during the 22-week "peak season",

Table 7.5 Break-even occupancy

22-Week "Peak Time"	*30-Week "Off-Peak Time"*
55% occupancy	30% occupancy
62% occupancy	25% occupancy
68% occupancy	20% occupancy

while the right side references the 30-week "off-peak season". These percentages were drawn from "field use" revenue only.

An assessment of the 22-week "peak season", utilizing only peak usage hours, revealed a need for 95.5 percent occupancy to offset total expenses including mortgage payment. When the revenue from concessions was added, the break-even point with the mortgage payment was 81 percent occupancy. This calculation only references the 22-week "peak usage hours". The calculation did not take into account any non-peak hours nor did it take into consideration any non-field use revenue sources (Table 7.6). Though it may be plausible to obtain these figures, the Center believed the utilization of the 52-week calendar year was much more strategic and provides the opportunities to generate much more lucrative long-term revenue streams.

Table 7.6 Field usage grid

Saturday	*Field 1*	*Field 2*	*Field 3*	*Sunday*	*Field 1*	*Field 2*	*Field 3*
8:00 AM	$180	$180	$180	8:00 AM	$180	$180	$180
9:00 AM	$180	$180	$180	9:00 AM	$180	$180	$180
10:00 AM	$180	$180	$180	10:00 AM	$180	$180	$180
11:00 AM	$180	$180	$180	11:00 AM	$180	$180	$180
12:00 PM	$180	$180	$180	12:00 PM	$180	$180	$180
1:00 PM	$180	$180	$180	1:00 PM	$180	$180	$180
2:00 PM	$180	$180	$180	2:00 PM	$180	$180	$180
3:00 PM	$180	$180	$180	3:00 PM	$180	$180	$180
4:00 PM	$180	$180	$180	4:00 PM	$180	$180	$180
5:00 PM	$180	$180	$180	5:00 PM	$180	$180	$180
6:00 PM	$180	$180	$180	6:00 PM	$180	$180	$180
7:00 PM	$180	$180	$180	7:00 PM	$180	$180	$180
8:00 PM	$180	$180	$180	8:00 PM	$180	$180	$180
9:00 PM	$180	$180	$180	9:00 PM	$180	$180	$180
10:00 PM	$180	$180	$180	10:00 PM			
Per Week	$2,700	$2,700	$2,700		$2,520	$2,520	$2,520

(continued)

Table 7.6 (continued)

Monday–Friday	Field 1	Field 2	Field 3
7:00 AM			
8:00 AM			
9:00 AM			
10:00 AM			
11:00 AM			
12:00 PM			
1:00 PM			
2:00 PM			
3:00 PM			
4:00 PM			
5:00 PM	$100	$100	$100
6:00 PM	$100	$100	$100
7:00 PM	$180	$180	$180
8:00 PM	$180	$180	$180
9:00 PM	$180	$180	$180
10:00 PM	$100	$100	$100
	$840	$840	$840
	x5	x5	x5
Per Week	$4,200	$4,200	$4,200

Critical success factors. The Center identified several critical success factors through the feasibility analysis. The Sports Complex may consider these factors to ensure their financial success in the competitive indoor sport facility market in the market area. An analysis to evaluate conditions that could impact the projected development/use and marketability of the sport complex was conducted. Results revealed the following critical components to ensure long-term success of the facility.

1 This Center believed that the Sports Complex had a solid foundation in regards to access and utilization of the soccer clientele base, however, it was recommended that they look to further diversify the consumer platform to ensure long-term success in addition the development in areas such as lacrosse.
2 Continued development and utilization of soccer network.
3 Incorporation of a strategic market plan.
4 Integration of diverse pool of youth sports to ensure enhanced and continued use of facility.
5 Utilization of the entire calendar year to increase revenue streams.

6 Enhance the utilization of "off-peak hours" throughout the calendar year.
7 Development of an Advisory Board/Committee.
8 Quality experience – employ engagement and retention strategies to attract repeat customers e.g. such as concessions, service, and programming.
9 Ensure staff and management are trained and knowledgeable of the youth sports industry.
10 Ensure competitive pricing strategies.
11 Incorporate market strategies to enhance strengths, opportunities, and accessibility.
12 Developed community partnerships to create marketing exchanges that further enhance delivery and exchange mediums.

Conclusion and recommendations

The fundamental purpose of this market study was to provide the Consultants and the Sports Complex, at the request of the financial institution, with resources that afford them the opportunity to plan and execute strategies that satisfy corporate and customer needs. The market study served as a function that would enhance the linkage between Consultants and development of the proposed facility. The data gathered allowed for the identification and definition of market-driven opportunities and problems. This information provided generation, refinement, and evaluation criteria. It allowed for dissemination and monitoring of market performance and provided the primary stakeholders with an improved understanding of market characteristics as that related to their strategic plan.

The systematic process of collecting, analyzing, and reporting information to Consultants was objective and logical. The success of any market study depends upon a correctly defined problem, knowledge of the market, and requires effective teamwork, analysis, and forecasting. The Center's knowledge and level of expertise assured that the market study was implemented efficiently and correctly. The team researched and assessed current demand characteristics and projected the future demand of the proposed facility. Procedures were put in place and utilized to ensure validity and reliability throughout the study.

The Center accurately identified and defined the key independent and dependent variables to be included in this study. The extent to which the variables under investigation were completely and accurately defined prior to hypothesizing any functional relationships was critical to ensure construct validity and an accurate definition of demand characteristics. For this study, the Center utilized data from both primary and secondary sources to secure relevant background information, historical trends, and any additional specific information relative to the scope of the study. A demand analysis was implemented to estimate the level of demand and the underlying reason for that demand of similar facilities. Additional measures were utilized to help ascertain the viability of facilities and amenities and further accentuate and define demand characteristics.

The Center provided an overview of the industry that highlighted trends, characteristics, and preferences of consumer groups. This assessment focused on physical, operational as well as marketing and promotional characteristics as they relate to feasibility of the development and operation of the prosed facility. Results revealed the following:

1 That population density with the 25, 100, and 250 mile radius was sufficient to support demand characteristics of the said facility.
2 That the youth population in the primary, secondary, and tertiary areas was slightly below the national average.
3 The median income within the Village was found to be higher than the national averages, while the county and state were found to be lower.
4 The climate assessment revealed that location was conducive for the use and development of an indoor multipurpose facility. The estimated chance of precipitation in peak season was found to be 74 percent while the estimated chance during the off-season was 46 percent. In addition the top six months for total precipitation were found to be May, July, June, August, April, and September.
5 It would be advantageous for Sports Complex not to directly compete with the Community Center but try to integrate programs that are of a complementary nature.

An assessment of sport participation trends revealed the following:

1 Right or wrong, parents provide a better experience for their children than they had themselves. The trend towards specialized spending early on with increased dollar amounts continues to grow.
2 A review of competitive facilities revealed basketball (23.4 million), soccer (12.6 million), baseball (13.7 million) volleyball (6.4 million) and softball (7.1 million) have the highest national participation rates among targeted court and field sports.
3 Sports with the largest number of casual participants include basketball (7.8 million) soccer (6.7 million), volleyball (2.9 million), baseball (4.8 million), touch soccer (3.8 million), and softball (3.0 million).
4 National sports participation has been stable since 2009. This can be attributed to US economic conditions improving over the past few years.
5 Of the sports analyzed, gymnastics, cheerleading, lacrosse, basketball, flag soccer, and wrestling have shown the greatest amount of growth since 2009.

6 The weighted average household income of indoor and outdoor sports participants was $72,569, which was slightly higher than the US average of $68,964.
7 When adjusted to reflect the Midwest Region index, volleyball, wrestling, baseball, and soccer comprise the largest number of frequent participants in the Midwest and Northeast Ohio region.
8 Parents will continue to support their children's desire to play sport and in turn provide the required sport equipment, apparel, shoes, and accessories.
9 Although not considered recession-proof, participation trends have remained stable and have been much more resilient than other industries in a downward economy.
10 It was estimated that parents spend nearly $1,000 annually to participate in youth sports.
11 The existing network that the owners of the proposed development retain was complementary to the potential success of the proposed facility.
12 Results showed 64 percent of the survey participants do not have enough access to the indoor facilities indicating that there was high demand and not enough supply of indoor soccer facilities in the region.
13 Access and convenience to the facility was assessed. Most of the respondents answered that the Village location was convenient for them to travel. The soccer clubs who do not have enough access to the indoor facilities perceived the Village location more convenient than the other group, indicating the Village location meets the market demand.
14 Over 60 percent of the participants responded that the Sports Complex Soccer facility will be the direct competitor of the indoor facility they are currently using, indicating the Sports Complex is competitive in the indoor facility industry in Northeast Ohio.
15 Respondents were asked if they would utilize the Village Indoor Soccer Facility during the summer months (May–August) and 61 percent (n=20) answered "yes" and 39 percent (n=13) answered "no".
16 A demand exists for the addition of a new facility.
17 The majority of the neighboring facility owners support the development and feel that it would further complement the network of current facilities, largely because these facilities are at peak season maximum occupancy.
18 However, there are a few competitors that feel that this development would be in direct competition to their existing facility.

In addition, the financial comparison revealed the following:

1 Center recognizes that financial statement analysis is an integral and important part of the broader field of business analysis. Business analysis

is the process of evaluating a company's economic prospects and risks for the purpose of making decisions. Therefore, analyzing a company's business environment, its strategies, and its financial position and performance are critical to ensure a wide range of business decisions, such as whether to invest in equity or in debt securities, whether to offer short- or long-term credit.

2 As previously noted earlier, sales normally influence the current asset and current liability account balances and sale figures typically depend on the industry, the economy, the season, and many other factors. Without plans for adequate cash reserves, borrowing capacity, or other means of meeting those expenses, a cash shortfall can cause the early demise of your new business. It doesn't matter that the idea behind the business was fundamentally sound; without adequate capital, you won't make it. Therefore, the critical factors in planning and the pitfalls to be avoided were discussed. Indicators of these pitfalls and ways to avoid them were also presented.
3 Revenue growth streams are limited to peak and off-peak hours of operation. Therefore, to maximize revenue streams it would be advantageous for Sports Complex to utilize the 52-week calendar year.
4 Results revealed that it would be advantageous for Sports Complex to operate both in the peak and off-peak seasons and maximize use during non-peak hours.
5 Reasonable occupancy rates can be maintained that ensure full payment of principle and interest payment.
6 Items within the ProForma and cash summary do not need to be displaced. They can be rounded accordingly and clarification of these items as to how each percentage e.g. such as capacity, and what it represents, would enhance the presentation.
7 It is not clear whether group ownership is going to procure a salary or stipend.
8 The capacity percentage row is irrelevant because it is not reverenced or representative of the numbers in the summary.
9 The non-soccer revenue has unrealistic percentage growth from year one to year five based on the field usage grid. To have a conservative projection, they should keep the year one non-soccer revenue constant for all five years.
10 Justification for increasing compensation of staff and concessions from year to year.
11 Two primary components that Sports Complex possesses are *land* and *location.*
12 Center assessment revealed that growth opportunities, not only specific to soccer, do exist. For example, enhancement in tournament hosting would produce significant revenue for Sports Complex and have a positive economic impact in the region.

Overall, Center extrapolated and utilized a variety of sources of information to ensure consistency of outcomes specific to this study. All of the utilized sources of information provided to Center by others were not audited, but were deemed to be reliable. Moreover, estimates and analysis regarding the proposed complex are based on trends and assumptions and, therefore, there will usually be differences between the projected and actual results. The assessment revealed only a few minor inconsistencies in the ProForma statement and cash flow summary. The Center recommended that these inconsistencies be addressed and that definitive constructs be articulated to further enhance the understanding of the financial statements and the origins of the data. Demands for youth service programs have remained constant. The Center recommended that Sports Complex develop a long term strategic marketing plan to complement development and engagement strategies of the said facility. Table 7.7 provides an illustration of assessment measures specific to this analysis and key market demand characteristics. Results revealed a score of 11 out of 15 for favorable and four out of 15 non favorable, further articulating the plausibility and feasibility of the proposed endeavor.

In conclusion, the Center sought to ascertain for the said Consultant and Sports Complex stakeholders, whether commercial concession services and facilities were of investment scale to which a capable private operator under lease agreement could achieve economic success, as well as offer

Table 7.7 An illustration of assessment measures specific to this analysis and key market demand characteristics

	Favorable	*Non-Favorable*
Population Density	√	
Population Youth/US Average		√ Slightly Below
Seasonality	√	
Location	√	
Access	√	
Demand	√	
Participate Rates	√	
Stakeholder Support	√	
Network	√	
Outdoor Space		√
Limited Sport Focus within Plan		√
22 Week Operation		√ Plausible
52 Week Operation	√	
Overall Revenue Opportunities	√	
Business Environment	√	

such services and facilities at reasonable prices to the general public and fulfill financial obligations. Results of the study would affirm this objective. The assessment outcomes revealed that Sports Complex could, even with the conservative 22-week ProForma, generate sufficient revenue to satisfy debt service for such a loan. However, the most advantageous alternative, to ensure long-term success of the facility, would be to utilize the 52-week calendar year. The Center was an advocate of the latter, for the integration and utilization of the 52-week alternative, along with the recommendations provided, would further enhance revenue streams to assure not only repayment of the debt, but profitability to the owner/operators.

References

Apanavičienė, R., Daugėlienė, A., Baltramonaitis, T., & Maliene, V. (2015). Sustainability Aspects of Real Estate Development: Lithuanian Case Study of Sports and Entertainment Arenas. *Sustainability (2071–1050), 7(6),* 6497–522.

Clarke A. & Kelleher, R. (2016). Common Feasibility Study Mistakes and How to Avoid Them. Ground Floor Partners, http://groundfloorpartners.com/common-feasibility-study-mistakes-and-how-to-avoid-them/.

Currie, R. R., Wesley, F., & Pandher, G. (2014). Contextualizing Site Factors for Feasibility Analysis. *Journal of Environmental Planning and Management, 57(10),* 1484–96.

Hageman, W. (2015). Spending More Money on Kids' Athletic Future Often Backfires. Chicago Tribune, StarTribune,www.startribune.com/spending-more-money-on-kids-athletic-future-often-backfires/262585181/, March 27, 2015.

Hinkin, T. R. (1995). A Review of Scale Development Practices in the Study of Organizations. *Journal of Management, 21(5),* 967–88.

Kim, M., Zhang, J. J., & Connaughton, D. (2010). Modification of the Volunteer Functions Inventory for Application in Youth Sports. *Sport Management Review, 13,* 25–38.

Mitchell, M.P. (2012). Team Business: A Post-Recession Update. *Impressions,* 6–9.

Novak, L. (1996). Market Feasibility Studies; A How-To Guide. Eugene, OR: University of Oregon.

Sangree, D. J. (2012). Perform Market Analysis with a Feasibility Study for Indoor Waterpark Resorts and Outdoor Waterparks. *Appraisal Journal, 80(2),* 149–56.

Sports, Fitness and Leisure Activities Topline Participation Report (2016).

The Sports & Fitness Industry Association Report (2016).

US Census (2010). Valley View Ohio population.

US Census (2014). Cuyahoga County Ohio population.

Chapter 8

A resource-based view of Bayi Fubang Rockets

Tyreal Yizhou Qian and James J. Zhang

Introduction

Over the past 20 years, the resource-based view (RBV) has gained considerable influence and reached a prominent position among theories in the field of organizational strategy and strategic management with respect to providing scholars and practitioners theoretical, methodological, and empirical insights. The increasing importance and ubiquity of firm resources, despite inconsistent and sometimes contradictory findings, creates the need for more definitive research that describes and defines the nature and scope of resources and their possible impact on the optimal performance of firms and organizations. Since the introduction of RBV (Wernerfelt, 1984), a number of attempts have been made to identify and understand the key attributes of resources and capacities that determine organization performance (Amit & Schoemaker, 1993; Barney, 1991; Palmatier, Dant, & Grewal, 2007; Peteraf, 1993), yet little research has been conducted in the sport setting although limited exceptions exist (Amis, Pant, & Slack, 1997; Anderson & Birrer, 2011; Gerrard, 2005; Papadimitriou & Apostolopoulou, 2009; Smart & Wolfe, 2000). In North America, Europe, and many developed countries, sport has been a steadily growing and increasing diverse industry, whereas in Asia, South America, Africa, and throughout many emerging economies, sport industry has enjoyed buoyant growth at an unprecedented rate due to increased amounts of discretionary income, a rising awareness of the importance of physical activity and active lifestyle, and greater access to recreational and leisure sports opportunities. Numerous distinctive types of sport organizations constitute the sport industry, and altogether form an ecosystem that is vital to the continuous development of the sport business landscape.

Among all the sport organizations, Professional Sport Clubs (PSCs), with the incontestable capacity of revenue generation, as well as immense entertainment value and media coverage involved, have commanded significant attention in the academic literature and popular press. However, most empirical and academic endeavors have primarily focused on PSCs in more economically developed regions and countries (Amis et al., 1997; Mauws,

Mason, & Foster, 2003; Smart & Wolfe, 2000), while few efforts have been made in regard to the examination of PSCs in emerging markets, especially those that are established in adverse conditions and have to be subject to certain political ideologies. It can be argued that some organizational paradigms, strategies, and tactics that are widely implemented among established PSCs might not be compatible with the ones needed in some international sport organizations considering the political, economic, and cultural incongruence; and thus, it is important to critically dissect and evaluate the resources that are central for the development of competitive strategies of those idiosyncratic PSCs in order to attain superior economic rents and a persistent competitive advantage (Barney, 1991). To fill this gap, the aim of this chapter is to identify and assess the essential indicators of strategic resources in the developmental process of a distinct PSC in China, Bayi Fubang Rockets, which the media and public referred as the "army team". A case study is presented and the RBV approach was utilized to discern how the presence and absence of the core traits of particular organizational resources and capacities would impact the ability of Bayi Fubang Rockets as to developing, maintaining, and sustaining a competitive advantage both financially and in terms of team performance. Finally, the chapter concludes with an analysis of underlying factors of the ups and downs of Bayi Fubang Rockets to provide a pragmatic insight into the viability and applicability of the RBV approach in terms of understanding endemic PSCs.

Review of literature

Sustained competitive advantage

When classic economic and organizational theories placed tremendous emphasis on the product of a firm back in the 1980s, few looked into the resource profile and sought the connection between a firm's capacity to obtain strategic resources and optimal product-market activities. Birger Wernerfelt, an economist and management theorist, proposed the idea of a firm's strategic resources in his seminal work "A Resource-Based View of the Firm" (Wernerfelt, 1984), and first introduced the concept of resource-based view to academia. He argued "resources and products are two sides of the same coin" (Wernerfelt, 1984, p. 171) as it was vital for firms to analyze the properties of their resources, build links between profitability and resources, and strategically manage resource position over time. Specifically, by taking a resource-based perspective, some key issues including the identification of a firm's most valuable and strategic resources, the sequence of a firm's market development, and the acquisition decision made by a firm in order to gain a strategic advantage, might be addressed in an effort of a firm's formulation of diversified strategies. However, it was believed that his original paper was, to a large extent, "terse and abstract" (Wernerfelt,

1995), and therefore, impeded the practicality and the generality of the resource-based view of the firm. Yet, fortunately, there have been a number of other research streams that contribute greatly to expanding the connotation and denotation of RBV and further apply the concept of RBV to a broader range of disciplines.

In the groundbreaking article, "Firm Resources and Sustained Competitive Advantage", Barney (1991) proposed two assumptions that contradicted the traditional strategy literature to fill the research void regarding how idiosyncratic firm attributes would influence a firm's competitive position. Contrary to homogeneity and mobility, a firm's resources were in fact heterogeneously distributed and imperfectly mobile. The new assumptions enabled researchers to examine resources of a firm from a unique perspective that a firm's resources might not be the same and perfectly mobile, and these two characteristics were important prerequisites for the analysis of a firm's competitive advantage. Consequently, Barney's (1991) RBV framework provided a sound basis for attempting to maintain a long-lasting competitiveness in its own right.

Attributes of resources

In line with the definitions of Wernerfelt (1984) and Barney (1991), a firm's resources include all assets, capabilities, organizational processes, firm attributes, information, knowledge, etc. Generally, the firm resources can be grouped into the following three categories: physical capital resources, such as physical technology, firm's plant and equipment, geographic location, and access to raw materials; human capital resources, such as training, experience, judgement, intelligence, relationships, and insight of employees; organizational capital resources, such as formal reporting structure formal and informal planning, controlling, coordinating systems, and informal relations within a firm and between firms. Nevertheless, it is not a guarantee for a sustained competitive advantage when a firm acquires one of the aforementioned resources. To better understand the essence of RBV, it is critical to first clarify what a competitive advantage is, and then identify and specify the conditions under which firm resources can be a source of a sustained competitive advantage for a firm.

Needless to say, not all aspects of a firm's physical capital, human capital, and organizational capital are strategically relevant resources. Some of these firm attributes may prevent a firm from conceiving of and implementing valuable strategies; others may lead a firm to conceiving of or implementing strategies that could potentially reduce its effectiveness and efficiency; still others may have no impact on a firm's strategizing processes. A firm is deemed to possess a sustained competitive advantage when it is implementing a value creating strategy not simultaneously being implemented by any current or potential competitors (Barney et al., 1989); other firms are unable to duplicate the benefits of the strategy (Barney, 1991); and most importantly, a competitive advantage is not based on calendar time.

Adopting the approach developed by Mauws et al. (2003), this study deemed Bayi Fubang Rockets as an independent strategic economic asset so that the ambiguity caused by the term "team" could be clarified and it could be argued that the mission of Bayi Fubang Rockets, a goal-directed social entity, was to seek to produce the league product and achieve economic viability. Thus, the attributes of resources that Bayi Fubang Rockets possessed to obtain or maintain a sustained competitive advantage were necessary to be identified. In accordance with Barney's (1991) conceptualization, for an organization to hold a potential of a sustained competitive advantage, its resources or capacities must contain four attributes: valuableness, rareness, imperfect imitability, and non-substitutability (Barney, 1991; Barney & Hesterly, 2015). These attributes of Bayi Fubang Rockets would be discussed and analyzed subsequently in the following sessions.

Bayi Fubang Rockets

Bayi Fubang Rockets, also known as Bayi Army Rockets or Bayi Rockets, is a professional basketball club based in Ningbo, Zhejiang, China and plays in the South Division of the Chinese Basketball Association (CBA) (CBA, 2017). Bayi in English means eight one as it refers to August 1, the Army Day commemorating the establishment of People's Liberation Army (PLA). Unlike the other 19 teams in the league, due to its affiliation with the PLA, Bayi Fubang Rockets is a unique professional basketball club with salient military features (CBA, 2017). Generally, there are two organizational designs used by the Chinese PSCs. One is based on the partnership between the government and a private corporation, where the government dominates the club management while the partner firm/corporation takes a relatively subordinate position even though sometimes the firm/corporation is the primary stakeholder of the club; the other builds upon a sole proprietorship in which the leading firm/corporation runs the club. Apparently, Bayi Fubang Rockets belongs to the former design as its official name, Bayi Fubang (Ningbo) Basketball Club, reveals that the club operates under the partnership between Ningbo Fubang (Holdings) Limited, a business group dominated by light industry, and Bayi Sports Team, the sport branch of the PLA (Bayi Sports Team).

The registered capital of Bayi Fubang Rockets is 20 million RMB, approximately three million in USD (Baike, 2017). The strategic apex (Mintzberg, 1979), i.e., the board of directors, consists of five members among whom three are from Fubang (Holdings) Limited and two are from Bayi Sports Team. Nevertheless, the personnel and team management, including player drafts and training, are controlled by the head coach who is (1) appointed by the Bayi sports team, (2) must maintain the status as a soldier

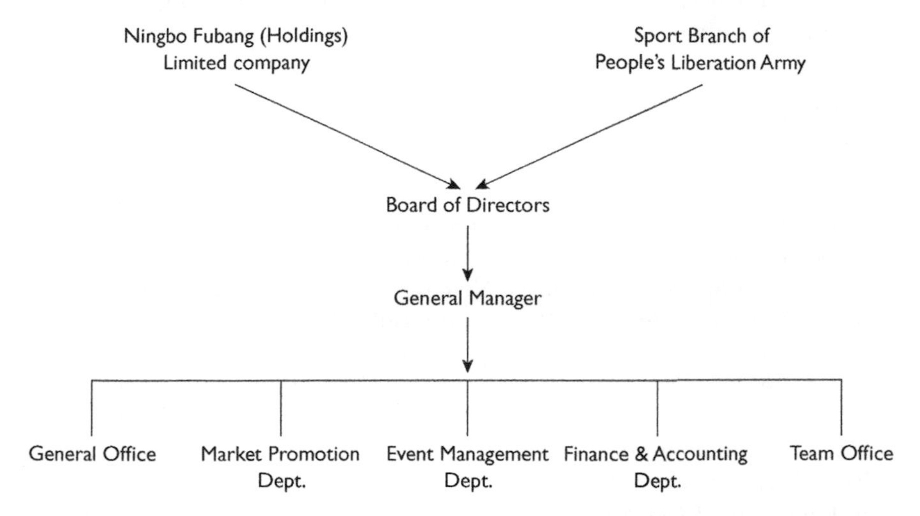

Figure 8.1 Bayi Rockets organizational design

for himself/herself, and (3) ensure all the players are soldiers, too, although playing basketball for the army is far from gun-wielding and battlefield-charging. The daily management of the club is carried out by five departments (offices), namely, general office, market promotion department, event management department, finance and accounting department, and team office, and is supervised by the general manager who is appointed by the board of directors (see Figure 8.1 for a detailed illustration of Bayi Fubang Rockets organizational structure). There is a separation of team management and club management in Bayi Rockets and consequently a separation of earnings: the revenue generated from transfer fees and commercial activities all go to the pocket of Bayi Sports Team while the club per se only receives the revenue from ticketing and sponsorship deals in the stadium. Yet, in the entire 1990s and early 2000s when Bayi Fubang Rockets enjoyed unparalleled monopoly in terms of recruiting the best players in China, due to its representation of Chinese military as well as the uncontestable salary and exceptional benefits it offered, despite the rigidity of this seemingly unfair revenue distribution, Bayi Fubang Rockets as an independent PSC was one of the few CBA clubs that enjoyed a winning record and remained financially well off. The good financial standing and team performance was largely attributed to the subsidies received from the army, without which Bayi Fubang Rockets would be very unlikely to operate in the black. However, as a consequence of the Chinese professional basketball reforms that took place in the early 2000s and aimed to facilitate the commercialization and professionalization of the CBA, the connection with the PLA became a controversial element for Bayi Fubang Rockets to sustain its domination built in the early years (Baike, 2017).

Method

This study was phased sequentially in order of a thorough review of Barney's work and relevant RBV literature to glean a general theoretical framework; a selection and examination of articles, reports, and blog posts published since 1998 from major Chinese and English sport news outlets, e.g., Tencent Sports, Sina Sports, Netease Sports, Hupu Basketball, ESPN, Sports Illustrated, Bleachers Report, and official announcements obtained from the homepage of Bayi Fubang Rockets to collect data with respect to the accomplishments and setbacks of Bayi Fubang Rockets and the overall performance of the league; discussions of the denotation and connotation of RBV via a doctorate seminar course for a semester as well as extensive direct discussions with the experts of PSCs and organization theory from the University of Georgia, coupled with their review and feedback on this study's conceptualization and applicability.

The data were analyzed per Strauss's (1987) qualitative analysis paradigm. The first procedure involved an unrestricted and comprehensive analysis of the data in which a myriad of concepts were filtered based on their relevance to the study, i.e. their association with the key incidents that assist Bayi Fubang Rockets to the position of a sustainable competitive advantage. Then the "cleaned" data were further analyzed according to Barney's (1991) classic identification of firm resource traits that generate a sustained competitive advantage, namely, valuableness, rareness, imperfect imitability, and non-substitutability. These data were supplemented by additional documentary materials, such as publicity materials released by the CBA. In this way, the evaluation of the achievements or obstacles due to resources acquired could be made through a RBV framework. Given the apparent difference and conflict existing between the past and the present political, economic, and social climate whereby the unique resources processed are the primary factors that determine strategy formulation and decision-making, this approach appeared to be both a reliable and practical method.

Results and discussion

According to Barney (1991), the effectiveness and efficiency of an organization are dependent on its resources that are valuable, scarce, imperfectly imitable, and not substitutable. In the case of Bayi Fubang Rockets, these factors play a paramount role in its rise and fall in the Chinese Basketball Association League. The next section will further discuss how these attributes affect the Bayi Fubang Rockets financially and in terms of team performance.

Valuableness and rareness

Being valuable is the necessary and sufficient condition for a resource to be considered to provide sustained competitive advantages. In other words, a valuable resource is indispensable for an organization to either conceive of or implement strategies that facilitate efficiency and effectiveness. It is suggested that a firm's performance can be enhanced only when its strategies "exploit opportunities or neutralize threats" (Barney, 1991). Other factors (i.e. rareness, imperfect imitability, and non-substitutability) may also play important roles and enable firms to achieve competitive advantages, but the valuableness of organizational resources is the primary concern for a firm to take into consideration. As aforementioned Bayi Fubang Rockets was once the best professional basketball club in the CBA, making 11 out of 16 finals and winning eight championships from 1995 to 2011 (see Table 8.1). It was also considered as the cradle of Chinese men's basketball teams, training a squad of gifted players who competed internationally on behalf of both the country and the army. Arguably, in the early stage of the CBA, a high-caliber pool of domestic basketball talent is the most valuable intangible resource for Bayi Fubang Rockets, which encountered few challenges in terms of recruiting the best Chinese players, given the limited number of qualified competitors whose offers were far less attractive than the ones provided by the "army team".

However, acquiring valuable resources is not the only prerequisite for securing a competitive advantage. Valuable resources can be possessed by a number of competing or potentially competing firms, yet the acquisition of these resources does not automatically transform into a sustained

Table 8.1 Bayi Rockets history record

Season (1998–2010)	*Regular Season Record (W-L)*	*Playoff Record (W-L)*	*Season Finish*
1998–99	21-1	8-0	CBA Champions
1999–2000	21-1	8-0	CBA Champions
2000–01	18-4	8-1	CBA Champions
2001–02	17-7	7-4	Runner-up
2002–03	17-7	7-4	CBA Champions
2003–04	14-8	5-3	3rd place
2004–05	24-14	5-6	3rd place
2005–06	28-14	7-5	Runner-up
2006–07	25-5	10-2	CBA Champions
2007–08	18-12	1-3	7th place
2008–09	25-25	N/A	11th place
2009–10	15-17	0-4	8th place

competitive advantage. Only when a firm is implementing a value-creating strategy not simultaneously implemented by other firms can it enjoy a competitive advantage. Intuitively, if a particular valuable firm resource is obtained by several firms, then these firms will be capable of utilizing the resource in a similar way, thereby carrying out a common strategy that makes a competitive advantage unattainable. The extent to which a valuable firm resource can be deemed as rare should be subject to the number of firms needed to generate perfect competition dynamics in an industry (Barney, 1991). The reasoning behind the rareness of resources can be well explained by the descending of Bayi Fubang Rockets into the darkest depths of the club's history. In the wake of the late-1990s' economic boom and the CBA reform, a few professional basketball clubs in the league began to receive substantial financial support from municipal governments as well as local enterprises, and started to challenge the domination of Bayi Fubang Rockets with respect to the financial incentives and benefits offered to the top domestic players. This deprived Bayi Fubang Rockets of being the sole premier free agency destination since it lost the appeal to the top domestic players. In addition, due to its affiliation with the army, Bayi Fubang Rockets abstained from hiring foreign players, who were usually much more effective and efficient than the locals to improve the overall

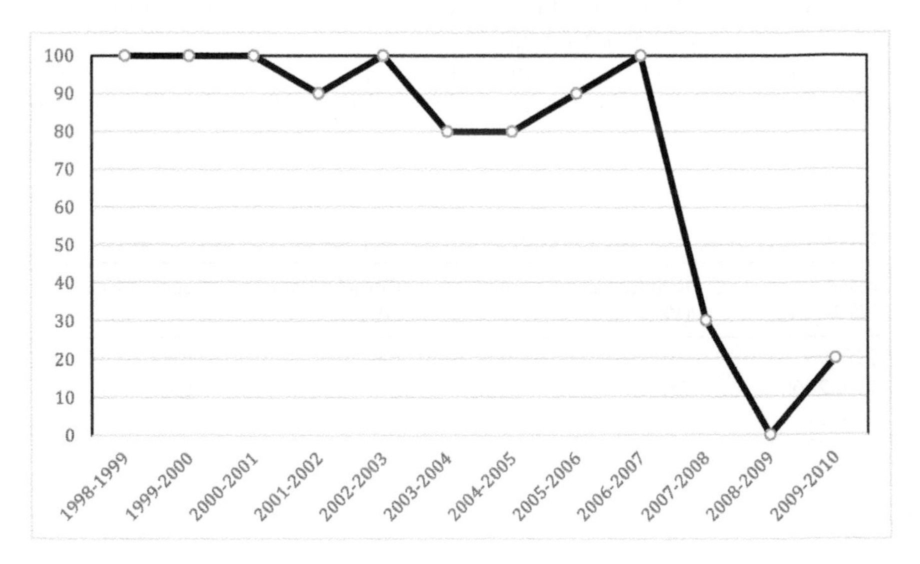

Figure 8.2 Record of Bayi Fubang Rockets

Each mark represents the final ranking Bayi Rockets finished from 1998–99 season to 2009–10 season. 100 on the y-axis indicates finishing in the 1st place or winning championship with every 10 points lowered to a lesser place, i.e., 90 the 2nd place, 80 the 3rd place, and so on and so forth.

team performance. Expectantly, after enjoying a decade of dominance in recruits, the recent years have witnessed enormous financial and personnel obstacles for Bayi Fubang Rockets to maintain a high quality of its line-up. Without good enough domestic drafts and a boost from foreign players that are now a staple for the rest of CBA clubs, a free fall of ranking is inevitable (see Figure 8.2).

Essentially, Bayi Fubang Rockets is now unable to outbid the lucrative contracts offered by other CBA clubs to the emerging domestic players, and it also refuses seeking foreign assistance from the NBA level players that are now a norm in the league. In this sense, the superior player advantage, the unique intangible resource Bayi Fubang Rockets once possessed, becomes neither rare nor valuable in today's league competition; and thus, it is not surprising that Bayi Fubang Rockets plummeted from grace following consecutive championships in 1990s and is currently holding a losing record. As a result, the absence of these two traits clearly leads to the drastic and unfortunate freefall in the recent years. It would be logical to argue that unless Bayi Fubang Rockets retrieve the valuableness and rareness of its recruits it would continue to struggle climbing back up the league ladder.

Imperfect imitability

The term "imperfectly imitable" was initially proposed by Lippman and Rumelt (1982) and Barney (1986), meaning that valuable and rare firm resources can only become sources of a sustained competitive advantage if a firm that does not possess these resources cannot obtain them. The imperfect imitability of a firm's resource can be achieved through one or a combination of three factors: unique historical conditions, causal ambiguity, and social complexity.

RBV of a sustained competitive advantage argues that a firm's ability to acquire and exploit some resources is contingent on its place in time and space. As opposed to traditional strategy theorists, resource-based theorists postulate that unique circumstances under which a firm is founded and operates will determine a firm's performance in the long run; while they posit that unique historical events and industry structure are critical determinants of a firm's subsequent actions. Moreover, the unique historical position of a firm is also highlighted as it grants the firm resources that are not controlled by competing firms and cannot be imitated. Barney (1991) asserted that firms and organizations were intrinsically historical and social entities, yet they still relied on their position in time and space to exploit some resources; once the particular unique time in history is eclipsed, it is almost impossible to access and take advantage of them (Zucker, 1977). Arguably, both the rise and fall of Bayi Fubang Rockets were inexorable as it was originally the flagship of the CBA and Chinese basketball, and at the same time, a product of a unique economic, social, and political system that is constantly evolving. Yet the present struggling is, without doubt, a result of disappointing record because of its historic link to the army, as illustrated by an increasing number of young athletes who refuse to play for the club. The reason is self-explanatory, that Bayi Fubang Rockets not only offers comparatively less generous contracts but also requires athletes to strictly follow military disciplines as it firmly controls its player's options. Moreover, even as an independent professional sport club, Bayi Fubang Rockets still needs to obtain the permission from the army or Bayi Sports Team in the first place if it wants to trade a player to another club; and a free agent should also receive permission from the army or Bayi Sports Team before he makes the move to play for the other club since players are not allowed to make any decisions at will.

Causal ambiguity requires that the relationship between a resource of a sustained competitive advantage and a firm that either possesses this resource or does not possess this resource is not perfectly understood by both parties. This ensures the sustained competitive advantage is not directly transferable and imitable in a way that firms without these resources are not able to engage in activities to reduce their disadvantage by hiring knowledgeable managers in a firm with a competitive advantage. Given the complexity of resources controlled by a firm, the incomplete understanding is very likely to exist among firms regardless whether they have a competitive advantage or not (Barney, 1991). On the other hand, social relationships, interpersonal relations, and a firm's reputation and culture are undoubtedly complex social phenomena and well beyond the capacity of a firm to comprehensively and systematically manage and leverage. Hence, a competitive advantage built around those social phenomena is more difficult for other firms to imitate and thus endows firms with a competitive edge that is imperfectly imitable (Amis et al., 1997; Barney, 1991). In light of the two factors explained above, the idea of causal ambiguity and social complexity can be underpinned by the continuous popularity of Bayi Fubang Rockets. Regardless of the fact that the club is currently out of championship contention, it still remains one of the most popular clubs with considerable media coverage, thanks to its reputation as a championship team and a time-honored fandom among Chinese basketball communities, which cannot be directly imitated or cultivated over a short period of time. Nevertheless, Bayi Fubang Rockets continues to develop under central planning and makes few attempts to utilize the market demand to regain its recruit advantage. At present, Ningbo Fubang (Holdings) Limited is more of a sponsor than a partner/owner unless the right to make management/marketing decisions are equally shared by Fubang and the army (Bayi Sports Team). This reveals the latent conflict between the two powers within Bayi Fubang Rockets.

Non-substitutability

Barney (1991) posited two forms of substitutability: a resource substituted by a similar resource and a resource substituted by a different resource. However, despite the form of substitutability, the resource that validates a competitive advantage cannot be replaced by any type of substitution. The exclusiveness of valuable, rare, and inimitable resources should not be obtained via implementation of similar/different strategies or using identical/distinct resources; otherwise, the resources cannot be labeled as resources with a sustained competitive advantage. From the Bayi Sports Team perspective, the most fundamental property that cannot be substituted, nor compromised, is its commitment to the army, the army representation, or the faith in an all-Chinese team, all of which are the essentials for the past Bayi dynasty and the beacon of restoring the past glory. Nevertheless, there have been voices from the strategic partner and the principal stakeholder of Bayi Fubang Rockets, Ningbo Fubang (Holdings) Limited, expressing its frustration over a noticeable deterioration in performance due to a mediocre crew of domestic players and not having foreign assistance. The threat of relegation looms large as the rest of the CBA clubs have become increasingly competitive by taking advantage of hiring foreign players and recruiting top-tier local players. Without imported pedigree, Bayi Fubang Rockets is facing mounting challenges and difficulties in gaining competitive edges. Yet despite requests for importing foreign players from Ningbo Fubang (Holdings) Limited, the army or Bayi Sports Team still insists on a "pureblood" team even at the price of being relegated to the lower league, as they believe with the involvement of foreign players Bayi Fubang Rockets would forfeit its long-term competitive advantage as the only all-Chinese team in the league and lose its last appeal for the fans, who are loyal to the club because of its army identity that cannot be substituted by any means. It might be plausible to have NBA level players to join Bayi Fubang Rockets and significantly improve its performance in a season or two, but in the long run it would destroy the iron-willed army culture upon which Bayi Fubang Rockets was founded. The negotiation regarding improving the club's performance and restoring its lost glory will continue in the coming years, but it is quite unlikely that Bayi Fubang Rockets would give up this identity.

Bayi Fubang Rockets and PBC CSKA Moscow

In order to illustrate the uniqueness of Bayi Fubang Rockets and facilitate a better understanding of the traits of resources that enable sustained competitive advantage, the PBC CSKA Moscow was included in the study as a historic counterpart to Bayi Fubang Rockets. The PBC CSKA Moscow is a Russian professional basketball team based in Moscow, Russia and is currently owned by Norilsk Nickel. It is a member of the VTB United League (the first tier of Russian professional club basketball) and the Euroleague. CSKA won two titles between 2006 and 2009 in Europe's principal club competition, the Euroleague, making the final in all four seasons, and has advanced to the Euroleague Final Four 13 times in the twenty-first century (Cingiene & Laskiene, 2004; Korneeva & Ogurtsov, 2016). Historically, the PBC CSKA Moscow is the most widely known basketball club that had a close connection with the country's military force due to its parent multi-sport club, CSKA Moscow which is popularly perceived as "the Red Army" or "the Red Army team" because of the association with the Armed Forces sports society under the Soviet Army during the Soviet era. Much similar to the path of Bayi Fubang Rockets, the PBC CSKA Moscow also undertook a series of setbacks and was unable to win a single title for three years after concluding an impressive streak of winning 25 championship titles. But the PBC CSKA Moscow broke away from the planned economy and began to capitalize on the vast European sports market after the collapse of Soviet Union. It was the first Soviet Union sports club that carried out a systematic reform and started to operate based on a market orientation. The strategic apex of the PBC CSKA Moscow, the board of directors, hired the head coach who took charge of the team and had the authority to decide on the inclusion of overseas players. As a result of the improved performance (retrieved championship in the 2010 VTB United League and won the champion of Euroleague in 2016) (Moscow, 2016), the club was able to maximize revenue generated from sponsorship deals, ticket sales, and broadcasting rights to maintain a sustainable competitive advantage in Europe.

Similarly, the PBC CSKA Moscow resources can be evaluated in the context of the RBV framework to explain the factors underlying the revival of the club. Recall that the first two elements of the RBV framework are valuableness and rareness. The value element of the PBC CSKA Moscow is clearly evident in its ability to attract top-level overseas players and retrieve financial support from various channels that are vital for the comeback. The PBC CSKA Moscow benefits from its past successes as a Soviet Army team and European recognitions as a perennial winning club. However, scarceness combined with value can only lead to a temporary competitive advantage. The factors in the RBV framework, imperfect imitability and non-substitutability, are particularly important in validating the competitive advantage. In accordance with the discussions of Barney and Hesterly (2015) as well as Anderson and Birrer (2011), causal ambiguity makes the key variables, for instance, the characteristics of players, coaching skills, and staff conditions impossible or problematic to identify and measure; social complexity differentiates the PBC CSKA Moscow from other sport clubs in terms of the club's culture, tradition, and earlier accomplishments, while unique historical condition guarantees the path of the PBC CSKA is not duplicable and irreversible. Taken together, these reasons demonstrate the trajectory of the PBC CSKA Moscow rejuvenation and provide useful insights into the possible solution to the predicament Bayi Fubang Rockets now faces. Compared to the PBC CSKA Moscow, Bayi Fubang Rockets is neither the first nor the best professional basketball club imbued with military features. However, the former communism comrades share considerable similarities considering their identical political and military backgrounds. Specifically, the PBC CSKA Moscow was once in deep crisis when Russia opened up to the world, something not quite different to what Bayi Fubang Rockets is currently undergoing, the most valuable and rare intangible resources, top-tier players and coaches, fled to the clubs that offered a higher salary and better benefits. The strict centralized management was unable to curb the downward momentum that brought the club to the bottom of the league. Yet, the major difference lies in the differing attitude towards the history of the two clubs: the PBC CSKA Moscow completely abandoned its military heritage while Bayi Fubang Rockets embraced it regardless of the objections from its strategic and business partner, Ningbo Fubang (Holdings) Limited. Nevertheless, from an RBV standpoint, the tradition and heritage of being an army team that are difficult to imitate and substitute have been a key factor in terms of generating resources (army subsidies, fans support, additional sponsorship opportunities, and national media exposure) to strengthen the club's mission. Unlike Bayi Fubang Rockets, following the collapse of the Soviet Union, the PBC CSKA Moscow lost access to the superior financial and personnel resources and had to resort to a thorough de-military reform to remain competitive and make ends meet. In contrast, Bayi Fubang Rockets still enjoyed a strong and generous support from the Chinese Army. What might be helpful to augment the military characteristics and relieve tension between the Army and the corporate partner, Ningbo Fubang (Holdings) Limited, is to grant a greater say to it in the decision-making process, such as the selection of domestic players as well as the nomination of coach measures; in addition, other measures, such as incentives, benefits, and player choices should be taken to attract better athletes, improve its caliber of play, and, in turn, to reinforce its competitiveness off court.

Looking forward

The current economic environment and sport market demand in China are favorable to the development of professional basketball clubs, especially when the state projects the total scale of sports industry to exceed $45 billion and demand for high-quality sport services and products is soaring among middle-class Chinese (Liang, 2014). In addition, the issuance of the "Suggestions on Accelerating Development of Sports Industry and Promoting Sports Consumption" in 2014 by China's cabinet, the State Council, demonstrated China's commitment to deepening the commercialization and professionalization of professional sport leagues, as well as the determination to support the long-term development of PSCs, a move reflecting the strategic vision of the central government (Xinhua, 2015). However, despite the fact that Bayi Fubang Rockets is still considered one of the most influential professional basketball clubs in China, it is undoubtedly challenged by clubs such as Guangdong Hongyuan Southern Tigers, Beijing Shougang Ducks, and Liaoning Benxi Flying Leopard, which take great advantage of the positive policies and exert diligent efforts to gain competitive edges in terms of drafting players, hiring coaches, searching for foreign assistance, developing local markets, and building up a loyal fan base. In this light, the key for Bayi Fubang Rockets to once again outperform other clubs rests upon the strategic decisions made to effectively manage their non-imitated and non-substituted resources and ultimately regain the valuable and rare resources they once possessed.

Conclusions

In a profusion of RBV studies, only a few researchers have placed focus on PSCs, with even fewer of them delving into PSCs in non-industrialized countries. In this chapter, a unique PSC in China, Bayi Fubang Rockets, was examined through a classic RBV approach (Barney, 1991). Critical attributes of resources that enabled a sustained competitive advantage were identified and discussed. In particular, this chapter shed important light on the influence of the presence and the absence of the revealed traits on the rise and fall of Bayi Fubang Rockets both on and off the court. The ability of RBV in terms of interpreting and explaining the mechanism and functions of PSCs in different contexts suggests the need for greater efforts to integrate the abundance of accumulated theoretical and empirical research, and to better the strategies that are most effective for building a sustained competitive advantage. The ideas outlined in this chapter can be utilized for endemic PSCs to critically discern the resources possessed and their respective characteristics on the basis of their ability to create and maintain a sustained competitive advantage (Mauws et al., 2003). It is worth emphasizing, however, that developing a tangible resource such as super star players, or an intangible resource such as military culture or army tradition, take much time, hard work, and demand unique historic settings. Thus, an early and consistent identification of the four antecedents, i.e., valuableness, rareness, imperfect imitability, and non-substitutability, and an arduous effort to satisfy them, are possibly the most effective and efficient ways of managing disorderly and complicated organizational resources as a prelude to achieving success.

It is also worth noting that, for over two decades, Bayi Fubang Rockets has been able to maintain a reputation as an elite professional club despite its downfall in league rankings of late. The military culture embedded in the club has been central to sustaining its popularity, but at the same time, acted as a formidable barrier for providing incentives to promising domestic players and seeking for foreign assistance. Seemingly, Bayi Fubang Rockets will continue to be recognized as one of the most symbolic PSCs in China. Nevertheless, possible reforms with respect to the incentives offered to domestic players should be taken into consideration and concerns regarding inadequate involvement of the partner corporate, Ningbo Fubang (Holdings) Limited, should also be addressed so that the club can better organize and leverage its existing resources and sustain its competitive advantage. In essence, advancing the understanding of PSC resources can increase the effectiveness and efficiency of the focal PSC dramatically, and provide practitioners and researchers with insights into ways to analyze the dynamic characteristics of PSCs' resources and enforce more comprehensive strategies to attain or maintain a sustained competitive advantage.

Albeit RBV has been broadly utilized in a wide range of disciplines, limitations still exist when researchers attempt to apply this theory to an array of research areas. First, and perhaps most fundamental, is the issue of tautology. There is an apparent overlap between imperfect imitability and non-substitutability given their close semantic meanings, causing difficulty distinguishing the two concepts. Second, if one assumes that the RBV may be specified in a testable form, any empirical assessment of its predictions requires the identification and measurement of relevant resources. This, in turn, gives rise to considerable work and difficulty in terms of operationalization and measurement of strategic resources with a competitive advantage. Third, the logic of the RBV does not predict a universal relationship between firm performance and any particular resource, which unavoidably results in difficulties in identifying key resources and elevating costs to evaluate how related resources would affect desired outcomes.

Scholars need to actively reflect upon and elevate their methodological approaches to empirically utilizing the RBV framework. Although previous studies (Amis et al., 1997; Anderson & Birrer, 2011; Gerrard, 2005; Papadimitriou & Apostolopoulou, 2009; Smart & Wolfe, 2000) set out an initial investigation into the sports landscape by adopting the RBV framework, which are much respected and appreciated, the assessments of organizational effectiveness in these studies are, to a great extent, insufficient. The majority of previous studies are qualitative and conceptual in nature, and thus request further empirical evidence generated from quantitative inquires. Solely relying on qualitative data in deciding on whether or not a PSC is successful would inevitably produce biased results and undermine the reliability and validity of the potential theoretical and empirical implications. Future studies should continue improving and innovating research designs and methodologies to yield more comprehensive insights for evaluating a sport organization.

References

Amis, J., Pant, N., & Slack, T. (1997). Achieving a Sustainable Competitive Advantage: A Resource-based View of Sport Sponsorship. *Journal of Sport Management, 11(1)*, 80–96.

Amit, R., & Schoemaker, P. J. (1993). Strategic Assets and Organizational Rent. *Strategic Management Journal, 14(1)*, 33–46.

Anderson, K. S., & Birrer, G. E. (2011). Creating a Sustainable Competitive Advantage: A Resource-based Analysis of the Gonzaga University Men's Basketball Program. *Journal of Sport Administration and Supervision, 3(1)*, 11–21.

Baike, B. (2017). Bayi Fubang Rockets. Retrieved from http://baike.baidu.com/item/八一富邦火箭俱乐部/13886877?fromtitle=八一火箭队&fromid=5697208 (accessed February 21, 2017).

Barney, J. (1986). Strategic Factor Markets: Expectations, Luck, and Business Strategy. *Management Science, 32(10)*, 1231–41.

Barney, J. (1991). Firm Resources and Sustained Competitive Advantage. *Journal of Management, 17(1)*, 99–120.

Barney, J., & Hesterly, W. (2015). *Strategic Management and Competitive Advantage Concepts and Cases.* Upper Saddle River, NJ: Pearson Prentice Hall.

Barney, J. B., Busenitz, L., Fiet, J. O., & Moesel, D. (1989). *The Structure of Venture Capital Governance: An Organizational Economic Analysis of Relations Between Venture Capital Firms and New Ventures.* Paper presented at the Academy of Management Proceedings.

CBA. (2017). Bayi Fubang Rockets. Retrieved from www.cba.gov.cn/cbastats/teamdetail.aspx?id=Te001 (accessed February 21, 2017).

Cingiene, V., & Laskiene, S. (2004). A Revitalized Dream: Basketball and National Identity in Lithuania. *The International Journal of the History of Sport, 21(5)*, 762–79.

Gerrard, B. (2005). A Resource-utilization Model of Organizational Efficiency in Professional Sports Teams. *Journal of Sport Management, 19(2)*, 143–69.

Korneeva, V. A., & Ogurtsov, E. S. (2016). The Politicization of Sports as a Soft Power Public Resource. *Indian Journal of Science and Technology, 9(29)*, 1–7.

Liang, W. (2014). *The Present Situation of Chinese Professional Basketball Club and the Development of Management System.* (Master's thesis), retrieved from CNKI.

Lippman, S. A., & Rumelt, R. P. (1982). Uncertain Imitability: An Analysis of Interfirm Differences in Efficiency Under Competition. *The Bell Journal of Economics*, 418–38.

Mauws, M. K., Mason, D. S., & Foster, W. M. (2003). Thinking Strategically About Professional Sports. *European Sport Management Quarterly, 3(3)*, 145–64.

Mintzberg, H. (1979). The Structuring of Organizations: A Synthesis of the Research. *University of Illinois at Urbana-Champaign's Academy for Entrepreneurial Leadership Historical Research Reference in Entrepreneurship.*

Moscow, P. C. (2016). History and Awards. Retrieved from www.cskabasket.com/history/?lang=en (accessed March 21, 2017).

Palmatier, R. W., Dant, R. P., & Grewal, D. (2007). A Comparative Longitudinal Analysis of Theoretical Perspectives of Interorganizational Relationship Performance. *Journal of Marketing, 71(4)*, 172–94.

Papadimitriou, D., & Apostolopoulou, A. (2009). Olympic Sponsorship Activation and the Creation of Competitive Advantage. *Journal of Promotion Management, 15(1–2)*, 90–117.

Peteraf, M. A. (1993). The Cornerstones of Competitive Advantage: A Resource-based View. *Strategic Management Journal, 14(3)*, 179–91.

Smart, D. L., & Wolfe, R. A. (2000). Examining Sustainable Competitive Advantage in Intercollegiate Athletics: A Resource-based View. *Journal of Sport Management, 14(2)*, 133–53.

Strauss, A. L. (1987). *Qualitative Analysis for Social Scientists.* Cambridge: Cambridge University Press.

Wernerfelt, B. (1984). A Resource-based View of the Firm. *Strategic Management Journal, 5(2)*, 171–80.

Xinhua. (2015, December 9). China Estimates 400 Billion Yuan Added Value in Sports Industry in 2015. *China Daily.* Retrieved from http://usa.chinadaily.com.cn/business/2015-12/09/content_22668603.htm.

Zucker, L. G. (1977). The Role of Institutionalization in Cultural Persistence. *American Sociological Review*, 726–43.

Part III

Managing opportunities

Chapter 9

Managing the business of soccer

A conceptual framework

Sten Söderman and James Santomier Jr.

Introduction

Throughout the past decade the business of soccer has benefitted significantly from globalization, primarily from increased sponsorship support from global brands such as Adidas, Nike, and Coca-Cola, and intensified media attention worldwide (Deloitte, 2015). This development has provided new business and investment opportunities for club owners and entrepreneurs. However, while research related to the globalization of business and soccer is extensive, an untapped opportunity is to identify and discuss the relationship between the two and how each can benefit from the management strategies and practices of the other (Morrow, 2003; Bolchover & Brady, 2004; Chadwick, 2009; Bridgewater, 2010; Burnes & O'Donnel, 2011; Soriano, 2011; Söderman, 2013; Gregson, 2010; Jarosz, Kornakov, & Söderman, 2015).

In the preceding four decades, the business of professional sport experienced a period of relatively slow development and sophistication. Recently, however, the rapid development of a variety of technological innovations has fomented significant transformation in professional sport worldwide (Cousens & Slack, 2005). Contemporary professional sport is a dynamic, hyper-competitive global industry comprised of federations, leagues, and clubs of all sizes that rely on a resource-based management approach in order to seek a competitive advantage and maintain long-term financial stability (Foster, Greyser, & Walsh, 2006; Mauws, Mason, & Foster, 2003). For example, while some businesses continue to struggle in the aftermath of the 2007–09 economic crisis, the English Premier League signed new broadcast rights agreements worth US$2.7 billion for the British live broadcast rights between 2010 and 2013, which increased to US$8.6 billion for the period 2013–14 (Deloitte, 2015; Harris, 2009).

Today, Europe's most successful soccer clubs enjoy the benefits of important supplemental (in addition to ticket sales) revenue-generating activities, such as increased sponsorship and broadcasting rights deals that facilitate the promotion of their brands in new global markets. The combined revenues of Europe's top 20 soccer clubs increased by US$36 million to US$5.5 billion for the 2008–09 season, while their market value grew from an average of US$632 million to an average of US$691 million (Olson, 2010). Deloitte (2015) estimates the European soccer market size to exceed US$26 billion for the 2016–17 season. Thus, European soccer clubs are optimistic about increased revenue etc. going forward, as they anticipate that growth in the Asian, African, and Latin American markets will gain momentum and accelerate soccer's popularity and profitability (Hong & Zhou, 2013; Liang, 2014).

However, one observation from the literature and data reviewed for this chapter is clear; there is an uneven distribution of wealth among leagues and clubs in the European soccer context. While many first division and some second division teams in leagues throughout Europe have enjoyed financial success, others have either been forced or have chosen to go into administration (Beech, Horsman, & Magraw, 2010). However in the soccer league, for example, "the use of fair play regulations in all three divisions, the requirement for new owners to demonstrate the source and sufficiency of their funding and the ongoing monitoring of clubs' tax affairs" has brought stability to club finances (The Guardian, 2015, p. 1). In Spain for example, La Liga's financial situation is improving, however the Spanish soccer clubs have approximately US$3 billion of debt. The improvement is, in part, due to better commercialization of TV rights with revenue increases offsetting differences among the La Liga teams and, in theory, improving the level of competition (SportsBusiness Daily Global, 2016). In addition, going forward, La Liga will rate Spanish soccer clubs financially to increase transparency and lure more investors (ESPNFC, 2016).

The primary purpose of this chapter is to present a management-focused conceptual framework, adopted from Dolles and Söderman (2008), for understanding the business of soccer, and six business imperatives extracted from the conceptual framework that have import for soccer and business management. The secondary purpose, through a comparative analysis, is to describe and explain how selected key factors and strategies within the context of European soccer management may be applicable to business enterprises worldwide. This chapter is based on an extensive review of literature and data collected and synthesized over several years, which has revealed two important attributes of modern-day European soccer: (a) it is a global phenomenon and (b) it is recession-proof (CNN, 2012; The Economist, 2012).

Review of literature

The extensive data and information available regarding the soccer industry is not well compiled, curated, or analyzed. For example, newspapers, magazines, and other similar media, because they are normally under relatively strict time constraints, produce reports, etc. where, by necessity, they are limited to identifying and describing specific sport events and their immediate contexts based solely on time and spatial perspectives. Most of these reports do not include a management-related focus or context (Chadwick, 2009; Smith & Stewart, 2010). Most traditional models of management that conceivably could be used to analyze soccer management strategies etc., do not address specific contextual and decision-making issues satisfactorily. Dolles and Söderman (2005, p. 10) identified four key areas related to the significant challenges involved in managing soccer within an international context: (a) the product and its markets, (b) the consumers, (c) the business process, and (d) its strategic vision and intent. They point out that except for licensed merchandise, the soccer business does not benefit from the option other businesses have of producing and storing inventory for future sale, as the two key characteristics of soccer are outcome uncertainty and the emotional involvement of its consumers. A traditional business model-based approach, therefore, may ignore the complexity of the management process in soccer business in order to isolate a few key variables and their interactions, which may be based on limited selection criteria. For example, in soccer, perhaps more so than in other business endeavors, there is a unique and complex relationship between human resource management and financial management. Porter concluded that "no one model embodies or even approaches embodying all the variables of interest, and hence the applicability of any model's findings is almost inevitably restricted to a small subgroup of firms or industries whose characteristics fit the model's assumptions" (Porter, 1991, p. 17). Instead of developing a management model of a soccer club based on limited variables, and in order to make progress in research, it was necessary to go beyond those limitations in developing this chapter.

Based on a comprehensive understanding of the competitive environment, business context, and relative position in the market of soccer, the approach selected for this chapter was to adapt a conceptual framework for team sport management developed by Dolles and Söderman (2013). A framework-based approach seeks to capture much of the complexity of the organization and encompasses a multitude of variables. Porter's (1991) frameworks, for example, of the five competitive forces, the value chain perspective of the firm, or the diamond framework exploring the competitive advantages of nations, are prominent examples of this approach. Other framework designs include those by Dolles and Söderman (2013) and O'Reilly (2013). However, relationships among factors incorporated within a conceptual framework cannot be rigorously drawn or calculated. Rather, a framework-based approach seeks to assist the researcher and the practitioner to better understand and analyze a problem or issue by understanding the primary factors and forces operating in the general research setting.

Empirical analyses related to comparative international business strategies and soccer business strategies are rare. Gammelsaeter and Senaux (2011) and Smith and Stewart (2010) contend that existing theories can explain satisfactorily the globalization of soccer; however, these macro analyses are deficient in addressing the unique elements and challenges of soccer club management. Hence, the methodological approach used for this chapter was abductive, which infers a case from a rule or result using an inference that is likely probable, and where theory and method are interrelated (Alvesson & Sköldberg, 2009; Dubois & Gadde, 2002; Josephson & Josephson, 1996). There are two primary types of organization operating in professional soccer: leagues and clubs. The league, for example the English Premier League, governs a group of clubs by carrying out tasks such as marketing and enforcing the rules of the game. A club is an organization comprised of players competing as a team against other clubs in a league. Within some leagues, for example the Bundesliga or the English Premier League, there is a small group of elite clubs that are among the most recognized brands in the world (Richelieu & Pons, 2006). Although the leagues act as power brokers with respect to media rights and select mega events etc., it is the clubs that win games and championships, garner the attention of consumers and create, with some exceptions, the opportunity for league-wide media rights, which represent a significant portion of the revenue for both teams and leagues.

Therefore, the management of soccer clubs is the focus of this chapter. "Clubs today have much in common with large or medium-sized businesses. In effect, they have become companies, creating economic value added, though with the specific characteristics of sports organizations, and so deserve to be studied on their own terms" (Gomez, Kase, & Urrutia, 2010, p. 2). Although elite soccer clubs are as well-known as some globally recognized consumer brands they are, in fact, only small and medium-sized enterprises (SMEs). For example, there are only five clubs in the English Premier League with more than 250 full-time employees (Moore & Levermore, 2012). Therefore, the management of European soccer clubs can be examined effectively by applying SME perspectives to assist in explaining what might be considered inherent qualities, advantages, disadvantages, and idiosyncrasies.

Method

The comparative conceptual framework developed for this chapter was based on existing literature, including selected soccer management case studies, which were adapted from the Dolles and Söderman framework (2013). Selected soccer management case studies were analyzed because they included multiple data collection methods. This is particularly relevant given that the use of the case study strategy has become increasingly popular in sport business research (Dibben & Dolles, 2013; Gratton & Solberg, 2013; O'Reilly, 2013; Skille, 2013). As previously stated, the theoretical/methodological approach of this chapter was abductive, namely where theory and method are interrelated (van Maanen, Södersen, & Mitchell, 2007). The approach rests on the limited possibilities of the generalization of various theories in time and space. Extant theory is developed in parallel with the empirical fieldwork and case analysis, where the final aim is to create a solid theoretical and empirical base, and simultaneously strengthen the practical validation of the research by making the results relevant for organizations and society. With the lack of a set of established theories a comparative analysis can take several forms. One approach is to focus on one or a few variables in a survey of multiple soccer clubs and another is to focus on one soccer club and identify many variables. This paper has taken a middle ground approach and has included key elements based on several cases and insights from the soccer and media industries, both from a practitioner and researcher perspective.

Imperatives, or specific requirements, can be initiated for many management functions, such as directing the behavior of personnel or making recommendations and suggestions. Imperatives normally incorporate a formal idea or belief that has a strong influence on people, making them behave in a particular way (Pearson, 2008). For example, Breul (2011, p. 1) identified seven management imperatives appropriate for a changing global business environment: (a) act with strategic intent, (b) leverage hyper-connectivity, (c) manage through collaboration, (d) use real-time performance data, (e) respond to the new security environment, (f) work with the private sector in new ways, and (g) cut costs and improve performance.

Other recent business-focused imperatives include, for example, hiring more women as a gender equality issue (Daily & Dalton, 2003; Schwartz, 1992), developing a 'green' or 'sustainability' initiative (Menguc & Ozanne, 2005), teaching business ethics in light of recent financial scandals (Crane, 2004), and confirming authenticity (Gilmore & Pine, 2007).

With the support of a conceptual framework, this chapter identifies and discusses a selection of key factors and imperatives that may assist business managers in extracting best practice from soccer management. The first section of the chapter presents the conceptual framework upon which the analysis is based, and the second section discusses best practice that is most prevalent in soccer management. This section is synthesized and formulated into six new business management imperatives. A short summary with the most important "best practices" concludes the chapter.

Results

Development of a conceptual framework

The dimensions of soccer club management, as well as its challenges, can be considered from several perspectives. A four-field matrix, adapted from Söderman (2004) constitutes the conceptual framework for examining soccer club business models, as well as management strategies and practices. The design of the conceptual framework is based on two elements within each of two dimensions: (1) a time-related dimension and (2) a spatial-related dimension. The time-related dimension is comprised of relevant activities taking place *during a soccer match* and those taking place *between soccer matches*. The spatial dimensions are comprised of relevant activities taking place *on the field* and those taking place *off the field*. Key factors, issues, etc. within each one of these four dimensions represents a specific context in which a variety of management strategies and practices may be developed and implemented (Figure 9.1):

1 *Off the field, during the match*: Creation of atmospherics in the stadium that may facilitate the cognitive/emotional and/or behavioral activity of consumers that may contribute to increasing fan identification (Gladden & Funk, 2002) and concomitant consumer behavior.
2 *On the field, during the match*: Focus on activities related to the execution of the match strategy and required planned activities by coaches and management/team support personnel.
3 *On the field, between matches/seasons*: Focus is on the execution of strategic development plans and specific training programs that may be initiated by management, coaches and/or trainers.
4 *Off the field, between matches/seasons*: Development of strategic business plans as well as human resource management. This dimension may, for example, involve activities related to the integration of a team's youth academy players or selection of transfer players.

In the four fields of the framework, specific soccer business functions, including those of field management, are represented. For example, on-the-field functions include executing planned coaching strategies and playing styles, and ensuring that the individual responsibilities of players are met and their technical performances meet expectations. Off-the-field activities, for example, include developing marketing strategies that take into consideration the cognitive and emotional experience of soccer consumers during the match itself – the atmospherics (Gladden & Funk, 2002).

From a theoretical perspective, soccer business managers understand and embrace the Profit Impact of Marketing Strategy (PIMS) model, which states that to "do things right" equals "operational excellence". The PIMS model enables managers to use a dual approach, i.e. to use both rational decision-making and "out-of-the-box" marketing strategies to sustain a competitive advantage. This dual approach, from a PIMS perspective, normally accounts for 20 percent of the total effectiveness or performance of business enterprises (Buzzell & Gale, 1987).

"To do things right" may also be expressed in a soccer club's intended business strategy, which is synonymous with executing the "Business Idea".

This represents 80 percent of the total effectiveness or performance of business enterprises, according to PIMS. Eric Rhenman, founder of the Scandinavian Institute for Administrative Research, has interpreted the research results of the Institute in "Business Idea" theory (Rhenman, 1973). This theory is based on two elements: (1) the "harmonic mode of operation", meaning that all functions within an enterprise should support each other; and (2) the relationship between the mode of business operation and the external business environment, i.e., the market and opportunity needed for a successful business launch, or the market and competition needed for a financially successful soccer match.

Furthermore, there are a number of models that view the soccer club as a strategic entity (Szymanski & Kuypers, 1999). Smith and Stewart (2010, p. 2) identified four dimensions of sport that have an impact on its management and that are applicable to the management of soccer business worldwide. The first dimension considers that sport is a heterogeneous and temporary experience "mired in the irrational passions of fans and commanding high

1. Atmospherics (marketing)	**2. Match (product/event management)**
• **Level of emotion in the stadium – media, noise level, etc. and activity of fans** • **Journalists, photographers, TV, social media** • **The stadium as 'place' in the marketing mix** • **Point of purchase communications – displays, posters, digital signage, etc.**	• **The match is the institutionalized activity performed by the players, referees, and coaches** • **Support activities by team physician and staff.**
4. Business Planning and Management	**3. Coaching (human resource management)**
• **Based on current strategy** • **Competitor analysis** • **Marketing** • **Product development** • **Acquisitions** • **Organizational and leadership development** • **Financial competence** • **Players as business assets.**	• **The players practise as a team or individually based on long/short-term strategy** • **Developing and training of tactics and playing styles** • **Analysing competitors and adapting to variety** • **Developing team spirit (cooperation, integration).**

Figure 9.1 Managing soccer: a conceptual framework (adapted from Söderman, 2004)

levels of product and brand loyalty, optimism and vicarious identification". The second dimension considers that sport managers prefer on-field winning rather than business profit, while the third dimension considers that sport "is subject to variable quality, which in turn has implications for the management of competitive balance and anti-competitive behaviour". The fourth dimension considers that sport has to manage a "fixed supply schedule".

The concept of fixed supply is an important consideration when analyzing soccer club management strategies, because soccer managers are restricted to what economists have referred to as a "fixed short-run supply", or a highly inelastic production curve, sometimes referred to as Baumol's cost disease (Baumol & Bowen, 1966; Rich, 2012). The supply of the core product, the on-field soccer match, cannot be increased in the same manner that the manufacture of other products can be increased, for example, by simply increasing the speed of the assembly line. Therefore, regardless of the level of demand for the "on-field match" product, the number of matches and the capacity of the venue limit how many consumers are actually able to attend. However, when consumer demand is reduced, for whatever reason, the unsold tickets represent lost revenue because the match product cannot be stored and sold again at another time (Dolles & Söderman, 2008; Dolles & Söderman, 2013).

Formulation of the matrix

During the game, off the field: Atmospherics, marketing and promotion. The atmospherics within a specific sport venue are comprised of intended and unintended elements that elicit specific cognitive, emotional, and behavioral responses of primary consumers (spectators). The specific atmosphere created in a soccer stadium is based on multiple factors, for example, the operation of concessions, including the sale of souvenirs and licensed merchandise, the ambient noise level in the stadium, fan-generated posters, and fan activity such as waving banners, chanting, singing, use of mobile devices, and sponsors' activations, for example, signage or LED ribbon board displays. Atmospherics, therefore, may create a feeling of increased involvement on the part of fans and, concomitantly, increase their level of identification with the team or star players. Atmospherics and the in-stadium consumer experience may be more satisfying than the experience of fans consuming a soccer match via TV (secondary consumption) or via a second screen (computer or mobile device), or than the experience of fans consuming highlights of the match (tertiary consumption). The images of many focused, highly emotional, and energetic fans attending a soccer match may, in fact, result in additional consumers desiring to attend a match in person, or view a match on TV or their preferred second screen.

During the game, on the field: The match. This dimension of the matrix represents the core soccer product, which is the key factor in determining the level of financial success of a soccer club. From an executive leadership and management perspective, it represents placing the most effective soccer team on the field, with the maximum number of key players performing at their highest strategic and technical levels. It is assumed that all players on the field are well prepared and understand the tactics and playing style required for success in each specific match.

Collins and Porras (1997) discussed the ability to mediate negative backlash and consequences of a particular action as an element that distinguishes a successful enterprise. Soccer managers, for example, have the responsibility to select, evaluate, mentor, and possibly remove players from the team, not only because of a temporary or permanent inability to perform technically in a specific position or apparent negative attitude/behavior regarding the team or coach, but also because of a player's inability to perform effectively as a team member. Individual discipline, adherence to a specific style of play selected by the manager and adhering to the manager's instructions are critically important as the team members are required to execute an effective playing strategy during a match.

Between matches/seasons, on the field: Coaching, human resource management. Although Gomez, Kase, and Urrutia (2010, p. 2) suggest that a sport organization's strategy may represent different models and different results, they argue that four key dimensions must be taken into consideration for effective soccer club management: (1) the teams' managers, including all coaches on the team's payroll; (2) the composition of the team's roster, which is related to the team's signing policy; (3) the players' participation during the season; and (4) the team's results. In soccer, the quality of service (coaching as part of human resource management) provided to players should also be evaluated on a regular basis and improved when necessary. Activities on the field, before and after matches, are normally focused on match strategy preparation and review, and physical conditioning. In addition to providing skilled leadership regarding soccer strategy and the science of training, it is necessary for coaches to earn the respect of their players, which in many cases requires coaches to gain the confidence of players regarding the validity of their soccer skills, coaching techniques and match strategies.

Between matches/seasons, off the field: Business planning and management. It should be stressed that effective strategic management generally leads to achieving organizational objectives. If the PIMS research is valid, then 80 percent of the success of a company is associated with two of the dimensions in the model: *Atmospherics* and *Business Planning and Management*. One may initially ask what specific business and playing strategies lead to winning matches and eventually a league championship? As a playing strategy, for example, "to maintain possession of the ball within the team" can be an effective strategy in a highly competitive match environment. This type of playing strategy characterized the English Premier teams several years ago. Fulham FC, for example, was one of the teams that decided to "maintain possession of the ball within the team", which required a selection (management decisions) of players capable of executing that style of play (Soriano, 2011). Yet, successful soccer club management has proven to be much more than deciding on a particular "playing strategy". For a sport enterprise,

> it is not enough merely to have appropriately differentiated subunits to deal with its sub-environments. Because different managerial goals, time orientations, and interpersonal orientations exist in these subunits, there must also be the necessary level of integration to ensure that these subunits are working toward a common goal.
>
> (Slack, 1997, p. 139)

Therefore, soccer club managers must not only collaborate effectively with the team's coach to assure that the planned playing strategy will be implemented during the match, but must also consider strategic business plans as well as the short-term execution (Excellence in Operations) of soccer management (Jarosz, Kornakov, & Söderman, 2015) Thus, consideration must be taken of all the business activities that occur between matches and seasons as well as outside the stadium, such as marketing, contract negotiation with media and sponsors, acquisition of players via the transfer system or developing and managing youth academies, financial accounting and resource allocation, and managing investor relations. Only after addressing and managing these elements effectively can the platform for success in *The Match,* and ultimately the soccer industry, be assured.

Translating soccer management to business management. The four-dimensional framework, and the elements within each frame presented above, can be used to draw critical insights from the management of soccer that may also apply to business management. One key insight is directly related to preparation of (2) *The Match.* In the world of sport, and perhaps especially in soccer, there are instances when a greater proportion of the match result may be determined by chance rather than the coach's strategy and/or the players' technical skill. In preparation for the match, the two dimensions of Coaching (3) and Management (4) serve as determining factors for supporting the success in dimension (2) *The Match.* The phrase "to fail to prepare is to prepare to fail" is typified in soccer because, for example, when a team fails to practise and train sufficiently between matches it may be difficult to compete effectively during a match. Dimension (4) thus constitutes an acknowledgement of the importance of preparation in advance of the match. The two other dimensions, however, can be seen as key drivers. With regard to soccer, where training, for example, is a predetermined element, an understanding can be developed that is valuable for the business manager.

Today's global business environment is significantly more complex and less predictable when compared to the business environment of 20 years ago. This increased complexity has caused, at least in part, a shift away from traditional styles of management and toward enterprise thinking (Goldsmith, 2012). From this perspective, business is conceptualized as a network of complex adaptive systems, characterized by numerous interactions among various agents (employees, suppliers, customers, and competition) resulting in non-linear relationships between action and outcome (Decision Craft, 2005). The role of management in this complex environment, therefore, is to develop a viable, robust, adapting organization that is able to survive and prosper in an unknowable variety of future environments, sustained by several, but relatively simple principles and values, i.e. a 'harmonic mode of operation'.

In a highly competitive business environment, if management does not adapt to current environmental conditions or prepare sufficiently and execute effectively, the chances of success may be reduced significantly. One key element that is different, however, between soccer and business, is that business is continual, whereas a soccer match and a season are not. A match has temporal and spatial limitations, players are aware of the playing conditions, and it is assumed that players have the skills and abilities required to compete effectively. The business environment, on the other hand, is continual and dynamic, which requires constant learning and adaptation on the part of business enterprises, elucidated by the 'Business Idea' theory (Rhenman, 1973). It is the forward thinking and effective managers that most rapidly learn what must be accomplished and develop specific adaptations to changes in the business environment that have the best chance for success.

Soccer industry success factors – six imperatives

The process of benchmarking, since its emergence in the 1980s, has been used as a framework for researching best practices in a range of industries in an attempt to understand and improve performance (Böhlke, 2006; Camp, 1989). In the context of elite sport systems, the nature of research carried out to identify factors necessary to facilitate international success has similarities to or makes direct reference to the process of benchmarking (de Bosscher, Truyens, van Bottenburg, & Shibli, 2013; de Bosscher, de Knop, van Bottenburg, & Shibli, 2008; Green, 2007). Soccer is a multibillion-dollar sector of the global sport industry. However, the match, although essential, is only one of the components driving financial success in this sector. Based on the four-field matrix and its analysis, six imperatives (requirements) were developed in order to identify best practices in soccer management. These imperatives reflect important management insights from soccer that may benefit the decision-making process and strategy development of business managers.

The first imperative: Ensure immediate response and decision-making when appropriate. The frame of reference for this imperative is (2) *The Match.* Teams that are best prepared technically and sufficiently trained are more likely to adapt effectively to changes in playing conditions occurring on the field during a match. For example, an opponent's rapid change from one style or tempo of play to another is met by an immediate response, designed to address the threat and perhaps take advantage of the situation. This normally occurs with excellent soccer teams because they have developed and practised the immediate implementation of alternative strategies required to address a variety of on-field situations (threats) that may occur during a match.

For soccer, substituting a player during a match is one of the most important tasks required of a manager, who is the only "line manager" with that power. His decision, however, is based normally on the current playing strategy and conditions that also are understood generally by the entire team. A new on-field playing strategy can be initiated effectively and quickly because players are used to the fact that anything can happen during a match, and are prepared for it. An "immediate response" also may occur at the club or league management level. This "immediate response" may be related to a resource allocation and/or utilization issue that may not be limited to the level of soccer club management. An immediate change in strategy or quick adaptive decision can also be the prerogative of an entire soccer league or the national soccer association of a particular country. For example, 20 years ago when professional soccer in England and Wales faced declining attendance and shrinking revenues, soccer leaders created a brand for top-performing clubs: the Premier League. As a result of the formation of the Premier League, player wages and mobility, as well as the commercial capacity of teams and players, increased significantly. Clubs in the league focused on selling licensed merchandise, i.e. club shirts, memorabilia, and other accessories, through their own branded outlets (Needle, 2010). This pattern of an immediate response is typical of soccer because the objective of the "game" is to win by responding to the opposing team's playing strategy in an immediate and effective manner, and because there are only 90 minutes (minus time played) to execute a response effective enough to increase a team's probability of winning.

In business, a management misjudgement or a succession of rapid changes in the business environment may not always be addressed immediately, effectively, or in a timely manner. There may be no perceived urgency or threat, in part, because there is no structured temporal limitation as there is in a soccer match. In addition, management may not consider the change in the business environment to be significant enough to warrant an immediate response or they may be unaware of its potential impact. A business seldom changes its strategy or reorganizes its resources rapidly enough and, in some cases, managers consider (or hope) that negative situations or dynamic changes in the external environment will dissipate naturally, which may lead to "business cycle thinking". One management strategy taken directly from soccer involves developing alternative scenarios or virtuous circles that foresee necessary adaptations in the business plan and in resource allocation. Business managers can learn from a well-prepared soccer team about how to adapt their business operations more rapidly and effectively, perhaps as an immediate reaction to a competitor's unexpected move, a consumer's new need, a major paradigm shift in technology utilization or a rapid change in the external business environment due to political, economic or cultural factors.

The second imperative: Nurture your fan (or consumer) base. This imperative refers primarily to (1) Atmospherics. Most, if not all, European soccer clubs, regardless of their size or prestige, have one common similarity: A generally loyal consumer base made up of highly identifiable fans. Soccer consumers generally support their local, regional, and/or national clubs regardless of the outcome of matches or club standings. Highly identifiable fans, or "fanatics", constitute a significant asset for soccer teams (Bauer, Stokburger-Sauer, & Exler, 2005).

A detailed study of fan loyalty by Wann (1995) outlined the following eight key fan motives: eustress (positive stress), escape, entertainment, economic, aesthetic, group affiliation, family, and self-esteem. The aforementioned motives have a direct influence on the loyalty of fans toward a soccer club. The concept of loyalty in soccer was also examined more recently by Castillo who posited that loyalty in soccer exists on three different levels: 1) between players and fans; 2) between players and clubs; and 3) between fans and clubs, and that clubs use a variety of ways to enhance fan loyalty (Castillo, 2007). Highly identified fans spend more money on season tickets and licensed merchandise, and are more resilient when it comes to the team's win/loss record (performance outcome sensitivity) and to increases in ticket prices (decreased price sensitivity) (Gladden & Funk, 2002).

Technological advancements, especially digital media and social media, have provided opportunities for managers to create new strategies and platforms for marketing soccer clubs. A soccer club's website is a vital link in communicating important information, such as standings, statistics, schedules, photos, human interest stories, and updates regarding player transfers, etc. as well as providing opportunities for loyal fans to remain connected to the team off the field and between matches and seasons (Kapur, 2012). Similar to many other professional sport leagues worldwide, the English Premier League provides consumers with the opportunity to purchase licensed merchandise online, engage in blogs and discussions, and access video on demand. Consequently, the management decision to integrate digital media into a club's communication strategy has facilitated a team's ability to develop and maintain strong bonds with fans, especially using a selection of social network sites (SNS).

Although consumer loyalty and decreased price sensitivity are not necessarily benefits that accrue to business, with the development of SNS such as Facebook and Twitter, businesses worldwide are now able to mimic the long-established pattern of soccer clubs – staying connected to their consumer base – by integrating a variety of digital technologies and strategies into their business plans. Businesses have learned from soccer, and other successful sport leagues and teams, and are now creating integrated marketing communications (IMC) packages across multiple digital platforms in order to maintain strong connections with their consumers and provide them with the latest news about their products and services and obtain thorough and direct feedback via conversations on social media. By initiating IMC strategies, businesses are now able to enhance the consumer experience and maintain their loyalty.

The third imperative: Learn from the supreme organizer of symbiotic third-party interest. This imperative refers to (4) *Business Planning and Management* and (1) *Atmospherics*. Investment in local, regional, and national teams, as well as leagues and federations by third-party interests, primarily through sponsorship, has contributed to profitability for many soccer enterprises. Local, regional, and global brands often contribute a large percentage of the soccer enterprise's revenue via sponsorship (Demir & Söderman, 2015). Commercial sectors that have traditionally sponsored soccer include: automotive, alcoholic and non-alcoholic beverages, telecommunications, apparel, and finance (insurance and credit cards). Soccer sponsorship schemes enable brands to access millions of consumers worldwide through well-planned and implemented sponsorship activation strategies. Moreover, as more effective activation strategies are initiated, enhanced integration of digital platforms and SNS may lead to additional sponsors joining a soccer enterprise's "virtuous circle". As the symbiotic relationship between sponsoring brands and soccer strengthens, competence and confidence is developed and new partnerships among brands and clubs emerge (Liu, Srivastava, & Woo, 1998).

Another example of symbiotic development exists in the telecommunications industry. Telecommunication companies from different regions of the world sponsor European soccer. In the past, Vodafone was the shirt sponsor for Manchester United. Now, many telecom companies sponsor soccer clubs in order to gain access to their loyal consumers. Although there is a large European soccer fan base in the Middle East and United Arab Emirates, telecom companies in Saudi Arabia and Dubai have adopted a different approach to sponsorship. Instead of sponsoring soccer in their own geographical territories, these companies are making full use of the global popularity of the dominant European soccer clubs. Saudi Telecom Company now sponsors clubs such as Real Madrid and Manchester United (Real Madrid Soccer Club, 2016; Manchester United Soccer Club, 2016). Similarly, Etisalat, the largest telecom company in Dubai, is the regional sponsor of FC Barcelona (2016). In addition to these new sponsorships, television broadcasts generate significant advertising revenues on match days before, during, and post-match.

What symbiotic partnership models exist outside the world of sport? Savvy business managers look for channel partners, develop networks, and are open for new business contacts and contracts because they are thinking synergistically. How can business managers foresee future patterns and networks and explore new opportunities in the same way that soccer managers do? One industry which has sought to leverage European soccer's rising popularity is the automotive industry. Audi has sponsored numerous soccer clubs in Europe and has now replaced Volkswagen as the automobile sponsor of US-based Major League Soccer (Major League Soccer, 2016; Long, 2015). Global brands leverage association with sport brands worldwide by using co-branding as well as traditional marketing strategies.

The fourth imperative: Make it a rule to develop young, talented managers. This imperative is linked to the human resource management element of (3) *Coaching*: In the soccer world "potential" ability carries significant importance, and not only with the increased value of a club's brand. Young, talented players are often provided with opportunities to develop and demonstrate their skills within the development academies of many of soccer's top- and mid-level teams (European Club Association, 2012). A prominent example is Argentinean Lionel Messi, who is now one of the highest-paid soccer players in the world. Messi earned £29.7 million in 2009 and replaced David Beckham as the world's highest-paid player in 2010 (Gray, 2010). Both players learned their skills at soccer youth academies. Cristiano Ronaldo, a Real Madrid player, now ranks No. 1 on the list of the world's highest-paid players. "He banked US$79 million last year in salary, bonus and endorsements – a sum that also makes him the highest-paid team athlete in the world" (Settimi, 2016, p. 1).

Soccer clubs search continually for young players with high potential and clubs normally have numerous scouts in different regions of the world informing the coaches and team management regarding potentially highly skilled players. Some individuals who have contributed to the development of excellent soccer players continue to benefit from their potential stars. Zlatan Ibrahimovic, who received his soccer education at Malmö FF, refers in interviews to the excellence of this club. Interestingly, Malmö FF continues to receive a small share of every transfer fee that he makes throughout his career.

Management consultants, such as McKinsey and Bain, are known for hiring the best young graduates directly from universities throughout the world, even with no guarantee that they will remain with the company for an extended period of time. Procter & Gamble offers attractive incentive programs to senior management for mentoring and maintaining the company's best young professionals.

> Elite professional service firms are a fertile ground for analysing cultural similarities in hiring. Entry-level professional positions typically require a prestigious university credential, and these employers solicit the majority of applications directly through university career centers rather than through informal networks.
>
> (Rivera, 2012, p. 1003)

However, forward thinking companies have adopted a positive approach toward developing young talent. In this regard their in-house "graduate programs", similar in a way to a soccer club's youth academy, contribute toward positive change in hiring practices. Rivera (2012, p. 1017) argues that "hiring is more than a process of skills sorting; it is also a process of cultural matching between candidates, evaluators and firms".

The fifth imperative: The reward system should be directly related to performance. This imperative is related to (4) *Business Planning and Management.* Soccer managers worldwide understand that high-level soccer talent is expensive and that there are certain benefits accruing to the organization for rewarding and recognizing the excellence of its players. Clubs that have an effective reward system in place tend to enjoy more success than counterparts who do not. A study by Sporting Intelligence focused on the average annual salaries of 272 teams in 14 major leagues across seven different sports being played in ten different countries. The results put European soccer on top of the list with FC Barcelona paying the highest average annual salary per player (US$7,910,737) and the highest average weekly salary per player (US$152,130). Real Madrid occupied the second spot with the US-based New York Yankees (Major League Baseball) third, Los Angeles Lakers (National Basketball Association [NBA]) fourth and Orlando Magic (NBA) fifth (Harris, 2011). The wage scale of a club is an important issue because players want to be associated with clubs that have comprehensive compensation packages. In addition, a club that compensates managers well will normally attract competent and effective leadership.

It is also advantageous for businesses to adopt certain salary and benefit practices similar to those in soccer. For example, bonuses for top performers may motivate other employees to improve their performances or productivity. Similarly, through the introduction of "employee referral programs", employees can further increase their income and certainly, stock options remain a viable option. With this condition, businesses worldwide are now providing extensive and complex bonus and incentive programs. If soccer, on the other hand, were to adopt similar programs, compensation could, in theory, be based on such factors as: (1) goals scored in championship games; (2) time of goals scored during a match (early versus late); (3) match-winning goals scored; and (4) the length of time a player controlled the ball during a match.

The sixth imperative: Genuine and virtual globalization. This imperative is related to (1) *Atmospherics* and (4) *Business Planning and Management.*

European soccer is a global phenomenon facilitated by significant contributions from international media corporations, sponsorship agreements with global brands, mega events such as the FIFA World Cup, and the rapid adoption of digital technologies and social media marketing. The desire of soccer clubs to: hire the best international talent; close lucrative television broadcasting deals; design highly interactive websites, developed to engage consumers; establish licensed merchandise retail outlets; appoint diverse management teams consisting of key members from different countries; and organize a variety of competitions, has boosted the sport's global reach. Apparently, the sport knows no boundaries, as sponsorship and merchandising deals are struck across borders worldwide.

Brand and sponsorship issues play a major role in the marketing strategies of professional sport teams as a strong sport brand leads to consumer trust and loyalty, which often results in higher team revenues. Additionally, a strong brand has positive effects with actual and potential exchange partners that help achieve the brand's goals. Though they may be strongly rooted in their local community, soccer clubs increasingly aim at developing international operations and building global brands. The proliferation of information technology and social media has made it possible to serve the needs of fans as well as corporate consumers worldwide. In this context, the opportunities for the promotion of corporate sponsors, and the benefits for soccer and its partners, are significant. Businesses can learn from the combination of various methods used by soccer clubs to conduct branding efforts that consequently result in a truly global following.

Discussion

Mainstream academic literature often suggests that sport should be studied in specialist niches on the basis that it is "not generalizable" or "transferable" to other academic disciplines. Indeed, sport does have a number of distinctive characteristics, specifically marketing and finance, which may influence the way in which it is managed, governed, and globalized. Soccer clubs and leagues have emerged as global assets due to strong commercial development, international expansion, and cross-cultural integration. While there are certainly numerous analogies related to soccer and business (Söderman, 2013) a significant difference between business and soccer is the relative importance of profit and ROI for business versus the "relative" preference for winning and on-field success for soccer. While it is clear that winning is paramount in professional sport, there is a growing recognition that high-level entertainment attracts "revenue and profits" and that resources that attract private equity, for example, are all key to successful performance. Moreover, there is clear evidence that in soccer, winning is also the fastest route to profitability. This means that it is no longer a case of either entertainment or revenue/profit, but it appears both are important and necessary. Both aims could be met through a management strategy of "do the right things", which builds a strong platform of quality resources from which to sustain a high win–loss ratio (Smith & Stewart, 2010).

The Managing Soccer Conceptual Framework, while contributing to understanding soccer management, is not meant to be all-inclusive. The two key dimensions of the matrix focus on time and spatial elements. Time-related elements signify activities that take place during and between games, such as coaching and training, team coordination and performance, and in this element, management planning plays a crucial role. Spatial elements describe activities taking place on and off the playing field, such as the creation of in-venue atmospherics and match dynamics. It can also be noted that in addition to in-venue atmospherics, the recent creation of fan zones for league and international competitions has also emphasized the importance of atmospherics in generating fan loyalty and additional revenue. Business management, depending on industry characteristics, encounters more or less similar challenges. By considering the "Managing Soccer Conceptual Framework" and the subsequent six imperatives as a tool for interpretation and insight, new management/enterprise thinking across other business sectors and industries may be triggered.

Soccer is an almost effortlessly globalized sport. Fans of English and Spanish soccer clubs, for example, can be found in the most remote parts of the world. The main forces behind globalization are focused marketing strategies by clubs and leagues, advances in technology, especially HD TV, and streaming on mobile devices. English clubs regularly visit Asia, and thus seek to constantly establish new connections with the Asian consumer market. African players play in English and Spanish leagues and inspire a teenage following in their home countries. Businesses can learn from the combination of various methods used by soccer clubs to conduct branding efforts, which consequently result in a truly global following. An ideal strategy for any business manager would be to explore the imperatives mentioned above and create a strategic roadmap that takes the best practices of soccer into consideration, wherever applicable, and at small incremental levels that can provide radically positive results. Although the six imperatives should not be regarded as conclusive, they might be useful and revealing as insights into the nature of a complex business environment in transition.

In retrospect, it is clear that managing elite soccer clubs is a complex process that requires solid theoretical and practical perspectives to understand completely. It is perhaps more akin to managing an elite theatre or ballet group rather than, for example, a globally recognized technology company. Regardless of the nature of the organization, there are certain management strategies and practices in common. Therefore, it was our purpose to elucidate some of these common elements and discuss how they may benefit soccer clubs, companies, and stakeholders. While the chapter was not intended to create or contribute to a grand theory of managing soccer or business, it did stay true to the abductive methodology (and the theoretical/practical dialectic), which infers a case from a rule and a result. However, the key to using the abductive method and the benefit that we see is that it is a process for gaining new knowledge.

References

Alvesson, M., & Sköldberg, K. (2009). *Reflexive Methodology: New Vistas for Qualitative Research.* London: Sage.

Bauer, H., Stokburger-Sauer, N., & Exler, S. (2005). The Loyalty of German Football Fans: Does a Team's Brand Image Matter? *International Journal of Sports Marketing & Sponsorship,* **7** *(1),* 14–22.

Baumol, W. J., & Bowen, W. G. (1966). *Performing Arts: The Economic Dilemma: A Study of Problems Common to the Theater, Opera, Music and Dance.* New York, NY: The 20th Century Fund.

Beech, J., Horsman, S.J.L., & Magraw, J. (2010). Insolvency Events Among English Football Clubs. *International Journal of Sports Marketing & Sponsorship, 11(3),* 236–49.

Bolchover, D., & Brady, C. (2004). *The 90-minute Manager: Lessons From the Sharp End of Management* (Revised edn). Harlow, Great Britain: Pearson.

Bridgewater, S. (2010). *Football Management.* Hampshire, UK: Palgrave Macmillan.

Breul, J. D. (2011). *Seven Management Imperatives.* IBM Center for the Business of Government. Retrieved from www.businessofgovernment.org.

Burnes, B., & O'Donnel, H. (2011). What can Business Leaders Learn from Sport? *Sport, Business and Management: An International Journal, 1(1),* 12–27.

Buzzell, R., & Gale, B. (1987). *PIMS Principles: Linking Strategy to Performance.* New York, NY: Macmillan.

Böhlke, N. (2006). Benchmarking of Elite Sport Systems. Unpublished doctoral thesis, University of Loughborough, Loughborough, England.

Camp, R. (1989). *Benchmarking – The Search for Industry Best Practices that Leads to Superior Performance.* Milwaukee, WI: Quality.

Castillo, J. C. (2007). The Concept of Loyalty and the Challenge of Internationalization in Postmodern Spanish Football. *International Journal of Iberian Studies, 20(1),* 23–40.

Chadwick, S. (2009). From Outside Lane to Inside Track: Sport Management Research in the Twenty-first Century. *Management Decision, 47(1),* 191–203.

CNN. (2012, June 15). Sky Coughs up Big for Football. *CNN.* Retrieved from http://business.blogs.cnn.com/2012/06/15/what-recession-sky-coughs-up-big-for-football/.

Collins, J., & Porras, J. (1997). *Built to Last: Successful Habits of Visionary Companies.* New York, NY: Harper Business.

Cousens, L., & Slack, T. (2005). Field-level Change: The Case of North American Major League Professional Sport. *Journal of Sport Management, 19(1),* 13–42.

Crane, F.G. (2004). The Teaching of Business Ethics: An Imperative at Business Schools. *Journal of Education for Business, 79(3),* 149–51.

Daily, C. M., & Dalton, D. R. (2003). Women in the Boardroom: A bBusiness Imperative. *Journal of Business Strategy, 24(5),* 1–15.

de Bosscher, V., de Knop, P., van Bottenburg, M., & Shibli, S. (2008). *The Global Sporting Arms Race.* Oxford, UK: Meyer & Meyer Sport.

de Bosscher, V., Truyens, J., van Bottenburg, M., & Shibli, S. (2013). Comparing Apples with Oranges in International Elite Sport Studies: Is it Possible? In S. Söderman and H. Dolles (Eds.), *Handbook of Research on Sport and Business*, Aldershot, UK: Edward Elgar.

Decision Craft. (2005, July 18). Managing Complexity. *Decisioncraft.com.* Retrieved from www.decisioncraft.com/dmdirect/complexity.htm.

Deloitte. (2015, June 4). Annual Review of Football Finance. *Deloitte.* Retrieved from www2.deloitte.com/se/sv/footerlinks/pressreleasespage/annual-review-of-football-finance-2015.html.

Demir, R., & Söderman, S. (2015). Strategic Sponsoring in Professional Sport – A Review and Conceptualization. *European Sport Management Quarterly, 15(3)*, 271–300.

Dibben, M., & Dolles, H. (2013). Participant Observation in Sport Management Research: Collecting and Interpreting Data of a Successful World Landspeed Record Attempt. In S. Söderman and H. Dolles (Eds.), *Handbook of Research on Sport and Business* (pp. 418–32). Cheltenham, UK: Edward Elgar Publishing.

Dolles, H., & Söderman, S. (2005). Globalisation of Sports – The Case of Professional Football and its International Management Challenges. *Deutches Institut Fur Japanstudien.* Retrieved from www.dijtokyo.org/publications/WP05_1GlobalizationOfSportsProfessionalFootballDollesSoederman.pdf.

Dolles, H., & Söderman, S. (2008). The Network of Value Captures: Creating Competitive Advantage in Football Management. *Wirtschaftspolitische Blätter Österreich* [Austrian Economic Policy Papers], *55(1)*, 39–58.

Dolles, H., & Söderman, S. (2013). The Network of Value Captures in Football Club Management: A Framework to Develop and Analyze Competitive Advantage in Professional Team Sports. In S. Söderman and H. Dolles (Eds.), *Handbook of Research on Sport and Business* (pp. 367–95). Cheltenham, UK: Edward Elgar Publishing.

Dubois, A., & Gadde, L. E. (2002). Systematic Combining: An Abductive Approach to Case Research. *Journal of Business Research, 55(7)*, 553–60.

ESPNFC. (2016, April 13). La Liga will Give Clubs Financial Ratings to Attract Investors. *ESPNFC.us.* Retrieved from www.espnfc.us/spanish-primera-division/story/2849706/la-liga-will-give-clubs-financial-ratings-for-transparency.

European Club Association. (2012). Report on Youth Academies in Europe. *European Club Association.* Retrieved from www.ecaeurope.com.

FC Barcelona. (2016). Sponsors. *FC Barcelona.com.* Retrieved from www.fcbarcelona.com/club/sponsors.

Foster, G., Greyser, S. A., & Walsh, B. (2006). *The Business of Sports: Cases and Text on Strategy and Management.* Scarborough, Canada: Nelson Education.

Gammelsaeter, H., & Senaux, B., (Eds.). (2011). *The Organisation and Governance of Top Football Across Europe: An Institutional Perspective.* New York, NY: Routledge.

Gilmore, J. H., & Pine II, B. J. (2007). *Authenticity: What Consumers Really Want.* Boston, MA: Harvard Business School.

Gladden, J. M., & Funk, D. C. (2002). Developing an Understanding of Brand Associations in Team Sport: Empirical Evidence from Consumers of Professional Sport. *Journal of Sport Management, 16(1)*, 54–81.

Goldsmith, D. (2012). *Enterprise Thinking and Rethinking: Paid to Think.* Dallas, TX: BenBella.

Gomez, S., Kase, K., & Urrutia, I. (2010). *Value Creation and Sport Management.* Cambridge, UK: Cambridge University Press.

Gratton, C., & Solberg, H. A. (2013). The Economics of Listed Sports Events in a Digital Era of Broadcasting: A Case Study of the UK. In S. Söderman and H. Dolles (Eds.), *Handbook of Research on Sport and Business* (pp. 202–18). Cheltenham, UK: Edward Elgar Publishing.

Gray, A. (2010, March 24). David Beckham Toppled by Lionel Messi as Barcelona Star Leads Football Earner Charts on £570,000 a Week. *Daily Mail Online.* Retrieved from www.dailymail.co.uk/sport/football/article-1260076/David-Beckham-toppled-Lionel-Messi-Barcelona-star-tops-football-earner-charts-570-000-week.html.

Green, M. (2007). Olympic Glory or Grassroots Development? Sport Policy Priorities in Australia, Canada and the UK 1960–2006. *International Journal of the History of Sport, 24(7),* 921–53.

Gregson, J. (2010). The Business of Football: What Business can Learn from Football. *The Wall Street Journal.* Retrieved from http://online.wsj.com/ad/article/businessoffootball-management.html.

Harris, N. (2009, February 7). So, is Football Recession-proof? *Independent.* Retrieved from www.independent.co.uk/sport/football/news-and-comment/nick-harris-so-is-football-recessionproof-1569578.html.

Harris, N. (2011, April 20). 200 Best-paying Teams in the World. *ESPN The Magazine/Sporting Intelligence Global Salary Survey.* Retrieved from http://espn.go.com/espn/news/story?id=6354899.

Hong, F., & Zhou, X. L. (2013). The Professionalisation and Commercialisation of Football in China (1993–2013). *The International Journal of the History of Sport, 30(14),* 1637–54.

Jarosz, O., Kornakov, K., & Söderman, S. (2015). *2015 ECA Club Management Guide.* Nyon, Switzerland: European Club Association.

Josephson, J., & Josephson, S. (1996). *Abductive Inference: Computation, Philosophy, Technology.* Cambridge, UK: Cambridge University Press.

Kapur, V. (2012, February 16). Gulf Money, Fans Make Football Clubs Recession-proof. *Emirates 24/7.com.* Retrieved from www.emirates247.com/business/gulf-money-fans-make-football-clubs-recession-proof-2012-02-16-1.443373.

Liang, Y. (2014). The Development Pattern and a Club's Perspective on Football Governance in China. *Soccer and Society, 15(3),* 430–48.

Liu, J., Srivastava, A., & Woo, S. O. (1998). Transference of Skills Between Sports and Business. *Journal of European Industrial Training, 22(3),* 93–112.

Long, M. (2015, March 5). Report: Audi to Replace VW as MLS Auto Partner. *Sportspromedia.com.* Retrieved from www.sportspromedia.com/news/report_audi_to_replace_vw_as_mls_auto_partner.

Major League Soccer. (2016). Sponsors. *Major League Soccer.* Retrieved from www.mlssoccer.com/sponsors.

Manchester United Football Club. (2016). Official Partners. *Manchester United.com.* Retrieved from www.manutd.com/en/Partners/Global-Partners.aspx.

Mauws, M., Mason, D. S., & Foster, W. M. (2003). Thinking Strategically About Professional Sports. *European Sport Management Quarterly, 3(3),* 145–64.

Menguc, B., & Ozanne, L. K. (2005). Challenges of the "Green Imperative": A Natural Resource-based Approach to the Environmental Orientation-business Performance Relationship. *Journal of Business Research, 58(4),* 430–38.

Moore, N., & Levermore, R. (2012). English Professional Football Clubs: Can Business Parameters of Small and Medium-sized Enterprises be Applied? *Sport, Business Management: An International Journal, 2(3)*, 196–209.

Morrow, S. (2003). *The People's Game – Football, Finance and Society*. Hampshire, UK: Palgrave Macmillan.

Needle, D. (2010). *Business in Context: An Introduction to Business and its Environment*. London, UK: Thomson Learning.

Olson, P. (2010, April 23). The World's Most Recession-proof Sport. *Forbes*. Retrieved from www.forbes.com/forbes/2010/0510/companies-soccer-valuations-manchester-united-recession-proof-sport.html.

O'Reilly, N. (2013). Portfolio Theory and the Management of Professional Sports Clubs: The Case of Maple Leaf Sports and Entertainment. In S. Söderman and H. Dolles (Eds.), *Handbook of Research on Sport and Business*. Cheltenham, UK: Edward Elgar Publishing.

Pearson Education Limited. (2008). *Longman Dictionary of Contemporary English*. Essex, UK: Pearson Longman.

Porter, M. E. (1991). Towards a Dynamic Theory of Strategy. *Strategic Management Journal, 12*, 95–117.

Real Madrid Football Club. (2016). Sponsors. *Real Madrid Football Club*. Retrieved from www.realmadrid.com/en/about-real-madrid/the-club/sponsors.

Rhenman, E. (1973). *Organization Theory for Long Range Planning*. Hertfordshire, UK: John Wiley.

Rich, D. J. (2012). Baumol's Disease in America. *Megatrend Review, 9(1)*, 97–106. Retrieved from www.megatrendreview.com/files/articles/016/07.pdf.

Richelieu, A., & Pons, F. (2006). Toronto Maple Leafs vs. Football Club Barcelona: How Two Legendary Sports Teams Built their Brand Equity. *International Journal of Sport Marketing & Sponsorship*, **7***(3)*, 231–51.

Rivera, L. A. (2012). Hiring as Cultural Matching: The Case of Elite Professional Service Firms. *American Sociological Review, 77(6)*, 999–1022.

Schwartz, F. N. (1992). Women as a Business Imperative. *Harvard Business Review, 70(2)*, 105–13.

Settimi, C. (2016, May 11). Cristiano Ronaldo, Lionel Messi Top the World's Highest Paid Soccer Players. *Forbes*. Retrieved from www.forbes.com/sites/christinasettimi/2015/05/06/cristiano-ronaldo-edges-lionel-messi-as-the-worlds-highest-paid-soccer-player/.

Skille, E. Å. (2013). Case Study Research in Sport Management – A Reflection Upon the Theory of Science and an Empirical Example. In S. Söderman and H. Dolles (Eds.), *Handbook of Research on Sport and Business* (pp. 161–75). Cheltenham, UK: Edward Elgar Publishing.

Slack, T. (1997). *Understanding Sport Organizations: The Application of Organization Theory*. Champaign, IL: Human Kinetics.

Smith, A., & Stewart, B. (2010). The Special Features of Sport: A Critical Revisit. *Sport Management Review, 13*, 1–13.

Söderman, S. (2004). Perspectives on Sport Management (in Swedish). In *On Sport Economics* (pp. 188–225). Stockholm, Switzerland: SISU Sports.

Söderman, S. (2013). *Football and Management – Comparisons Between Sport and Enterprise*. Basingstoke, UK: Palgrave Macmillan.

Soriano, F. (2011). *Goal: The Ball Doesn't Go In By Chance: Management Ideas from the World of Football*. Basingstoke, UK: Palgrave Macmillan.

SportsBusiness Daily Global, (2016, April 1). La Liga's Financial Situation Continues to Improve Thanks to TV Revenue. *Sportsbusinessdaily.com*. Retrieved from www.sportsbusinessdaily.com/Global/Issues/2016/04/01/Finance/La-Liga.aspx.

Szymanski, S., & Kuypers, T. (1999). *Winners and Losers: The Business Strategy of Football*. London: Viking.

The Economist. (2012, May 16). German Football Success: A League Apart. *The Economist*. Retrieved from www.economist.com/blogs/gametheory/2012/05/german-football-success.

The Guardian. (2015, June 5). Football League Increases Penalty for Clubs Entering Administration. *The Guardian*. Retrieved from www.theguardian.com/football/2015/jun/05/football-league-penalty-administration.

Van Maanen, J., Södersen J. P., & Mitchell T. R. (2007). The Interplay Between Theory and Method. *Academy of Management Review, 32(4)*, 1145–54.

Wann, D. (1995). Preliminary Validation of the Sport Fan Motivation Scale. *Journal of Sport and Social Issues, 19(4)*, 377–96.

Chapter 10

A symbiosis analysis of stakeholder relationships in the Chinese professional football league

Tao Yang, Cuixia Yi, Kun Zhang, Luxiang Cui, and Tyreal Yizhou Qian

Introduction

It has been 22 years since China initiated the professionalization of its football. Riding on the waves of controversies, Chinese professional football has come a long way over the years of ups and downs, but still finds itself susceptible to illegal gambling, match fixing, and football-related violence. Similar to the tourism industry, the stakeholders of Chinese professional football, despite existing interdependently, motivated by diverse agendas and objectives, possess differing roles and positions in the allocation of limited resources. As a result, conflicts and discords emerge and accumulate, resulting in the need for reconciliation and coordination (Song, 2003; Ji & Chen, 2009). Due to the idiosyncratic behaviors and traits in the professionalization process of Chinese football, it is of great significance to establish an equitable participation and distribution mechanism and a harmonious relationship between the shareholders so that the balance of interests can be reached, and therefore forming a stable and reciprocal symbiotic system (Ji & Chen, 2009).

Moreover, in the wake of an anti-corruption campaign and the implementation of State Council document No. 46, Development of Sports Industry and Promoting Sports Consumption, followed by the issuance of Chinese Football Reform and Development Program and the staggering eight billion RMB CSL media contract, the importance placed on and the attention received in Chinese football fully display the challenges and opportunities presented in the further professionalization of Chinese football. Echoed by economist Wu Jinglian who suggested "governing system is more important than technology in the market economy", the present study, through the lenses of the symbiosis theory and the stakeholder theory, attempts to systematically delve into the relationships between the stakeholders of CSL at different professionalization stages. Discussions and managerial implications with respect to the symbiosis model are consequently presented with an aim to provide suggestions and insights for the sustainable development of Chinese professional football.

Review of literature

Stakeholder theory

Introduced by Stanford Research Institute in the 1960s, stakeholder theory stemmed from the endeavor to maximize the business interests of corporate shareholders. An ample body of theoretical and empirical knowledge contributed by Ansoff (1965), Clarkson (1994), Freeman (1984), Mitchell et al. (1997), Rowley (1997) has greatly advanced and prompted stakeholder theory to be widely accepted in the management and economics literature (Cai, Tian, & Feng, 2009). In addition, researchers also devote significant attention to the theoretical development of stakeholder theory in other areas such as ethics, law, and sociology, however, among which, corporations/firms have constantly been the focal subject of interest. It was not until after the 1990s that the research subject shifted and expanded to government, community, city, social groups, as well as relevant political, economic, and social environments.

According to Freeman's classic definition, corporate stakeholders are the individuals or the groups that can either influence a firm's achievement of goals and objectives, or otherwise be influenced by a firm's achievement of goals and objectives. These individuals or groups often encompass employees, customers, suppliers, business partners, government, the general public, etc., defining stakeholders in a broad sense (Freeman, 1984; Jia & Chen, 2002). Furthermore, stakeholder theory posits that the assets of a firm are not only from shareholders but also from employees, suppliers, creditors, and customers, who make special investments in human resources, and a firm is not simply a conglomerate of tangible assets but an "institutional arrangement of the governance and the management of specialized investments" (Chen & Liu, 2011). More recently, Mitchell et al. (1997) propose a typology of stakeholders based on the attributes of power, legitimacy, and urgency, thus separate seven stakeholder classes into three groups – latent stakeholders (one attribute), definitive stakeholders (two attributes), and expectant stakeholders (all three attributes) (Freeman, 1984). This explicitly demonstrates the dynamism of corporate stakeholders given different temporal and environmental conditions under which types of stakeholders are interchangeable.

CSL stakeholder relationship model

Drawing on supply chain management theory, specifically, the dyadic relationship between supply and demand, CSL, being a sophisticated project, possesses a considerable number of stakeholders and operates under a complicated and interlaced supply chain network. The stakeholders of CSL are the individuals and groups that can influence or be influenced by CSL, including the government, the Chinese Football Association (CFA), the Chinese Football Association Super League (the biggest shareholding firm of CSL), the Professional Football League (PFL, which consists of 16 professional football clubs), media, sponsors, investors, suppliers, spectators, community, and the like.

Figure 10.1 shows CSL is a multi-stakeholder system in which stakeholders exist interdependently and are subject to mutual interaction and restriction.

Professional sports leagues are market-oriented and profit-driven social entities by providing entertainment and related products to consumers (Wang, 2007). Considering the Chinese professional football has already met the prerequisite of a professional sports league, it is necessary for the present study to subsume the 16 professional football clubs under the concept of Professional Football League (PFL). More importantly, as evidenced by the success of European Union football leagues and the four major American professional sports leagues (NFL, NBA, MLB, and NHL), the experience of these prototypical professional sports leagues are conducive to the professionalization of Chinese football (Liu, Sun, & Tao, 2009).

Symbiosis theory

The idea of symbiosis was first proposed by the German biologist Heinrich Anton de Bary in 1879, and subsequently developed and refined by Famintsim and Prototaxis, who referred to symbiosis as the relationship in which different organisms exist and evolve with, or inhibit one another (Ahmdajina, 1986; Wang & Bao, 2012). Currently, an increasing number

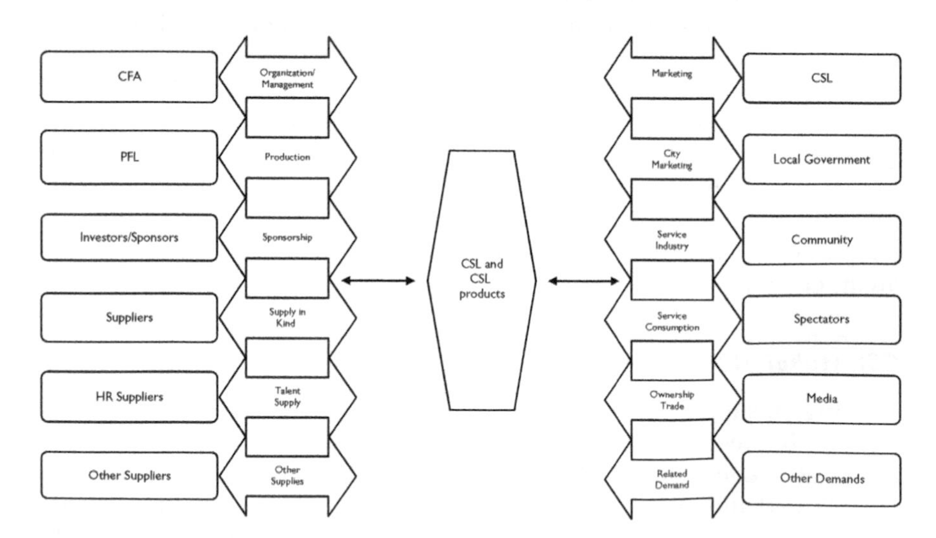

Figure 10.1 The CSL stakeholder relationship model

of scholars have utilized symbiosis as an important source for innovation (Wang, Tan, & Xu, 2006). Since the 1950s, the domain of symbiosis theory has gradually spanned to other areas such as philosophy, sociology, and economics. It is worth noting that the mutual penetration of natural science and social science as well as the application of symbiosis theory in sociology and economics provide concrete theoretical foundation for the study of the stakeholders of CSL. So far, the majority of symbiosis theory in sociology research focuses on the systematic analysis between two symbiotic units; however, with a growing body of literature on this topic, it is predictable that future research will be conducted to describe and analyze the relationship between at least three symbiotic units.

To understand symbiosis theory from the biological perspective, it is important to identify the four fundamental factors of the phenomenon, namely, symbiotic unit, the foundation; symbiotic model, the internal interaction or combination of the units; symbiotic environment, the external influential factors outside of the units; and symbiotic interface, the medium for the interactions of the former factors (Liu, Sun, & Tao, 2009). In line with symbiosis theory, PFL places tremendous emphasis on competition and cooperation between 16 professional clubs in order to produce a high quality product and ensure the sustainability of the clubs and the league. Essentially, PFL is a highly symbiotic system of interest. Through the production and marketing of the games, interests of different stakeholders are addressed, therefore making symbiosis the driving force behind Chinese professional football league (Zhou & Li, 2010). For PFL, the participating associations, organizations, and firms/clubs are the basic symbiotic units, which comprise the homogeneous symbiotic units, i.e., the professional clubs, as well as the heterogeneous symbiotic units, i.e., media, firms, clubs, and the football association; institutional and market environments are the symbiotic environment for PFL, including the social economic system, football development policy, sport market resources, etc.; cooperation and operation model of PFL is the symbiotic model, that is, parasitism, commensalism, and mutualism, among which the last one is the most stable and sustainable model; market, hence, is the symbiotic interface for PFL.

Analyses and discussion

Relationship of major CSL stakeholders

Given that the sport system fails to keep pace with the reform of the economic system, Chinese football, subject to planned administration, still has a long way to realize its professionalization. Nevertheless, while the professionalization and the reform of the Chinese football continues to deepen in an orderly manner, the relationships between stakeholders are increasingly susceptible to adjustments and transformations, reaching a balance at both supply and demand ends. Under certain environments and conditions, stakeholders facilitate the synthesis of supply and demand. In a sense, CSL is an administrative professional sports league, or in other words, administrative monopolistic professional sports league, which is a management model characterized by a quasi-government element where the administrative department and government sport association (management center) organize and manage the professional sports, and professional sports clubs participate in the league (Li & Yuan, 2006) (Table 10.1).

The following section presents the Chinese professional football league at different professionalization stages:

1 Pseudo-professional stage: Players of professional football clubs mainly came from provincial and municipal football teams and were affiliated with regional sport bureaus; there were 12 clubs playing in the Jia A League from the 1994 to 1997, and this number expanded to 14 in 1998; FMC employed administrative instructions on the league, blocking the transfer channel of the players.
2 Semi-professional stage: Players did not solely come from provincial or municipal sports school but also club reserves; of those players, some were still affiliated with regional sport bureau while the rest were under professional clubs; there were 17 clubs in 2004, the birth year of CSL; at the same time, clubs began to focus more on profitability and market operation, whereas FMC faced increased challenges; the market economy started to be dominant.
3 Professional stage: Currently there are 16 professional football clubs with a even more diverse talent pool; players are independent legal entities; transfers are now legally protected, facilitated, and streamlined; FMC launches its own football league, while CFA becomes the supervisory and managing institution of CSL, transitioning to a complete market-driven and service-based organization; government and football associations at different levels strive to provide a favorable symbiotic environment for the development of professional football via policies and systems.

Authorized by the Chinese government, the General Administration of Sport of China (GASC) organizes, supervises, and develops sports in China. The vertical governing relationship, known as "tiaotiao", and the horizontal administrative relationship, known as "kuaikuai", constitutes the Chinese sport administrative system, causing a significant amount of unnecessary administrative procedures and bureaucratic red tape (Yang, 2011). On the other hand, CFA and FMC, authorized by GASC, act as agents of the development of Chinese football. There was an latent principal-agent relationship between FMC and the professional football clubs, especially in the Jia A League era under a planned economy; ostensibly,

Table 10.1 Overview of the history of the Chinese professional football league

League Title	*Time*	*Stage of Professionalization*	*Managing Organization*	*Operation Mechanism*	*Feature*
Jia A League	1994–2003	Early professional stage: pseudo-professional stage	Football Management Center (FMC), Chinese Football Association (CFA)	Primarily driven by planned economy	Administrative sports league
Chinese Super League (CSL)	2004–15	Developing stage: semi-professional	FMC, CFA	Primarily driven by market economy	Administrative sports league
	2016 to date	Mature stage: professional	CFA	Completely driven market economy	Service-orientated sports league

this link marks an innovation in the system with respect to the society-building and resource-sharing between the state and the society in an effort to further advance the development of football and expand the football market. Each professional club is in fact an agent and promotes football at different levels by assuming and sharing the responsibility of provincial and municipal sports bureaus.

As shown in Table 10.2, the early stage of Chinese football professionalization witnessed a commensalistic relationship between the Chinese government, GASC, CFA, CFA, and the professional clubs. Club rights restriction, withdrawal of investors and sponsors, club name changing, and club ownership transfer were commonly seen during this period. However, as professionalization of the Chinese football continues to progress, a complete market-oriented professional league, as well as a service-oriented government and associations will be established, thus transforming the relationship between CFA and the clubs into mutualism in the mature stage.

CFA, CSL, and the CSL clubs. To foster an open, diversified, and orderly professional football market, CSL was founded with CFA holding 36 percent of the share with the 16 clubs holding the rest (each club holds four percent). Its main functions include integrating overall resources, exploring CSL operation, and event business development, such as intellectual property development, event marketing, and associated professional services. Although CFA along with the clubs formed CSL, and relegated some of the operation rights to the clubs, it still maintains a tight control of CSL. What the clubs hold are event content, player management, event ticket operation, merchandise manufacturing, and sponsorship and advertising management (Table 10.3).

The symbiotic relationship between the CFA, CSL, and the CSL clubs are reflected by the distribution of their interests. In other words, their relationship is the quintessential commensalism as CFA is in absolute domination in terms of the event operation rights while being in charge of distributing these rights to CSL and the CSL clubs. As such, CFA is de facto the biggest beneficiary in the relationship. However, it can be argued that the current commensalism between the three will gradually transform into mutualism and CSL clubs will replace CFA and become the primary beneficiary, because of the decentralization of CFA and the clarification of the ownership of the intangible property of CSL.

The Chinese government, CFA, and the CSL clubs. A series of policies, regulations, and mechanisms formulated by the state and CFA contribute to the sustainable development of CSL and its clubs, which warrants a favorable market environment. Yet, it was not until after the 2002 World Cup that the terrible performance of the Chinese national football team prompted pervasive public criticism against the Chinese professional football league and CFA; in addition to the fact that the physical fitness of the youth in

Table 10.2 Name changing and ownership transferring of major Chinese professional football clubs

Current Name	*Names Used*
Dalian Shide F.C.	Dalian Wanda, Wanda Dalian Shide, Dalian Shide
Shanghai Greenland Shenhua F.C.	Shanghai Shenhua, Shanghai Shenhua TP, Shanghai Shenhua SVA
Shandong Luneng Taishan F.C.	Shandong Jinan Taishan, Shandong Taishan Jiangjun, Shandong Luneng Taishan
Tianjin Teda F.C.	Tianjin Samsung, Tianjin lifei Samsung, Tianjin Teda, Tianjin Teda Dingxin, Tianjin Teda CEC, Tianjin Kangshifu
Qingdao Jonoon F.C.	Qingdao Hainiu, Qingdao Yizhong Hainiu, Qingdao Yizhong, Qingdao Beer, Qingdao Hademen, Qingdao Beilaite, Qingdao Jonoon
ChangSha Jinde F.C.	Shenyang Dongbei Liuyao, Shenyang Huayang, Shenyang Sea Lions, Shenyang Jinde, Changsha Jinde
Liaoning Whowin F.C.	Liaoning Yuandong, Liaoning, Liaoning Hangxing, Liao Ning Tianrun, Liaoning Fushun Jianlibao, Liaoning Fushun Shuangling, Liaoning Fushun, Liaoning Fushun Tegang, Beijing Sanyuan Liaoning Zhongshun, Liaoning, Liaoning Zhongyu, Liaoning Huludao Port
Guangzhou Evergrande Taobao F.C.	Guangzhou Taiyangshen, Guangzhou Geely, Guangzhou Xiangxue, Guangzhou Rizhiquan, Guangzhou Pharmaceutical
Jiangsu Suning F.C.	Jiangsu Maite, Jiangsu, Jiangsu Jiajia, Jiangsu Jiajia Taihushui, Jiangsu Jiajia Tianrun, Jiangsu Shuntian
Beijing Renhe F.C.	Shanghai Pudong, Shanghai Cosco Huili, Shanghai COSCO Sanlin, Shanghai Yongda, Shanghai International, Xi'an Chanba International, Shaanxi Baorong Chanba, Shaanxi Zhongxin Chanba, Shaanxi Lvdi Chanba, Shaanxi Zhongjian Chanba, Shaanxi Renhe Chanba, Guizhou Renhe, Guizhou Maotai, Beijing Renhe

China has been declining over the years, it was pressing for the Chinese government to undergo a comprehensive reform of Chinese football. On one hand, revitalizing football is a necessary and sufficient condition for China to realize its "football dream" for the entire nation and an important step to become a real sports powerhouse. Unswervingly pushing forward football reform falls in line with the Chinese people's request and utilizing it as a

Table 10.3 Market value of 2014 CSL

Corporate Name	*Revenue*	*Source of Revenue*	*Note*	*Overall Revenue*
CSL	440 million yuan with a net profit of 270 million yuan	57 percent came from sponsorship, 34 percent from naming rights, and nine percent from event copyright loyalty	Shareholder dividends and player transfer income were deducted	2.44 billion yuan
CSL Professional Clubs (16)	2.015 billion yuan with 220 million yuan in red	40 percent came from Sponsorship, 10 percent from player transfer, six percent from ticket sales, 44 percent from other items	Revenue exceeded two billion yuan; although the majority of the clubs were losing money, there were five clubs that began to operate in black in 2014, comparing to only two in 2013	

Table 10.4 Milestone policies and regulations pertaining to football reform (in the recent three years)

No.	*Time*	*Milestone Policies and Regulations*
1	2014-10-20	Opinions on Accelerating the Development of Sports Industry and Promoting Sports Consumption
2	2015-03-08	Overall Plan of Chinese Football Reform and Development
3	2015-08-13	Opinions on Accelerating the Development of Youth and School Football
4	2015-08-17	Plan of Chinese Football Association Adjustment and Reform, marking the separation of CFA from GASC
5	2016-06-13	FMC set off to proceed the cancellation of registration and had set up a liquidation group.

breakthrough to facilitate the sports management system reform is consistent with the essence of 18th National Congress of the Communist Party of China.

As illustrated in Table 10.4, in recent years, the central government has introduced a number of policies that support the development of professional football and school football. A good example would be the media rights of CSL, which was 7.3 million yuan in 2012, climbed to 10 million yuan in 2014, then jumped to 80 million yuan in 2015, and was finally sold at an astronomical five-year 8 billion yuan figure in 2016. This means CSL profits from the media rights more than that of the English Premier League (EPL) (167 million), Spanish La Liga (340 million), and National Basketball Association (NBA) (6.2 billion) combined in China (Xie, 2015). On the other hand, according to Wang Dengfeng, the director of the Department of Physical, Health and Arts Education, China plans to build 20,000 football schools with football as their specialty and support 200 high level football teams in the Chinese institutions of higher education (Lu, 2015).

All the policies and regulations will greatly enhance the symbiotic environment of the Chinese government, CFA, and the CSL clubs and substantially improve the efficiency of CSL. In addition, these measures will also help promote a balanced and harmonious development between professional football clubs given a bigger pool of talent supply, reduced player cost, and a stronger momentum from the professional clubs.

CSL club, sponsors, and investors. The contractual relationship between professional football clubs, sponsors, as well as investors, is, in fact, mutualism, as their gains are aligned with the performance of these clubs. CSL has seen continued growth in player's salaries since 2011, reflecting that investors are optimistic about the current investment climate of CSL. A survey conducted on 16 CSL clubs and 10 CSL sponsors in 2013 revealed that despite the fact the real estate industry still took the lead, CSL investors became more diversified in the past years (Table 10.5).

Table 10.5 2013 CSL investor sectors

Sector	*Real Estate*	*Consumer Goods*	*Service*	*Manufacturing*	*Financial Industry*	*Electronic Industry*	*Internet*	*Fashion*	*Media*	*Energy*
Number of Sponsors	9	3	2	2	2	2	2	1	1	1

Table 10.5 suggests most CSL club are operating in red, resulting in the withdrawal of investors and sponsors from the market. Given that the rights and interests of investors and sponsors are not adequately protected, the majority of investors and sponsors deem sponsoring professional football as a one-time project, not a product or a brand to operate and manage in a long run. Moreover, as disclosed in Table 10.6, it is not difficult to conclude that professional football is an extremely expensive sport in China, which requires a considerable financial input. This statement is evident by the regional distribution of the CSL clubs, which mirrors the current economic and social status in China. But with the Chinese professional football turning to maturity, there will be an increasing number of professional football clubs based in the central and western cities to avoid vicious competition; and most importantly, as an integral component of corporate culture, there will be a more stable and diversified presentation of sponsors and investors in the light of the special commodity nature of professional football league (Table 10.6).

CSL clubs, local government, and community. With the emergence of city marketing, sporting events have become the new marketing landscape for many domestic and foreign countries and cities. In this light, professional football, which constitutes long-term sporting events, is also gaining tremendous popularity among local governments and communities. It can be argued that professional football clubs and their respective local governments are in a mutualistic relationship in which they influence and promote one another. Specifically, local government and community offer a sporting event with the basic event resources including venue, facilities, equipment, and human resources, and in turn, a successful sporting event creates additional job opportunities and promotes local businesses for local government and community; moreover, the event also enables local government to improve the utilization of sport facilities, delivers positive energy, and facilitates the development of mass sports and school sports; and finally, as an critical supplement of city culture, sporting event culture strengthens the cohesion and solidarity of the hosting city and community. For example, that Guangzhou Evergrande Taobao F.C. won the AFC (The Asian Football Confederation) championship significantly publicizes the Guangzhou city and elevate the reputation of the Guangzhou government and CFA.

Table 10.6 Regional distribution of 16 CSL clubs

Region	*East*										*Central*	*West*
Province	Guangdong	Shanghai	Hebei	Jiangsu	Zhejiang	Beijing	Shandong	Liaoning	Tianjin	Jilin	Henan	Chongqing
Number of Teams	2	2	2	1	1	1	1	1	1	2	1	1
Total	**14**										**1**	**1**

CFA, CSL clubs, and professional football players. The relationship between CSL clubs and professional football players is bound through contracts. In the early stage of professionalization, it is a parasitic or a commensalistic relationship, however, in the mature stage, it develops into more of a mutualism. Player salary will increase only when professional football players create high quality sports products and boost club revenue, while CFA selects the best players from the clubs and forms the national team, providing a platform for those players to demonstrate their talent and skill and play for the national pride, which in turn boost players' popularity and reinforces their commercial value.

CSL clubs and spectators. The CSL clubs and spectators are in a sheer transactional relationship but at the same time in a mutualistic relationship. The quality of CSL, to a large extent, determines the attendance rate, which is reflected by ticket sales; a high quality sporting event will give rise to a ripple effect not merely on those event goers but other potential consumers around them. Therefore, the priority of CSL is how to approach and retain those consumers. It certainly not only requires producing high quality and competitive sporting event product, but also premium services which give consumers a sense of belonging as well as a sense of honor, and makes them appreciate CSL not just as a commodity but as an exceptional portfolio of services. In addition, CSL also relates to media, suppliers, schools, and other stakeholders, constituting a gigantic system where all parties coordinate, safeguard, and share, offering valuable references and implications for other professional sports events.

Building a developmental path

Balance the development of Chinese professional football clubs. Symbiosis theory states that symbiosis, whose essence is consultation and cooperation, is one of the basic driving forces of social development. Professional football clubs are both competing with and dependent on one another simultaneously. Therefore, the professional clubs are better off by maintaining a mutualistic symbiosis, which strengthens cooperation, minimizes vicious competition, and sustains a balanced development between the clubs. Consistent with the success of the major American professional sports leagues, especially NBA's globalization strategy, a balanced development of the professional football clubs is essential. To achieve this goal, ensuring financial stability is the first step; it should be a joint decision based on the consensus of all the CSL clubs when it comes to issues regarding revenue distribution, market segmentation, and salary cap (Wang, 2007). Second, it is of great importance to preserve competitive balance by a balanced allocation of elite athletes; supplemented by the undergoing school football reform, the increased amount of player training and development platforms will contribute greatly to the player reserve and supply. Third, maintaining a regional balance for the professional football clubs is the key; midwest capital cities, such as Xi'an, Changsha, and Wuhan, can take the initiative to construct their own professional football clubs and tap into the local markets by adopting idiosyncratic training and transferring systems.

Promote service-oriented government, associations, business entities. The government and CFA should re-orientate themselves through the development of relevant policies and regulations to foster a favorable mutualistic environment for CSL. Actions and initiatives in this effort – proactively carrying out and implementing Overall Plan of Chinese Football Reform and Development and Opinions on Accelerating the Development of Youth and School Football; abandoning a profit-oriented mindset and concentrating on efficiency and pragmatism; ruling the football market by laws and regulations; playing the role of the market and improving the market mechanism; being persistent in the separation of CFA's role in administration and management; and returning the control of CSL to the CSL clubs – are hereby proposed. In addition, the CSL clubs, as business entities, should adopt service-driven customer orientation, not only producing exciting and high quality event products but also innovating and improving the company's marketing strategy in order to retain the existing and exploit the new consumers.

Launch various types of football competition at different levels and ages groups. Local associations, schools, organizations, and businesses should be incentivized and encouraged to organize football competitions at all levels. This would be instrumental for professional football by giving administrative power to voluntary associations to promote amateur football leagues; relying on college sports associations to boost college football participation and competition; accelerating the development of youth football and school football plans and formulating a youth football and school football competition system that includes intramural, intermural, and regional competitions; building comprehensive and orderly intercollegiate, interscholastic, junior high, and elementary football league mechanism; and implementing an hierarchical event management scheme with the establishment of a prefectural, municipal, provincial, and national teenagers school football competition system.

Conclusion

The sustainable development of the Chinese professional football is a systematic process, requesting coordination and collaboration from all the stakeholders involved. A sound symbiotic environment is the core, which provides a critical insight for the stakeholders that the Chinese professional football is best managed through a reciprocal, stable, and integrated symbiotic system by constructing, refining, and streamlining the symbiotic condition, symbiotic interface, and symbiotic model of the stakeholders. Effective government supervision, corporate development, community participation, and multi-party collaboration along with the establishment of benefit/interest sharing/consultation mechanism, are in demand to achieve mutualism between the stakeholders.

References

Ahmdajina, V. (1986). *Symbiosis: an Introduction to Biological Association.* Biddeford, ME: University of New England.

Ansoff, H. I. (1965). *Corporate Strategy: An Analytic Approach to Business Policy for Growth and Expansion.* New York, NY: McGraw-Hill.

Cai, J., Tian, C., & Feng, W. (2009). Summary of the Application of Stakeholder Theory. *Communication of Finance and Accounting, 4(2),* 51–54.

Chen, C., & Liu, P. (2011). Major Sports Events Stakeholder Management Theory and Framework Construction. *Journal of Wuhan Institute of Physical Education, 45(4),* 14–20.

Clarkson, P. (1994). *The Therapeutic Relationship in Psychoanalysis, Counselling Psychology and Psychotherapy.* London: Whurr Publishers.

Clarkson, M., Starik, M., Cochran, P., & Jones, T. M. (1994). The Toronto Conference: Reflections on Stakeholder Theory. *Business and Society, 33(1),* 82.

Freeman, R. E. (1984). *Strategic Management: A Stakeholder Approach.* Boston, MA: Pitman.

Ji, J., & Chen, Q. (2009). Ecotourism Stakeholders Symbiotic Mechanism. *Modern Agriculture, 6(3),* 109–12.

Jia, S., & Chen, H. (2002). Review of Methods Defining Stakeholders. *Foreign Economics and Management, 24(5),* 13–18.

Li, N., & Yuan, G. (2006). *Sports Economics.* Shanghai, China: Fudan University.

Liu, J., Sun, Q., & Tao, R. (2009). Professional Sports Leagues: A Symbiosis Approach. *Journal of Shandong Institute of Physical Education, 25(1),* 15–17.

Lu, Y. (2015, August 17). 20000 Football Featured Schools will be Built by the End of 2020. *China News Service.* Retrieved from http://news.china.com/domestic/945/20150817/20212340.html.

Mitchell, R. K., Agle, B. R., & Wood, D. J. (1997). Toward a Theory of Stakeholder Identification and Salience: Defining the Principle of Who and What Really Counts. *Academy of Management Review, 22(4),* 853–86.

Rowley, T. J. (1997). Moving Beyond Dyadic Ties: A Network Theory of Stakeholder Influences. *Academy of Management Review, 22(4),* 887–910.

Song, R. (2003). Ecotourism: Multi-objective and Multi-body Symbiosis (Doctoral thesis, Graduate School of Chinese Academy of Social Sciences, Beijing, China). Retrieved from http://cdmd.cnki.com.cn/Article/CDMD-80201-2004044094.htm.

Wang, Q. (2007). *Theory on Chinese Professional Sports League.* Beijing: Beijing Sports University.

Wang, Z., & Bao, X. (2012). Theory Development and Application of Industrial Symbiosis. *East China Economic Management, 26(10),* 131–36.

Wang, Z., Tan, Q., & Xu, X. (2006). Evolution Model and Empirical Study of Enterprise Cluster Symbiosis. *Chinese Journal of Management Science, 14(2)*, 141–48.

Xie, Y. (2015, September 26). How will CSL Spend 8 Billion Yuan. *NetEase*. Retrieved from http://news.163.com/15/0926/14/B4EP6CFQ00014Q4P.html.

Yang, T. (2011). Chinese Professional Basketball League Supply Chain Stakeholder Relationship. *Journal of Tianjin Institute of Physical Education, 26(5)*, 422–26.

Zhou, Y., & Li, W. (2010). The Development of UEFA Championship League: A Symbiosis Approach. *Journal of Wuhan Institute of Physical Education, 44(10)*, 32–36.

Chapter 11

Customer loyalty in fitness centers

Differences among Baby Boomers and Generations X, Y, and Z

Jerónimo García-Fernández, Pablo Gálvez-Ruíz, Antonio Jesús Sánchez-Oliver, and Moisés Grimaldi-Puyana

Introduction

The current demographic situation in the 28 European Member States (EU28) is characterized by continuing population growth. While the population of the EU28 as a whole increased in 2016, the population of the ten European Member States declined. Since the series began in 1961, the latest information available is also of interest as 2016 was the second year when there was a slight natural decrease in the EU28. The positive population change with 1.5 million more inhabitants was therefore due to net migration. On January 1, 2017 the population of the EU28 was estimated at 511.8 million inhabitants, which was 1.5 million more than a year before. The increase in population numbers in 2016 was smaller than that recorded in 2015 when the population of the EU28 had risen by 1.7 million. Over a longer period, the population of the EU28 grew from 406.7 million in 1960 to 511.8 million in 2017, an increase of 105.1 million people. The rate of population growth has slowed gradually in recent decades; for example, the EU28's population increased on average by about 1.5 million persons per year during the period 2005–17 when compared with an average increase of around 3.3 million persons per year during the 1960s (Eurostat Statistics Explained, 2017). Currently, the population of Europe and Spain stands at 739 and 46 million inhabitants, respectively.

When observing the data on self-reported frequency of exercising or playing sports of adults aged 15 and older in EU28 countries collected from the European Commission's Special Eurobarometer (European Commission, 2014), it can be verified that the socio-demographic data reveals strong differences. The frequency of participating in exercise or sports tends to decrease with age. A majority of 15–24 year-olds (64 percent) exercises or plays sports at least once a week. This falls to 46 percent in the 25–39 age group, 39 percent for 40–54 year-olds, and 30 percent for the 55+ age group. Correspondingly, the proportion that never exercises or plays sport ranges from 19 percent among 15–24 year olds, to 58 percent of those aged 55 or over. Furthermore, men are more likely than women to exercise or play sport. The difference between men and women is strongest in the younger age groups: 74 percent of men aged 15–24 exercise or play sports at least once a week, compared with 55 percent of women in the same age group. The gender gap is narrower for older age groups, with men exercising or playing sports only slightly more than women in the 40–54 and 55+ age groups. The same pattern applies in relation to regular activity (at least five times per week): the gap between men and women is large in the youngest age group (15 percent compared with eight percent) but then narrows in the older age groups.

In terms of population and sports, one area of increased sociological interest is that of generational differences analysis. A generation can be defined as people born in the same time span who share significant historical and/or social life experiences that shape their outlooks and characteristics (Kupperschmidt, 2000). Knowing the characteristics of each of the generations and how they behave is one of the first steps to considering what would be the most appropriate marketing strategies for companies. Each of the generations of people that have been forming over time has some particular experiences that are marked by a series of unique characteristics in which they differ from the others. This is why the behavior of people according to their generation could be different and consequently, their continuity in the sport practices. Precisely, according to the European Commission (2014), one of the greatest increases in sport practices by the European population has been in fitness centers. In fact, Europe is currently one of the regions of the world with the greatest number of fitness program customers, installations, and billings (International Health, Racquet & Sports club Association – IHRSA, 2017). The abandoning of the customers in these installations is both a challenge and an opportunity for their managers (Clavel, Iglesias-Soler, Gallardo, Rodríguez-Cañamero, & García-Unanue, 2016). Due to the difficulty to retain clients in the fitness industry, the objective of this study was to analyze the relationship between quality, satisfaction, perceived value, and future intentions of consumers according to the generational cohorts.

Review of literature

Client loyalty is crucial to fitness centers. Understanding factors that influence client loyalty is crucial for fitness centers (García-Fernández, Bernal-García, Fernández-Gavira, & Vélez-Colón, 2014). Customer loyalty is one of the main objectives that organizations propose to survive in a market as competitive as the current one. Companies that obtain high percentages in customer retention would have high productivity rates and higher profit margins. Several studies have analyzed the relationship between different subjective variables and consumer behavior intentions in these types of sport services within fitness centers (García-Fernández et al., 2018). To know how generational groups behave can help find effective ways to connect with them and make the best business decisions.

Generational cohort theory

Organizations need to be as dynamic as the economy. As membership in the workforce is continually changing, organizations must be cognizant of the characteristics of all potential clients and generational cohorts to prepare them to better meet the organization's goals and objectives (Reisenwitz & Iyer, 2009). Demographers note that generational cohorts share cultural, political, and economic experiences, as well as having similar outlooks and values (Kotler & Keller, 2006). There are currently four generations, beginning with the baby boomers, who were born during 1945–64, Generation X came after the boomers and were born during the years 1965–81, Generation Y or the Millennials, were born between 1982 and 1994, and finally the Centennials or Generation Z make the fourth generation of those born after 1995. At this moment, members of the Baby Boomer generational cohort are retiring and members of Generation Y have been entering the workforce.

It is therefore important to determine the characteristics of all the generations and their possible consumer behavior. Similarly, organizations must fine-tune their segmentation strategies to the dynamic consumer needs of these generational cohorts. One way in which organizations and marketers may assess the needs of the market is to compare the characteristics of the different generations (Reisenwitz & Iyer, 2009). The literature provides a plethora of defining characteristics for each generation based upon seminal events, experiences, values, spending habits, dress, and other attributes (Young, Sturts, Ross, & Kim, 2013). Lamm and Meeks (2009) suggested that differences can be generalized to the mean cohort level, which does provide greater insight and evidence to make predictions about the tendencies of individuals born within those periods of time.

Baby Boomers (BB). The name of this generation refers to the "baby boom" (birth rate) of those years. The BB generation was raised in a strong economy where the opportunities for jobs and education were favorable (Karp, Fuller, & Sirias, 2002). They are perceived as the most competitive of all generations. BB are often termed "workaholics" as their main focus is their career (Zemke, Raines, & Filipczak, 2000). Although the BB are nearing or have reached early retirement age, a good majority are still working and plan to continue working. BBs do not devote much time to leisure and recreational activity. According to Young et al. (2013), Baby Boomers wanted to work to ward off boredom and keep busy and they find personal satisfaction in working.

Generation X (GX). Generation X is often referred as the latchkey generation due to generational differences in many children growing up in this era and job satisfaction of both parents working outside the home. GX experienced the highest parental divorce rate, resulting in them being raised in single-parent homes (Zemke et al., 2000). A group approximately one-half the size of Boomers, GX is known as being resourceful and independent, while seeking work-life balance, including putting family and friends first, and work second (Karp et al., 2002). Professionally, they appreciate direct and immediate feedback along with challenging projects. They were the first generation to place importance on fun in the workplace. Lastly, technology plays an important role for GX as they grew up with Internet, computers, automated teller machines, and cell phones (Ceballos, 2017).

Generation Y – The Millennials (GY). GY is the most diverse generation and the most accepting of diversity (Hill & Stephens, 2003). GY uses a variety of social media networks to both provide and access information immediately and is recognized as the most wired generation to date (Angeline, 2011). People belonging to this group are primarily characterized by their positive attitude toward information technology and the Internet that provide them with a lot of information about products and services, and are less rooted in traditional social morals and ethics (Lendel, Siantová, Závodská, & Šramová, 2017). Their most distinguishable quality is their comfort and expertise with technology (Hershatter & Epstein, 2010). GY shares the same outlook as GX in achieving a work-life balance and is well related to consumer behavior (Múčka, 2007). Researchers and practitioners argue that this group of people is an easier target to market because they have grown up in a consumer-oriented society (Brand, 2000). Furthermore, GY is much more tuned into media than the previous generations because there is so much more media to be tuned into (Manning-Schaffel, 2002). Thus, members of GY represent a viable group to study in terms of media influences (Bush, Martin, & Bush, 2004).

Generation Z (GZ). GZ is a second cohort of digital natives who have been educated and trained in a context marked by the growth and socio-technical development of the networks, the Internet, the web, and mobile and intelligent extensions (Fumero, 2017). This generation has influenced the historical development in the daily use of technology, in the same way that technology has influenced these individuals in how they relate to, inform, or communicate with others (Fumero, 2011). They are digital natives, considerably limited by their cognitive capacity as they improve their operational capacity on the Internet by simple imitation and observation of the members of their family nucleus. The games and the consumption of audiovisual content are their main activities. They do not show awareness of what the Internet is or what it means to be “online”, which shows its level of everydayness (Fumero, 2017). The use of social networks and instant messaging applications has grown substantially, especially in GZ. In this way, the number of children with a public profile in these networks has increased notably, from a quarter (25 percent) in 2010 to almost a third (29 percent) in 2014. GZ people are predominantly the children of GX, but they also have parents who are the GY. The economic recession has taught GZ to be independent and has led to an entrepreneurial desire after seeing their parents and older siblings struggle in the workforce (Grubb, 2016). GZ is more conservative, more money-oriented, and more entrepreneurial and pragmatic about money compared to the GY group (Prakash Yadav & Rai, 2017).

Customer loyalty

There has been extensive research related to generational differences in regard to attitudes, characteristics, and overall outlooks on life (Oh & Reeves, 2014). A number of studies have investigated generational differences in the sport practices (Bednall, Valos, Adam, & McLeod, 2012; Bennett, Henson, & Zhang, 2003) and the impact those differences may have upon fun (Lamm & Meeks, 2009) and personality and motivation (Wong, Gardiner, & Lang, 2008). It is possible to suppose that stated generational differences do impact the sport practices; yet, to date few studies have investigated generational differences in customer loyalty in fitness centers. The fitness industry continues to grow worldwide, as indicated by IHRSA (2017). Comprehensively, Europe is the most profitable market with the largest growth in practitioners, and is among the markets with most growth, having Spain as one of the countries with the greatest growth in consumers of fitness centers and with the greatest penetration in the industry (European Commission, 2014; IHRSA, 2017; Ministerio de Educación, Cultura y Deporte, 2015). Yet, the principle challenge of this market lies in the poor loyalty of its clients (García-Fernández et al., 2014), understanding that the stronger the loyalty the greater the financial expense for the client (García-Fernández, Gálvez-Ruíz, Bernal-García, & Vélez-Colón, 2016a).

To examine customer loyalty, studies have been conducted utilizing subjective measurements of behavior (Theodorakis, Howat, Ko, & Avourdiadou, 2014). Usually customer loyalty studies have analyzed conceptual models including service quality, perceived value, or satisfaction (García-Fernández et al., 2018; García-Fernández, Gálvez-Ruíz, Fernández-Gavira, & Vélez-Colón, 2016b; García-Fernández, Gálvez-Ruíz, Vélez-Colón, & Bernal-García, 2017; Nuviala, Grao-Cruces, Pérez-Turpín, & Nuviala, 2012; Theodorakis et al., 2014). Yet, in no case has a study been carried out on how the conceptual relations would vary based on generational cohorts.

Development of hypotheses

Perceived quality is defined by Zeithaml (1988) as "the judgement of the consumer on the excellence or superiority of a product/service" (p. 3), and perceived value is "the global evaluation of the consumer on the usefulness of a product based upon the perception of what is received and what is given" (Zeithaml, 1988, p. 14). As to satisfaction, Kotler (1991) indicates that it is a response or a post-consumption evaluation. Regarding the studies carried out in sport centers, Murray and Howat (2002) tested the positive relations between perceived quality, perceived value, satisfaction, and future intentions in public sports centers. Yu et al. (2014) corroborated the positive relations between perceived quality, perceived value, satisfaction, and future intentions in adults over 60 years old. Avourdiadou and Theodorakis (2014) noted the relationship among perceived quality, satisfaction, and future intentions in fitness centers, differentiating between customers with greater or lesser experience as facility users. While Theodorakis et al. (2014) found no positive and significant relationship between perceived value and future intentions for fitness center consumers, Calabuig, Núñez-Pomar, Prado-Gascó, and Añó (2014) found positive and significant relationships among perceived value, customer's satisfaction, and future intentions of behavior in customers of public fitness centers. Finally, García-Fernández et al. (2016b; 2017) noted that the relationships among the four variables were significant and positive both in customers with short length of membership in the installation and customers with a length of membership of more than two years. Based on these evidences, the following hypotheses were proposed and tested in the current study:

> H_1: Perceived quality would have a direct positive effect on customer satisfaction.

> H_2: Perceived quality would have a direct positive effect on perceived value.

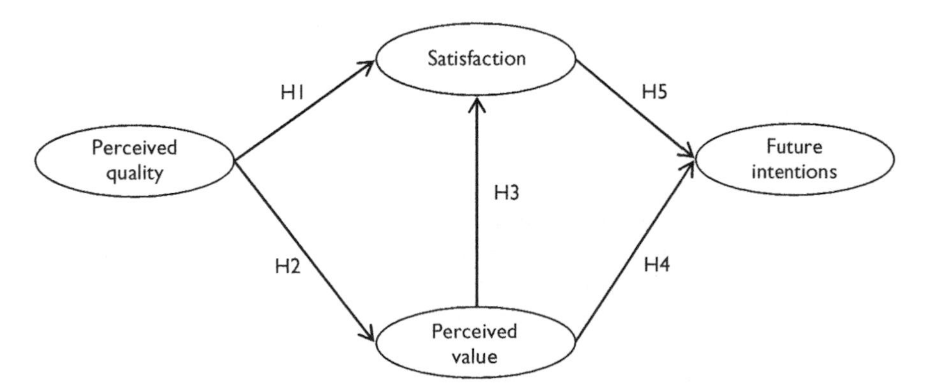

Figure 11.1 Hypothesized model depicting relationships among perceived quality, perceived value, customer satisfaction, and future intentions of fitness center members

H_3: Perceived value would have a direct positive effect on customer satisfaction.

H_4: Perceived value would have a direct positive effect on customer future intentions.

H_5: Customer satisfaction would have a direct positive effect on customer future intentions.

Method

Participants

The research sample consisted of 15,725 clients (8,423 women and 7,302 men) of 55 fitness centers in Spain. Of the sample, 5.7 percent (*n*=900) were GZ, 63.3 percent (*n*=9,956) GY, 20.7 percent (*n*=3,297) GX, and 9.9 percent (*n*=1,572) BB. As to sex, it stood out that only in the BB was the percentage of men (52.1 percent; *n* = 819) greater than that of women (47.9 percent; *n* = 753). Regarding the frequency of facility usage, it is highlighted that in all the generations the greatest frequency was four times per week (GZ = 31.4 percent; GY = 33.3 percent; GX = 35.1 percent; BB = 33.7 percent). As to the length of membership as a customer, it is noteworthy that 40 percent of GZ had been there between zero and three months and 27.5 percent of the BB over two years. With respect to the means used to go to the fitness center, it is seen that GZ had a high percentage of walking (68.8 percent; *n* = 619), the same as BB (57.6 percent; *n* = 906); however, GX and GY had greater percentages by car or motorbike (43 percent; *n* = 4,286; 49.7 percent; *n* = 1,637, respectively). Regarding the time they took to get to the fitness center, it is notable that in all the cases this was less than 15 minutes (GZ = 74 percent; GY = 76.4 percent; GX = 78.8 percent; BB = 78.9 percent) (Table 11.1).

Measurement and procedures

The survey used for data collection was composed of a socio-demographic section (gender, age, weekly frequency of usage, length of membership, commute and time to get to fitness center) and a section of client perception formed by four variables, perceived quality, perceived value, satisfaction, and future intentions. García-Fernández et al.'s scale (2018) was adapted for the present study using eight items (four items for facility, two items for employees, two items for programs) for perceived quality. To measure perceived value, Zeithaml's (1988) scale was used, which was composed of two items. Measurement of satisfaction was based on Oliver (1997) by using one item. Future intentions were evaluated by one item proposed by Zeithaml, Berry, and Parasuraman (1996). Answers to the items were

Table 11.1 Distribution of the participants according to generation cohorts

Variable	*GZ*		*GY*		*GX*		*BB*		*Total*	
	n	%	n	%	n	%	n	%	n	%
Gender										
Male	371	41.2	4,575	46	1,537	46.6	819	52.1	7,302	46.4
Female	529	58.8	5,381	54	1,760	53.4	753	47.9	8,423	53.6
Total	900	100	9,956	100	3,297	100	1,572	100	15,725	100
Weekly Frequency										
One/less time/week	39	4.3	446	4.4	153	4.6	85	5.4	723	4.6
Twice/week	212	23.6	2,008	20.2	560	17	307	19.5	3,087	19.6
Three/week	127	14.4	1,648	16.6	621	18.8	275	17.5	2,671	17
Four/week	283	31.4	3,320	33.3	1,154	35.1	530	33.7	5,287	33.6
Five/more week	239	26.6	2,534	25.5	809	24.5	375	23.9	3,957	25.2
Total	900	6.7	9,956	63.3	3,297	100	1,572	100	15,725	100
Length of Membership										
0 to 3 months	360	40	2,234	22.4	579	17.6	274	17.4	3,447	22
3 to 6 months	178	19.8	1,574	15.8	372	11.3	173	11	2,297	14.6
7 to 12 months	145	16.1	1,996	20.1	614	18.6	265	16.9	3,020	19.2
1 to 2 years	170	18.9	2,571	25.8	922	27.9	427	27.2	4,090	26
More than 2 years	47	5.2	1,581	15.9	810	24.6	433	27.5	2,871	18.2
Total	900	100	9,956	100	3,297	100	1,572	100	15,725	100

(continued)

Table 11.1 (continued)

Variable	*GZ*		*GY*		*GX*		*BB*		*Total*	
	n	%	n	%	n	%	n	%	n	%
Commute										
Walking	619	68.8	4,853	48.7	1,524	46.2	906	57.6	7,902	50.3
CyR/Sk	45	5	285	2.9	63	1.9	27	1.7	420	2.7
Car/Mot	138	15.3	4,286	43	1,637	49.7	602	38.3	6,663	42.4
Bu/PTr	98	10.9	507	5.1	67	2	34	2.2	706	4.5
Other	0	0	25	.3	6	.2	3	.2	34	.2
Total	900	100	9,956	100	3,297	100	1,572	100	15,725	100
Time to Get to Fitness Center										
Less than 15 min	666	74	7,605	76.4	2,597	78.8	1,240	78.9	12,108	77.0
15 to 25 min	194	21.6	2,065	20.7	637	19.3	309	19.6	3,205	20.4
More than 25 min	40	4.4	286	2.9	63	1	23	1.6	412	2.6
Total	900	100	9,956	100	3,297	100	1,572	100	15,725	100

Notes: Generation Z = GZ; Generation Y = GY; Generation X = GX; Baby Boomers = BB; Cycle or roller skating = CyR/Sk; Car or motorbike = Car/Mot; Bus/public transportation = Bu/PTr.

collected through a 10-point Likert-type scale (1 = completely disagree to 10 = completely agree). The investigators of this study contacted the main fitness center chains in Spain, informing them about the study and its aim. Of the chains, six agreed to participate with their installations. A total of 55 fitness centers took part in the study, to which a link with the questionnaire was sent. This link had to be sent to all the customers of each installation. The information collection period lasted two months.

Data analyses

Given that the aim of this study was to analyze the differential characteristics of fitness center clients with different generation groups, an ANOVA analysis was first carried out to find out the possible differences among the groups established. As a contrast test, Scheffé and Games-Howell tests were conducted to examine homogeneity in the variances. Effect size was calculated using the value of Eta^2 (η^2). The second step, a confirmatory factor analysis (CFA) with AMOS 20.0 software, was conducted prior to the hypothesis testing in order to check the measurement model. The assessment of the model fit was estimated based on multiple indicators (Hu & Bentler, 1999), using the maximum likelihood method (ML). Specifically, the chi-square (χ^2) statistical test, the ratio of chi-square to its degrees of freedom (χ^2/df) (Hair, Black, Babin, Anderson, & Tatham, 2006; Jöreskog & Sörbom, 1993), root mean square error of approximation (RMSEA), comparative fit index (CFI), goodness of fit index (GFI), Tucker-Lewis index (TLI), parsimony comparative of fit index (PCFI), and parsimony goodness of fit index (PGFI) were adopted. Minimum acceptable values for these indices should be less than 5 for the χ^2/df (Bentler, 2002), between .08 and .10 for the RMSEA (Byrne, 2001), greater than .90 for the CFI, GFI, and TLI, and above .60 for the PCFI and PGFI (Arbuckle, 2009; Blunch, 2008; Hair et al., 2006; Kline, 2005). Reliability was examined via calculating internal consistency coefficients. Lastly, structural equation model (SEM) analyses were carried out to test the hypotheses and evaluate the adjustment of different groups by following the same fit indices.

Results

There were no missing values in the data and there was an approximately univariate normal distribution, since the items had absolute values of skewness lower than 3.0 and kurtosis lower than 7.0 (Kline, 2004). The group of GY was the one that obtained lower mean scores in all items while the BB group achieved the highest scores in practically all items (Table 11.2). The results of the ANOVA test showed significant ($p < .005$) differences among the groups; thus, the Games-Howell was conducted and the measure as equality of variances was not assumed. In this way, it was noted that

Table 11.2 Descriptive statistics and ANOVA examining differences among generation groups

Construct	*Mean (SD)*				F	*GZ / GY*	*GZ/ GX*	*GZ / BB*	*GY / GX*	*GY / BB*	*GX / BB*	η^2
	GZ	*GY*	*GX*	*BB*	*(3.3877)*							
Perceived Quality												
F1	6.76 (2.73)	6.03 (2.76)	6.36 (2.72)	6.87 (2.62)	19.701	.000	.008	.780	.047	.000	.000	0.01
F2	7.06 (2.61)	6.39 (2.64)	6.50 (2.54)	6.94 (2.44)	15.583	.000	.000	.741	.765	.000	.001	0.11
F3	5.98 (2.68)	5.62 (2.71)	5.94 (2.60)	6.43 (2.55)	15.887	.019	.986	.001	.037	.000	.000	0.01
F4	6.74 (2.66)	6.06 (2.69)	6.26 (2.59)	6.82 (2.50)	19.611	.000	.000	.895	.349	.000	.000	0.01
P1	6.54 (2.98)	6.10 (2.91)	6.58 (2.77)	7.16 (2.63)	23.800	.006	.993	.000	.001	.000	.000	0.02
P2	7.00 (2.79)	6.39 (2.81)	6.69 (2.69)	7.25 (2.53)	19.077	.000	.066	.185	.067	.000	.000	0.01
PR1	6.08 (2.91)	5.59 (2.79)	5.92 (2.73)	6.43 (2.66)	15.622	.001	.585	.038	.045	.000	.000	0.12
PR2	6.27 (2.67)	5.56 (2.68)	5.83 (2.60)	6.34 (2.57)	19.374	.000	.002	.935	.096	.000	.000	0.01
Perceived value												
PV1	6.85 (2.85)	6.56 (2.82)	6.68 (2.69)	7.25 (2.49)	12.439	.124	.546	.006	.780	.000	.000	0.01
PV2	6.73 (2.87)	6.49 (2.89)	6.69 (2.74)	7.24 (2.55)	13.162	.291	.990	.000	.419	.000	.000	0.01
Satisfaction												
S1	7.12 (2.74)	6.48 (2.80)	6.61 (2.70)	7.17 (2.54)	16.366	.000	.000	.964	.725	.000	.000	0.01
Future intention												
F1	7.21 (2.88)	6.63 (2.92)	6.76 (2.83)	7.34 (2.64)	14.707	.000	.004	.707	.712	.000	.000	0.01

the GY and GZ groups presented significant ($p < .005$) differences in all of the measures related to perceived quality, satisfaction, and future intention while GX and GY groups showed significant ($p < .005$) differences with respect to the BB group in all the scales. As to the value scale, the BB group showed significant ($p < .005$) differences with respect to the rest of the groups, explaining the high score obtained in the items of this scale. In all the cases, the value obtained for the size effect was low.

The CFA results of the measurement model showed an overall acceptable fit of the data among different groups of generations (Table 11.3). The RMSEA index was high but did not exceed the critical point of 1.0 (Byrne, 2001). The CFI, GFI, and TLI indices also exceeded the 0.9 recommendation for acceptable fit and the results of PCFI and PGFI were above .60. The ratio χ^2/df was high. All of the items' standardized regression weights were significant ($p < 0.05$) and loaded highly on their expected constructs, above the 0.70 threshold (Hair et al., 2006). SEM showed the overall acceptance of the relationship model (Table 11.4). The path coefficients for each model are illustrated in Figure 11.2, indicating that all the hypotheses were supported in the different groups but not with the same effect, except in the relationship between perceived quality and perceived value, where all the groups showed a similar relationship (i.e., H_2: β values between .89 and .93). The GZ group showed the strongest effect in the relationship between the dimensions perceived quality and satisfaction (H_1: $\beta = .56$), as well as between satisfaction and future intentions (H_5: $\beta = .56$). Notwithstanding, for both H_1 and for H_5 the GX group was the one that had least strength in the relations,

Table 11.3 Confirmatory factor analyses for the measurement model of different generation groups

Generation	χ^2	*GL*	*RMSEA*	*CFI*	*GFI*	*TLI*	*PCFI*	*PGFI*	χ^2/GL
GZ	401.42	68	.074	.985	.939	.980	.736	.608	5.90
GY	426.18	68	.073	.986	.937	.982	.737	.607	6.26
GX	593.25	68	.089	.980	.914	.973	.732	.612	8.72
BB	551.87	68	.093	.981	.922	.974	.733	.617	8.11

Table 11.4 Fit of the SEM model according to different generation groups

Generation	χ^2	*GL*	*RMSEA*	*CFI*	*GFI*	*TLI*	*PCFI*	*PGFI*	χ^2/GL
GZ	392.81	48	.089	.978	.932	.970	.711	.574	8.18
GY	414.38	48	.088	.980	.929	.972	.712	.572	8.63
GX	579.47	48	.095	.970	.903	.959	.705	.556	12.07
BB	541.56	48	.098	.972	.911	.962	.707	.561	11.28

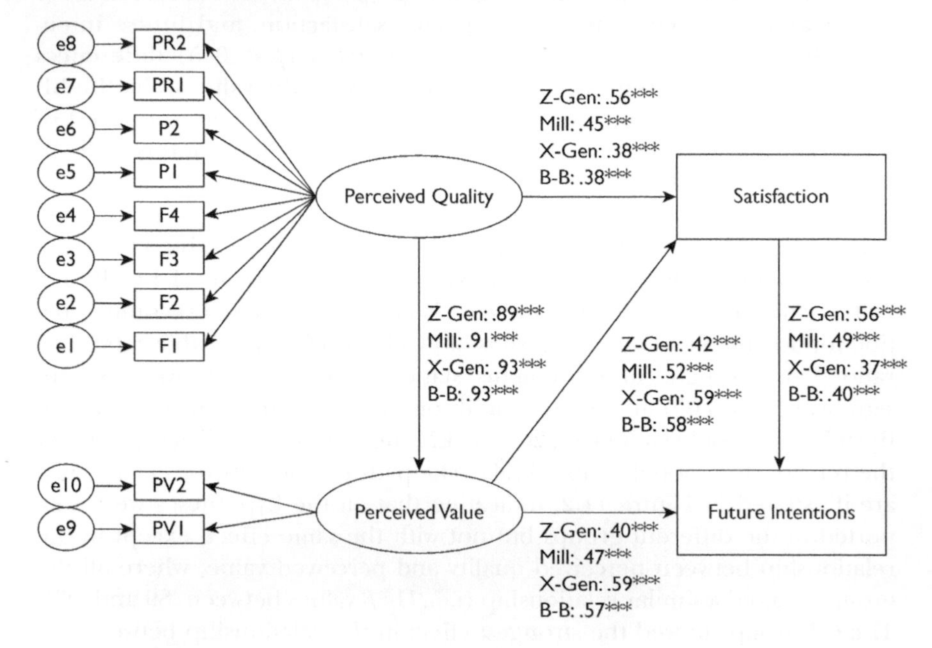

Figure 11.2 Standardized estimates of the structural models

contrary to the results obtained in the relationship between perceived value and satisfaction (H_3: $\beta = .59$) and between perceived value and future intentions (H_4: $\beta = .59$). In both cases the GX group had the highest effect with very similar values to the BB group (H_3: $\beta = .58$; H4: $\beta = .57$); meanwhile, the GZ group had the weakest relations for these two hypotheses.

Discussion

The aim of this study was to analyze the differences in the relationship among perceived quality, perceived value, satisfaction, and future intentions in different generational cohorts. Although the model has been analyzed on other occasions (i.e., García-Fernández et al., 2016b, 2017; Theodorakis et al., 2014), until now it had not been tested to compare its differences according to different age segments. As to the relationship between perceived quality and satisfaction, different works had revealed a causal relationship between both variables (Avourdiadou & Theodorakis, 2014).

The findings in this study corroborate the results of previous studies. Nevertheless, it stands out that the strongest relationship is in GZ. Yet, one must recall that all of the generations had a significant causal relationship between perceived quality and customer satisfaction. Regarding the relationship between perceived quality and perceived value, the findings have shown positive relations in all the generations analyzed, the strongest being the BB generation. Taking into account that perceived quality is a component of perceived value and a positive factor of it (Murray & Howat, 2002), the findings could indicate that the BB generation is the one most aware of service quality or is more demanding with the service provided. These results also corroborate the previous studies, which indicated a positive relationship between perceived quality and perceived value (García-Fernández et al., 2016b, 2017; Theodorakis et al., 2014).

In this study, it has been revealed that there exists a positive causal relationship between perceived value and customer satisfaction, just as other works indicated (Calabuig et al., 2014; Theodorakis et al., 2014; Yu et al., 2014). The findings have indicated a greater relation in the GX and BB groups; the sequential relationships among perceived quality, perceived value, and satisfaction present a greater importance to the older generation. In the same way, the relationship between perceived value and future intentions also showed positive results, unlike the findings in Theodorakis et al.'s (2014) study. Findings of this study coincide with those by Calabuig et al. (2014), García-Fernández et al. (2016b; 2017), and Murray and Howat (2002). In particular, the strongest weight corresponds to the BB generation; so, loyalty or intention to recommend is going to depend more strongly on what people give and receive in exchange. In fact, the results have indicated that the BB generation more consciously evaluates this relationship and is therefore more critical in the evaluation of the sports services. Moreover, the relationship between satisfaction and future intentions was positive (Avourdiadou & Theodorakis, 2014; García-Fernández et al., 2016b, 2017). In particular, this relation is stronger for those who are younger and in the GZ group. This finding leads one to think that the younger the person is, the less the evaluation of the service, in which case loyalty depends more on a transitory and momentary process in spite of being a continuous and permanent evaluation. As the findings have indicated that the relationship is positive for all the generations, it is important to offer a good service for the customers to build up loyalty (Calabuig et al., 2014).

In terms of practical implications for management, this study reveals the differences in the management of fitness centers depending on the kind of clients in generational cohorts. The results obtained are especially valuable and could be used to improve customer loyalty for consumers of fitness centers in other parts of the world as they could help to find out the behavior of customers depending on their age or generation. Precisely, the findings showed that perceived quality influences satisfaction; so, managers must properly manage their resources to achieve high levels of customer satisfaction.

The main limitation of this work lies in two aspects. On one hand, a limited number of items were used to evaluate perceived quality, perceived value, and more specifically, satisfaction and future intentions. In other works, there are numerous scales with a greater number of items that could have been adopted, which would have offered a stronger validity and generalizability of the scales. Nonetheless, having used a lesser number has also made it possible for the sample to be greater. Future works should not only increase the number of items in the variables analyzed, but also include other variables applicable to other geographic areas. The second major limitation is the use of a transversal methodology, which obliges the analysis of a fact at a specific moment. Though this type of study tends to work with this methodology, it does not prevent it from being a limitation and it cannot be observed what occurs over time. That is why it is necessary to analyze the proposed loyalty model over time and analyze how it evolves and what the differences are.

References

Angeline, T. (2011). Managing Generational Diversity at the Workplace: Expectations and Perceptions of Different Generations of Employees. *African Journal of Business Management, 5(2)*, 249–55.

Arbuckle, J. (2009). *Amos18 Reference Guide (Version 18)*. Chicago, IL: Statistical Package for the Social Sciences.

Avourdiadou, S., &Theodorakis, N. D. (2014). The Development of Loyalty among Novice and Experienced Customers of Sport and Fitness Centers. *Sport Management Review, 17(4)*, 419–31.

Bednall, D. H., Valos, M., Adam, S., & McLeod, C. (2012). Getting Generation Y to Attend: Friends, Interactivity and Half-time Entertainment. *Sport Management Review, 15(1)*, 80–90.

Bennett, G., Henson, R. K., & Zhang, J. J. (2003). Generation Y's Perceptions of the Action Sports Industry Segment. *Journal of Sport Management, 17(2)*, 95–115.

Bentler, P. (2002). *EQS 6 Structural Equations Program Manual*. Encino, CA: Multivariate Software.

Blunch, N. J. (2008). *Introduction to Structural Equation Modeling Using SPSS and AMOS*. Thousand Oaks, CA: Sage.

Brand, R. (2000). *Advertisers Examine Teens and Their Spending Clout*. Retrieved February 10, 2018, from www.tcpalm.com/business/01jteenu.shtml.

Bush, A. J., Martin, C. A., & Bush, V. D. (2004). Sports Celebrity Influence on the Behavioral Intentions of Generation Y. *Journal of Advertising Research, 44(1)*, 108–18.

Byrne, B. M. (2001). *Structural Equation Modeling with AMOS: Basic Concepts, Applications and Programming*. Mahwah, NJ: Lawrence Erlbaum Associates.

Calabuig, F., Núñez-Pomar, J., Prado-Gascó, V., & Añó, V. (2014). Effect of Price Increases on Future Intentions of Sport Consumers. *Journal of Business Research, 67(5)*, 729–33.

Ceballos, S. D. (2017). *A Study of the Differences in Globe Leadership Preferences between Baby Boomers, Generation X and Millennials*. Unpublished doctoral dissertation, Our Lady of the Lake University, San Antonio, TX.

Clavel San Emeterio, I., Iglesias-Soler, E., Gallardo, L., Rodriguez-Cañamero, S., & García-Unanue, J. (2016). A Prediction Model of Retention in a Spanish Fitness Centre. *Managing Sport and Leisure, 21(5)*, 300–18.

Del Webb. (2010). *Baby Boomer Survey: Working to Live, not Living to Work. Business Wire.* Retrieved February 10, 2018, from www.dwboomersurvey.com/.

European Commission. (2014). *Special Eurobarometer 412: Sport and Physical Activity.* Brussels, Belgium: European Commission.

Eurostat Statistics Explained. (2017). *Population and Population Change Statistics. European Union (EU).* Retrieved February 10, 2018, from http://ec.europa.eu/eurostat/statistics-explained/index.php/Population_and_population_change_statistics.

Fumero, A. (2011). IRC 2.0. Medios para la información, la relación y la comunicación en la web 2.0. *El Profesional de la Información, 20(6)*, 605–09.

Fumero, A. (2017). JóveneZ. *Revista de Estudios de Juventud, 16(114)*, 11–27.

García-Fernández, J., Bernal-García, A., Fernández-Gavira, J., & Vélez-Colón, L. (2014). Analysis of Existing Literature on Management and Marketing of the Fitness Centre Industry. *South African Journal for Research in Sport, Physical Education and Recreation, 36(3)*, 75–91.

García-Fernández, J., Gálvez-Ruíz, P., Bernal-García, A., & Vélez-Colón, L. (2016a). El gasto económico en centros de fitness low-cost: diferencias según fidelidad y características del cliente. *Sport TK: Revista Euroamericana de Ciencias del Deporte, 5(1)*, 137–44.

García-Fernández, J., Gálvez-Ruíz, P., Fernández-Gavira, J., Vélez-Colón, L., Pitts, B., & Bernal-García, A. (2018). The Effects of Service Convenience and Perceived Quality on Perceived Value, Satisfaction and Loyalty in Low-cost Fitness Centers. *Sport Management Review, 21*, 250–62.

García-Fernández, J., Gálvez-Ruíz, P., Fernández-Gavira, J., & Vélez-Colón, L. (2016b). A Loyalty Model According to Membership Longevity of Low-cost Fitness Center: Quality, Value, Satisfaction, and Behavioral Intention. *Revista de Psicología del Deporte, 25(1)*, 107–10.

García-Fernández, J., Gálvez-Ruíz, P., Vélez-Colón, L., & Bernal-García, A. (2017). Antecedents of Customer Loyalty: A Case of Low-cost Fitness Centers. In J. Zhang, and B. G. Pitts (Eds.), *Contemporary Sport Marketing: Global Perspectives* (pp.139–55). Oxford, UK: Routledge.

Grubb, V. M. (2016). Defining the Generations. In *Clash of the Generations: Managing the New Workplace Reality.* Hoboken, NJ: John Wiley & Sons.

Hair, J., Black, W., Babin, B., Anderson, R., & Tatham, R. (2006). *Multivariate Data Analysis* (6th edn). Upper Saddle River, NJ: Pearson Prentice Hall.

Hershatter, A., & Epstein, M. (2010). Millennials and the World of Work: An Organization and Management Perspective. *Journal of Business and Psychology, 25(2)*, 211–23.

Hill, R. P., & Stephens, D. L. (2003). The Compassionate Organization in the 21st Century. *Organizational Dynamics, 32(4)*, 331–41.

Hu, L., & Bentler, P. M. (1999). Cutoff Criteria for Fit Indexes in Covariance Structure Analysis: Conventional Criteria Versus New Alternatives. *Structural Equation Modeling: A Multidisciplinary Journal, 6(1)*, 1–55.

International Health, Racquet & Sports Club Association (2017). *The IHRSA Global Report 2016.* Boston, MA: IHRSA.

Jöreskog, K. G., & Sörbom, D. (1993). *LISREL 8: Structural Equation Modeling with the SIMPLIS Command Language.* Chicago, IL: Scientific Software International.

Karp, H., Fuller, C., & Sirias, D. (2002). *Bridging the Boomer Xer Gap.* Palo Alto, CA: Davies-Black.

Kline, R. B. (2004). *Beyond Significance Testing: Reforming Data Analysis Methods in Behavioral Research.* Washington, DC: American Psychological Association.

Kline, R. (2005). *Principles and Practice of Structural Equation Modeling* (2nd edn). New York NY, The Guilford Press.

Kotler, P. (1991). *Marketing Management: Analysis, Planning, Implementation and Control.* Englewood Cliffs, NJ: Prentice Hall.

Kotler, P., & Keller, K. L. (2006). *Marketing Management, Twelfth Edition.* Upper Saddle River, NJ: Pearson Prentice Hall.

Kupperschmidt, B. R. (2000). Multigeneration Employees: Strategies for Effective Management. *The Health Care Manager, 19(1),* 65–76.

Lamm, E., & Meeks, M. D. (2009). Workplace Fun: The Moderating Effects of Generational Differences. *Employee Relations, 31(6),* 613–31.

Lendel V., Siantová E., Závodská A., & Šramová V. (2017). Generation Y Marketing – The Path to Achievement of Successful Marketing Results Among the Young Generation. In A. Kavoura, D. Sakas, & P. Tomaras (Eds.), *Strategic Innovative Marketing* (pp. 11–17). Cham, Switzerland: Springer.

Manning-Schaffel, V. (2002). *Generation Y.* Retrieved February 10, 2018, from www.brandchannel.com/start1.asp?id=136.

Ministerio de Educación, Cultura y Deporte (2015). *Encuesta de hábitos deportivos 2015.* Madrid: Subdirección General de Estadística y Estudios, Secretaría General Técnica.

Múčka, F. (2007). *Generation Y tiahnenasvet.* Trend. Retrieved February 10, 2018, from www.etrend.sk/trend-archiv/rok-/cislo-November/generation-y-tiahne-na-svet.html.

Murray, D., & Howat, G. (2002). The Relationships Among Service Quality, Value, Satisfaction, and Future Intentions of Customers at an Australian Sports and Leisure Centre. *Sport Management Review, 5(1),* 25–43.

Muthén, B., & Kaplan, D. (1985). A Comparison of Some Methodologies for the Factor Analysis of Non-normal Likert Variables. *British Journal of Mathematical and Statistical Psychology, 38,* 171–89.

Nuviala, A., Grao-Cruces, A., Pérez-Turpin, J. A., & Nuviala, R. (2012). Perceived Service Quality, Perceived Value and Satisfaction in Groups of Users of Sports Organizations in Spain. *Kinesiology, 44(1),* 94–103.

Oh, E., & Reeves, T. C. (2014). Generational Differences and the Integration of Technology in Learning, Instruction, and Performance. In J. Spector, M. Merrill, J. Elen, & J. Bishop (Eds.), *Handbook of Research on Educational Communications and Technology* (pp. 819–28). New York, NY: Springer.

Oliver, R. (1997). *Satisfaction, a Behavioral Perspective on the Consumer.* New York, NY: McGraw-Hill.

Orejuela, A. F. S., Salamanca, Y. D. T., & Junco, C. A. A. (2018). Análisis de variables de segmentación de mercados. *I+ D Revista de Investigaciones, 11(1),* 85–99.

Population Pyramids of the World from 1950 to 2100 (2018). *Population Pyramid.* Retrieved February 10, 2018, from www.populationPyramid.net.

Prakash Yadav, G., & Rai, J. (2017). The Generation Z and their Social Media Usage: A Review and a Research Outline. *Global Journal of Enterprise Information System, 9(2),* 110–16.

Reisenwitz, T. H., & Iyer, R. (2009). Differences in Generation X and Generation Y: Implications for the Organization and Marketers. *Marketing Management Journal, 19(2),* 91–103.

Theodorakis, N. D., Howat, G., Ko, Y. J., & Avourdiadou, S. (2014). A Comparison of Service Evaluation Models in the Context of Sport and Fitness Centers in Greece. *Managing Leisure, 19(1),* 18–35.

Wong, M., Gardiner, E., & Lang, W. (2008). Generational Differences in Personality and Motivation: Do they Exist and what are the Implications for the Workplace? *Journal of Managerial Psychology, 23(8),* 878–90.

Young, S. J., Sturts, J. R., Ross, C. M., & Kim, K. T. (2013). Generational Differences and Job Satisfaction in Leisure Services. *Managing Leisure, 18(2),* 152–70.

Yu, H. S., Zhang, J. J., Kim, D. H., Chen, K. K., Henderson, C., Min, S. D., & Huang, H. (2014). Service Quality, Perceived Value, Customer Satisfaction, and Behavioral Intention Among Fitness Center Members Aged 60 Years and Over. *Social Behavior and Personality: An International Journal, 42(5),* 757–67.

Zeithaml, V. A. (1988). Consumer Perceptions of Price, Quality, and Value: A Means-end Model and Synthesis of Evidence. *Journal of Marketing, 52(3),* 2–22.

Zeithaml, V. A., Berry, L. L., & Parasuraman, A. (1996). The Behavioral Consequences of Service Quality. *The Journal of Marketing, 60(2),* 31–46.

Zemke, R., Raines, C., & Filipczak, B. (2000). *Generations at Work: Managing the Clash of Veterans, Boomers, Xers, and Nexters in your Workplace.* New York, NY: AMACOM.

Chapter 12

Analyzing the marketing situation of the Chinese Table Tennis Super League

Mandy Y. Zhang, Brenda G. Pitts, and James J. Zhang

Introduction

Table tennis, also known as ping-pong, is an Olympic sport that was originated in England during the late nineteenth century. With its surging popularity and the great number of people playing this sport, table tennis was officially recognized and admitted to the Olympic Games by the International Olympic Committee (IOC) in 1981, and became a medal event at the 1988 Olympic Games in Seoul, Korea. Since then, table tennis has distinguished itself in Summer Olympic Games, with ever-increasing worldwide television viewing audiences. Table tennis was recently ranked as the fifth most watched sport at the Athens Olympic Games (International Table Tennis Federation – ITTF, 2017). In the early 1950s, the Chinese Table Tennis Association (CTTA) was founded and officially accepted into the ITTF (Table Tennis World, 2005). Table tennis has become a very popular and revered sport in China.

Beginning in the late 1970s, a new economic model, often referred to as the socialist market economy, was employed by the Chinese government. This new model gradually incorporated free market concepts into China's planned economy. Under this policy, China has experienced economic growth, community development, and governance change at an accelerated rate in recent years. This economic resurgence has inevitably transformed how businesses are being operated in China, including the sport business. The Chinese sport industry has gradually been developed since the early 1990s. Professional table tennis, as a core segment, has spearheaded the development of this nascent sport industry. Prior to the 1990s, sports in China were completely government-funded. This situation began to change in 1994 when Chinese soccer first formed a professional league, soon followed by professional sport leagues for basketball, volleyball, table tennis, and weiqi (a chess game also called "go" (What's on Xiamen, 2010; Zhang, Kim, Pitts, & Zhang, 2015).

China's table tennis teams first sought corporate support in 1995. That year, the first China professional table tennis club competition was held among provincial/city club teams. To obtain financial support, each of the

19 clubs was able to find a sponsoring company. To a great extent, the initial success was due to the popularity of table tennis and its elite status in China. However, these clubs were only assembled for the two-day tournament, and were dissolved immediately after the competition was completed (Chu, 2011). Nevertheless, that was a milestone for China's table tennis to be professionalized. In 1998, the Chinese Table Tennis Super League (CTTSL) was formally established to govern the club competitions, and a competition schedule was adopted with home and away games as often seen in competitive sports of western countries. Even with the tremendous popularity of table tennis in China, several factors have kept the CTTSL from being successful. In an effort to promote CTTSL growth and development, the league has developed various policies and regulations to govern the operations of the league and its teams. According to Zhang, Xie, Zhang, Pitts, and Zhang (2016), these written documents cover a wide range of activities, such as player drafting, broadcasting contracts, and team sponsorship, which are an attempt to learn from European and American professional sport leagues. Even so, the league is in the early stage of its development and management; a majority of its teams are facing challenges in attracting consumers, finding sponsorships, obtaining broadcasting rights, and earning a profit. Many teams are struggling financially. Due to the lack of attendance at CTTSL events in large markets, most CTTSL matches are held in arenas with poor conditions located in smaller cities and towns. Because a number of CTTSL clubs have not been able to establish a stable home court site, frequently moving the home court from one city to another, income from ticket sales is almost negligible. The negative financial cycle has led to minimal investment in event promotion and publicity activities. As a game event is typically not presented with excitement, many issues also exist in game operations and event management. There are many other issues in the management and operation of the CTTSL and its clubs and events, primarily in the areas of ownership, policy and governance, sponsorship agreement, event presentations and operations, domestic and international marketing, revenue distribution, player drafting, contract, free agency, club transfer, salary cap, athlete endorsement, copyrights, and ultimately, competitive balance that are essential to protect the game attractiveness. Tao (2011) indicated that despite CTTSL being the top level table tennis competition in China, even in the world, effective marketing of the CTTSL has apparently lagged behind. All in all, the CTTSL events are not positioned high in the minds of consumers, although table tennis is a very popular participation sport in China. According to Feng (2008), Xu (2008), and Xu and Li (2010), the Chinese government dominates the administration of the CTTSL and controls the majority of financial resources, such as title sponsorship, broadcasting rights, advertisements, and athlete's rights of portraiture, which is detrimental to the advancement of the CTTSL. The CTTSL should gradually transfer from governmental administration to adopting a market-driven management model.

According to Zhang et al. (2016), there is an apparent gap between the CTTSL product offerings and the desires of consumers. In an effort to improve the quality of its product offerings, market appeal, consumer demand, and overall consumption level, a comprehensive review of literature was conducted to analyze the market environment of the Chinese Table Tennis Super League (CTTSL). Critical issues in the areas of market segmentation, branding, governance, and policies were identified and deemed influential on consumer perceptions of the CTTSL and its overall level of achievement. Discussions are conducted on the necessity and practical procedures of repositioning the CTTSL and repackaging its products. Experience gained and lessons learned in this process of striving for improving CTTSL operations may be useful for other professional table tennis leagues located in Europe and throughout other parts of the world.

Review of literature

Market segmentation

Segmentation is the process of partitioning markets into groups of potential customers with similar needs or characteristics who are likely to exhibit similar purchasing behavior. Segmentation is based on consumer decision-making that is impacted by rational and emotional factors. These factors are then used to group people together with the intention of targeting advertising and marketing programs at them in order to increase their purchasing behaviors (Pitts & Stotlar, 2012; Weinstein, 1994). Segmentation variables may include characteristics of individuals, groups, and/or organizations, which are used to divide the mass market into homogeneous groups. Examples of these variables are age, sex, race, income, household size, education, geographic location, personality traits, emotional needs, interests, opinions, activities, and memberships. Researchers have classified segmentation approaches into four areas: (a) state of being – demographics, (b) state of mind – psychographics, (c) state of doing – behavior, and (d) state of amalgamation – lifestyle. Mullin, Hardy, and Sutton (2007) and Pitts and Stotlar (2012) have indicated that an effective marketing investigation often requires multiple segmentation variables. While mass marketing is a necessary part of many marketing plans, this strategy is no longer as efficient or cost effective as it once was. The marketplace has changed and moved from a manufacturing-driven to a consumer-driven economy (Kotler, 1999). Smith (1956) wrote of the need to target homogeneous components of a heterogeneous market rather than the market as a whole, and was the first to call this strategy "segmentation."

Unlike the well-developed professional sports in western countries, professional sport leagues in China are presently going through the start-up period and their marketing strategies are overall lacking. Yang (1995), the former vice-president of ITTF, once predicted that table tennis as China's national sport gets most of the attention in the nation and takes on the responsibility of winning international honors for the country; expectedly, the transformation from a government-funded system to a market-driven system would be easily staged and well-supported for table tennis. Yet, this has in fact not been the case as evidenced by the limited advancement that the CTTSL has made as a professional sport league. As one of the most popular participation sports in China, its spectator support is apparently deficient. Zhong (2005) indicated that there is a general lack of marketing analyses for the table tennis marketplace in China; for example, CTTSL administrators are generally unaware of its target market. The consumption of table tennis relies mainly on the participation programs or sales of ping-pong equipment. Wang (2011) explained that most CTTSL matches were played in arenas with poor conditions located in small-size cities or towns. Its clubs change home court continually, which is often referred as "floating home court" or "migratory circus," due in part to the fact that the CTTSL is in fact more popular in small-size cities or towns. Presented with a multitude of entertainment options and intense market competition in big cities, the CTTSL seemingly cannot draw people's attention in large markets; even attendances at some of the world table tennis tournaments held in big cities have been sporadic. Tao (2011) speculated that while it may be a good attempt for some clubs to place their home courts in university facilities to cultivate future consumers, it may take a long time before a group of core consumers is formed. In fact, university campuses are not always appealing to all corporate sponsors.

Branding and brand equity

While branding is to develop, build, manage, and measure brand equity, brand equity focuses on values derived from both financial and customer-based perspectives. Essentially, brand equity is of four hierarchical dimensions: (a) brand awareness, (b) perceived quality, (c) brand associations, and (d) brand loyalty (Aaker, 1991; Raggio & Leone, 2009). Through offering functional (product related attributes – success, star player, head coach, team management; and non-product related attributes – logo, themes, colors, stadium, tradition, and product delivery), symbolic (i.e., fan identification and peer group acceptance), and experiential (i.e., escape, nostalgia, and pride in place) benefits, branding is the most commonly used method of building product identification and product differentiations, which usually begin with the adoption of a brand logo, brand name, or trademark, and continue through refining the product production and delivery process (Gladden & Funk, 2001, 2002). Of this process, positioning a brand in the minds of consumers represents the overarching desire of the producer and the marketer to establish a good image of the brand, particularly to those in the target market segment. Subsequently, product positioning provides indications about a product or brand on such key marketing questions as who, where, what, when, and even how at times.

Zhang, Cianfrone, Braunstein, and Kim (2007) further defined functional benefits of a sport game into two concepts for spectators, market demand and event operations. Sport games are the core product function of professional sport teams. Market demand is related to consumer expectations towards the attributes of the core product (Byon, Lam, & Zhang, 2011; Byon, Zhang, & Connaughton, 2010; Zhang, Lam, & Connaughton, 2003). Essentially, market demand is a cluster of pull factors associated with the game that a professional sport team can offer to its new and returning spectators (Braunstein, Zhang, Trail, & Gibson, 2005; Hansen & Gauthier, 1989; Schofield, 1983; Zhang et al., 1995). Game attractiveness (e.g., individual skills, presence of star players, team records, league standing, record-breaking performance, and closeness of competition), schedule convenience (e.g., game time, day of week, and weather), and economic consideration (e.g., ticket price, marketing promotions, availability of substitute forms of entertainment, television effect, and competition caused by other sport events) factors have been previously identified by researchers as affecting spectator decision-making for the attendance of professional basketball games (e.g., Hansen & Gauthier, 1989; Schofield, 1983; Zhang et al., 1995). While sport games are the core product function of a professional sport team, the coaching staff, athletes, and referees are primarily responsible for producing the core product. When operating games, team management usually has little involvement in the process of producing the core product. Instead, the team management primarily works on other product functions related to game support programs, such as ticket service and stadium quality. The quality of support programs often affects the overall operational effectiveness of a team, and even promotes the consumption levels of consumers (Brooks, 1994; Byon, Zhang, & Baker, 2013; Stotlar, 1989; Zhang et al., 2007). In many ways, support programs are a form of customer service. Customer service normally has four characteristics: intangible, inseparable, perishable, and variable (Kotler & Armstrong, 1997; Sasser, Olsen, & Wyckoff, 1978). Previous researchers indicated that customer satisfaction is an important consequence of service quality. Numerous researchers have suggested that the provision of high service quality is critical to the profitability of an organization because it enhances customer satisfaction and in turn, promotes customer loyalty (retention). Marketing resources are better spent by retaining existing customers than attracting new ones. In order to satisfy customers, service quality has to meet or exceed their expectations (Anderson, Fornell, & Lehmann, 1994; Reichheld & Sasser, 1990; Stoner, Freeman, & Gilbert, 1995; Zhang et al., 2004; Zhang, Lam, Connaughton, Bennett, & Smith, 2005). As little empirical evidence can be found about the core product features of the CTTSL and its event operations, it is highly speculated that few research investigations into the CTTSL's core product and event operations have been conducted. To some extent, this is likely caused by the inadequate attention given to these critical areas of functions by the CTTSL's league administration and its clubs.

In terms of symbolic and experiential benefits, sport spectators make an important contribution to the success of sporting events primarily through motivational and financial support. Unlike market demand variables as pull factors (Braunstein et al., 2005; Hansen & Gauthier, 1989; Schofield, 1983; Zhang et al., 1995), social motivations are personal push factors that work as internal motives for spectators to consume sport events (Funk, Mahony, Nakazawa, & Hirakawa, 2001; Kahle, Kambara, & Rose, 1996; Pease & Zhang, 2001; Wann, Melnick, Russell, & Pease, 2001; Zhang et al., 2007). According to Schwartz (1973), Sloan (1989), and Zillmann and Paulus (1993), there are five theoretical categories that can be used to explain the social motivations of sport fans: (a) salubrious effect theories (recreation theory and diversion theory), (b) stress and stimulation seeking theories, (c) catharsis and aggression theories (catharsis theory, frustration-aggression theory, and social learning theory), (d) entertainment theories, and (e) achievement seeking theories. Salubrious effect theories explain that spectators are attracted to a game for its pleasure and the benefits of physical and mental well-being. By attending sport events, spectators can relieve their fatigue and boredom and become re-charged. Sport attendance can also be used as an escape from work and other tediums of life. Based on stress and stimulation seeking theories, sport games are seen as stressors. Spectators are attracted to a game for stressing, risking, arousing, and stimulating experiences in a socially acceptable manner. Positive stress and arousal allows for the expenditure of excess energy by being involved with the crowd. Catharsis and aggression theories propose that spectators are attracted to a game for its violence and aggressive actions. Some believe that the aggression levels of spectators will be reduced by watching the acts of aggression of others, while others believe aggression levels are increased. According to entertainment theories, spectators are attracted to a game for seeking of pleasure, sensation, satisfaction, and happiness. The aesthetic application of skills in movement makes sport an art form for spectators. Achievement seeking theories emphasize that spectators are attracted to a team for identification with the achievement of others, sharing success, gaining knowledge, and satisfying their own needs. Of the five social motivation theories of spectatorship, achievement-seeking theories have been predominantly studied in relationship to spectator attendance (Pease & Zhang, 2001; Wann et al., 2001). To date, little research findings can be found about symbolic and experiential benefits associated with the CTTSL, indicating the lack of studies in this conceptual area.

A few studies on branding and brand equity of China's professional sports had been conducted in the past. Mao (2008), Song and Xu (2003), and Zhu and Song (2003) indicated that to some extent, the CBA have built a recognizable brand in China; even so, brand association and brand loyalty by its consumers are much lacking when compared to those of the National Basketball Association (NBA) in the USA and apparently, re-positioning the CBA in the mind of consumers is highly needed. Tang (2010) pointed out that a brand name is one of the most valuable assets for a professional sport league. The Chinese Football Super League should make efforts to enhance the quality of its core product, improve administrative effectiveness and efficiency at both the league and the club levels, and re-establish the prestige of the league in the minds of fans. Li (2005), Xin (2006), and Zhang (2008) explained that as the Chinese Volleyball Association is still in its infant stage of development, the league should learn from the successful experience of professional sport leagues in the western countries or regions in the areas of market-driven operations and branding management. Chai (2010) conceptually analyzed the brand equity of the CTTSL from the perspective of brand culture and emphasized the necessity of enhancing consumer awareness, establishing a home court arena, developing event ceremonies and rituals, increasing communications between clubs and consumers, promoting events with star players, and designing such distinct branding components as logo, catchphrase, mascot, and signal coloration so as to elevate the overall image of the CTTSL in the mind of spectators. All in all, of a few research attempts made previously, branding studies on China' professional sports have primarily focused on identifying issues in branding management; yet, none has focused on forming solutions.

Governance and policies

According to Stoner, Freeman, and Gilbert (1995), by-laws, policies, regulations, and rules are constitutional documents that are essential to the governance of an organization. These documents would provide explanations on general goals, purpose, and competencies of the organization, and also lay out plans and procedures to deal with work relationships within and beyond the organization. In particular, policies and regulations are operational plans that contain details for carrying out organizational strategies and operational plans in daily activities. For instance, the Operational Manual for CTTSL Clubs covers a wide range of administrative topics, such as athlete eligibility, drafting and transferring, athlete contracts, club management, standards of facilities, equipment, apparel, competition schedules, event management, advertisement and sponsorship, telecasting, marketing, media relations, officiating, and grassroots development (CTTSL, 2012). Presumably, any effort to enhance the marketing achievement and repositioning of the CTTSL would have to start from making changes and improvements in these operational policies, regulations, and procedures.

The CTTSL is the top table tennis division under the CTTA. The CTTA is responsible for organizing local, regional, national, and international tournaments and at the same time, seeking to involve itself with other associations to encourage, promote, and maintain table tennis as a popular sport and holistic form of exercise in China and even the world. The CTTA functions through a number of committees, including competition, coach, referee, equipment, scientific research, junior athlete development, and mass media. Yet, the CTTA is only the direct superior administrative organization for the CTTSL. In China, the national government has a centralized administration of all sport affairs. The national council establishes a special department to administer sports, the General Administration of Sport of China (GASC), which is equivalent to a ministry. Under this ministry, the Table Tennis and Badminton Administrative Center (TTBAC) is an administrative branch and the CTTA is essentially under the TTBAC's supervision. In actuality, the TTBAC is the superior governing body of the CTTSL, which directs the establishment of the league's policies and oversees its administration (Feng, 2008; Lan, 2007; Xu 2008; Xu & Li, 2010). The China Table Tennis Club League, the predecessors of CTTSL that started in 1995 and ended in 1997, first adopted a game-meeting system, where clubs were assembled temporarily and dissolved right after the competition. From 1998 to 2008, the CTTSL adopted a home-away (i.e., single) double round-robin system. From 2008, the CTTSL has been using the competition system with a double round-robin during the regular season and a single-elimination system during the post-season games, which helps extend the season, increases the numbers of matches, builds excitement, and closely resembles modern professional sport competition systems, such as that of the NBA. In an effort to restrain selling the hosting rights of home games, in 2005 CTTSL postulated a rule that every club must have a home court city and 45 percent of home games (i.e., five games) should be placed in this city. Since 2012, this number has been reduced to four games; even so, it is still far from a fixed home court. In an effort to have elite players available for international competitions, the season of CTTSL is often altered and compressed into four or five months, typically from June to October each year. During the Olympic Games year, the CTTSL season has to be postponed until after the Olympiad. When compared to the NBA, the length of a CTTSL season is considerably shorter and subsequently has a lessor amount of events and opportunities to appeal its game products to consumers. Due to an inconsistent season schedule and a short competition season, it is usually difficult for foreign athletes to make a plan in advance to play in the CTTSL. For this reason, international development and promotion for the CTTSL are very constrained (Ci, 2007; Liang, 2007; Qin, 2009).

To balance the interests among the CTTA, CTTSL clubs, athletes, and sponsors would be crucial for the CTTSL's long term development; however, the CTTA deprives primary rights and interests that are supposed to belong to CTTSL clubs and/or athletes originally. For instance, the best advertising signage spaces around a table tennis court, which are most frequently covered by television broadcasting, belong to the CTTA. This is also true for the athlete's rights of portraiture, for which the CTTA has the control. This type of policy would greatly hamper the development of the CTTSL as the CTTA establishes policies primarily benefiting itself (Qi, 2011). There is not a set salary-cap for each of the CTTSL clubs; nonetheless, to enhance competitive balance, athletes in the CTTSL are divided into three categories: super, top, and second-level players. For each club, the number of super and top level athletes is restrained. Presently, the sum of super and top level athletes in every club cannot be more than four, where super level athletes cannot be more than two. All international players are taken as top level athletes, assuming each is active in international competitions. While there is no limitation on the number of international players within a club, only one international player can play in a match for each club. To some degree, this rule excessively protects domestic players, restricting international players and working against the intended internationalization of the CTTSL. In 2006, the league started to implement an "athlete auction system." The overall salary level for the auctioned athletes received suddenly increased several-fold. Most of the auctioning prices were over ¥1.0 million, with some being around ¥5.0 million; however, a major portion of the contracted athlete salary needs to be submitted to the CTTA and also the province (or a city) where an athlete was cultivated. With the increased revenue for the CTTA, provinces/cities, and athlete, many clubs are actually running into financial crisis as they invest a lot but earn little. In 2012, the CTTSL cancelled the "athlete auction system" and implemented the "individual salary cap" policy that regulates an athlete's maximum salary. Additionally, the CTTA extended the permitted contract length between a club and an athlete from two years to four years. Regardless, most of the clubs are still financially struggling and oftentimes have to sell the hosting rights of home games to make up the budget deficit. To some extent, the new policies have helped reduced a club's financial stress.

The CTTA has recently taken a few initiatives to enhance commercial operations of the CTTSL and its clubs. For instance, negotiations have been made to have a few domestic corporations, such as 361 degrees, China Unicom, Double Happiness, Tinsu, Kweichow Moutai, and Chowtaifook, be league-wide sponsors. CTTA has just signed a broadcasting agreement with the China Central Television (CCTV), although it is rather a misfortune that the sales of television rights are merely exchanges for the CCTV's free broadcasting of CTTSL's matches, instead of being an avenue for revenue generation (Yuan, 2012). Consequently, game time has to be shortened at times and even altered to cater for the CCTV's live broadcasting schedule. Additionally, over the past few years game support programs are increasingly executed or offered by the club administrations to enhance the quality of event operations and also promote the appeal of game events to consumers. Entertainment activities such as dance teams (cheerleaders), band performances, and interactive games are often performed before, during, and after matches; nonetheless, entertainment activities other than the game itself are overall limited and the arena atmosphere is still dreary. Since 2012, the CTTSL has started to hold youth training camps that are aimed to cultivate young players and promote grassroots to build up the consumer base although the duration of the training camp was merely one week and only 30 juniors could attend. All in all, the commercial operations of the CTTSL are still at its primitive stage.

Challenging issues and opportunities

According to Zhang et al. (2016), the CTTSL adopted a general marketing approach, without a targeted market segment(s). Its events were more attractive to consumers in small to medium size markets and had little appeal to consumers in large markets due in part to the fact that many big cities in China had hosted one or more large-scale international and national sport events in recent years, typically including major league professional sport events in basketball, soccer, and baseball. There is a tremendous imbalance in the geographical locations of the CTTSL club teams, minimizing the exposure of both live and televised events, hampering the cultivation of a national audience, hindering the achievement level of sponsorship, and consequently reducing the likelihood of obtaining major sponsors. Currently, there are eight male and also eight female club teams in the CTTSL. Of them, a majority represent provinces, cities, organizations, or corporations located in the eastern and central regions of China, mainly those in economically well-developed communities. In fact, three of the eight men's teams are in Chekiang province. Unlike those well-developed major league sport leagues in western countries, the CTTSL does not have a defined geographic marketing territory for the teams, causing overlapping marketing efforts and limiting the achievement level of each team.

In terms of the league's core product, namely the game event itself, many CTTSL practices are considered issues and challenges that hamper the league's event operations and its overall achievement level. The major income of CTTSL came from sponsorships (title sponsor, signage, and endorsement), lacking income from ticket sales and broadcasting revenues. Event tickets were often used as giveaways for interest exchange with local authorities or business entities. For a short-term gain of income from auctioning the hosting rights, changing home court often occurred between seasons or even within a season from some teams. The CTTSL has signed a broadcasting agreement with the CCTV in an effort to develop and build up the event brand. Television broadcasting rights were merely used for free CCTV broadcasting. Oftentimes, CTTSL games had to be shortened or altered in their scheduling to meet broadcasting demand by the CCTV. In addition to television, the CCTV simultaneously televised the game events via its website and mobile phone devices, further leading to market competitions with the live event and televised programming. The league and its teams focused merely on elite table tennis competitions, overlooking the commercial and entertainment aspects of sport events. Most of the CTTSL teams approached the game event as a traditional form of sport competition rather than a commercialized sport product. As a matter of fact, most of the teams did not have a marketing unit within the team management, nor a budget for event promotions (e.g., advertising, publicity) (Zhang et al., 2016).

CTTSL policies go through frequent changes, lacking long-term visions, a well-planned course of actions, and consumer perceptions of stability. The league was at the beginning of developing a policy to reward establishing a home court. Within CTTSL policies, Olympic Games and the WTTC events were considered of much more priority than its own operations. Ultimately, the CTTA under the TTBAC administration controlled the CTTSL as a professional sport league, and established the league's policies that were more beneficial to these national administrations, sometimes at the expense of CTTSL clubs. On numerous occasions, the TTBAC and the CTTA deprived the basic rights and interests that were supposed to belong to the clubs and athletes (e.g., preferable signage locations in a competition venue, athlete's rights of portraiture). Mechanisms for maintaining competitive balance among teams, such as salary cap, salary floor, revenue sharing, and luxury tax, were rarely adopted, leading to the absence of evenly distributions of athletic talents. Consequently, some teams had been historically and repetitively dominating (Zhang et al., 2016).

Zhang, Zhang, Pitts, and Zhang (2014) summarized the challenges faced by the CTTSL in the areas of market segmentation, product branding, and governance and policy, which is organized and presented in Table 12.1. Promisingly, the CTTSL has recently launched a week-long summer youth table tennis camp that is aimed to expand the league's consumer base via grassroots promotions, and has also taken the initiatives to add entertainment activities such as dance teams (cheerleaders), band performances, artistic shows, interactive games, lucky draws, and giveaways during a game event; however, both the quality and quantity were primitive and far from adequate. The CTTSL has started to develop polices to implement a salary cap. It is only at the beginning stage for the CTTSL to require a player's contract that is longer than two competition seasons, aiming to form a comparatively more stable labor relationship. Over the recent years, the athlete's salary has had a multi-fold increase; yet, most of the teams have run an annual deficit and their expenditures usually far exceeded their budgets. Over time, the league administration has started to value a consumer-based operation and formulate policies that promote, govern, and enforce consumer-based marketing.

Table 12.1 Summary and synthesis of assertions from reviewing critical literature related to market segmentation, product branding, and governance and policy

Perspective		*Themes from Critical Literature*
Segmentation	Target market	• General marketing • Unaware of key segment of consumers • Lack of targeted marketing
	Location	• Little attractiveness to consumers in large markets • More attractive to consumers in small to medium size markets
	Geography	• Teams predominantly represent cities and/or corporations in the eastern region (three of eight male teams belonging to Chekiang province)
Branding	Core product	• Lack of event publicity • Fans complain that they could not get event information and event tickets are unobtainable • Lack of ticket sales channels • Lack of game event attractiveness • Sale of home court rights, leading to frequent shift of home court locations throughout a season and over seasons to gain income • Major income coming from sponsorships, lacking income from ticket sales and broadcasting revenues • Frequent change of title sponsors, leading to consumer confusion and sense of instability • Income from ticket sales is negligible • Oftentimes, CTTSL games have to be shortened or altered in schedule to meet broadcasting demand of the CCTV • In addition to television, CCTV simultaneously televise the game events via its website and mobile phone devices • Most of the teams do not have a marketing and promotion unit within the team management • The league and teams focus merely on elite table tennis competitions, overlooking the commercial and entertainment aspects of sport events • Event tickets are often used as giveaways for interest exchange with local authority or business entities • Shifting CTTSL season schedules due to major world competition events. • Shifting season schedules make it difficult for international players to join the league • Lack of international market development and promotion • Female athletes wearing skirts in the competition

(continued)

Table 12.1 (continued)

Perspective		*Themes from Critical Literature*
	Game event operations	• Events are held in poor arena conditions • Lack of accountability for sponsorship's investment • Most of the teams do not have a plan nor executed operations for event concessions • Most of the teams do not have a plan nor executed operations for sales licensed product • Sporadically host a week-long youth table tennis camp in the summer since 2010
	Symbolic and experiential benefits	• The focus is on elite athlete competitions, paying no attention to a fan's game experience • Spectators are after-thought • Lack of localized fan identification • Lack of fan loyalty • Lack of fan cultivation • Pay no attention to fans and consumer experience
Policy	General	• CTTA (TTBAC) controls the league • Organization of CTTSL depriving rights and revenues belonging to clubs • National government benefits are superior to club's benefit • CTTA (TTBAC) establishes policies that are beneficial to itself, but unfavorable to the clubs • CTTA/TTBAC deprives the rights and interests that are supposed to belong to the clubs (e.g., best advertise site, athlete's rights of portraiture) • Limiting number of foreign players entering game
	Competitive Balance	• Having mechanism for even distributions of talents • Lack of enforcement of consumer-based characteristics of sport event product • Started to install salary gap
	Labor Relations	• Only at beginning stage to require a longer term contract for athletes • Complexity and confusion caused by the dual-affiliation and dual-roles that athletes are expected to carry

Discussion

With an attempt to seek new strategies and improve the league's image in the mind of consumers, this review of literature study would help attain a competitive balance in the CTTSL, expedite the professionalism progress of the league, develop CTTSL events and products that are much more embraced by consumers, promote the overall development and success of professional table tennis in China and the world, and ultimately accelerate the global advancement of table tennis as an enjoyable, convenient sport game.

Mullin et al. (2007) and Pitts and Stotlar (2012) indicated the importance of identifying and serving a targeted market segment. In the present analysis, the realization that the CTTSL adopted a general marketing approach and was not aware of its key segment(s) of consumers indicates a need to conduct marketing surveys, use the collected information to formulate strategic plans, and ultimately create a new image in the minds of consumers. It is pitiful that the income from ticket sales was almost non-existent. Studying and building up the market demand to meet consumer expectations towards the attributes of the core product is absolutely necessary. To do so needs to take into consideration those variables affecting game attractiveness, schedule convenience, and economic consideration (Byon, Zhang, & Baker, 2013). The league needs to approach the game event as a commercial product that is based on in-depth understanding of consumer interests and needs. The league and its teams need to have formal marketing and promotion functions to monitor changes in market demands. They need to have a stable, well-thought competition schedule. A good professional league would welcome and provide equal opportunities for international athletes to join.

The quality of support programs often affects the overall operational effectiveness of a game event, and even promotes the consumption levels of consumers (Byon et al., 2013; Stotlar, 1989; Zhang et al., 2007). Marketing resources are better spent by retaining existing customers than attracting new ones. In order to satisfy customers, service quality has to meet or exceed their expectations (Reichheld & Sasser, 1990; Zhang et al., 2005). While it is promising that the CTTSL has recently taken the initiatives to add entertainment activities, making greater investment, building traditions and rituals for each club, enhancing quality improvement, and adopting creative entertainment ideas would further add entertainment value to a game event and help retain consumers. It is rather concerning that CTTSL consumers do not think its game events to be of high entertainment value due primarily to the fact that the CTTSL overlooks the importance of spectator experience at a game event. Due to the historical role that table tennis has played in China, socio-motivational factors identified in the western contexts (e.g., Sloan, 1989; Wann et al., 2001) may not fully explain the motives of Chinese consumers; for instance, nationalism, national pride, national attention, government support of table tennis, and extensive media highlights may have some significant impacts on consumer interests and consumption behaviors. Concerted efforts are necessary to study and understand those factors affecting the motivation of CTTSL consumers.

Based on the above discussions, it is apparent that some institutionalized marketing functions are necessary to help develop and promote the CTTSL brand. In this process, athletes, coaches, and team administrations can all play a major role, such as organizing and attending publicity activities and social functions (e.g., meeting fans, signing photographs, visiting communities, and coaching youth teams). As the CTTSL has the elitist group of table tennis players, having a developmental league (i.e., a minor table tennis professional league) may also help generate fan awareness and interest. Every effort needs to be made to enhance competitive balance among CTTSL clubs. The nature of the sport industry is such that competitors must be of approximately equal capacity to be successful. It is the degree to which teams in a league are evenly matched and talents are evenly distributed. It appears necessary that the CTTSL needs to make concerted efforts to sort out the labor relations among its constituents and stakeholders, which should at least include the league administration, provinces/cities, teams, and athletes. Future studies may consider conducting quantitative investigations into specific topic areas by utilizing the themes summarized in this article.

References

Aaker, D. A. (1991). *Managing Brand Equity*. New York, NY: Free.

Anderson, E. W., Fornell, C., & Lehmann, D. R. (1994). Customer Satisfaction, Market Share, and Profitability: Findings from Sweden. *Journal of Marketing, 58(3)*, 53–66.

Braunstein, J. R., Zhang, J. J., Trail, G. T., & Gibson, H. J. (2005). Dimensions of Market Demand Associated with Major League Baseball Spring Training: Development of a Scale. *Sport Management Review, 8(3)*, 271–96.

Brooks, C. M. (1994). *Sport Marketing: Competitive Business Strategies for Sport*. Englewood Cliffs, NJ: Prentice-Hall.

Brown, M. T., Rascher, D. A., Nagel, M. S., & McEvoy, C. D. (2010). *Financial Management in the Sport Industry*. Scottsdale, AZ: Holcomb Hathaway.

Byon, K. K., Zhang, J. J., & Connaughton, D. P. (2010). Dimensions of General Market Demand Associated with Professional Team Sports: Development of a Scale. *Sport Management Review, 13(2)*, 142–57.

Byon, K. K., Lam, E. T. C., & Zhang, J. J. (2011). Does Event Quality Enhance Team Identification? *Research Quarterly for Exercise & Sport, 82(1)*, A78.

Byon, K. K., Zhang, J. J., & Baker, T. A. (2013). Impact of Market Demand and Game Support Programs on Consumption Levels of Professional Team Sport Spectators as Mediated by Perceived Value. *European Sport Management Quarterly, 13(2)*, 232–63.

Chai, H. N. (2010). *Creating Sport Brand Culture: The Case of CTTSL*. Beijing, China: General Sport Administration of China.

Chinese Table Tennis Super League. (2005). *Operational Manual of Chinese Table Tennis Clubs*. Beijing, China: CTTSL.

Chinese Table Tennis Super League. (2012). *Operational Manual of Chinese Table Tennis Clubs.* Beijing, China: CTTSL.

Chu, Y. P. (2011, September). League Started from Flash Marriage. *Table Tennis World, 227,* 28.

Ci, X. (2007, June 5). A Strict Participation Rule to International Athlete Resulting in "Zero International Player" in CTTSL this Year. *China Youth Daily,* p. 1.

Feng, F. (2008). An Analysis of the Issues Associated with Athlete Transfer in CTTSL. *Journal of Nanyang Normal University, 7(6),* 64–66.

Funk, D. C., Mahony, D. F., Nakazawa, M., & Hirakawa, S. (2001). Development of the Sport Interest Inventory (SII): Implications for Measuring Unique Consumer Motives at Team Sporting Events. *International Journal of Sports Marketing & Sponsorship, 3,* 291–316.

Gladden, J. M., & Funk, D. C. (2001). Understanding Brand Loyalty in Professional Sport: Examining the Link between Brand Associations and Brand Loyalty. *International Journal of Sports Marketing & Sponsorship, 3,* 67–95.

Gladden, J. M., & Funk, D. C. (2002). Developing an Understanding of Brand Associations in Team Sport: Empirical Evidence from Consumers of Professional Sport. *Journal of Sport Management, 16,* 54–81.

Hansen, H., & Gauthier, R. (1989). Factors Affecting Attendance at Professional Sport Events. *Journal of Sport Management, 3,* 15–32.

International Table Tennis Federation. (2017). ITTF Museum: Table Tennis in Olympics Games. Retrieved from www.old.ittf.com/museum/Olympicgames.html.

Kahle, L. R., Kambara, K. M., & Rose, G. M. (1996). A Functional Model of Fan Attendance Motivations for College Football. *Sport Marketing Quarterly, 5(4),* 51–60.

Kotler, P. (1999). *Marketing Management* (10th edn). Englewood Cliffs, NJ: Prentice Hall.

Kotler, P., & Armstrong, G. (1997). *Marketing* (4th edn). Englewood Cliffs, NJ: Prentice-Hall.

Lam, E. T. C., Zhang, J. J., & Jensen, B. E. (2005). Service Quality Assessment Scale (SQAS): An Instrument for Evaluating Service Quality of Health-fitness Clubs. *Measurement in Physical Education and Exercise Science, 9(2),* 79–111.

Lan, T. (2007). *Exploring the Professionalism and Administration System of Table Tennis in China.* Unpublished doctoral dissertation, Beijing Sport University, Beijing, China.

Li, G. D. (2005). *Building Brand of Chinese Volleyball Association: Its Origination and Development.* Unpublished doctoral dissertation, Beijing Sport University, Beijing, China.

Liang, Y. (2007, January 12). A Setback in Marketization of CTTSL: Limiting the Participation of International Athlete to Ensure 2008 Olympics Gold Medals. *Nanfang Daily,* p. 8.

Mao, Y. Q. (2008). *Communication Strategies for Chinese Basketball Association's Brand's Building.* Unpublished master's thesis, Fudan University, Shanghai, China.

Mullin, B. J., Hardy, S., & Sutton, W. A. (2007). *Sport Marketing.* Champaign, IL: Human Kinetics.

Pease, D. G., & Zhang, J. J. (2001). Socio-motivational Factors Affecting Spectator Attendance at Professional Basketball Games. *International Journal of Sport Management, 2(1),* 31–59.

Pitts, B. G., & Stotlar, D. K. (2012). *Fundamentals of Sport Marketing* (4th edn). Morgantown, WV: Fitness Information Technology.

Qi, G. (2011). Where is the Story for CTTSL? *Table Tennis World, 227(9),* 30.

Qin, D. Y. (2009, May 24). Incompatibility of Competition Schedule Resulting in Almost no European athletes in CTTSL. *Jiefang Daily*, p. 5.

Raggio, R. D., & Leone, R. P. (2009). Drivers of Brand Value, Estimation of Brand Value in Practice and Use of Brand Valuation: Introduction to the Special Issue. *Journal of Brand Management, 14(5)*, 2.

Reichheld, F. F., & Sasser, E. W. (1990). Zero Defections: Quality Comes to Services. *Harvard Business Review, 68*, 105–11.

Sasser, W. E., Olsen, R. P., & Wyckoff, D. D. (1978). *Management of Service Operations: Text and Cases.* Boston, MA: Allyn & Bacon.

Schofield, J. A. (1983). Performance and Attendance at Professional Team Sports. *Journal of Sport Behavior, 6*, 196–206.

Schwartz, J. M. (1973). Causes and Effects of Spectator Sports. *International Review of Sport Sociology, 8(3)*, 25–43.

She, Y. G. (2006). *Marketing Operations for the Sport Event of Chinese Basketball Association.* Unpublished master's thesis, Southwest University of Finance and Economics, Chengdu, China.

Sloan, L. R. (1989). The Motives of Sports Fans. In J. H. Goldstein (Ed.), *Sports, Games, and Play: Social and Psychological Viewpoints* (2nd edn) (pp. 175–240). Hillsdale, NJ: Lawrence Erlbaum.

Smith, W. (1956). *American Enters the World – A People's History of the Progressive Era and World War I* (Vol. 7). New York, NY: McGraw-Hill.

Song, J. Y., & Xu, Y. G. (2003). Strategies for Brand Building of Division I of Men's Basketball of China. *Journal of Guangzhou Physical Education Institute, 23(5)*, 4–6.

Stoner, J. A. F., Freeman, R. E., & Gilbert, D. R. (1995). *Management* (6th edn). Englewood Cliffs, NJ: Prentice Hall.

Stotlar, D. K. (1989). *Successful Sport Marketing.* Dubuque, IA: W. C. Brown.

Tang, C. Q. (2010). *Strategies for Brand Promotion of Chinese Football League.* Unpublished master's thesis, Hunan Normal University, Changsha, China.

Tao, X. Y. (2011, September 16). Difficulty to Giving Consideration to Both Social and Economic Benefits: Clubs having Floating Home courts in CTTSL. *Xinmin Evening News*, p. 8.

Wang, Y. (2011, July 12). Why do CTTSL Clubs become Circus? The Over-emphasis on Capital Gain. *Wenhui Daily*, p. 16.

Wann, D. L., Melnick, M. J., Russell, G. W., & Pease, D. G. (2001). *Sports Fans: The Psychology and Social Impact of Spectators.* New York, NY: Routledge.

Weinstein, A. (1994). *Market Segmentation: Using Demographics, Psychographics, and Other Niche Marketing Techniques to Predict Customer Behavior* (2nd edn). New York, NY: McGraw-Hill.

What's on Xiamen. (2010). *Professional Sports, Sports Culture, Popular Sports in China.* Retrieved from www.whatsonxiamen.com/health1352.html.

Xin, Q. F. (2006). *Strategies for the Improvement of Brand Design of Chinese Volleyball Association.* Unpublished master's thesis, Beijing Sport University, Beijing, China.

Xu, J. L. (2008). Influence of Sport System Transformation on the Operation of CTTSL. Unpublished Doctor's thesis, Beijing Sport University, Beijing, China.

Xu, J. L., & Li, H. S. (2010). Influence of Sport System Transformation on the Operation of CTTSL. *Journal of Sports Adult Education, 26(4)*, 18–19.

Yang, S. (1995, April). Remain Sober-minded and Accelerate the Speed of Reform. *Table Tennis World, 221*, 10–11.

Yuan, H. (2012). CTTSL Organizing Committee: Strong collaboarations to enhance the productivity of clubs. Available at http://sports.sohu.com/20090730/n265585442.shtml.

Zhang, L. L. (2008). *Exploring the Factors Affecting the Branding and Marketing Strategies of Chinese Volleyball Association*. Unpublished master's thesis. Henan University, Zhengzhou, China.

Zhang, J. J., Cianfrone, B. C., Braunstein, J. R., & Kim, D. H. (2007). Marketing Strategies for the Development of Sport Business in North America. *Proceeding of SPOEX 2007: International Sport Industry Seminar*, 41–72.

Zhang, J. J., Connaughton, D. P., & Vaughn, C. (2004). The Quality of Special Programs and Services for NBA Season Ticket Holders and their Predictability to Game Consumption. *International Journal of Sport Marketing and Sponsorship, 6(2)*, 99–116.

Zhang, J. J., Lam, E. T. C., & Connaughton, D. C. (2003). General Market Demand Variables Associated with Professional Sport Consumption. *International Journal of Sport Marketing and Sponsorship, 5(1)*, 33–55.

Zhang, J. J., Lam, E. T. C., Connaughton, D. P., Bennett, G., & Smith, D. W. (2005). Development of a Scale Measuring Spectator Satisfaction Toward Support Programs of Minor League Hockey Games. *International Journal of Sport Management, 6(1)*, 47–70.

Zhang, J. J., Pease, D. G., Hui, S. C., & Michaud, T. J. (1995). Variables Affecting the Spectator Decision to Attend NBA Games. *Sport Marketing Quarterly, 4(4)*, 29–39.

Zhang, J. J., Pennington-Gray, L., Connaughton, D. P., Braunstein, J. R., Ellis, M. H., Lam, E. T. C., & Williamson, D. (2003). Understanding Women's Professional Basketball Game Spectators: Sociodemographics, Game Consumption, and Entertainment Options. *Sport Marketing Quarterly, 12(4)*, 228–43.

Zhang, M. Y., Kim, M. K., Pitts, B. G., & Zhang, J. J. (2015). From East to West: Growth and Organization of Asian Sport Events in North America. *Journal of Shanghai University of Sport, 39(4)*, 19–23.

Zhang, M. Y., Xie, Y., Zhang, L., Pitts, B., & Zhang, J. J. (2016). Repositioning the Chinese Table Tennis Super League: An Inductive Inquiry. *Journal of Xi'an University of Sport, 24(2)*, 1–15.

Zhang, M. Y., Zhang, L., Pitts, B., & Zhang, J. J. (2014, October). Examining Key Strategies for Repositioning the Chinese Table Tennis Super League: Development of a Theoretical Framework. Paper presented at the 2014 World Association for Sport Management Conference, Madrid, Spain.

Zhong, Y. J. (2005). *Theory and Practice for the Exploration of Table Tennis Market in China*. Unpublished doctoral dissertation, Beijing Sport University, Beijing, China.

Zhu, Z. J., & Song, J. Y. (2003). Influence of Brand Image on Division I Men's Basketball of China. *Journal of Chengdu Sport University, 29(4)*, 51–57.

Zillmann, D., & Paulus, P. B. (1993). Spectators: Reactions to Sports Events and Effect on Athletic Performance. In R. N. Singer, M. Murphey, & L. K. Tennant (Eds.), *Handbook of Research on Sport Psychology* (pp. 600–19). New York, NY: McMillan.

Chapter 13

Examining the limits and opportunities of innovations in sport management practice

Jana Nová

Introduction

Whereas in other sectors the impact of innovations on management and product portfolio development is heavily researched, in sport a systematic exploration of the link between innovations, management, and digital transformation is missing. In the literature, we can find contributions, which deal with the organizational context of innovation in sport. Newell and Swan (1995) presented a framework for understanding the diffusion of innovations in sport organizations, Caza (2000) explored the receptivity context of innovation in an amateur sport organization, and Hoeber and Hoeber (2012) classified the determinants that contribute to the innovation process, in a community sport organization. Winand, Vos, Zintz, & Scheerder (2013) developed an explorative typology of sports federations based on their attitudes and perceptions of determinants of innovation and their innovation capacity and Winand and Zintz (2014) explored the different types of innovations implemented by sports federations. Many other authors have focused on a description of various types of innovations in different sports and sports organizations (Desbordes, 2001; Goff, McCormick, & Tollison, 2002; Hughes, Lee, & Chesterfield, 2009). Sport and technological innovations are another well-developed research area. Balmer, Pleasence, and Nevill (2012) gauged the impact of technological and technical innovation on Olympic performance. In many popular sports newspapers and journals various rankings of top innovations in sport from the past decades can be found describing sporting gear, apparel, merchandise innovations, sports stadium innovations, winter and summer Olympic innovations, training innovations, innovations in sports broadcasting, etc..

The impact of technology on sport has been examined in details by Fuss, Subic, and Ujihashi in 2007, providing a deeper insight into sports technology and its recent developments from the perspective of different disciplines, industrial practice, academia, and athletes. The nature of athletic performance considering the relationship between sport, technology and the body was explored by Magdalinski (2009). A business perspective in an examination of sport and technology is offered by Pope, Kuhn, and Forster (2009). From the literature review regarding innovations and sport management, it is obvious that the research of innovations in sport is focused either on innovations introduced by sports organizations for the improvement of their processes or services or on technological innovations introduced for the improvement of performance in sport and its measurement.

Considering the scope of the types of innovations presented in the two most cited sources in terms of the classification of innovations – Oslo Manual (2005) and Doblin Ten types of innovation (Kelsey, Walter, Pikkel, & Quinn, 2013) – we can identify the gap in the classification of innovations in sport and subsequently the gap with regard to new opportunities for developing defensible innovations in many other areas related to management in sports, such as finance, process, offering, and delivery when considering the new opportunities brought by digital transformation. In sports literature, we cannot find the conceptual framework for analyzing the various types of innovations in the sports sector and therefore our aim is to encourage a systematic approach towards assessing the possibility of innovation in sports and sports organizations in the light of Industry 4.0 that is deeply rooted in the digital transformation.

The concept of Industry 4.0 originates from a German government project to promote digitalization or computerization (Lasi, Fettke, Kemper, Feld, & Hoffmann, 2014). As Magruk (2016) states, Industry 4.0 can also be described as the digitization of material production, driven by cyber-physical systems in the Internet of Things (IoT) environment, which consists of two main components in the form of Internet of Services (IoS) and Internet of Media (IoM). Clouds, big data and their processing, and social media and mobile applications are named among the components of Industry 4.0 as well as smart products (Hermann, Pentek, & Boris, 2015). The impact of this fourth industrial revolution is discussed by a number of researchers in different sectors and in sport as well (PwC study on digitalization in football, 2014). Digital transformation is changing the nature of the magic triangle that consists of product, users, and market (Figure 13.1).

To exploit fully the potential of digital reality sports organizations should develop their own digital strategies. Until now only a few sport clubs and leagues have declared that they have elaborated their digital strategy – for example FC Barcelona (Jivaldi, LLC 2016) or NBA (Reddish, 2016) but their digital strategies are focusing just on marketing using social media and smart technologies. In our view digitalization is affecting not only marketing processes but also other core and minor processes in sports organizations and the logic of digital transformation in sports organizations is presented in Figure 13.2.

Apart from the elements of Industry 4.0 digitalization of sports organizations is also to a great extent driven by the digitalization of users that have changed from traditional customers represented by generation X to digital

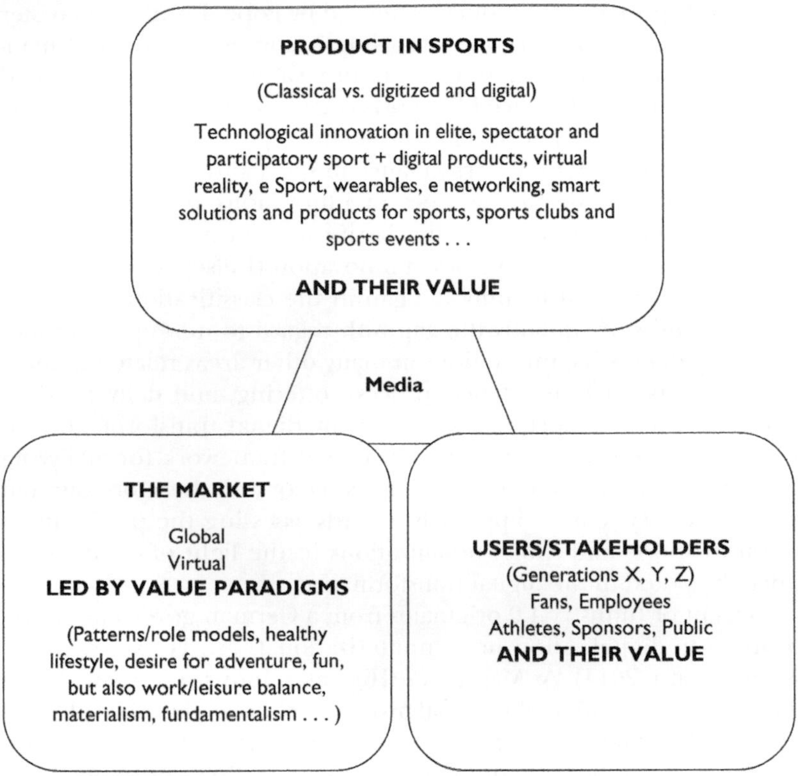

PRODUCT IN SPORTS

(Classical vs. digitized and digital)

Technological innovation in elite, spectator and participatory sport + digital products, virtual reality, e Sport, wearables, e networking, smart solutions and products for sports, sports clubs and sports events . . .

AND THEIR VALUE

Media

THE MARKET

Global
Virtual

LED BY VALUE PARADIGMS

(Patterns/role models, healthy lifestyle, desire for adventure, fun, but also work/leisure balance, materialism, fundamentalism . . .)

USERS/STAKEHOLDERS

(Generations X, Y, Z)
Fans, Employees
Athletes, Sponsors, Public

AND THEIR VALUE

Figure 13.1 Digital transformation and its influence on the magic triangle – product, market, and users

natives that are represented by generations Y and Z (PwC study on digitalization in football, 2014). Processing of big data in sport can be resolved by implementing the concept of sport business intelligence that means relevant, systematic, and continuous data collection in order to develop sports organizations, sport events and/or sport activities (Rasku Puronaho, & Turco, 2015). This concept must be inevitably accompanied by the utilization of IT tools and systems and the usage of smart solutions.

Method

For assessing the opportunities and limitations of innovation in sports management various concepts have been used and analyzed, namely: innovation typology, the specific features of sport and their influence on sports management, digital transformation.

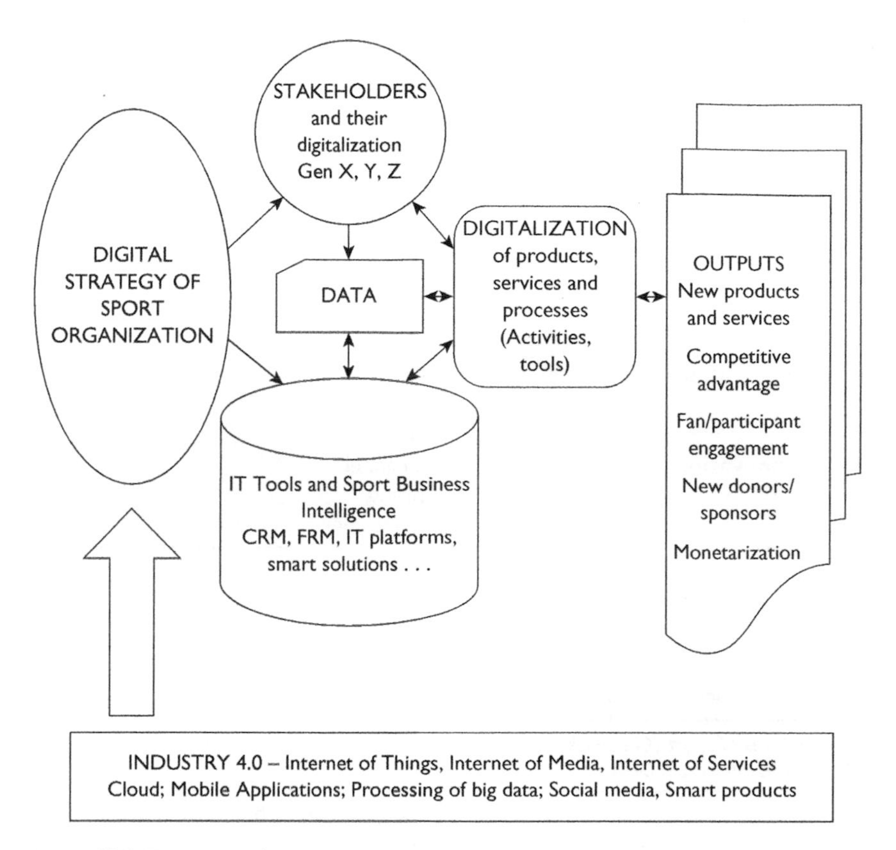

Figure 13.2 The logic of the digital transformation in sport organizations

First, the 'Ten types of innovation' framework (Keeley, Walters, Pikkel, & Quinn, 2013) as an example of innovation typology was used (Table 13.1). The influence of the specific features of sport on innovations in Finance, Process, Offering, and Delivery in sport was analyzed bearing in mind the influence of the specific features of sport on innovations in sport (Table 13.2; Nová, Novotný, Racek, Rektořík, Sekot, Strachová, & Válková, 2016). Second, digital transformation and its influence on the magic triangle – product, market and users (see Figure 13.1) – have been also taken into consideration when assessing the limits and opportunities in sports management.

All the above-mentioned frameworks provided us with the opportunity to explore how the specific features of sport and digital transformation affect the introduction of the different types of innovations within sport organizations and where the limits for innovation are. It also allowed us to evaluate the opportunities for not only product or services innovation but also for many other types of innovation that go beyond sports products.

Table 13.1 Ten types of innovation – original structure and categorization used from 1998–2011

Type of Innovations	
Finance Innovations	Business model Networking
Process innovations	Enabling Process/ Structure Innovations Core Process
Offering innovations	Product Product System Service
Delivery innovations	Channel Brand Consumer Experience

Note: Adapted from Keeley et al., 2013 (p. 11).

Table 13.2 Influence of the specific features of sport on sport management

Specific features of sport (Chadwick, 2011; Smith & Stewart, 2010)	*Influence on Sport Management*
Irrational passion for sporting teams, competition or athletes; high degree of optimism and brand loyalty	Risk taking can be higher than in usual business
Different perception of the performance in sport; uncertainty of the outcome	High creativity in the development of the variety of economic, social, and environmental indicators for evaluation of the institutional performance
Competitive balance, the principle of "collaborating to compete"	The need to accept and balance the principles of "accepting the competitor"
Limited organizational control over product – limits the scope to attain competitive advantage	Necessity of inventing the unique non-sport product 's competitive advantage
Variable quality of sport product, fans (customers) are producers and consumers	Inclusion of the fans and consumers of sport activities in the creation of the quality of the sport product
Symbiotic relationship with the media	Sports-oriented innovations are bound to the media sector
Limited availability	The need to maintain the financially balanced and mixed (sporty and business-like) portfolio of the products

Note: Cited from Nová et al., 2016.

Results and discussion

The analysis of innovations, which can occur in sports organizations, was conducted within Doblin's framework. Limits as well as opportunities set by the specific features of sport and digital transformation were considered in each type of innovation and are presented in Tables 13.3–13.6.

Table 13.3 Finance innovations in sport management

Business model
Limitation: Organizations that operate in the sports industry can, when it comes to their organizational structure, meet with a phenomenon that is called organizational isomorphism (DiMaggio & Powell, 1983). Dominant profit models such as Limited Liability Company, Association, league, union, society, club, incorporated natural person, non-profit organizations etc. have been taken for granted for decades. Sport is reliant on third party payments and this limits its freedom in terms of the introduction of new business models as well as pricing policies which is accompanied by limited control over the product.
Opportunities: The interdependences of sports stakeholders and the media represent new opportunities for new business models in order to fully exploit the business opportunities. The implementation of innovative business models supported by innovative Internet-based IT systems can also assure wide participation in sport. Teaming in the local context – local players, employers, sports clubs, local governments, insurance companies – means sharing the expenses related to participation in sports (local grants for supporting sports activities). Shared ownership of new ventures in sport means collaborating/partnering in generating revenues and managing costs. Moreover, social media allows the introduction of the new type of financing, so-called crowdfunding – the practice of funding a project or venture by raising many small amounts of money from a large number of people, typically via the Internet (https://en.oxforddictionaries.com), and this can happen on a global scale due to the global and virtual nature of the sports market.
Networking
Limitations: The need to accept and balance the principles of "accepting the competitor", competitive balance, the principle of "collaborating to compete" are the specific features of sport which naturally support the existence of leagues and sports associations, merging different kinds of sports under umbrella organizations that cluster their own strengths with the capabilities and assets of others. A symbiotic relationship with the media as an exclusive feature of sport represents a unique kind of networking. This networking is typical for elite sport and brings a billion-dollar business for both – media and sports clubs or athletes.
Opportunities: The exploration and exploitation of networking as innovation is overlooked in community sport and sports clubs at the local level. Therefore, a strategic approach should be applied towards the usage of different forms of networking including alliances, complementary partnering, and cooperation.

(continued)

Table 13.3 (continued)

Business model
Sharing the expertise of coaching techniques and procedures among professional clubs and local sports clubs is one example of this kind of innovation. Building Innovation Learning Networks at the sports associations' level is another. Networking processes can be enhanced by the utilization of information technologies and digitalization of communication processes (Skype for business, O365 platforms such as Yammer, Share point, Teams, etc.).

Table 13.4 Process innovations in sport management

Enabling process/structure innovations
Limitations: The limited organizational control over the sport product limits the scope to attain a competitive advantage and therefore the necessity of inventing the unique non–sport product's competitive advantage supports strongly the focus on structure and process innovations in sport. But these innovations need internal investment and may be funded by government, media, partners, associations, but can be problematic for NGOs in the sport.
Opportunities: Structure and process innovations should focus on creating environments that are productive towards performance that would attract the best talents and athletes to sports organizations or a variety of participants. Innovations of internal structures in sports organizations mean using the flexible and project-based forms of organizational structure that would create productive working and sporting environments so as to foster organizational as well as individual performance. An innovative talent and incentives system, decentralized management based on knowledge management, appropriate organizational design and IT integration are the means by which sports organizations can achieve unique competitive advantages. An example, which represents this type of innovation, is effective sports records for improving performance and information sharing, simplifying administrative procedures, ticketing, and open access to information for various customers and fan groups and implementation of relevant hardware and software solutions based on the logic of sport business intelligence and analytics.
Core processes
Limitations: To exploit the process innovations in sports organizations means that they can use their unique capabilities efficiently and adapt quickly to meet sport, social, and economic goals.
Opportunities: Inclusion of the fans and consumers of sports activities in the creation of the quality of the sports product, a different perception of performance in sport and uncertainty of the outcome – these are the specific features of sport in favor of implementing the variety of process innovations such as standardization, localization, logistic systems, strategic design, process automation, on-demand production, and usage of intellectual property. Process innovations often form the core competency of the sports organization, but sports are surrounded by a myriad of regulators who have significant influence on not only sports products but also the standards they must follow. 24-hour access around the globe for sports

spectators/consumers using innovations in IT and the social media, sharing sport results on-line, sharing the experience of different sports communities around the globe (global fan clubs), introduction of the different ISO standards namely – ISO 9001, ISO 9001 - quality management system, ISO 14001 - Environmental management systems, ISO 20121 - Sustainable events (www.iso.org) for improving the processes – these all represent this type of innovation. Through digitalization there is competition in sport among the clubs, although they use common systems (for reservations, ticket sales, providing catering services, in marketing, etc.).

Table 13.5 Offering innovations in sport management

Innovations in the offering - Product, Product System and Service
Limitations: Product, Product System and Service in sport should be judged together, considering the fact that in sport the offer for customers is not just the product but also the sport experience, which is a much broader concept than the product in "pure business". Moreover, customers in sport are seeking cost-efficient sport involvement and activities of a high-quality standard. Innovation in offering means innovating the product design, service design and discovering how the particular service can be delivered more effectively and efficiently. Specific features of sport, namely a different perception of performance in sport and limited organizational control over the sport product heavily influence the scope of innovations that can be implemented in the offering.
Opportunities: To explore the innovation opportunities regarding the offering in sport the classification of products in the sports industry (Pitts & Stotlar, 2013) can be used: participation in sport, elite sport, professional competitions, equipment and accessories for sport, promotional items and media outlets to promote sport, services of sports facilities, marketing research in sport, managerial services for sport and athletes. With regard to the above-mentioned classification of the innovation landscape in sport, sport scientists are involved in projects related to athletes' equipment, coaching and measurement technologies, training science and medical management (Drawer, 2008). These findings are now incorporated into new diagnostic, sport performance, and coaching devices and programmes – especially for elite sport. Thus professional sport has enjoyed a huge development due to significant technological innovation (performance in product innovation). But when it comes to the organization of elite and club sports and especially to the widening of participation in sport via new sport products these have not changed much. But the digital transformation has brought new sports products such as eSports (also known as electronic sports, competitive (video) gaming, professional (video) gaming, or pro gaming). Internet-based creation of leagues in different sports is another example of how digitalization can enhance participation (www.vaseliga.cz/en). Virtual and Augmented Reality offers a completely different experience and views over the match and sporting events. The limited approach towards product innovation in sport can be overcome by realizing that there is a variety of digital elements that make the sport product unique, such as event, ticketing, organization, facility, equipment, apparel.

(continued)

Table 13.5 (continued)

Innovations in the offering - Product, Product System and Service
Product Performance
Limitations: This type of innovation develops distinguishing features and functionality and involves entirely new products, as well as updates and line extensions that add substantial value. When it comes to the core elements of sport product, their scope of innovation is limited to sport event experience's four components (Mullin, Hardy, & Sutton, 2000): (a) game form (rules/ techniques), (b) players, (c) equipment, and (d) venue.
Opportunities: Although sports products show low evidence of change, innovations in these elements can produce new product categories in sport. The whole variety of the innovations is in place as a result of the digital transformation – wearable technology for athletes which collects data relating to acceleration, direction, position, etc. are changing the sport experience offering on-line data to coaches as well as fans. The concept of the connected stadium (Wi-Fi connection in stadia) and the connected fan is changing the sport experience radically (CISCO, 2015). The introduction of Hawk-Eye – a complex computer system – has changed the rules in some sports.
Product System and Services in sport
Limitations: The effort towards innovation regarding the product system and services in sport should deal with and distinguish three levels of the sport product/ service (Blakey, 2011): • **Fundamental benefit provided by the sport product/service** – personal sport experience • **Expected sport product/ service** – comprises the actual components received by the sport consumer • **Augmented sport product/service** – presents enhanced features to improve the basic offer
Opportunities: Complementary products and services create valuable connections between otherwise distinct and disparate offerings. Development of the programs dedicated towards improving customer service and creating a competitive advantage for sport organizations and fan e-cards (credit, personal information, attendance record, prepaid services, and update via the Internet), pre- and post-sport event services for different target groups (customization) represent this type of innovation. Utilization of IT tools for processing of the data related to fans and sponsors such as CRM, FRM, Sport Business Intelligence concept and techniques alongside with the implementation of the appropriate quality systems (Nová, 2013) can radically change the approach towards the quality of the product system and services in sport.

Table 13.6 Delivery innovations in sport management

Channel
Limitations: Channel innovations encompass all the ways sports organizations connect and provide offerings to customers and users. Individuals are seeking not only sport success but also sport experience and entertainment, many of them also for preventive purposes. The new generation has access to information and can compare the offer in sport with other alternatives and they choose excellence.

The specific features of sport, namely limited availability and the need to maintain the financially balanced and mixed (sport- and business-like) portfolio of the products, force sports organizations to provide affordable sports activities in the evenings and at weekends and to accommodate the different needs of families, seniors, etc.

Opportunities: E-business has impacted the provision of sport profoundly and replaced the traditional channels of delivery in sport such as physical attendance at sports events. However, considering the sport product as a sport experience, innovations in physical environments (venues) are still important. When it comes to the spectator sport product, what is important is to find innovative multiple but complementary ways to bring sport products and services to customers. The recently introduced iFollow is a digital live streaming and content platform that will revolutionise the way football fans overseas can follow their EFL teams (Claxton, 2017). More and more fans are consuming the sport using their smart phones (Sport Business INTL, 08/09/2017).

Brand

Limitations: Can be caused by the heavy reliance on an irrational passion for sporting teams, competition, or athletes and thus overlooking the new approaches to enhance the brand and image of the sports organization, especially in "non-winning" times.

Opportunities: A high degree of optimism and brand loyalty are the specific features of sport that have brought a generation of loyal fans, athletes, and employers. They recognize, remember, and prefer particular sports brands to those of competitors or substitutes. Branding PR campaigns, offering sponsored/free services for fans and sports participants are characteristic of this type of innovation. In this sense, social media provides endless opportunities for building the global fan base measured by digital reach (DSM, Digital Reach, 2016).

Customer Experience

Limitations: Both sports organizations and sports customers have built over some time not only beneficial but also emotional connections. This also allows managers in sport to take a higher risk, which is another specific feature of sport – risk taking can be higher than in normal business, but it must still be wisely assessed and is heavily influenced by the expected sporting performance and expected standard of the services.

Opportunities: In sport customers are naturally engaged in the innovation process as far as they are at the same time consumers and producers of the sport product. Inclusion of the fans and consumers of sport activities in the creation of the quality of the sport product can be enhanced by gathering, processing, and using the available data as is envisaged by the Sport Business Intelligence concept (Rasku et al., 2015). Customized Customer Relationship Management (CRM) and Fan Relationship Management (FRM) IT systems such as ProSport 365 (http://prosport365.dk/) Optimised sales, sponsors, and event management for professional sports clubs, provide a unique opportunity for the enhancement of fans' engagement. The technique called Crowdsourcing allows obtaining (information or input into a particular task or project) by enlisting the services of a number of people, either paid or unpaid, typically via the Internet (PwC study on digitalization in football, 2014).

In developing the conceptual framework of innovative sports management in the digital era (Figure 13.3) a few sub-concepts must be taken into account. The concept includes the elements that are mentioned in the analytical part of the paper – the specific features of sport and typologies of innovations, Industry 4.0 as a digital transformation phenomenon as well as consideration regarding the different nature of sports managers' work in sport sectors. The conceptual framework also includes concepts of open innovation and absorptive capacity that are based on the use of purposive inflows and outflows of knowledge in order to accelerate internal innovation.

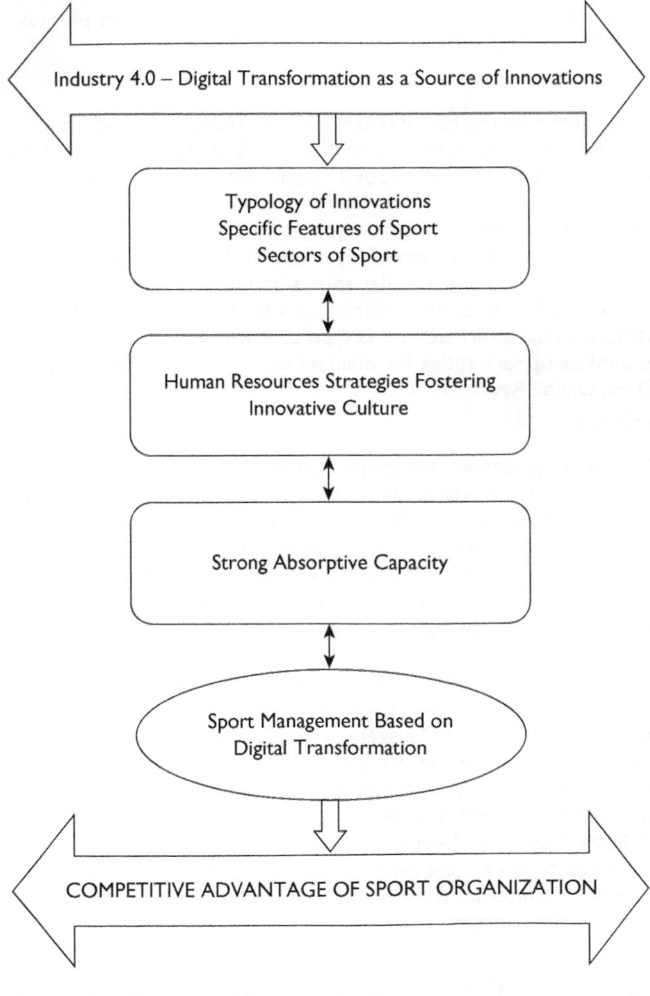

Figure 13.3 Conceptual framework of sports management based on digital transformation

To assure the innovative spirit in sports organizations and the creation of their competitive advantage, the implementation of a human resources recruitment policy based on these concepts is needed to exploit fully the opportunities arising from digital innovations. The absence of human resources strategies and policies that focus on open innovations and absorptive capacity can be a crucial limiting factor for innovations in sports management in the digital era. The concept of absorptive capacity as the ability of a company to use the knowledge that exists outside of the company depends, according to Cohen and Levinthal (1990), on the ability of the organization to recognize the value of new information, integrate it, and use it for commercial purposes. The capability of an organization to exploit external information – absorptive capacity – is considered to be a key component of innovation capability (Lane, Koka, & Pathak, 2002) but it must be accompanied by appropriate human resources ready for this role (Nová, 2016).

Scientific advances have been the driving force behind the development of professional sport for the last 50 years. Technology has improved sport, results, performance, and the sport experience as such. Innovations in this area have a tremendous potential, but in our chapter we have focused not only on technological innovations in sport but, via the analysis of innovations in sport in a broader sense, we have tried to explain the potential of different types of innovation in sport in the light of Industry 4.0 and digital transformation elements.

Following the typology of innovations could help in our view clarifying the core competencies or competitive advantages across different sectors in sport and will help sports managers not only understand better but also exploit fully the specific features of sport in the digital era.

At the same time, managers in sport should be aware of the fact that innovations of the sport product are limited considering not only the nature and components of the sport product but also digital elements implemented in the rules and techniques of the particular sport, wearables for players/athletes, digitalized equipment, and connected venue and virtual reality can enhance radically the sport experience. Therefore, we would recommend developing further the classification of innovations in relation to these components in sport. This would enable the innovation of the core and innovations of the intangible items of the sport product to be distinguished. In the professional sport, in particular innovations focus on product extension as winning and losing is beyond managerial control. In sports organizations which operate in the public or non-profit sport sector, the creation of the conditions for the development of intrapreneurship (Gautam & Verma, 1997) is of the utmost importance.

Industry 4.0 provides a variety of opportunities for constant innovation in sport. But not all sports organizations are well-positioned to innovate effectively. Professional sports have made a major investment in digital innovations to boost sporting performance and marketing improvement. But very little has changed in the other sectors (public, NGO) where the appropriate human resources are missing for sport organizations to be able to innovate effectively. Successful innovation strategies driven by digital transformation needs fast changes in order to stay ahead of the competition or to keep the brand relevant. Sports organizations, therefore, should invest in the culture and infrastructure for innovations including human resources.

This chapter demonstrates how innovations in sports management should be systematically identified, considering the opportunities brought by Industry 4.0, using a well-known typology of innovations. This systemized approach is underpinned by the proposed conceptual framework of sports management based on digital transformation. The framework offers the logic for realizing the importance of managerial activities that would foster the implementation of digitally-based innovations in sport in order to develop the competitive advantage of the particular sport organization. The major finding of this paper of applying a systematic approach to assessing innovation in sports management in the digital era could provide opportunities for business development in all sports sectors, which is a unique area of study that deserves more attention. Moreover, the theoretical perspective of the concepts of open innovation and absorptive capacity is covered sufficiently, but in sports management, there is a lack of studies of how to operationalize them, especially when it comes to human capital and human resources management. The proposed conceptual frameworks regarding Industry 4.0 and innovations in sport provides researchers with the foundation upon which further research in this area can be developed.

References

Balmer, N., Pleasence, P., & Nevill, A. (2012). Evolution and Revolution: Gauging the Impact of Technological and Technical Innovation on Olympic Performance. *Journal of Sport Sciences, 30,* 1075–83.

Blakey, P. (2011). *Sport Marketing.* Exeter, UK: Learning Matters.

Caza, A. (2000). Context Receptivity: Innovation in an Amateur Sport Organization. *Journal of Sport Management, 14,* 227–42.

Cohen,W. M., & Levinthal, D. A. (1990). Absorptive Capacity: A New Perspective on Learning and Innovation. *Administrative Science Quarterly, 35,* 128–52.

Desbordes, M. (2001). Innovation Management in the Sports Industry: Lessons from the Salomon Case. *European Sport Management Quarterly, 1(2),* 124–49.

Dimaggio, P. J., & Powell, W. W. (1983). The Iron Cage Revisited: Institutional Isomorphism and Collective Rationality in Organizational Fields. *American Sociological Review, 48(2),* 147–60.

Drawer, S. (2008). Performance Research, Science & Innovation in Olympic and Paralympic Sport – A Call to the UK Science Community. *The Sport and Exercise Scientist, 16,* 4–7.

Fuss, F. K., Subic, A., & Ujihashi , S. (2007). *The Impact of Technology on Sport.* London, UK: CRC.

Gautam, V., & Verma, V. (1997). Corporate Entrepreneurship: Changing Perspectives. *The Journal of Entrepreneurship, 6(2),* 233–47.

Goff, B. L., McCormick, R. E., & Tollison , R. D. (2002). Racial Integration as an Innovation: Empirical Evidence from Sports Leagues. *The American Economic Review, 92,* 16–26.

Chadwick, S. (2011). Editorial: The Distinctiveness of Sport – Opportunities for Research in the Field. *Sport, Business and Management: An International Journal, 1(2),* 120–23.

CISCO. (2015). Cisco Connected Stadium Solution. Retrieved from www.cisco.com/c/dam/en_us/solutions/industries/docs/sports/Connected_Stadium_Datasheet.pdf.

Claxton, D. (2017). EFL To Allow English Soccer Clubs to Live Stream Games On iFollow. www.sporttechie.com/sports/soccer. September 18, 2017. Retrieved from: www.sporttechie.com/efl-to-allow-english-soccer-clubs-to-live-stream-games-on-ifollow/.

Dellea, D., Vogel, S., Meletiadis, I., Gupta, N., Zahn, F., Görgülü, K., & Drechsel, D. (2014). Football's Digital Transformation. *Growth Opportunities for Football Clubs in the Digital Age.* Retrieved from www.pwc.ru/ru/publications/footbal-digital-transformation.pdf.

Digital Sport Media (2016, September). Retrieved from: www.digitale-sport-medien.com.

FC Barcelona. (2016). Case Study. Retrieved from: www.jivaldi.com/casestudy/fcb/.

Hermann, M., Pentek, T., & Boris, O. (2015). Design Principles for Industrie 4.0 Scenarios: A Literature Review. Technische Universität Dortmund Fakultät Maschinenbau Audi Stiftungslehrstuhl Supply Net Order Management. Retrieved from: www.thiagobranquinho.com/wp-content/uploads/2016/11/Design-Principles-for-Industrie-4_0-Scenarios.pdf.

Hoeber, L., & Hoeber, O. (2012). Determinants of an Innovation Process: A Case Study of Technological Innovation in a Community Sport Organization. *Journal of Sport Management, 26,* 213–23.

Hughes, C., Lee, S., & Chesterfield, G. (2009). Innovation in Sports Coaching: The Implementation of Reflective Cards. *Reflective Practice, 10,* 367–84.

Keeley, L., Walters, H., Pikkel, R. & Quinn, B. (2013). Ten Types of Innovation: The Discipline of Building Breakthroughs. Copyright©2013, Deloitte Development LLC. Hoboken, NJ: John Wiley & Sons, Inc.

Lane, P. J., Koka, B., & Pathak, S. (2002). *A Thematic Analysis and Critical Assessment of Absorptive Capacity Research.* Boston, MA: Academy of Management.

Lasi, H., Fettke, P., Kemper, H. G., Feld, T., & Hoffmann, M. (2014). Industrie 4.0: Bedarfssog und Technologiedruck als Treiber der vierten industriellen Revolution. *WIRTSCHAFTSINFORMATIK, 56,* 261–64.

Mullin, B.J., Hardy, S., & Sutton, W. (2000). *Sport Marketing* (2nd edn). Champaign, IL: Human Kinetics.

Magdalinski, T. (2009) *Sport, Technology and the Body: The Nature of Performance.* London, UK: Routledge.

Magruk, A. (2016). Uncertainty in the Sphere of the Industry 4.0 – Potential Areas to Research. *Business, Management and Education, 14(2),* 275–91.

Newell, S., & Swan, J. (1995). The Diffusion of Innovations in Sport Organizations: An Evaluative Framework. *Journal of Sport Management, 9*, 317–37.

Nová, J. (2013). Current Concepts of the Quality in Sport and their Utilization in the Czech Republic. Ekonomika a management, Praha: Vysoká škola ekonomická v Praze, roč., č. 4.

Nová, J., Novotný, J., Racek, O., Rektořík, J., Sekot, A., Strachová, M., & Válková, H. (2016). *Management, Marketing a ekonomika sportu*. 1. vyd. Brno: Masarykova univerzita.

Nová, J. (2016). Concepts of Open Innovations and Absorptive Capacity and their Influence on Human Resources Requirements in Sports Organizations. Paper presented at the 10th International Conference on Kinanthropology, Brno, Czech Republic.

OECD. (2005). Oslo Manual: Guidelines for Collecting and Interpreting Innovation Data, 3rd Edition. OECD, Eurostat. Retrieved from www.oecd.org/sti/inno/oslomanualguidelinesforcollectingandinterpretinginnovationdata3rdedition.htm.

Pitts, B. G., & Stotlar, D. K. (2013). *Fundamentals of Sport Marketing* (4th edn). Morgantown, WV: Fitness Information Technology.

Pope, N, Kuhn, K. A., & Forster, J. (2009). *Digital Sport for Performance Enhancement and Competitive Evolution: Intelligent Gaming Technologies*. Hershey, NJ: IGI.

Rasku, R., Puronaho, K., & Turco, D. M. (2015). Sport Business Intelligence and Data Driven Decision: The Case of AKK Sports LTD and WRC Championship Nestle Oil Rally Finland. In R. Rasku & A. Ahonen (Eds.), *Sport Business Intelligence* (pp. 16–32). Jyväskylä, Finland: JAMK University of Applied Sciences.

Reddish, J. (2016). More than a Game: Digital Strategy for NBA Championships. March 11, 2016. Retrieved from http://flipthemedia.com/2016/03/not-just-anyones-game-digital-strategy-nba-championship-teams/.

Smith, A. C., & Stewart, B. (2010). The Special Features of Sport: A Critical Revisit. *Sport Management Review, 10(1)*, 1–11.

Sport Business International Team. (2017). New Global Data Service Reveals the Full Picture about Sport Consumption. *Sport Business International, 17*, 26–27.

Winand, M., Vos, S., Zintz, T., & Scheerder, J. (2013). Determinants of Service Innovation: A Typology of Sports Federations. *International Journal of Sport Management and Marketing, 13*, 55–64.

Winand, M., & Zintz, T. (2014). What Service Innovation Types are Implemented by Sport Federations? Paper presented at the European Association for Sport Management Conference, Coventry, UK.

Chapter 14

Conceptual distinctions in general and local sponsorship objectives

A qualitative inquiry

Gregg Rich, Jori N. Hall, and Billy J. Hawkins

Introduction

Sponsorship has been defined "as the provision of assistance either financial or in-kind to an activity by a commercial organization for the purpose of achieving commercial objectives" (Meenaghan, 1983, p. 9). According to Gardner and Shuman (1988), sponsorship can be implemented to "support corporate objectives (e.g. enhancing corporate image) or marketing objectives (e.g. increasing brand awareness)" (p. 44). Through securing category exclusivity in sponsorships and integrating them within their overall marketing strategies, companies are believed capable of establishing distinct and sustainable competitive advantages in their markets (Amis, Pant, & Slack 1997; Amis, Slack, & Berrett, 1999; Fahy, Farrelly, & Quester, 2004). Consequently, companies continue to invest resources towards securing sponsorships. Global sponsorship spending in 2017 is expected to reach $62.8 billion, with North American spending to represent 37 percent of that projection (IEGSR, 2017). Sponsorship spending is anticipated to continue increasing. Over the past four years, global spending for sponsorships has grown at an approximate annual rate of 4.3 percent (IEGSR, 2017).

As company investments into sponsorships increase, marketing expenditure accountability has received greater managerial emphasis (Verhoef & Leeflang, 2009). Yet, the characteristic that arguably produces sponsorship's importance within the marketing mix, its integration with other marketing mediums, creates challenges in effectively isolating and measuring its returns (Pearsall, 2010). While there has been question as to whether practitioners truly desire to understand sponsorship returns (Javalgi, Traylor, Gross, & Lampman, 1994), some scholars (Cornwell, 2008; Meenaghan, McLoughlin, & McCormack, 2013) suggest that measurement difficulties may be attributable to an incomplete understanding of their effects.

Furthermore, sponsorship leveraging practices are continually evolving with the emergence of social media and other new technologies (Meenaghan et al., 2013). In 2016, to support its partnership with NCAA March Madness, and create brand interaction with college students, Reese's created a multi-platform, social media campaign. The candy manufacturer posted content on Twitter and Facebook that utilized streaming videos and cleverly positioned copy that engaged fans with entertaining commentary throughout the tournament. These social "chatter" initiatives were coupled with an Instagram contest and a Snapchat promotion (Social Media Fuze, 2016). As an activation approach in support of its NBA partnership, American Express allowed fans to experience the signature moves and personal stories of four NBA players using interactive digital video. During NBA All-Star Weekend in New York, fans could pivot around life-size digital representations of John Wall, Anthony Davis, LaMarcus Aldridge, and Mason Plumlee as they performed passes, dunks, and drives; allowing fans the ability to experience the players from vantage points of their own preference (O'Loughlin, 2016).

Opportunities for consumer brand interaction through social media and emerging technologies continue to increase. With new tools and resources for leveraging and activating sponsorships, opportunities for sponsors to engage and interact with individuals in new and different ways may be created. This evolution is reflected in academic literature. Earlier investigations of the phenomenon generally adopted a traditional marketing mix approach (Cornwell & Maignan, 1998; Olkkonen, Tikkanen, & Alajoutsijärvi, 2000; Walliser, 2003); whereas, scholars now acknowledge that sponsorship's common elements – fostering strategic, long-term relationships and incorporating interactive marketing communications – align more with relationship marketing practices (Cousens, Babiak, & Bradish, 2006; Grönroos, 1994).

The frequently-cited challenges of obtaining objective, quantitatively-calculated, and transactional returns (Pearsall, 2010) is likely to continue as companies use their sponsorships as interactive, relationship management platforms. In other words, measurement challenges may reflect a misalignment between sponsorship objectives and sponsorship leveraging, a misalignment between sponsorship objectives and their measurement practices, or measurement practices inadequately capturing sponsorship leveraging practices. Sponsorship objectives are chiefly important because they generally serve as the basis for how companies develop their leveraging practices and evaluate sponsorship success (Chadwick & Thwaites, 2004). In short, sponsorship objectives are the foundation of sponsorship management and evaluation processes. Additionally, given their foundational importance, it is reasonable to assume that companies' sponsorship decision-makers use selection criteria that reference back to these objectives (Figure 14.1).

Review of literature

Research on sponsorship objectives has revealed similar findings (Cornwell & Maignan, 1998; Walliser, 2003). Previous studies regularly reference increasing brand awareness (Abratt, Clayton, & Pitt, 1987; Crowley, 1991; Quester,

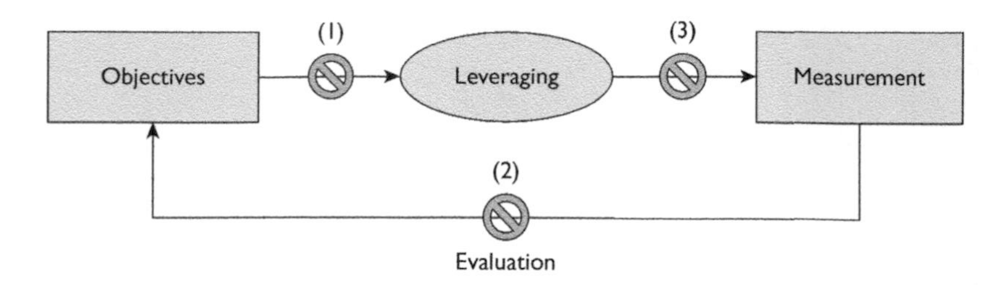

Figure 14.1 Identified areas for sport sponsorship evaluation misalignment

Farrelly, & Burton, 1998), enhancing brand or product image (Mihalik 1984; Polonsky et al., 1995), and entertaining clients (Scott & Suchard, 1992) as primary sponsorship objectives. Sponsorship selection criteria heavily mirror these objectives. Common criteria that are identified in research include the ability to provide media coverage (Abratt et al., 1987; Crowley, 1991), access to on- and off-site audiences (Irwin, Asimakopoulos, & Sutton, 1994; Meenaghan, 1991), and offering the ability to reach specific target markets (Irwin et al., 1994; Thwaites, Aguilar-Manjarrez, & Kidd, 1998). Sponsorship costs and sponsor-property fit are also considerations (Irwin et al., 1994; Meenaghan, 1991). With companies using sponsorships more as integrated and interactive relationship management platforms, the ability of their sponsorships to reach *specific* target markets may possess even greater importance. From a relationship management perspective, developing strong relationships with groups that associate with these sponsored properties – most notably fans – determines whether companies' sponsorships succeed; for these fans ideally represent existing consumers and/or target markets (Crowley, 1991).

Delineating sponsorship objectives

Cornwell and Maignan (1998) emphasize that many sponsorship objective studies are descriptive in nature, and are conducted by "giving sponsors a pool of objectives and asking them to rank the goals that explained their involvement in sponsorship" (p. 12). When considering concerns previously highlighted with this article, a difficulty isolating and measuring sponsorship effects from other marketing mediums (Pearsall, 2010) and an incomplete understanding of how sponsorship works (Cornwell, 2008; Meenaghan et al., 2013), the question becomes whether the sponsorship objectives that are stated within literature are, in actuality, stating marketing-level or corporate-level objectives. This is important because to further academic understanding of how sponsorship functions, and its subsequent effects, researchers must first ensure that they possess an accurate understanding of its objectives (Figure 14.2).

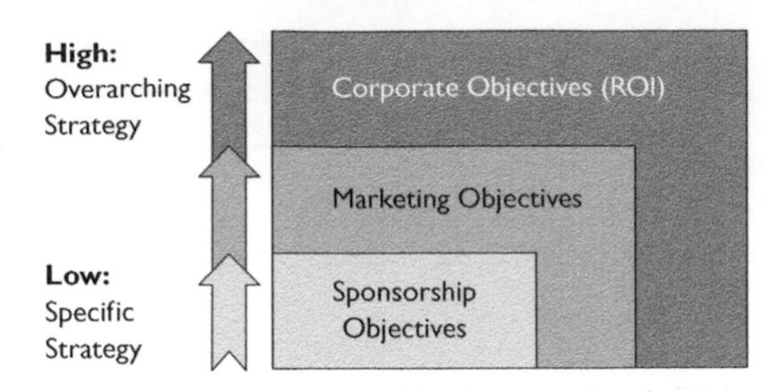

Figure 14.2 Level categorization of sport sponsorship objectives

Many of the studies that examine sponsorship objectives do provide categorical distinctions. For instance, two studies categorize sponsorship objectives into being corporate-related or product/brand-related (Irwin & Asimakopoulos, 1992; Irwin & Sutton, 1994). Sandler and Shani (1993) applied three categories, including broad corporate objectives, marketing objectives, and media objectives. The categories from these studies are primarily determined by authority-level. Further, a more recent study by Chadwick and Thwaites (2004) outlined four categories that are delineated more by function: Marketing communication objectives (i.e. strategic promotions), relationship marketing objectives (i.e. building relationships with consumers), network objectives (i.e. collaborating with related organizations), and resource objectives (i.e. allocating sponsorship resources to establish a competitive advantage). These researchers adopted the approach from earlier studies on sponsorship objectives (Irwin et. al., 1994; Shani & Sandler, 1993), believing that they should be associated with the structures and authorities that institute them. Consequently, conceptual categories for objectives at the corporate, marketing, and sponsorship levels are acknowledged in this study. Higher-level objectives (i.e. corporate) are expected to be more overarching, while those at a lower-level are likely more specified towards function (i.e. marketing, sponsorship).

However, with sponsorship leveraging practices evolving into more relational applications (Olkkonen et al., 2000) and with greater emphasis on interactive activations (Meenaghan et al., 2013), sponsorship objectives should be framed in relational contexts. Olkkonen et al. (2000) argued that earlier sponsorship research followed narrow theoretical and methodological perspectives, demonstrating a concerning lack of theory development. This may explain why sponsorship objectives in previous studies are often generalized to the degree that they are conceptually ambiguous. Moreover, considering the medium integration and relational complexity to which sponsorship leveraging has currently evolved, more attention should be ascribed to the many environmental contexts in which individuals may engage with sponsorships (Cornwell, 1995). Focusing on the relational attributes as they pertain to sponsorship objectives, a social identity approach serves as this study's theoretical lens of inquiry. Both theories have previously been applied within sponsorship contexts (Alexandris & Tsiotsou, 2012; Cobbs, Groza, & Rich, 2015; Cornwell & Coote, 2005; Gwinner & Swanson, 2003; Madrigal, 2000; 2001).

Social identity approach

A social identity approach applies the theories of self-categorization and social identity to explain group association and intergroup behavior respectively. Finding meaning in their environments, individuals will accentuate differences between and similarities within social categories (Haslam, Oakes, Turner, & McGarty, 1995). Through the psychological process of stereotyping, individuals categorize themselves (i.e., self-stereotyping) and others into groups (Turner & Oakes, 1986). There are innumerable social identities into which individuals may self-categorize themselves throughout the day (Reynolds & Turner, 2006), with these social identities likely residing at different levels of abstraction (e.g. individual, city citizen, state resident, national citizen, etc.). From this theoretical perspective, the self is perceived as both "personal and collective," with changes in how individuals self-categorize themselves, influencing their judgements of others (Reynolds & Turner, 2006, p. 233). Individuals engage in social behavior that can reflect interpersonal or intergroup behaviors, as they fluctuate along a continuum of self- and social-group orientation (Tajfel & Turner, 1979). Desiring to maintain a positive self-concept (i.e. positive distinctiveness), social identity theory asserts that individuals exhibit an assortment of strategies towards this end. While several strategies exist within the theory's framework, many of these strategies are predicated upon individuals' perceptions of legitimacy, stability, and permeability associated with these groups (Tajfel & Turner, 1979). Groups into which individuals identify themselves as members are referred to as in-groups, with all other groups – those in which these individuals do not identify as members – being referred to as out-groups.

Two strategies that individuals may employ to maintain positive distinctiveness are in-group favoritism and out-group derogation (Hogg & Abrams, 1988; Tajfel & Turner, 1986). By employing these strategies to either perceive the in-group positively or out-group negatively, individuals are believed to strengthen their social self-esteem. These identity-maintenance strategies are thought to be employed by individuals when they feel strong group identification or receive negative group feedback (Ashforth & Mael, 1989; Hogg & Abrams, 1988). A social identity approach is anticipated to offer explanation for how fans of sport properties, through sponsorship leveraging and activation, self-categorize themselves into groups with their teams' sponsors. Once associated with sponsoring brands, social identity theory is believed capable of providing explanations for fans' behaviors towards those brands and their competitors.

Examining hometown sponsorship

A sponsorship context that has currently been neglected within extant literature is hometown sport sponsorship. This context warrants examination, considering the emotional connections many individuals likely possess for their hometowns and local teams. Also, many corporations possess large employee bases within their hometowns; therefore, many low abstraction groups based on geographic location and their related affiliations are present in hometown contexts. These group associations (i.e., city resident, fan, employee) represent social identities. If adhering to a social identity perspective, these group synergies suggest a potential for hometown corporations to employ their local sponsorships as means for achieving sustainable competitive advantages in their local markets. Thus far, no research—to the author's knowledge—is known to have examined hometown sponsorship objectives. Based on the lack of research in this area, a study exploring sport sponsorship's common objectives from a relational perspective was conducted. This study focuses on identifying and examining hometown sponsorship objectives in relation to the phenomenon's more common objectives. This study is intended to better capture any nuances and distinctions that may exist between the two contexts.

Method

From a managerial perspective, the purpose of this study was to identify key objectives of sponsorship in two contexts. First, the common objectives of corporate sport sponsorship were identified and examined from a relationship management perspective using a social identity approach as a theoretical lens of inquiry. Then, using similar methods, the context of corporate hometown sport sponsorship was examined. Given these aims, the following research questions guide this study:

1 What do sponsorship managers perceive to be common sponsorship objectives? How do these objectives function with one another when applying a social identity approach?
2 When asking sponsorship managers to narrow their focus to consider hometown sponsorship objectives and effects, what are distinctive or nuanced differences in sponsorship strategy that emerge?

Sampling and participants

The metropolitan area of Rivendell (a pseudonym) located in the southeastern United States with nearly 5.5 million residents was chosen to conduct the study. A center of trade and commerce, it is home to 18 Fortune 500 companies. Many of these companies possess large, national (and some international) sponsorship portfolios. Additionally, the area has a diverse selection of sport and entertainment options, with many sport teams, music venues, museums, and festivals present. Five major professional sport properties and two major collegiate athletic programs reside in Rivendell.

Typical case sampling, a purposeful sampling strategy (Patton, 2002) was employed in this study. Participants had to meet the following criteria: (a) Be involved in the management, negotiation, and/or leveraging of hometown sponsorships now or within the past year and (b) work for major sport properties (i.e. property representative), national marketing/sponsorship agencies (i.e. agency consultant), or sponsorship-active corporations (i.e., corporate sponsorship manager) located in Rivendell. To collect data that captured perspectives from all three roles, it was deemed necessary to have all roles represented in the sample. To be considered a major sport property, the property had to receive regular regional and national media coverage. Agencies with participants in the study operated nationally. Their clients were either large corporations with international or national sponsorship portfolios, and/or major sport properties with international and/or national reach. For the purposes of this study, sponsorship-active corporations needed to have an international or national sponsorship portfolio.

The 11 participants ($N = 11$) in this study consisted of sponsorship managers who represented sport properties (n=5), agencies (n=4), and corporations (n=2) headquartered in Rivendell (Table 14.1). Every major property in the metropolitan area had managerial representation in the sample. The average experience participants had managing corporate sport sponsorships was approximately 14 years; ranging from two years to 25 years.

Participant interviews

Ten semi-structured interviews were conducted with the 11 participants, as two requested to be interviewed together. The two participants were property representatives who worked for the same property. The participant who held the more senior role was the primary speaker during this interview, with the participant in the less senior role interjecting when asked; demonstrating deference to the senior manager. Prior to their interviews, participants signed consent forms. Participant interviews averaged one hour in length, with the shortest interview being 35 minutes and the longest being one hour and 38 minutes. Typed transcriptions from interview recordings totaled 180 pages (in Times New Roman, 12-font, single-space, normal margins). Nine of the 11 interviews were conducted in-person. The last two interviews were conducted by phone after multiple attempts to schedule an in-person interview were unsuccessful. Based on experiences from the earlier interviews performed, there were minimal concerns regarding the interview participants' question sensitivities, or the interviewer's need to observe participants' physical cues during their interviews. Moreover, by the eighth interview, there was a noticeable decrease in new data captured. Following the two phone interviews – given the lack of new data/insights captured – it was determined that data saturation was achieved.

Table 14.1 Pseudonym names of interviewees and their background information

Participant Pseudonyms	*Gender*	*Title (Level)*	*Interview Time*	
Penelope Cornwell	Female	Director		1:12:47
Eyan Joseph	Male	Vice President		0:35:04
Clint Castleberry	Male	Vice President		1:38:47
Theo Carey	Male	Director		1:24:02
AGENCY			Total	4:50:40
			Average	1:12:10
Nick Gunter	Male	Director		0:55:04
Herman Depp	Male	Vice President		0:54:04
CORPORATE			Total	1:49:08
			Average	0:54:34
Janet Bird	Female	Director		0:45:03
Mark Wall	Male	Manager		0:53:46
Rita Bell	Female	Vice President		1:01:13
Bobby Jones	Male	Vice President		0:55:07
Donny Bones	Male	Director		
PROPERTY				3:35:09
				0:53:45
			Total	10:14:57
			Average	1:01:30

Semi-structured interviews were recorded using an audio recorder. Upon transcription of interviews, these recordings were destroyed. In an effort to ensure interview participant confidentiality, participants were assigned pseudonyms, which were applied to all documents. Given the small population (i.e., Rivendell sponsorship managers) sampled for this study, certain information was not provided (i.e. employer names), generalized (i.e. occupational title) or documented within the study as a collective summary – unassigned to a specific participant (i.e. years of experience). Any identifiable information (e.g., company's name, employee's name) provided within participant interviews were removed and replaced with appropriate, more generalized terms. A pseudonym list with identifying information was stored on an encrypted, password protected, data folder during the study, and was destroyed following the study's completion.

Data analyses

The constant comparative method (Charmaz, 2014) was used to conduct an analysis of participant interviews. Coding occurred at three levels, including initial, focused, and theoretical (Charmaz, 2014). Coding involves "categorizing segments of data with a short name that simultaneously summarizes and accounts for each piece of data" (Charmaz, 2014). Following the recommendation of Charmaz (2014), initial codes were short, and designed to capture meanings and actions. Per her recommendations, these codes were generally designed to start with gerunds. Focused codes were built from the initial codes, through identification of initial codes that frequently arose and/or possessed more meaning than other codes. These codes were designed to focus and condense the data (Charmaz, 2014). Given the intentions of this study, focused codes were generally structural-functional (Glaser, 1998) in nature. Theoretical codes were created to reintegrate the data. Focused codes were weaved into theoretical conceptualizations; providing stronger explanation of the data (Charmaz, 2014). Focused codes were weaved into theoretical conceptualizations; then, these theoretical codes were compared within a conceptual framework using a social identity approach to find emergent trends and to examine consistencies and inconsistencies identified during coding and framework development.

After an initial reading of interview transcripts, NVIVO software was used to conduct initial coding, as it was determined to be an effective tool for 1) retrieving data assigned to these codes, and 2) organizing initial codes with either a general (S) or hometown (H) context classification. Focused and theoretical codes were developed on a Microsoft Excel worksheet, allowing for easier manipulation and reorganization of data. Memo-writing was utilized to encourage increased engagement in the data and assist in coding analysis, particularly during its early stages (Charmaz, 2014). Three memo categories were used in the study for (a) reflections (e.g. thoughts from interviews), (b) applications (e.g. rationale for directions taken within the study), and (c) feedback. Reflection memos were used to organize thoughts following interviews with participants; application memos were used to document rationale for directions taken in the study; and feedback memos were used to document committee feedback pertaining to the study. During and immediately after interviews, the interviewer's notes were used as a methodological journal; documenting their "methodological dilemmas, directions, and decisions" (Charmaz, 2014, p. 165). Later, these journal notes were often refined and elaborated upon in memos.

Establishing trustworthiness

To strengthen the credibility and confirmability of the findings (Lincoln & Guba, 1986), member checking and an audit trail were employed. When developing the interview guide, an informal interview with a senior sponsorship manager with property, agency, and corporate experience was conducted to assess contextual relevance (Kirkhart, 1995). Then, following the informal interview, the interview guides were reviewed with the same sponsorship manager to assess the intelligibility of their questions. Lastly, following revisions, a fellow researcher reviewed the interview guides and provided feedback (Fowler, 2002). The first two interviews were conducted in July and August of 2016 as a pilot, from which minor revisions were made to the interview guide. These revisions included adding several role specific questions, and providing a definition (with example) of hometown sponsorship that was used in the study. Each interview participant confirmed that they understood and accepted the definition provided during the interview upon having it read to them. The pilot interviews were with individuals with backgrounds in multiple sponsorship roles, and both were qualified candidates for the study. Based on these revisions, a formal interview introduction and three interview guides – modified to reflect the roles of the interview participants – were used in the study.

Given that sponsorship is an abstraction in many aspects, interview participants were asked to provide the interviewer with their definitions for it. The purpose for this exercise was twofold. First, it helped ensure that interview participants possessed a similar sponsorship conceptualization, and that their responses were referring to the same phenomenon. Second, it provided the interviewer a means for establishing practical boundaries (i.e. what "is sponsorship" versus what "is not sponsorship") when developing a conceptual sponsorship framework; considering that scholars have yet to agree upon a theoretical definition for the phenomenon (Cornwell & Maignan, 1998; Dolphin, 2003; Hoek, Gendall, Jeffcoat, & Orsman, 1997). Following this exercise, responses were found to be similar and in agreement with one another, while helping the researcher identify four core aspects of sponsorship as perceived by the study's participants: (a) sponsorship creates associations between a company and a property, (b) sponsorship allows for emotional connection to a company's target audience, (c) sponsorship encourages changes in normative behaviors through its leveraging, and (d) sponsorship offers business-related benefits. These definitional elements of sponsorship were considered when developing the conceptual sponsorship framework for this study.

Results

The data analysis procedure for this study revealed a descriptive framework for how sponsorship objectives may function towards meeting an overarching marketing-level goal, which in turn provided support for an overarching company-level goal. Further, from this framework and a hometown-focused examination of managers' perceptions towards sponsorship, two dominant themes emerged for how hometown sponsorship may function within companies' overall sponsorship objectives. Findings from this study were presented in the order in which they were identified.

Managerial objectives associated with sponsorship

During their interviews, participants were asked to provide a list of common sponsorship objectives. Then, participants were to prioritize these objectives. Prior to analyzing participants' interviews, these objectives were then consolidated – based on their functional similarities – into a set of five general managerial objective categories associated with sponsorship:

1 Generating a positive return-on-investment (ROI)
2 Engaging consumers (e.g. activation)
3 Increasing customer visibility (e.g. leveraging)
4 Investing in the community (e.g. non-profit leveraging extensions)
5 Engaging employees (e.g. employee recognition and appreciation tie-ins)

These findings served as an initial starting point for developing a framework, as they collectively reflected the interview participants' general perceptions of what constituted the phenomenon's "common" objectives. As depicted, these findings provide broadly-stated functions or outcomes; offering little explanation for how sponsorship works.

Following the analyses of participants' interviews, a structural hierarchy for managerial objectives was discovered. "Generating a positive ROI" emerged as an overarching company-level objective; whereas, the remaining four managerial objective categories identified by interview participants were found to be at the sponsorship-level. When considered collectively, these sponsorship-level objectives revealed an overarching thematic objective at the marketing-level: "Building brand ambassadors for life." As sponsorship and its associated marketing activities primarily function as corporate relationship management platforms, sponsorship- and marketing-level objectives were relationally thematized to better reflect their organizational functions. Thematic sponsorship objectives, and the overarching thematic marketing objective noted above, emerged from qualitative analysis protocols used after the creation of managerial objective categories. Consequently, although four thematic sponsorship objectives were revealed through this analysis, these thematic objectives – while capturing sponsorships' general functions – do not perfectly correspond with the managerial objective categories identified prior. Furthermore, "Generating a positive ROI" was not thematized given its function as a quantitative metric of overall company performance.

To address the first research question, descriptions and supporting evidence for thematic objectives and their related sub-themes were provided. Then, these thematic objectives were applied into a theoretical framework that adhered to a social identity approach – which, from a general context, emphasized self-categorization theory – and a conceptual framework for corporate sponsorship was presented. To address the second research question, two thematic objectives specific to hometown sponsorship were presented from a secondary analysis of data. This analysis only examined data that was specifically relevant to a hometown sponsorship context. During interviews, the following definition for, and explanation of, hometown sponsorship was provided to participants prior to asking questions specific to hometown sponsorship:

> For purposes of this study, the closest metropolitan area to possess a professional sport franchise or franchises from the Big Four sport leagues – including MLB, NBA, NFL, and the National Hockey League (NHL) – in relation to an individual's residence is considered their "hometown." Properties within these metropolitan areas would be considered "hometown properties." Additionally, athletic programs from public state universities, whether within the boundaries of that metropolitan area, would also be considered "hometown properties." For example, if individuals lived in New Hampshire, their "hometown" for purposes of this study would be the "Boston Metropolitan Area" in Massachusetts. Subsequently, the Boston Red Sox would be considered a "hometown property." Yet, the athletic program at the University of New Hampshire would also be considered a "hometown property" for New Hampshire residents. From a corporate perspective, this study assumes that corporations' international, national, or regional headquarters function like individuals' residences; making the metropolitan areas where their offices are located their "hometowns."

Upon having it read to them during the interview, each interviewee confirmed that they understood and accepted the definition provided.

Thematic sponsorship objectives of general context

The data analysis procedure used in this study revealed four common, thematic sponsorship objectives: (a) meeting people where their passions live, (b) fostering brand love, (c) committing to communities, and (d) empowering employees. Descriptions and supporting evidence for these thematic objectives and their related sub-themes were provided below.

Joining people where their passions live. A thematic sponsorship objective that emerged from the analysis was "meeting people where their passions live," which involved corporations identifying their brands' target audiences' passions, and anthropomorphically situating their brands within environments that connected to those passions. To this end, corporations partnered with sport properties to develop associations with their fans' and their passions, with nearly 70 percent of all sponsorship spending in North America tying back to sport (IEGSR, 2017). The following comment from Herman summarized this thematic objective: "Yeah. the beauty of sponsorships—particularly the big ones—is if you do it the right way, you're targeting the right consumer segment from a brand perspective, and they're super passionate about these spaces, so they're more in tune with commercial messaging" (Herman, Corporation). Nick highlighted aspects of this thematic objective when he provided an example of what he perceived to be an exemplar sponsorship:

> I look at Home Depot and its partnership with College Gameday as a rather unique partnership . . . I think that it was a really unique way to take something that Home Depot was already doing with purchasing media on ESPN and *target home improvement customers*—making it more personal—and *tying it to this brand of college football,* which was really, *really growing from an affinity standpoint* (Nick, Corporation).

Additionally, three sub-themes were captured within the thematic sponsorship objective "meeting people where their passions live": (a) creating associations to specific audiences' social identities, (b) embracing a consistent brand personality, and (c) pursuing organic relationships. These three subthemes represented common strategies that together can successfully help brands "meet people where their passions live."

Creating associations to specific audiences' social identities. Corporations' brands associated themselves with properties that were central to the social identities of their target audiences' passions; encouraging in-group inclusion and emotional connectedness. In other words, brands strategically positioned themselves in environments that promoted them being positively stereotyped by their target audiences. The following comment from Eyan captured the belief that these emotional connections between fans and properties led to positive outcomes for properties' sponsors through associative inclusion:

> fans have an affinity for their products' sponsors – their teams' sponsors . . . *if you're a big follower of a NASCAR driver, and he uses a Tide car, you're going to go buy Tide, because you'd like to support him.* Same thing with college sports, so that's why you have long-term sponsors. We want to build affinity with these fans . . . they're die-hard fans, they're passionate . . .
>
> (Eyan, Agency)

Janet touched on this thematic objective from a negative positioning; expressing the importance of corporations partnering with properties that reached their target audiences:

> You know, you don't want to partner with a brand that doesn't reach your audience. And so, *making sure you do sponsorships that are relevant to the audience you're targeting is really important,* because, you know, sponsorship is proven to amplify marketing objectives. But at the same time, if you're not aligned with the right brand, you're not going to amplify, because you're targeting an audience that's not yours.
>
> (Janet, Property)

Reinforcing a consistent brand personality. Corporations' actively attempted to reinforce their brands' intended personality characteristics among targeted audiences. This was functionally enacted by monitoring consumer brand personality perceptions relative to sponsorship leveraging and activation; then, adjusting strategies to manipulate target audiences' perceptions as necessary – reflecting these brand personality characteristics. Additionally, interview participants commented on the importance of further managing these personality perceptions through the construction of their brands' sponsorship portfolios. The following discourse from Nick provided support for this sub-theme:

> Do people see us as innovative? Do people see us as faster than the competition? Do people see our people as smarter than the competition? There's a long list of them. And *we try and look and see if there are differences in the trends we're seeing at the macro marketing and communications level, and ones at the sponsorship level. And we talk about what we're doing to kind of influence some of those things.*
>
> (Nick, Corporation)

Clint also expressed the need for corporate brands to reflect the personalities of the target audiences that they were intending to reach. One of his "pet-peeves" involved sponsors failing to recognize the successes of their sponsored teams or players: "*if you're a sponsor, you're supposed to be a fan.* And it's a partnership, and *you're supposed to take pride and have a rooting interest in it.* And so . . . if you're not going to be a fan of the team, then what's the point?" (Clint, Agency)

Penelope commented on how corporations in the same industry would often develop their own market niches through their sponsorship portfolios; promoting unique brand personality characteristics through these portfolios:

> Everyone kind of has their niche. T-Mobile does a lot with the NBA. Verizon traditionally has the NFL. AT&T traditionally has the NCAA. *For example, AT&T was the collegiate brand, and they have a huge portfolio in collegiate sports when compared to their competitors*, especially considering that Verizon was very focused on the NFL.
>
> (Penelope, Agency)

Pursuing organic relationships. Once associations were developed, corporations utilized communication channels that reached their target audiences' in social contexts; attempting to establish anthropomorphic and archetypal brand characteristics that mirrored their target audiences' in-group members. As social media has evolved, with more individuals engaged in its use, sponsorship activations have increasingly incorporated the platform to interact with their target audiences. Sponsorship managers emphasized the importance of social interactions with potential consumers by adopting an organic communication approach:

> We try to stay a lot more organic with our [social media] posts. *We don't like to push a sponsor's posts.* Like, "Come out and buy my [product]. I'm [a sponsor]. You're not driving someone to buy their products . . . [it's] very indirect. Because, really when it comes down to it, you're getting to the point where you're going to bog so many peoples' social media feeds down, they don't even want to see what you're posting anymore . . . a lot more of our posts are organic . . . *just trying to engage people more, instead of constantly pushing sales messages down their throat.*
>
> (Rita, Property)

Theo felt that two important elements of "pursuing organic relationship" were the frequency and timing of communications. Moreover, he thought that brands should focus on making these social interactions fun, and something that was capable of going viral:

> I think *timeliness is the key.* I think that [if social media communications are] too frequent, it's overkill . . . that's the primary thing with social media – and to make it relevant. *Not to make [social media posts] a corporate message, but rather something that's fun, and people want to interact with it, and want to share.* I think too many times you get corporate messaging through social, where the corporation thinks, "Okay, we've got to get this message out there," but they've got to find a fun way to do it to make people want to share it.
>
> (Theo, Agency)

An advocate of social activation as a sponsorship leveraging element, Janet believed that sponsorship managers must stay relevant with trends. Her rationale was that staying relevant with trends allowed sponsorship managers to effectively develop organic communications through whatever medium was most appropriate for reaching their desired target audience—which, for her property, was often millennials:

> I tell the folks working for me, as soon as you become too old for a medium, you age yourself out of being relevant in this industry. So, I listen to music that I'm not necessarily interested in. I have apps on my phone that I don't necessarily use that much, but I'm aware of them, because *if you're not staying current, you're not going to be able to speak to the needs that your clients are looking for.*
>
> (Janet, Property)

Fostering brand love. Another thematic sponsorship objective that emerged from the analysis was "fostering brand love." Corporations attempted to foster brand love with individuals in their target audiences. Brand love, as defined in this study, is a construct that consists of seven dimensions: (1) self-brand integration, (2) passion-driven behaviors, (3) positive emotional connection, (4) long-term relationship, (5) positive overall valence, (6) attitude certainty and confidence (strength), and (7) anticipated separation distress (Batra, Ahuvia, & Bagozzi, 2012). This thematic objective involved both pursuing anthropomorphic relationship with, and creating unique and exclusive experiences for, individuals of their brands' target audiences. These consistent social and experiential interactions were intended to make brands more central to their target audiences' self-identities. Theo was a major proponent of experiential activation as a means for fostering brand love:

> A commercial might in that moment [make an impression], but someone actually *experiencing a product or service – hands on, can make that person a customer for life.* And I 100 percent believe in that. And that's why companies have also gone that route, because *you just have more impact when you're there in front of, and you're able to see it, touch it, feel it, and truly get immersed in whatever your product or service is.*
>
> (Theo, Agency)

Clint shared his thoughts on how to enhance that experience for brands' target audiences, believing that the experience brands intend to offer these individuals should align with the root sources of their fandom:

> the best practice that I would say is don't just do it because that's how it's always been done, but really think about the event type; where fans are going to be; what they're going to do; why are they there; *why they're a fan of that team; what makes that team unique; and really insert your brand there.*
>
> (Clint, Agency)

Lastly, when Nick spoke to the importance of creating unique and memorable experiences, he also mentioned the need for these experiences to be "unreplicatable" by competitors; allowing corporations to develop unique relationships with their consumers:

> I would say hospitality is a big part of what we do. Entertaining customers is more than just a ticket, but *providing them with kind of a complete end-to-end experience, where we kind of maximize all the touch points that we have.* Influence those events with intellectual property and the assets we can, whether it be appearances, or something as simple as putting a logo on an invitation, but *making that experience unique and unforgettable, and unreplicatable by our competition.*
>
> (Nick, Corporation)

Committing to communities. This thematic sponsorship objective involved corporations fulfilling their perceived societal commitments through corporate social responsibility (CSR)-linked sponsorship activations or charity extensions; encouraging cognitive consistency between their brands' intended personalities and those of their targeted audiences' social groups. Further, these community investments were amplified through their relationships with – and the resources of – sport properties. Support for "committing to communities" was provided through the following interview participant discourse:

> Overall, my perspective on it is most of the companies that we do business with do a lot of stuff in the community, whether it's involved with us or not. They're going to do stuff, usually from a community perspective . . .; *as a property, [we] can be a mouthpiece for what they're doing in the community.* But they're doing stuff well above and beyond [what the public sees them do with properties], that probably gets lost.
>
> (Bobby, Property)

Herman's thoughts mirrored Bobby's when it pertained to the level of large, corporate involvement within communities: "if you're a big company that has a big presence in a market, *there's an expectation that you are giving back to your community.* So, we're obviously involved in a lot of different areas that may look like a sponsorship, but *go far beyond that*" (Herman, Corporation).

While admitting that CSR-linked sponsorship was likely underutilized by corporations, Nick felt that it was becoming an area of greater consumer focus:

> I think like everybody *we could do [CSR-linked sponsorship] a little bit more.* I think particularly with the millennial audience; corporate social responsibility is becoming a much more important part of how people conduct business. Like, *what's your social profile? . . . people want to do business with people that kind of match their own.*
>
> (Nick, Corporation).

Empowering employees as ambassadors. This thematic sponsorship objective was focused on corporations integrating their employees into their sponsorships. Corporations considered how they could incorporate their employees into their various sponsorship arrangements, often desiring to instill a sense of pride and emotionally connect with them; namely, to encourage passion and commitment towards their corporations and their brands. Corporations' intentions were to encourage their employees to adopt the brand as a central element of their self-identities. Consequently, employees were empowered to become their brands ambassadors and evangelists. Property representatives, such as Rita, mentioned that these types of employee-inclusive leveraging practices were executed by her property's sponsors regularly: "Companies use [event sponsorship hospitality] as *rewards for their employees,* or to entertain clients. Those are super easy, and *are included in almost any deal that we do*" (Rita, Property).

Both corporate sponsorship managers extolled the importance of emotionally connecting and empowering their employees through sponsorship. When asked about whether his company engaged their employees through sponsorship, Herman answered:

> Yeah, definitely! Yeah. And *we have incentives and opportunities to bring these [sponsorship] assets to the employees. It's a big part of what we do,* for sure . . . and we do that across everything – from global partnerships, to national partnerships, to local. You'll always see us communicating with our internal employees because it gives them a sense of pride.
>
> (Herman, Corporation)

Nick also discussed employee engagement through sponsorship; alluding to the thematic objective of "empowering employees as ambassadors":

> employees are usually a huge part of how a company presents itself, so how do you get them engaged and involved in the partnership? And not just excited about it, but use it to influence their behavior? We have [hundreds of thousands of] employees. *How do we get them excited and engaged, and wanting to help spread the brand message?*
>
> (Nick, Corporation)

Thematic sponsorship objectives in local context

When sponsorship was examined from a hometown context, two dominant thematic objectives emerged: (a) weaving into the local fabric and (b) winning where you live. Descriptions and supporting evidence for these thematic objectives and their related sub-themes were provided below.

Weaving into the local fabric. This thematic sponsorship objective involved corporations reinforcing their in-group associations with their local communities. When "weaving into the local fabric" of their hometowns, corporations focused on leveraging and activation opportunities that were not commercially motivated – or minimally so. A common strategy related to this thematic objective was for corporations to integrate their prominent, hometown sport sponsorships with local charity and grassroots initiatives. Janet summarized this thematic objective well:

> there is the belief that *if you are a local sponsor, you should be invested in the local properties in your hometown. And there is that expectation from the citizens* . . . I think they want a little bit more than you're a partner of that team . . . they would like to see how you are partnering with that team to help this community. I think that's *where you get the real win . . . partnering with your hometown team and doing something great for the community that's an actual event.*
>
> (Janet, Property)

Expanding upon this thematic hometown objective of "weaving into the local fabric," Theo commented on the perception of authenticity that he believed hometown corporations garnered when they included smaller properties, such as local festivals, into their sponsorship portfolios:

> I think it depends. *I think a good mix because your larger properties are going to resonate with the consumers in the market place, but some of the smaller ones are going to touch the consumer.* Those are the ones that feel more like a hometown sponsorship to me . . . There's some authenticity to sponsoring a local festival . . . I think your smaller festivals and things like that – I think that's where you're interacting with consumers, and that's when the visibility to consumers changes . . . You don't view it as, "Oh yeah, they're in my hometown." [It's more like], "Okay, look. *They're actually integrated into my community, and supporting local events.*"
>
> (Theo, Agency)

Herman acknowledged that his company was highly involved with the local community through its sponsorship portfolio. The sole objective of one sponsorship, a golf tournament, was to tie into, and give back, to the local community:

> We are a sponsor of the [Golf Tournament] out at [Hometown]. And that's part of a broader relationship with the [Golf Organization]. That is overtly and purposeful in helping to drive awareness and funds for the [Hometown Charity]. *That's the focus, and giving back to our local hometown community.* That is *the* objective of that relationship.
>
> (Herman, Corporation)

Sport sponsorships were noted by interview participants as opportunities for corporate visibility within their hometowns, with sponsorships functioning like beacons, at times through naming rights, that communicated their hometown associations:

> That may not necessarily be the goals and objectives for the out-of-market sponsorships that you do, but when you do hometown sponsorships – this is your home base . . . the people here are dear to you. *So, you want to make sure that you're visible, and that they see you.*
>
> (Penelope, Agency)

With many of their employees located within their hometowns, corporations were capable of executing large, employee-focused activations around their sport sponsorships that also tied back to their communities. Many interview participants thought that these initiatives were effective resources for improving employees' attitudes towards their employers – instilling pride, while further reinforcing existing in-group associations:

> [Sponsor] has a strong employee base here in Rivendell. It's their hub. And anything that they do with us in the community is not only to tie into the community – *they always try to tie employee engagement into that as well.* So, we'll do a [weekend event] as an example. And, they'll bring the employees out to work the various events that we do surrounding that weekend. Having them in uniforms, so you get the connection to them, but also [to] have your employee base knowing, "Hey, [sponsor] is out there doing solid stuff in our community." And so, I think it works both ways. *Both from an internal employee perspective, but also externally for their customer base.*
>
> (Bobby, Property)

Winning where you live. Another thematic hometown objective that emerged from the data was "winning where you live." Where the thematic hometown objective of "weaving into the local fabric" focused more on reinforcing in-group associations through less commercially-driven endeavors, "winning where you live" involved corporations' openly attempting to establish sustainable competitive advantages against their competitors in their hometowns. From a social identity perspective, this involved strategies that reflected and encouraged managerial behaviors of in-group favoritism by prominent hometown corporations and sport properties. One interview participant, Clint, compared the rationale for this thematic objective to that of in-state, college sports recruiting:

> I mean, it's very similar to college football recruiting, or college basketball recruiting, any major college sport recruiting. *You've got to win where you're [located]*. If you've got a great sports or entertainment property in your hometown, and you're in the mindset of doing team deals, then you should probably look to take care of your own town for a multitude of reasons, but primarily because you don't want your CMO going to the game and seeing your competitor's messaging running everywhere; coming back and saying, "What are we doing in sponsorships?" So, it's protecting that home turf.
>
> (Clint, Agency)

During his interview, Mark, spoke directly to the emotional motivations for corporations to adopt this thematic hometown objective:

> I think, by nature, and probably for many things, *the closer you are to something, the more intimate you are with it.* And it means more. You want to be more involved. You want to know more. You want to be a part of it more. So, that's why a hometown sponsorship has more value. And in addition to that, you can look at it reversely, and *you don't want to lose that to a competitor.* So, yes, they're very intimate with it.
>
> (Mark, Property)

To that end, corporations were seen by interview participants as investing more into hometown sport properties than they would for similar properties elsewhere: "Without a doubt, *you will see hometown companies do more, and probably spend more on local partnerships than they otherwise would* – I think they look at it very differently" (Nick, Corporation).

Forming hometown alliances. A predominant sub-theme for "winning where you live" was identified in the data; namely, "forming hometown alliances." This sub-theme represented a strategy for achieving this thematic hometown objective that corporations' non-local competitors were unable to perfectly imitate (i.e., imperfect imitability) or adopt (i.e., imperfect mobility).

Prominent hometown corporations, particularly B2C companies, regularly sought to partner with prominent hometown sport properties. This sub-theme/strategy often allowed these corporations to form alliances with both the hometown sport properties they sponsored and the other hometown sponsors of those properties. Theo and Bobby acknowledged possible sponsor portfolio effect from these alliances:

> There's definitely value to that. I think there's more value to the mid-tier company than there is to the large fortune 500 company. So, yes. *Companies spend money with us, because not only do they want that association with the team, but they also know and want to see themselves in the same lights of a [Hometown Sponsor 1], a [Hometown Sponsor 2], a [Hometown Sponsor 3], and those types of companies.* And yes, we have people that spend money with us, because they want to be in that same neighborhood, if you will.
>
> (Bobby, Property)

Pertinent to this thematic strategy, Mark referred to the "natural" associative benefits among hometown sport properties and prominent hometown corporations. He spoke about his property's community activism, and how they often partnered with their sponsors. During his interview, he mentioned that while many sponsors – including non-local sponsors – have partnered with his property on community initiatives, hometown partners were preferred; resonating better with the local community:

> We're finding ways to, really, what does community mean to us, and what does it mean to the community? – to link all those together, and find the right partners that would integrate with that naturally and want to be a part of it . . . *The natural fit is going to be a hometown company.* If we took one of their competitors and we went to market with [a community initiative], it probably isn't going to feel as good for the community, or the client, or us . . . *You're going to get a better [sponsorship effects] amplification if you're a hometown corporation doing something for the community with the right sports team that has the right fit and the right idea for your brand, than*

> *taking a competitor and putting it in that same campaign.* If you looked at those two campaigns, I guarantee you that the value amplification that the hometown company is getting is more than the competitor.
>
> (Mark, Property)

These preferences were regularly alluded to by interview participants, and they suggested that hometown community members (i.e. a central social group) generally preferred hometown sponsorships, and conversely, the sponsorships between hometown properties and the competitors of those local corporations were discouraged. In some situations, interview participants expressed the belief that sponsorships among some of the more prominent hometown corporations and sport properties were almost mandatory – for both the corporations and sport properties. Bobby admitted that there were a few hometown sponsors that were almost required in their sponsor portfolio:

> [Hometown Sponsor] is a great example of one *that would be almost impossible not to do a deal with them. And it would almost be impossible for them not to do a deal with us.* So, do we want to be offering anything but [Hometown Sponsor] in our venue? No. Our fans would not be happy if we were offering [Hometown Sponsor's Competitor]. Would [Hometown Sponsor] want to have a property of our magnitude in Rivendell with [large numbers of] people coming through, that was offering a product other than theirs? They wouldn't.
>
> (Bobby, Property)

When the alternative to the "mandatory" hometown sponsorship mentioned above was brought to the attention of Theo, he found it unthinkable:

> I was thinking, what if [Non-Local Competitor] sponsored something here in Rivendell – like, unheard of. Me as a consumer and working in the industry – that's my perception. So, *you could imagine that people out there would probably be shocked if you went to the [Hometown Football Team's] game and they only had [Non-Local Competitor]?* I'm trying to think if there's anybody that's every really done that.
>
> (Theo, Agency)

Clint possessed a slightly different perspective than Bobby. He suggested that properties were regularly entering sponsorship conversations with multiple prospects simultaneously. In such scenarios, he believed that properties were proactive in communicating with hometown corporations when they were engaged in conversations with their competitors; reaching out to them as a local (i.e. in-group) courtesy:

> I've seen companies strategically do team deals where they don't have corporate presence, whether it be national, regional, international – but lo-and-behold, one of their competitors does. And so, I do think that happens. *And I think in the negotiation process too, properties are well aware of who the primary competitors are, and even maybe not primary competitors, but maybe those brands that really irritate the other brands.* And they certainly, if they're talking to both, they let them know that. And I would too, if I were in their shoes.
>
> (Clint, Agency)

Hometown sponsorship: An effective testing ground. While the evidence was not substantial enough to treat this observation as a thematic objective of hometown sponsorship, an important insight was offered by one of the corporate managers that warranted inclusion. He noted that hometown sponsorship can serve as a safe environment and testing ground for new sponsorship leveraging and activation practices:

> [Hometowns are] a great testing ground and it's easy for you to be there and see that without having to jump on a plane to see it. So yes. You tend to see more of that . . . *testing control and best practices developed with things you do at the local level.* Plus, usually those partnerships are big enough for you to actually get a little bit more creative with them . . . I think it's also an opportunity – particularly if you're trying to recruit B2B customers – for you to use that as a local tool to entertain them with your executive audience in attendance. So, it's *capable of showcasing your brand in a positive light within a safe environment* . . . so, I think it's a great opportunity.
>
> (Nick, Corporation)

This insight, when considering the greater financial investments made towards individual sponsorships; the alliances and strong relationships forged through in-group associations; and the heightened emphasis towards secondary functions of sponsorship, provided support for the possibility of both a sustainable and dominant competitive advantage within corporations' hometown communities.

Overarching objectives

Building brand ambassadors. From an analysis of the four thematic sponsorship objectives, and how they collectively functioned together, an overarching marketing-level, thematic objective emerged: "building brand ambassadors for life." The term "brand ambassadors for life" collectively referred to all individuals who strongly identified with their brands;

possessed brand love; resisted negative criticisms of their brands from others; and had integrated their brands into their lifestyles. The relationship these individuals maintained with their brands was anthropomorphic and possessed a strong degree of centrality in their self-identities. This thematic marketing objective was perceived to be the sponsorship outcome sought by interview respondents from a relationship management context, with Clint referring specifically to this objective as a desired end outcome:

> and that's *how you make a brand ambassador for life.* That's *what everyone does nowadays*... They (consumers) can't tell the story about going to the game that they weren't going to go to [because] they got tickets last minute, without saying that a brand is the one that reached out to them and said, "Hey, I see that you're a fan of this team and you don't have tickets. We're going to hook you up because we love the same team that you do."
>
> (Clint, Agency)

This marketing level objective, while not generally able to be directly measured in terms of ROI, is believed to indirectly encourage behaviors that generate revenues and profits for companies:

> I would say sales [is a sponsorship objective], but it's funny. Out of so many clients that say, "Well, sponsorships have to sell." You know, you have to be able to show me that I sold more widgets because I sponsored this team or league. It's really hard to do. It's really hard to quantify. And, I'm not so sure that's what sponsorship – my personal opinion is that's not why you do sponsorship. You can – *I think you can sell more products because of sponsorship, but it's not a direct,* "I sponsored this; therefore, I sold ten percent more widgets." I think there's more to it than that.
>
> (Clint, Agency)

Generating a positive ROI. Furthermore, through analysis procedures, it was determined that the managerial objective "generate a positive ROI" was not a sponsorship objective, but rather a company-level objective. Throughout interviews, participants took relational elements and regularly discussed the challenges into converting those measures to ROI.

> Well, here's the thing. My ROO is that I want to reach 200,000 Instagram users, and have at least 50 people attend my event – and those were my objectives. I can measure that – versus, a ROI that is quantified with dollar signs: What I spent versus what I got back. ROOs are much easier to measure than ROI. *So, if you don't actually have the math to get your ROI, you could fluff it and argue, "We got a return on our investment!" – based on whatever your objectives were.*
>
> (Penelope, Agency)

These measurement practices were questioned by several interview participants in property or agency roles. While they often acknowledged the internal pressures placed upon corporate managers to provide sponsorship ROI metrics, these participants questioned the accuracy and general validity of these practices. The below quote from Bobby shared a common sentiment:

> When companies are spending based upon specific metrics, it's to help them justify spends internally. And, I'm not from a client perspective. I understand that analytics and all that should play a part in all that. But if that's your end all, be all . . . *it's probably not going to do you a lot of good. Because you're going to be looking at something in a very specific, isolated case – when, it's probably a much bigger conversation* . . . than what you're trying to evaluate.
>
> (Bobby, Property)

Corporate managers also acknowledged the challenges associated with measuring many of sponsorships' relationship-oriented functions through a financial prism. Herman referred to the process as being both "an art and a science":

> What are property metrics? Are they trending up? Trending down? Are they flat? So we consider all those different methodologies to evaluate whether or not we renew. And then there's also the art behind the exercise too. *It's an art and a science,* as you probably know. *There are a lot of gray areas and emotions and other factors that influence your decisions.*
>
> (Herman, Corporation)

Nick, who acknowledged the need for corporations to more accurately measure sponsorship ROI, was hopeful that emergent technology would eventually allow for better information capture and measurement of their sponsorships' financial values:

> I think we're bad as an industry at [measurement]. To me, *I've always looked to measurement as a microcosm of the broader marketing organization. We should be following in line with what the broader organizational goals are, and trying to measure against those, as opposed to creating our own thing.* I think, you know, this movement towards getting more digital and more targeted will allow us to kind of do that, and do it in real-time too. And make real-time decisions.
>
> (Nick, Corporation)

A structural hierarchy based on authority-level. The functions associated with these two higher-level objectives – "building brand ambassadors for life," and "generating a positive ROI" – were regularly stated as prioritized managerial objectives during conversations with interview participants. Some participants mentioned the marketing-level function ahead of the company-level function, while others adopted a top-down approach in stating objectives. The ordering of these objectives was often delineated by interview participants' managerial roles: "Definitely, *advertising has got to be number one. And then, number two is sales.* And then depending on the company, both client entertainment and employee engagement" (Bobby, Property). "I think overall they are. They focus on the main buckets of what you should get out of sponsorship . . . *revenue, consumer engagement, and growing your base* . . . Obviously, every person should put those down for you" (Theo, Agency). "Our two main ones [objectives] at our broadest level are *driving consumer awareness and sentiment – 'brand love'* as it's referred to. And driving sales of our product. I mean, those are the two core objectives . . ." (Herman, Corporation).

The conceptual model that emerged from this study's analysis recognized this stated structural hierarchy containing sponsorship-level objectives, marketing-level objectives, and company-level objectives within its framework, applying the objectives into these hierarchical levels. Further, given the relationship management orientation of the phenomenon, the conceptual framework that emerged from this study focused on the integration of the sponsorship-level and marketing-level thematic objectives, with "generating a positive ROI" included in the model as an overall, end outcome.

Conceptualizing a highly-integrated social framework

Thematic sponsorship objectives were integrated within a conceptual framework that provided an explanation for how they functioned together to (a) achieve the overarching marketing thematic objective (building brand ambassadors) and (b) support the overarching company objective (generating a positive ROI). Analysis procedures revealed that the functions associated with these objectives were highly-integrated with one another. These levels of integrated functionality were evidenced during interviews with the two corporate managers – both of whom stated that their roles regularly involved the coordination and management of cross-functional teams. Consequently, a visualized representation of the conceptual framework that emerged from the data was developed. This conceptual framework represents a theoretical interpretation, by using a social identity approach, of how sponsorship generally functions from a relationship management perspective. From analysis procedures, the thematic sponsorship objectives of "committing to communities" and "empowering employees," while important, were determined to be secondary thematic objectives, while "joining people where their passions live" and "fostering brand love" served as the model's more emphasized thematic objectives. "Committing to communities" and "empowering employees" were deemed secondary sponsorship thematic objectives given their generally smaller scale and leveraging scope. Moreover, their contributions towards "generating a positive ROI" for their corporations were more difficult to quantify than the other two thematic sponsorship objectives (Figure 14.3).

"Joining people where their passions live" and "fostering brand love" were found to function as primary thematic sponsorship objectives; directly reaching their brands' specific target audiences. Their leveraging and activation elements were the primary drivers for "building brand ambassadors for life." Consequently, these thematic objectives were more regularly implemented to establish ROI justifications that supported their sponsorships. Once a conceptual framework was developed for explaining how sponsorships generally functioned in support of marketing-level and corporate-level objectives, thematic objectives more focused on hometown sponsorships were sought. A secondary data analysis that solely focused on interview discourse pertaining to hometown sponsorship contexts was conducted.

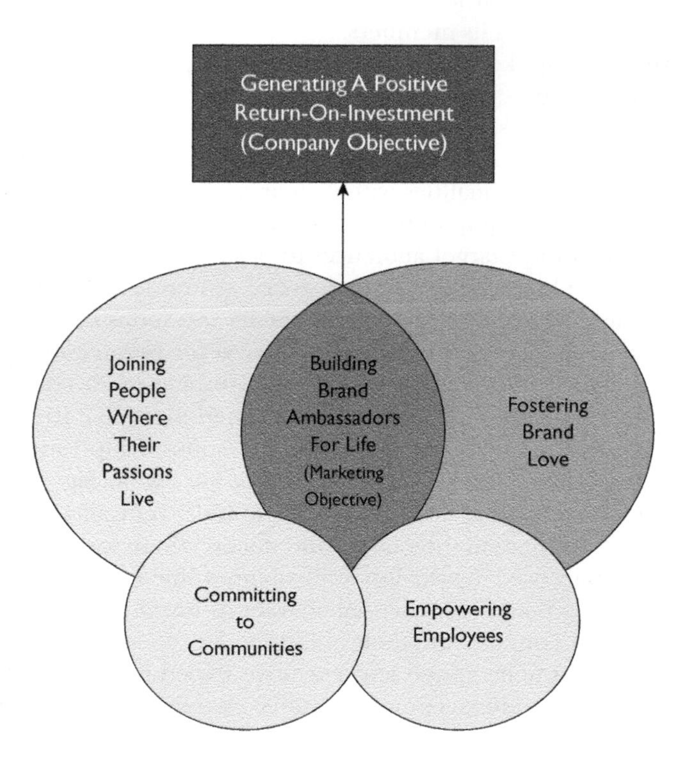

Figure 14.3 Hypothesized sponsorship conceptual framework in general context

Discussion

The following research questions guided the current study: (a) what do sponsorship managers perceive to be common sponsorship objectives and how do these objectives function with one another when applying a social identity approach? And (b) when asking sponsorship managers to narrow their focus to consider hometown sponsorship objectives and effects, what are distinctive or nuanced differences in sponsorship strategy that emerge?

Building brand ambassadors through sponsorships

The first research question sought to identify common sponsorship objectives and construct a framework using a social identity approach that explained how these common objectives functioned together. From data analysis procedures, four inter-related thematic sponsorship objectives were revealed: (a) joining people where their passions live, (b) fostering brand love, (c) committing to communities, and (d) empowering employees as brand ambassadors. When applied into a social identity framework, particularly self-categorization theory, these thematic objectives provided a general explanation for how corporate sponsorship functioned relationally to influence social groups and its members.

Interview participants spoke to the importance of corporations identifying their brands' target audiences, and through sponsorship placing their brands in those environments, "joining people where their passions lived." These environments were strategically chosen to reinforce consistent perceptions of their brands' personalities within their target audiences' social groups. This also entailed corporations leveraging these sponsorships in a manner than promoted their target audiences to positively stereotype their brands as anthropomorphic members of their social groups. This was often accomplished through the application of social media as a sponsorship activation element. Social media communications allowed for organic interaction with target audiences that engaged them on a human level; creating brand narratives and call-to-actions that were positioned more like friendly conversations than sales pitches. Another important sponsorship function identified through analysis of participant interviews was "fostering brand love," where corporations sought to increase the brands' centrality within the self-identities of individuals in their target audiences. Where social media activations were generally used to establish anthropomorphic social relationships, corporations also created experiential activations for target audience members to emotionally connect with their brands on a deeper level; engaging these individuals through unique and exclusive experiences. In other words, from a relationship context, corporations first established a friendship (i.e. anthropomorphic in-group association), then they pursued romance (i.e. brand love). As secondary objectives, corporations both leveraged their sponsorships with community/charity extensions (i.e. "committing to the community"), and regularly used their sponsorship resources on employees to encourage their emotional commitment towards them and their brands (i.e. empowering employees as ambassadors). These practices encouraged cognitive consistency in their brands' personalities with target audiences; presenting them as both authentic and credible.

From this study's findings, corporations generally used sponsorship as an integrated, relationship management platform, with its mechanisms intended to encourage target audiences (and employees) to develop anthropomorphic personality associations with their brands; ultimately motivating them to self-categorize themselves into what this study termed as brand ambassadors for life. "Building brand ambassadors for life" represented the logical culmination of the thematic sponsorship objectives that were identified through data analysis. For these individuals, their brands were expected to exhibit strong degrees of centrality in their self-identities, and influence their normative behaviors. Consequently, brand ambassadors for life were defined in this study as consumers who strongly identified with their brands; possessed brand love; resisted negative criticisms of their brands from others (i.e. demonstrated in-group favoritism); and highly integrated their brands into their lifestyles.

Furthermore, findings that emerged from this study aligned within a social identity approach framework, suggesting that corporations were using their sponsorships to create beneficial social group associations by manipulating target audiences' perceptions. In addition, many of the framework's proposed mechanisms agreed with extant sponsorship and brand literature. A key foundational element of the conceptual framework for determining sponsorship effectiveness involved establishing a good sponsor-property fit in the minds of target audiences, which has been noted by scholars in numerous operationalization articles on sponsorship fit (Becker-Olsen & Simmons, 2002; Cornwell, Humphreys, Maguire, Weeks, & Tellegen, 2006; Johar & Pham, 1999; Olson & Thjømøe, 2011; Ruth & Simonin, 2003). Further, the importance ascribed to developing sponsorship portfolios strategically positioned to present consistent brand images/personalities (i.e. good sponsorship-sponsorship fit) supported findings from Chien, Cornwell, and Pappu (2011). These high-fit associations are likely to encourage local consumers to include sponsoring hometown brands of their hometown teams as members of their in-group.

Corporations were found to encourage consumers anthropomorphizing (Levy, 1985; Plummer, 1985) with their brands through activation strategies allowing for social interactions and meaningful consumer-brand relationships (Fournier, 1998; Fournier & Alvarez, 2012). With the proliferation of social media (Walsh, Clavio, Lovell, & Blaszka, 2013) and emergent, interactive technologies, opportunities for greater reciprocity between consumers and brands were possible – a key element of human relationships (Giddens, 1991).

Additionally, Kim and McGill (2011) found that products were more likely to be anthropomorphized by consumers in situations where the products' behaviors aligned with the normative behaviors they sought. Their findings supported the conceptual framework's functionalism that involved aligning intended brand personalities towards specific, target audiences. Lastly, brand relationship and brand product attributes were found capable of influencing brand love and behaviors similar to those expected from this study's "Brand ambassadors for life" (Albert & Merunka, 2013).

Hometown sponsorships: Amplifying a natural advantage

When the data was examined from a hometown context, interview participants shared perspectives that suggested that corporations focused significant attention towards reinforcing their "hometown" social identities and corresponding in-group associations (i.e. local business–city, local employer–employee, and hometown sponsor–property). These associations were reinforced both within commercial and non-commercial contexts. Corporations "weaved themselves into the local fabric" by creating non-commercial philanthropic and grassroots extensions around their larger sponsorship properties. Employees were actively incorporated into their sponsorships, with these employee-oriented leveraging elements actively reinforcing quadratic hometown employer–employee–team–community associations. From a direct, commercial perspective, corporations allocated additional resources towards "winning where they lived," and established visible alliances with other local corporations and properties (in-group favoritism).

While findings from this analysis failed to support that hometown sport property representatives exhibited behaviors of out-group derogation towards direct competitors of their city's prominent hometown corporations, there was evidence of normalized in-group favoritism by managers of both hometown sport properties and hometown corporations. Based upon interview participant discourse and feedback, however, members of the local community may be prone to exhibit *both* positive distinctiveness strategies of in-group favoritism and out-group derogation. Sponsorships (in general) have been proposed as being capable of providing corporations a sustainable competitive advantage (Amis et al., 1997). While in agreement with their position, findings from this study would expand upon theirs, suggesting that hometown sponsorships provide optimal associative conditions for local corporations to establish sustainable competitive advantages within their home markets (Figure 14.4).

Managerial implications

The major implication from this study is that sponsorship managers must first know their target audiences to effectively manage their sponsorships.

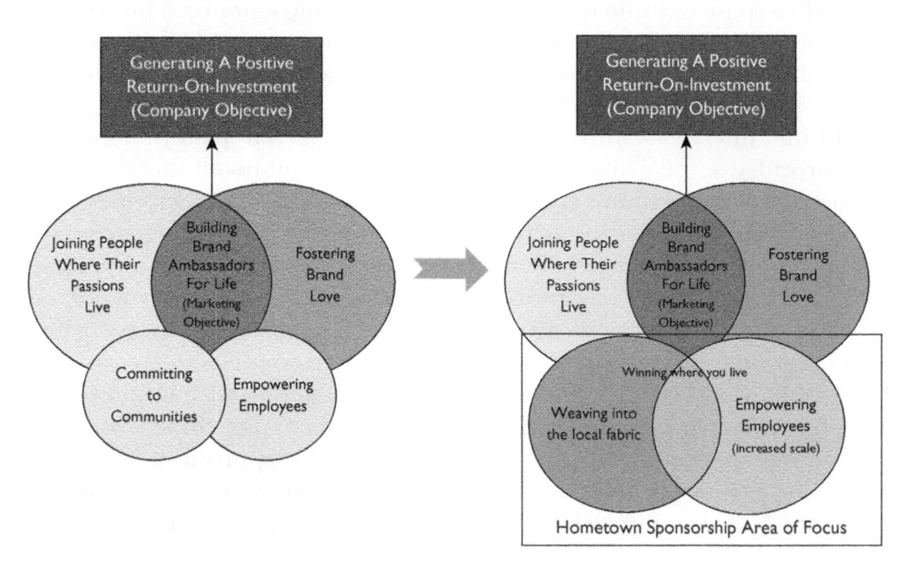

Figure 14.4 Summarization of hometown sponsorship's natural competitive advantage

This target audience understanding should be based on morew than demographics, but include a meaningful understanding of their passions, preferences, and behaviors – especially communication behaviors. When selecting properties to sponsor – and when leveraging and activating upon these sponsorships – managers should attempt to create brand personalities that resonate closely to their target audiences to promote social group identification and encourage behaviors of brand favoritism. A related implication for managers is to focus on sponsorship's ability to create brand relationships with consumers and their social groups, and be cautious when linking direct revenue generation initiatives to sponsorships. Rather, as managers attempt to create connections with communities where they sponsor, they may want to consider leveraging their sponsored sport properties with CSR-linked sponsorship initiatives (Walker & Kent, 2009); particularly if their brands do not have an inherently high associative fit with the community (Uhrich, Koenigstorfer, & Groeppel-Klein, 2014).

For managers, whose corporations have only recently begun using sponsorship as a strategic resource, findings from this study suggest that the creation of a formal, hometown sponsorship strategy may serve as a safe, initial entry point and foundation for developing their corporate sponsorship portfolio. Formation of a strong hometown sponsorship portfolio is expected to 1) protect what is likely an already advantageous product/service market; 2) develop strong in-group associations with the community;

3) instill a sense of pride in employees, encouraging emotional investment and commitment; 4) create networking opportunities and brand alliances with other hometown sponsors; and 5) provide a testing ground for developing sponsorship best practices.

During interviews with participants, a managerial pattern emerged that provided some explanation for sponsorship's oft-noted measurement challenges. Corporations generally establish sponsorship objectives and develop their strategies for achieving them internally. Then, agencies are often empowered by their clients to manage the sponsorship leveraging and activation of these sponsorships. Measurement is regularly a shared responsibility between agencies and corporations, applying *ad hoc* reporting practices. Final sponsorship evaluation, however, is conducted by corporate leadership. Consequently, agencies develop leveraging and activation practices based on corporate objectives provided to them. For these leveraging and activation practices to occur, they must receive approval from corporate managers. From this study's analysis, considering the leveraging and activation practices discussed within the data, these sponsorship objectives are focused on developing meaningful brand relationships with consumers; whereas, the corporations' evaluation processes consistently prioritize the quantification of direct, financial returns (Figure 14.5).

When sponsorship measurement directly focuses on ROI measures, corporations are likely conflating their overarching corporate (ROI-focused) objectives into their overarching marketing (i.e. brand-focused) objectives. Little evidence was found in the data to suggest sponsorship leveraging and activation generates substantial and direct financial returns. Rather, from managers' perceptions, sponsorship effects appear to establish meaningful consumer relationships that *indirectly* generate significant financial returns over prolonged time periods. Therefore, when trying to evaluate sponsorship effectiveness with financial measures (i.e. ROI), corporations may be performing their evaluations with an inappropriate unit of measure. Findings from this study suggest that companies should focus on measuring sponsorship effectiveness by improving consumer behavior measurement practices that tie directly into sponsorship's relationship-oriented objectives.

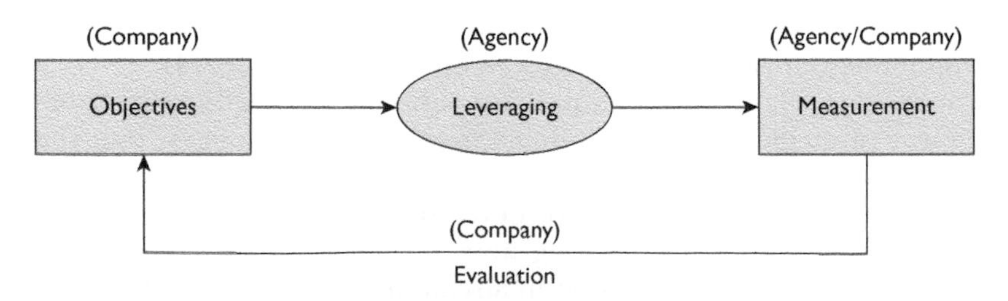

Figure 14.5 Common management responsibilities in both general and local contexts

Such an approach would be expected to capture sponsorship effects better. For instance, being able to track normative behavior changes throughout sponsorship exchanges – and comparing these metrics with overall corporate financial performance – may be a more accurate indicator of sponsorship's overall impact on corporations' financial health over time.

Theoretical implications

Using a social identity approach, findings from this study suggest the possibility for corporations to exploit their community associations to establish sustainable competitive advantages through sponsorship; thereby, extending the theoretical contributions of social identity theory and self-categorization theory into competitive advantage research. Previous research that examined competitive advantage and sponsorship (Amis et al., 1997; Amis et al., 1999; Fahy et al., 2004) used a resource-based view (RBV) of the firm as an inquisitive lens. Further, this study is the first known to specifically examine how sponsorship works from a hometown sponsorship context; explicitly incorporating sponsorship manager data from corporation, property, and agency roles. Therefore, findings from this study can serve as a conceptual starting point for model development and testing of hometown effects in subsequent studies.

Based on their inherent associative relationships, hometown sponsorships may be able to provide both a sustainable *and* dominant competitive advantage in corporations' local communities. Future studies should attempt to identify hometown market share and profitability for large (i.e. regional, national, and multi-national) corporations in relation to their hometown sponsorship investments; examining these sponsorships longitudinally. Findings from this study also suggest that hometown companies invest more into community initiatives than they would otherwise. One property representative who participated in this study went so far as to suggest that hometown sponsors saw more benefits from their community initiatives than non-local sponsors. Future studies should examine CSR-linked sport sponsorship benefits among these two contexts. Lastly, during interviews, patterns in managerial perspectives were noticeable based on sponsorship's managerial roles. Greater investigation should be conducted on how this triadic (i.e. corporation–agency–property) sponsorship management structure functions, and its influence on sponsorship leveraging and activation.

Research limitations

While this study's sample included sponsorship managers in corporate, agency, and property roles – and possessed interview participant representation from every major property in the researched area – there were two factors that limited corporate sponsorship manager interview participation: (1) Existing policies regarding research participation, and (2) the inability to secure in-person interviews due to their managerial time-constraints. For instance, multiple corporate managers were unable to participate in the study due to corporate policies prohibiting research collaboration outside of approved vendors. Additionally, to allow for the inclusion of the second corporate sponsorship manager and a fourth agency consultant, two phone interviews were included in the sample; reducing the interviewer's access to participant social cues and environment. The two corporate sponsorship managers that served as interview participants, however, managed large sponsorship portfolios for two Fortune 500 corporations; offering valuable insight into hometown sponsorship. Another limitation in this study included the sole interviewer's subjectivities, which previously worked as an agency consultant and was already experienced with many of the properties that were represented in the interview participant sample. It is believed that these interviewer subjectivities introduced bias during the study's data collection and analysis phases. Lastly, this study is not generalizable to other hometown contexts, as it solely employs qualitative methods of inquiry. Consequently, transferability of findings is limited to corporate hometown sponsorships within the United States that adhere to the hometown sponsorship definition applied by this study.

References

Abratt, R., Clayton, B. C., & Pitt, L. F. (1987). Corporate Objectives in Sports Sponsorship. *International Journal of Advertising, 6(4)*, 299–311.

Albert, N., & Merunka, D. (2013). The Role of Brand Love in Consumer-brand Relationships. *Journal of Consumer Marketing, 30(3)*, 258–66.

Alexandris, K., & Tsiotsou, R. H. (2012). Testing a Hierarchy of Effects Model of Sponsorship Effectiveness. *Journal of Sport Management, 26(5)*, 363–78.

Amis, J., Pant, N., & Slack, T. (1997). Achieving a Sustainable Competitive Advantage: A Resource-based View of Sport Sponsorship. *Journal of Sport Management, 11(1)*, 80–96.

Amis, J., Slack, T., & Berrett, T. (1999). Sport Sponsorships as Distinctive Competence. *European Journal of Marketing, 33(3/4)*, 250–72.

Ashforth, B. E., & Mael, F. (1989). Social Identity Theory and the Organization. *Academy of Management Review, 14(1)*, 20–39.

Becker-Olsen, K., & Simmons, C. J. (2002). When Do Social Sponsorships Enhance or Dilute Equity? Fit, Message Source, and the Persistence of Effects. *Advances in Consumer Research, 29(1)*, 287.

Batra, R., Ahuvia, A., & Bagozzi, R. P. (2012). Brand Love. *Journal of Marketing, (76)2*, 1–16.

Chadwick, S., & Thwaites, D. (2004). Advances in the Management of Sports Sponsorship: Fact or Fiction? Evidence from English Professional Soccer. *Journal of General Management, 30(1)*, 39–59.

Charmaz, K. C. (2014). *Constructing Grounded Theory* (2nd edn). London, UK: Sage.

Chien, P. M., Cornwell, T. B., & Pappu, R. (2011). Sponsorship Portfolio as a Brand-image Creation Strategy. *Journal of Business Research, 64(2)*, 142–49.

Cobbs, J., Groza, M. D., Rich, G. (2015). Brand Spillover Effects within a Sponsor Portfolio: The Interaction of Image Congruence and Portfolio Size. *Marketing Management Journal, 25(2)*, 107–22.

Cornwell, T. B. (1995). Sponsorship-linked Marketing Development. *Sport Marketing Quarterly, 4(4)*, 13–24.

Cornwell, T. B. (2008). State of the Art and Science in Sponsorship-linked Marketing. *Journal of Advertising, 37(3)*, 41–55.

Cornwell, T. B. & Coote, L. V. (2005). Corporate Sponsorship of a Cause: The Role of Identification in Purchase Intent. *Journal of Business Research, 58(3)*, 268–76.

Cornwell, T. B., Humphreys, M. S., Maguire, A. M., Weeks, C. S., & Tellegen, C. L. (2006). Sponsorship-linked Marketing: The Role of Articulation in Memory. *Journal of Consumer Research, 33(3)*, 312–21.

Cornwell, T. B., & Maignan, I. (1998). An International Review of Sponsorship Research. *Journal of Advertising, 27(1)*, 1–21.

Cousens, L., Babiak, K., & Bradish, C. L. (2006). Beyond Sponsorship: Re-framing Corporate-sport Relationships. *Sport Management Review, 9(1)*, 1–23.

Crowley, M. (1991). Prioritising the Sponsorship Audience. *European Journal of Marketing, 25(11)*, 11–21.

Dolphin, R. R. (2003). Sponsorship: Perspectives on its Strategic Role. Corporate Communications. *An International Journal, 8(3)*, 173–86.

Fahy, J., Farrelly, F., & Quester, P. (2004). Competitive Advantage through Sponsorship: A Conceptual Model and Research Propositions. *European Journal of Marketing, 38(8)*, 1013–30.

Fournier, S. (1998). Consumers and their Brands: Developing Relationship Theory in Consumer Research. *Journal of Consumer Research, 24(4)*, 343–73.

Fournier, S., & Alvarez, C. (2012). Brands as Relationship Partners: Warmth, Competence, and In-between. *Journal of Consumer Psychology, 22(2)*, 177–85.

Fowler, F. J. (2002). *Survey Research Methods* (3rd edn). Thousand Oaks, CA: Sage.

Gardner, M. P., & Shuman, P. (1988). Sponsorships and Small Businesses. *Journal of Small Business Management, 26(4)*, 44–52.

Giddens, A. (1991). *Modernity and Self-identity: Self and Society in the Late Modern Age.* Stanford, CA: Stanford University Press.

Glaser, B. G. (1998). *Doing Grounded theory: Issues and Discussions.* Mill Valley, CA: Sociology.

Grönroos, C. (1994). Quo Vadis, Marketing? Toward a Relationship Marketing Paradigm. *Journal of Marketing Management, 10(5)*, 347–60.

Gwinner, K. P., & Swanson, S. R. (2003). A Model of Fan Identification: Antecedents and Sponsorship Outcomes. *Journal of Services Marketing, 17(3)*, 275.

Haslam, S. A., Oakes, P. J., Turner, J. C., & McGarty, C. (1995). Social Categorization and Group Homogeneity: Changes in the Perceived Applicability of Stereotype Content as Function of Comparative Context and Trait Favorableness. *British Journal of Social Psychology, 34(2)*, 139–60.

Hoek, J., Gendall, P., Jeffcoat, M., & Orsman, D. (1997). Sponsorship and Advertising: A Comparison of Their Effects. *Journal of Marketing Communications, 3(1)*, 21–32.

Hogg, M. A. & Abrams, D. (1988). *Social Identifications: A Social Psychology of Intergroup Relations and Group Processes.* London, New York, NY: Routledge.

IEGSR. (2017). Sponsorship Spending Forecast: Continued Growth Around the World. *IEG*. Retrieved from www.sponsorship.com/iegsr/2017/01/04/Sponsorship-Spending-Forecast–Continued-Growth-Ar.aspx.

Irwin, R. L., & Asimakopoulos, M. K. (1992). An Approach to the Evaluation and Selection of Sport Sponsorship Proposals. *Sport Marketing Quarterly, 1(2)*, 43–51.

Irwin, R. L., Asimakopoulos, M. K., & Sutton, W. A. (1994). A Model for Screening Sport Sponsorship Opportunities. *Journal of Promotion Management, 2(3/4)*, 53–69.

Javalgi, R. G., Traylor, M. B., Gross, A. C., & Lampman, E. (1994). Awareness of Sponsorship and Corporate Image: An Empirical Investigation. *Journal of Advertising, 23(4)*, 47–58.

Johar, G.V., & Pham, M. T. (1999). Relatedness, Prominence, and Constructive Sponsor Identification. *Journal of Marketing Research, 36(3)*, 299–312.

Kim, S., & McGill, A. L. (2011). Gaming with Mr. Slot or Gaming the Slot Machine? Power, Anthropomorphism, and Risk Perception. *Journal of Consumer Research, 38(1)*, 94–107.

Kirkhart, K. E. (1995). Seeking Multicultural Validity: A Postcard from the Road. *Evaluation Practice, 16(1)*, 1–12.

Levy, S. J. (1985). Dreams, Fairy Tales, Animals, and Cars. *Psychology and Marketing, 2(2)*, 67–81.

Lincoln, Y. S. & Guba, E. G. (1986) But is it Rigorous? Trustworthiness and Authenticity in Naturalistic Evaluation. *New Directions for Program Evaluation, 1986(30)*, 73–84.

Madrigal, R. (2000). The Influence of Social Alliances with Sport Teams on Intentions to Purchase Corporate Sponsors' Products. *Journal of Advertising, 29(4)*, 13–24.

Madrigal, R. (2001). Social Identity Effects in a Belief-attitude-intentions Hierarchy: Implications for Corporate Sponsorship. *Psychology & Marketing, 18*(2), 145–65.

Meenaghan, J. A. (1983). Commercial Sponsorship. *European Journal of Marketing, 17(7)*, 5–73.

Meenaghan, T. (1991). The Role of Sponsorship in the Marketing Communications Mix. *International Journal of Advertising, 10(1)*, 35–47.

Meenaghan, T., McLoughlin, D., & McCormack, A. (2013). New Challenges in Sponsorship Evaluation Actors, New Media, and the Context of Praxis. *Psychology & Marketing, 30(5)*, 444–60.

Mihalik, B. J. (1984). Sponsored Recreation. *Public Relations Journal, (June)*, 22–25.

O'Laughlin, S. (2016, December 27). Brands Deliver High-tech Engagements to Score with Today's Hyper-connected Fans. *EventMarketer.com.* Retrieved from www.eventmarketer.com/inside-10-of-the-industrys-best-digital-sports-sponsorship-activations/.

Olkkonen, R., Tikkanen, H., & Alajoutsijärvi, K. (2000). Sponsorship as Relationships and Networks: Implications for Research. *Corporate Communications, 5(1)*, 12–18.

Olson, E. L. and Thjømøe, H. M. (2011). Explaining and Articulating the Fit Construct in Sponsorship. *Journal of Advertising, 40(1)*, 57–70.

Patton, M. Q. (2002). *Qualitative Research and Evaluation Methods* (3rd edn). Thousand Oaks, CA: Sage Publications.

Pearsall, J. (2010). Sponsorship Performance: What is the Role of Sponsorship Metrics in Proactively Managing the Sponsor-property Relationship? *Journal of Sponsorship, 3(2)*, 115–23.

Peteraf, M. A. (1993). The Cornerstones of Competitive Advantage. A Resource-based View. *Strategic Management Journal, 14(3)*, 179–91.

Plummer, J. T. (1985). How Personality Makes a Difference. *Journal of Advertising Research, 24(6)*, 27–31.

Polonsky, M., Sandier, D., Casey, M., Murphy, S., Portelli, K., and Van Velzen, Y. (1995). Small Business and Sport Sponsorship: the Australian Experience. *Journal of Promotion Management, 3(1/2)*, 121–40.

Quester, P.G., Farrelly, F. & Burton, R. (1998). Sports Sponsorship Management: A Multinational Comparative Study. *Journal of Marketing Communications, 4(2)*, 115–28.

Reynolds, K. J., & Turner, J. C. (2006). Individuality and the Prejudiced Personality. *European Review of Social Psychology, 17(7)*, 233–70.

Ruth, J. A. & Bernard, L. S. (2003). "Brought to You by Brand A and Brand B": Investigation Multiple Sponsors' Influence on Consumers' Attitudes Toward Sponsored Events. *Journal of Advertising, 32(3)*, 19–30.

Scott, D. R. & Suchard, H. T. (1992). Motivations for Australian Expenditure on Sponsorship—an Analysis. *International Journal of Advertising, 11(4)*, 325–32.

Sandler, D. M. & Shani, D. (1993). Sponsorship and the Olympic Games: The Consumer Perspective. *Sport Marketing Quarterly, 2(3)*, 38–43.

Social Media Fuze. (2016, June 16). 8 Best Social Media Campaigns. *Social Media Fuze.* Retrieved from: http://socialmediafuze.com/best-social-media-campaigns-2016/.

Tajfel, H., & Turner, J. C. (1979). An Integrative Theory of Intergroup Conflict. In W. G. Austin & S. Worchel (Eds.), *The Social Psychology of Intergroup Relations.* Monterey, CA: Brooks/Cole.

Thwaites, D., Aguilar-Manjarrez, R. & Kidd, C. (1998). Sports Sponsorship Developing in Leading Canadian Companies: Issues & Trends. *International Journal of Advertising, 17(1)*, 29–49.

Turner, J. C., & Oakes, P. J. (1986). The Significance of the Social Identity Concept for Social Psychology with Reference to Individualism, Interactionism and Social Influence. *British Journal of Social Psychology, 25(3)*, 237.

Uhrich, S., Koenigstorfer, J., & Groeppel-Klein, A. (2014). Leveraging Sponsorship with Corporate Social Responsibility. *Journal of Business Research, 67(9)*, 2023–29.

Verhoef, P. C., & Leeflang, P. S. H. (2009). Understanding the Marketing Department's Influence Within the Firm. *Journal of Marketing, 73(2)*, 14–37.

Walker, M., & Kent, A. (2009). Do Fans Care? Assessing the Influence of Corporate Social Responsibility on Consumer Attitudes in the Sport Industry. *Journal of Sport Management, 23(6)*, 743–69.

Walliser, B. (2003). An International Review of Sponsorship Research: Extension and Update. *International Journal of Advertising, 22(1)*, 5–40.

Walsh, P., Clavio, G. Lovell, M. D., & Blaszka, M. (2013). Differences in Event Brand Personality between Social Media Users and Non-users. *Sport Marketing Quarterly, 22(4)*, 214–23.

Chapter 15

ISO 20121 and Theory U

A new way to manage sporting events

Cristiana Buscarini and Sara Franzini Gabrielli

Introduction

All human activities, including sports, have an impact on the environment. We analyze the impact of sports on the environment as the effect on the territory, water, landscape, and climate surrounding the sporting event, including the social and economic impact. With reference specifically to the sporting activity and the impact that such activities may have on the host territory, a question arises: How to organize an event that minimizes adverse effects and optimizes positive outcomes? The answer to this question is the concept of sustainability. In its broader sense, sustainability implies a continuous process of development that sustains over time the protection and reproduction of world capital, composed of economic, human, social, and natural capital. We understand "economic capital" as all things created by individuals. Human-social capital is composed of all individuals in a society, while natural capital is made up of the environment and natural resources. In the last decade, as far as the sports sector is concerned, there is an extensive bibliography on social responsibility (Babiak & Trendafilova, 2011; Bradish & Cronin, 2009).

The principle of sustainable development in sport dates back to 1992, the year in which the Rio de Janeiro Conference on Environment and Development took place. Article 10 of the European Charter for Sports underlines that all people and organizations engaged in sports activities have the responsibility to protect the environment and to promote sustainable sports practices. In 2007, the White Paper on Sport drafted in Brussels by the European Commission, emphasized the role that sports play in the politics and everyday life of citizens in terms of health, well-being, education, inclusion, and the economic dimension in terms of GDP and job creation. The CIO also pursues sustainability goals, in fact, in the Olympic Charter, among the Fundamental Principles of Olympism; it refers to the educational value of a good example, social responsibility, and respect for universal fundamental ethical principles. In addition, the CIO, point 13, states that: "to encourage and support a responsible concern for environmental issues, to promote sustainable development in sport and to demand that the Olympic Games be held accordingly". The CIO regards the environment as one of the cornerstones of the entire Olympic Movement, along with sport and culture. Its respect became part of the Olympic Charter in 1996, but already in 1994 the IOC had started to cooperate with the UNEP (United Nations Environment Program) and in 1995 created the Commission on Sport and the Environment to outline principles that sport and its manifestations would no longer harm the natural environment.

The "Agenda 21" program, drawn in 1992, in Rio de Janeiro, during the Earth Summit, aims at raising awareness on the Olympic Movement, particularly on the theme of the natural environment. The program stipulates the guidelines that must be applied to Olympic events, also reiterated in the "Olympic Agenda 2020", drawn in December 2014. In addition to outlining a sustainability policy, the IOC has a so-called "Olympic Games Impact" (OGI) study, in which the themes analyzed are vast and include, among others, the construction of sports facilities and the Olympic Village, modification of infrastructure, and the quality of water and air. In this regard, the International Standard Organization has prepared the "ISO / DIS 20121: 2012 Event sustainability management systems-requirements with guidance for use published on June 15, 2012", defining the requirements of an event sustainability management system and aiming to minimize the impact of a particular event on the community and on the environment in which it takes place.

The standard developed on the basis of the English BS-8901, which provides a template for event organizers and their suppliers to further develop a more sustainable management system with stakeholders. This activity is within the norms and the role assigned to the stakeholders. The approach is to "manage" stakeholder engagement, also by defining the relationship of these expectations within the context of the event. The standard makes a plea to consider all the stakeholders – both individuals and collective subjects – everybody who has a specific interest in the event, so that is participants and visitors, lenders, workers, suppliers, communities (local or professional), associations and future generations. The third peculiarity of the rule is the obligation to analyze the whole life cycle of the event, at all stages and for the entire supply chain. For each phase, it is necessary to analyze: the design (maximum design and detail design); the implementation (preparation, conduction, and verification); the closure and return checks (inheritance and reporting).

There are two technical aspects to take into account: first, the ISO is a contractual standard, and, second, its scope of application is extremely wide. A contractual standard is a technical specification, a rule that can only be referred to by reference to the number, can be used in public regulations and provisions (e.g., for patronage), can be certified and verified by an independent third party. The scope of the ISO standard is very extensive and does not assume limitations on the size of the event nor on its phases and subjects; hence it applies both to those who directly manage the event and to those who provide services such as catering, cleaning, security, as well as and also to the locations, such as hotels, fairs, platforms, etc. These two aspects make it a "universal" standard. ISO-20121 provides benefits to everyone involved in the event, from organizers, event hosts to workforce, restaurateurs, builders, transporters, participants, community, etc. ISO-20121 promotes organizational growth in terms of efficiency, efficacy, competence, and awareness and increases the risk management capability of its business. It enables a methodology that fosters the implementation of appropriate criteria for all three dimensions of sustainability and the adoption of methodologies that allow the systematic analysis of the contexts in which the events are organized, thus taking into account the expectations and relevant issues for all stakeholders and the minimization of related risks (International Organization for Standardization, 2017).

ISO-20121 encourages organizers to deepen regulatory issues and work on compliance and management more consciously in issues such as security at assembly and disassembly, permissions and bureaucracy, warranties to be requested from suppliers, training, the volunteers, the agreements with the municipalities hosting the events, and the evaluation of the critical aspects of the locations. The standard also foresaw an in-depth mapping process of the stakeholders that allows you to manage critical areas at a pre-emptive stage and allows you to involve other actors in the same way. Other important benefits of implementing the ISO are the reduction of the risks and negative impact on the environment, the improvement of the quality of event management and the ability to stand out from competitors in a credible and transparent way. As well as to spread the culture of sustainability to stakeholders and to enhance the image of the organizers and those who are involved in the event and to offer a valuable help to the partners to achieve their sustainability.

The ISO-20121 is based on the most established principles of management systems such as ISO-9001, includes some of the features of ISO-26000 Guidance on Social Responsibility, has significant similarities with ISO-14001 for certification of environmental management systems (quality management), and uses the Deming Plan Do Check Act (or Deming Cycle) approach. The Sustainable Event Management System certification was first applied for the 2012 London Olympics. It is comprehensive, because it takes into account three dimensions that the event organization must consider: environmental, social, and economic. First, the economic aspect is value creation. Second, the social is inclusion and respect for shared values. Last, the environmental impact, or the footprint of the event, is reduced by optimum management, and the implementation of best practices.

Method

There have been few sporting events in Italy where ISO-20121 was applied, and for this reason we wanted to understand why. We tried to investigate how many Italian National Sports Federations were aware of these rules. To do so we then sent a questionnaire to the 44 National Sports Federations, asking questions that covered the various steps of organizing sports events (according to ISO-20121). We calculated their compliance with the regulations and, for those who did not comply, we sent out another questionnaire to assess their interest in knowing more and/or applying these norms. The questionnaire was composed of questions regarding the various activities to be carried out throughout the organizational process of a sporting event as outlined by international norms. The scope of this was to have a general overview of all the federation's activities that organize sporting events and the steps they follow. In particular, we divided the phases following the Deming model of the Plan Do Check Act and the guidelines of ISO-20121.

Step 1 – Planning

At this stage, the law calls for a statement of intent and value that serves as a guideline throughout the event. This statement is nothing other than a document within which the organization indicates what are the principles that guide the action and the goals you want to achieve. This way everyone will know what to point out, what principles to set up to guide their actions and, during monitoring and control, verify that the values and intentions have been respected. It is of crucial importance at this stage to include all your stakeholders, ask their opinions, and their expectations, in order to have a general picture of the event. The legislation also demands that every single step and operation be documented so that it has both the process under control and documentation useful to organize future events. It is a stage full of actions to be put in place, of arrangements to be taken, and of precise laws to be observed: it must be borne in mind that for each country, region, and city there are provisions of precise bureaucratic rules and procedures that must be respected to obtain all the necessary permissions for the regular performance of the event (e.g., security rules, privacy, authorization to sell beverages and foods).

Step 2 – Facilitating

This is the phase in which all the resources necessary for the smooth running of the event are sought and made available: human resources, supply chain, infrastructure, technology, and financial resources. The first, human resources, includes those who will work in the event with remuneration and those who will contribute freely (volunteers). In order to be able to harmonize the work of people in any degree, it is essential that training courses are provided for building a harmonious and prosperous business climate that makes everyone participate in organizing the event. The supply chain, on the other hand, must be chosen by choosing sustainable, environmentally and socially responsible suppliers not only during production and sale, but also when purchasing raw materials. Each vendor should provide the necessary information so that it can map all of its production processes to evaluate its sustainability. Core subjects that are considered for the evaluation of suppliers are: "responsible sourcing, use of secondary materials, minimizing embodied impacts, healthy materials".

1 Responsible sourcing – ensuring that products and services are sourced and produced under a set of internationally acceptable environmental, social, and ethical guidelines and standards.
2 Use of secondary materials – maximizing the use of materials with reused and recycled content, minimizing packaging, and designing products that can either be reused or recycled.
3 Minimizing embodied impacts – maximizing resource and energy efficiency in the manufacturing and supply process in order to minimize environmental impacts.
4 Healthy materials – ensuring that appropriate substances and materials are used in order to protect human health and the environment (The LOCOG Sustainable Sourcing Code, 2011).

Each local organization has its documents and procedures to participate both in the seven years early selection and in the hosting of the future Olympic Games regarding the criteria linked to the dossier. With regard to the infrastructure and technologies that support the whole process of planning, organizing, and managing the event, it is useful that they are appropriate and advanced to provide adequate technical and informatics support to reduce the amount of printed paper and to circulate all the information in the optimum way. The desire is to minimize the use of printed publications and other printed materials as much as possible and, as such, favor the use of electronic publications. At this stage, it is crucial to carry out an analysis of the costs and revenues that are expected to occur during the event and, above all, in the process of being implemented: Good financial planning, with adequate cash flow analysis, can help the organization take the necessary measures in terms of expenses to be made and sponsorships required to have adequate financial coverage. It is then necessary to create and maintain a proper information and communications management system (both outward and inward), so that everyone is involved in what is being achieved and, above all, to keep records of every single operation completed.

Step 3 – Review

At this stage, senior management must review the sustainable management system at predetermined intervals to ensure its sustainability, adequacy, and effectiveness. Monitoring actions can be performed in different ways, pre-set and shared by the entire organization, and at different times. The goal is to keep the process under control in such a way as to make the last phase, the stage of action, consonant and appropriate to the different circumstances.

Step 4 – Action

The objective is to analyze the data obtained during the control phase, to identify any non-conformity and to act accordingly by taking the necessary corrective actions. This creates a circular process in which each activity is monitored, controlled, evaluated, and if there are defects, corrected. There is thus a process of continuous improvement, a kind of "learning by doing" that leads to the creation of know-how within the organization. Reaction modes to non-conformities may differ depending on the stage of the event organization you are in: if the event is being created and planned, then any future B plans may be entered that can be put in place, at a time when what is planned in advance should not be successful.

If one is already in the process of performing the event, then in the realization phase, the B plans from the previous phase can be put into practice. At the end of the event, when a concluding budget is to be drawn up in which the targets have been reached and even for those that have not been reached, then it is possible to identify problems that could be solved in the years to come. At the end of the event, it is very important to draw up the final balance sheet, a report within which all the data and documentation relating to the event, both positive and negative, are put, in a sign of great transparency and, above all, to communicate to their stakeholders in the first place and the rest of the world after, their outcomes and intentions for subsequent years. In particular, it is useful to focus on the legacy that the event leaves to the territory and to the community. Every event leaves its mark, leaves its memory, positive or negative, on the community and territory that hosts it and, if positive, it can bring greater benefits for both organizers and society.

These four steps are the criteria covered in our questionnaire to calculate the compliance of an event: After careful analysis we have created dichotomous questions relevant to the phases indicated by the norm so that the respondents have a clear signal of their compliance, or not, with the legislation. In particular, for each phase of the event, actions that should be carried out according to the regulations are identified. For each of these, it was expected to respond YES if the action was performed, and NO if it was not made, to have a greater ease both in compliant computation (as a positive response leads directly to increasing the compliance rate regulation, and a negative lead to an increase in the percentage of non-compliance), and in identifying non-conforming actions. It is a process of continuous evolution, which every organization has to do according to the field in which it operates the resources available and its skills. This creates a list of actions recommended by the policy for managing, planning, and executing the event that is configured as a useful tool both as a guideline for the organization and as a compliance calculation tool. We then submitted a questionnaire to 44 Italian National Sports Federations in order to have a clear view of how ISO-20121 would be applied. In order to complete the analysis and have a framework as comprehensive as possible we also asked the federations to make available the internal documents related to their sustainable development policies (e.g., sustainability budgets and ethical codes) as well as technical and non-technical guidelines and regulations, for the organization of sporting events.

We proceeded with a content analysis of the supplied documents; in doing so we were also able to carry out a qualitative analysis, getting more and more in touch with the organizations at the summit of the Italian sport system. We also sent a questionnaire to those who did not apply these guidelines, in which we asked questions to understand whether their nonconformity stemmed from the fact that they did not know the norms or rather because of lack of competence, resources, or time. Through the data collected from this questionnaire we hoped to indicate the level of knowledge of ISO-20121, understood as a percentage of those who had or had not heard of it, and the availability of the Federations who showed interest in learning more.

The second questionnaire also sought to investigate the availability of federations to implement their process of organizing sporting events with a new human resource management methodology, which was founded at MIT, Boston, and then spread around the world. This new methodology helps the cohesion and connectivity processes within any kind of organization; additionally, and most importantly, it identifies "listening" as the single most valuable asset to be taken advantage of. This theory can be used both as an internal aggregation tool for the organization as well as a tool aimed at raising stakeholders' engagement. Otto Scharmer is the creator of the theory called Theory U, a name derived precisely from the form that Scharmer's process follows in order to arrive at a new approach to leadership: a "U", representing the descent towards the deep self with an open mind, an open heart, and an open will, from which to draw solutions to make changes.

Theory U proposes that the quality of the results that we create in any kind of social system is a function of the quality of awareness, attention, or consciousness that the participants in the system operate from. Since it emerged around 2006, Theory U has come to be understood in three primary ways: first as a framework; second, as a method for leading profound change; and third, as a way of being – connecting to the more authentic of higher aspects of our self. In exploring this territory more deeply, we realized that most of the existing learning methodologies relied on *learning from the past,* while most of the real leadership challenges in organizations seemed to require something quite different: letting go of the past in order to connect with and *learn from emerging future* possibilities. We realized that this second type of learning – learning from the emerging future – not only had no methodology, but also had no real name. And yet innovators, entrepreneurs, and highly creative people all express an intimate relationship with this deeper source of knowing. Otto started referring to it as Theory U and "presencing". Presencing is a blended word combining "sensing", that is, feeling the future possibility, and "presence", meaning the state of being in the present moment. Presencing means *"sensing and actualizing one's highest future possibility – acting from the presence of what is wanted to emerge".*

The proposition of Theory U, that the quality of results in any kind of socio-economic system is a function of the awareness that people in the system are operating from, leads to a differentiation between four levels of awareness. These four levels of awareness affect where actions originate relative to the boundaries of the system. The journey through the U develops seven essential leadership capacities:

1 *Holding the space of listening.* The foundational capacity of the U is listening. Listening to others, listening to oneself, and listening to what emerges from the collective. Effective listening requires the creation of open space in which others can contribute to the whole.
2 *Observing.* The capacity to suspend the "voice of judgement" is key to moving from projection to true observation.
3 *Sensing.* The preparation for the experience at the bottom of the U – presencing – requires the tuning of three instruments: the open mind, the open heart, and the open will. This opening process is not passive but an active "sensing" together as a group. While an open heart allows us to see a situation from the whole, the open will enables us to begin to act from the emerging whole.
4 *Presencing.* The capacity to connect to the deepest source of self and will allows the future to emerge from the whole rather than from a smaller part or special interest group.
5 *Crystallizing.* When a small group of key persons commits itself to the purpose and outcomes of a project, the power of their intention creates an energy field that attracts people, opportunities, and resources that make things happen. This core group functions as a vehicle for the whole to manifest.
6 *Prototyping.* Moving down the left side of the U requires the group to open up and deal with the resistance of thought, emotion, and will;

moving up the right side requires the integration of thinking, feeling, and will in the context of practical applications and learning by doing.

7 *Performing.* A prominent violinist once said that he couldn't simply play his violin in Chartres cathedral; he had to "play" the entire space, what he called the "macro violin", in order to do justice to both the space and the music. Likewise, organizations need to perform at this macro level: they need to convene the right sets of players (frontline people who are connected through the same value chain) and to engage a social technology that allows a multi-stakeholder gathering to shift from debating to co-creating the new.

Results

The questionnaire analysis on compliance with ISO-20121 (first questionnaire) shows that among the 32 federations, only seven implement or partially implement the actions provided by the Standard. From the data we collected from the questionnaires and other supplementary documents gathered on the sustainability of the event (access regulations, supplier lists, eco-guides for event organization, protocols on site safety, regulations for the selection and training of volunteers, etc.), to which only seven of the 32 granted us access, we were able to zero-in on many organizational issues. Among the various problems highlighted is the lack of education on environmental sustainability, mainly due to the lack of awareness of the effects of their actions in terms of economic, social, and environmental impact.

Another issue that arises is that of stakeholder engagement or lack thereof. Most figures do not account for stakeholders, they are not taken into consideration and questioned to understand their expectations and needs, and how their direct or indirect actions influence the event. To help manage these issues we have proposed the application: Theory U. This application is considered a useful tool for increasing internal cohesion around the theme of sustainability of the events. The goal of the application is to promote environmental awareness, as well as providing tools to help manage sustainable events.

As for stakeholder engagement, we have formulated some questionnaires then given at different times of the event (pre-event, during event, and post-event). In doing so, we have included the key stakeholders of the event in an integral way and collected feedback that has enabled us to get a general map of the expectations and needs of the stakeholders. The process described above requires a previous step: mapping the main stakeholders of the event. Senior executives should hold brainstorming sessions with the entire organization to identify major stakeholders and contact them. The need to engage with stakeholders in a serious and continuous manner opens the door to a potential new professional figure within many organizations: the Sustainable

Development Trainer. This figure, on sustainability issues, should follow the planning, implementation, and post-event process of collecting as much feedback as possible through the questionnaires mentioned above. These questionnaires provide important information for the improvement of the events as well as understanding the needs to turn active stakeholders to proactive ones. The analysis of the documents, noted above, shows that the actions implemented were mainly aimed at the protection of the natural environment, while not abiding by the respect to safety and the economy (efficiency and efficacy). There is a tendency to organize sporting events in "Green" mode.

To further our research, we sent out the second questionnaire to 25 federations that, at the previous stage, did not provide us with documentation on their organizational events. The purpose of this survey was to understand the motivations behind the federation's non-compliance and their possible willingness to undertake a sustainability path, complying with international norms, supported by the Theory U. The figures below show the results of the second questionnaire used in the study just mentioned. The following questions were asked: Are you aware of the existence of ISO-20121? If so, can you quantify the degree of knowledge of the ISO-20121 guidelines?

The data in Figure 15.1 indicate that 62.5 percent of the respondents are aware of these international norms. This result further encouraged research because, on the one hand, there was a cultural lack of regulation, on the other hand, knowledge of these norms already exists within the industry but they are not implemented at the application level.

With the answers to the question shown in Figure 15.2, we have found the availability of federations to know the rules in more detail and apply them within the organization of their sporting events. The data shows that most responders are interested in undertaking a process of training and enforcement of this legislation. To spread the culture of sustainability the Laboratory of Economics and Management, at the University of Rome

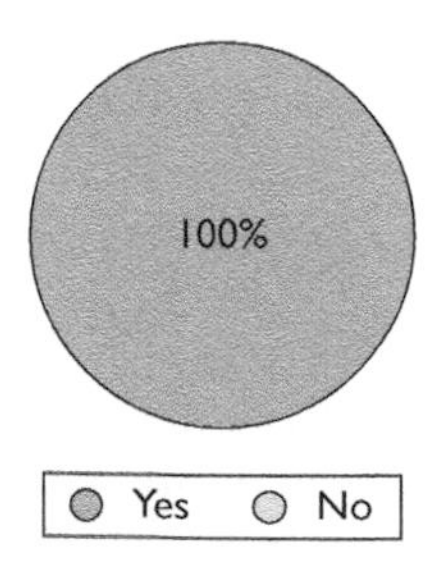

Figure 15.1 If you don't know ISO 20121, are you interested in knowing it deeply and applying it?

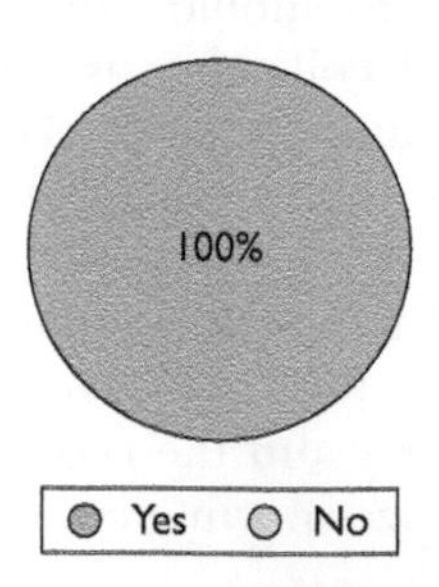

Figure 15.2 If there will be the possibility to implement the organizing process through a new HR methodology (Theory U), are you available to know and apply it?

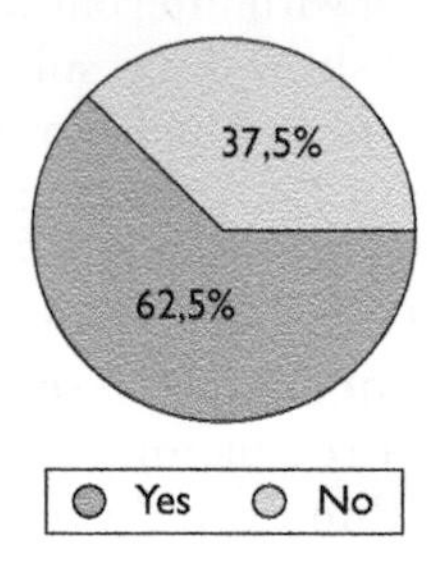

Figure 15.3 Are you aware of the existence of the ISO 20121?

"Foro Italico", is embarking on a mission to provide assistance to all Italian sports organizations interested in pursuing a path to sustainability. In order to understand the availability of these federations to include policies of sustainability within the organizational process, such as Theory U, we asked if they were interested in adopting and applying this tool.

The data in Figure 15.3 indicate that all of the responders are interested in learning more and applying the proposed theory within their organization.

Discussion

The aim of this is to shed a light on the sport sector in Italy, specifically the theme of sports and sustainability. We have analyzed the Italian pport federations, the vertical organization of the Italian sports sector, and concluded that those who applied, although only partially, the ISO-20121 guidelines have increased their market value. Indeed, in the talks with both the general secretaries and those responsible for organizing the events, there was an increase in the number of requests made by sporting affiliates to the federation regarding models and regulations for the organization of sustainable sporting events, mainly at a youth level. Additionally, public and local authorities have increased the availability of public spaces to conduct sporting events, while also showing greater openness to the dialogue aimed at better understanding the needs of those who organize events.

The data collected from the seven federations who applied these norms of sustainability of sporting events, achieved immediate and positive results in terms of image and territorial marketing. The federations that did not apply the guidelines provided by ISO-20121, have developed a high interest in learning more about them. This process can be facilitated with the help of the University. It is precisely in this sense that the Laboratory of Economics and Management, coordinated by Professor Cristiana Buscarini at the University of Rome "Foro Italico", proposed this initiative. Subsequently, a startup for the construction of a web app was launched, which allows the various federations and sport clubs in the country, national and international, to organize their events independently, with the support of a theoretical foundation that bases its roots in the ISO Standards. This application empowers every sport organization, big or small, to plan and track their own sporting events in relation to the resources, time available, and the needs of both the organization and the local community.

At the heart of everything is the awareness of the need for a new organizational paradigm that allows people who are part of a working reality to be heard in their expectations in order to motivate them and engage them dynamically in the process of co-creation of a common goal. Motivation is therefore the main lever (or dynamo) capable of triggering a virtuous process that involves universal and shared values. As mentioned in the study, Theory U can accomplish this task because it focuses on self-assessment, assessment of others, and the facilitation or tackling of particular situations within the organization of sporting events.

References

Babiak K., & Trendafilova, S. (2011). CRS and Environmental Responsibility: Motives and Pressures to Adopt Green Management Practices. *Corporate Social Responsibility and Environmental Management, 18(1),* 11–24.

Bradish, C., & Cronin J. J. (2009). Corporate Social Responsibility in Sport. *Journal of Sport Management, 23(6),* 691–97.

Buscarini, C., & Mura, R. (2011). Nuovi sviluppi in tema di rendicontazione sociale nelle Federazioni Sportive Nazionali (FSN). *Azienda Pubblica, 4.2011,* 406.

Buscarini, C., Manni, F., & Marano, M. (2006). La responsabilità sociale e il bilancio sociale delle organizzazioni dello sport. Milano, Italy: Franco Angeli.

Buscarini, C., & Mura, R. (2013). *Routledge Handbook of Sport and Corporate Social Responsibility.* Abingdon, UK: Routledge.

Godfrey, P. C. (2009). Corporate Social Responsibility in Sport: An Overview and Key Issues. *Journal of Sport Management, 23(3)*, 698–716.

Ioakimidis, M. (2007). Green Sport: A Game Everyone Wins. *The Sport Journal, 10*(*2*), 1.

Irwin, R. L., Lachowetz, T., Cornwell, T. B., & Clark, J. S. (2003). Cause-related Sport Sponsorship: An Assessment of Spectator Beliefs, Attitudes, and Behavioral Intentions. *Sport Marketing Quarterly, 12(3)*, 131–39.

International Organization for Standardization. (2017). ISO-20121, Sustainable events: Event Sustainability Management Systems. Geneva, Switzerland: IOS.

Mallen, C., Bradish, C., & MacLean, J. (2008). Are we Teaching Corporate Citizens? Examining Corporate Social Responsibility and Sport Management Pedagogy. *International Journal of Sport Management and Marketing, 4(2/3)*, 204–24.

Marano, M. (2001). Implementing Management Control and Performance Measurement Systems in Large Non-profit Sport Organizations. *Proceedings of the 9th Congress of the European Association for sport Management.*

Scharmer, O. (2009). *U-THEORY: Leading from the Emerging Future. The Social Technology of Presencing.* Oakland, CA: Berrett-Koehler.

Index

Page numbers in *italics* refer to figures. Page numbers in **bold** refer to tables.